Reading STREET

Program Authors

Peter Afflerbach

Camille Blachowicz

Candy Dawson Boyd

Elena Izquierdo

Connie Juel

Edward Kame'enui

Donald Leu

Jeanne R. Paratore

P. David Pearson

Sam Sebesta

Deborah Simmons

Alfred Tatum

Sharon Vaughn

Susan Watts Taffe

Karen Kring Wixson

PEARSON

Glenview, Illinois • Boston, Massachusetts
Chandler, Arizona • Upper Saddle River, New Jersey

We dedicate Reading Street to
Peter Jovanovich.

His wisdom, courage,
and passion for education
are an inspiration to us all.

Accelerated Reader

PEARSON

ISBN-13: 978-0-328-47040-2
ISBN-10:   0-328-47040-6

5 6 7 8 9 10 V003 14 13 12 11
CC1

Any Path, Any Pace

Reading STREET

CALLE de la Lectura

"Welcome to
Reading Street!
Bienvenidos too."

PEARSON

SCOTT FORESMAN

PEARSON

Find Your Place on Reading Street!

Who said so?

The Leading Researchers,

Program Authors

Peter Afflerbach, Ph.D.
Professor
Department of Curriculum and
Instruction
University of Maryland at
College Park

**Camille L. Z. Blachowicz,
Ph.D.**
Professor of Education
National-Louis University

Candy Dawson Boyd, Ph.D.
Professor
School of Education
Saint Mary's College of California

Elena Izquierdo, Ph.D.
Associate Professor
University of Texas at El Paso

Connie Juel, Ph.D.
Professor of Education
School of Education
Stanford University

Edward J. Kame'enui, Ph.D.
*Dean-Knight Professor of
Education and Director*
Institute for the Development of
Educational Achievement and
the Center on Teaching and Learning
College of Education
University of Oregon

Donald J. Leu, Ph.D.
*John and Maria Neag Endowed
Chair in Literacy and Technology
Director, The New Literacies
Research Lab*
University of Connecticut

Jeanne R. Paratore, Ed.D.
Associate Professor of Education
Department of Literacy and
Language Development
Boston University

P. David Pearson, Ph.D.
Professor and Dean
Graduate School of Education
University of California, Berkeley

Sam L. Sebesta, Ed.D.
Professor Emeritus
College of Education
University of Washington, Seattle

Deborah Simmons, Ph.D
Professor
College of Education and
Human Development
Texas A&M University

Alfred W. Tatum, Ph.D.
*Associate Professor and Director
of the UIC Reading Clinic*
University of Illinois at Chicago

Sharon Vaughn, Ph.D.
*H. E. Hartfelder/Southland
Corporation Regents Professor
Director, Meadows Center for
Preventing Educational Risk*
University of Texas

Susan Watts Taffe, Ph.D.
Associate Professor in Literacy
Division of Teacher Education
University of Cincinnati

Karen Kring Wixson, Ph.D.
Professor of Education
University of Michigan

Consulting Authors

Jeff Anderson, M.Ed.
Author and Consultant
San Antonio, TX

Jim Cummins, Ph.D.
Professor
Department of Curriculum,
Teaching and Learning
University of Toronto

Lily Wong Fillmore, Ph.D.
Professor Emerita
Graduate School of Education
University of California, Berkeley

Georgia Earnest García, Ph.D.
Professor
Language and Literacy Division
Department of Curriculum
and Instruction
University of Illinois at
Urbana-Champaign

George A. González, Ph.D.
Professor (Retired)
School of Education
University of Texas-Pan American,
Edinburg

Valerie Ooka Pang, Ph.D.
Professor
School of Teacher Education
San Diego State University

Sally M. Reis, Ph.D.
*Board of Trustees Distinguished
Professor*
Department of Educational
Psychology
University of Connecticut

Jon Scieszka, M.F.A.
*Children's Book Author
Founder of GUYS READ
Named First National Ambassador
for Young People's Literature 2008*

Grant Wiggins, Ed.D.
Educational Consultant
Authentic Education
Concept Development

Lee Wright, M.Ed.
Pearland, TX

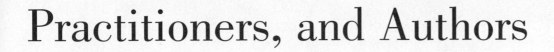
Practitioners, and Authors

Consultant

Sharroky Hollie, Ph.D.
Assistant Professor
California State University
Dominguez Hills, CA

Teacher Reviewers

Dr. Bettyann Brugger
Educational Support Coordinator–Reading Office
Milwaukee Public Schools
Milwaukee, WI

Kathleen Burke
K–12 Reading Coordinator
Peoria Public Schools, Peoria, IL

Darci Burns, M.S.Ed.
University of Oregon

Bridget Cantrell
District Intervention Specialist
Blackburn Elementary School
Independence, MO

Tahira DuPree Chase, M.A., M.S.Ed.
Administrator of Elementary English Language Arts
Mount Vernon City School District
Mount Vernon, NY

Michele Connor
Director, Elementary Education
Aiken County School District
Aiken, SC

Georgia Coulombe
K–6 Regional Trainer/Literacy Specialist
Regional Center for Training and Learning (RCTL), Reno, NV

Kelly Dalmas
Third Grade Teacher
Avery's Creek Elementary, Arden, NC

Seely Dillard
First Grade Teacher
Laurel Hill Primary School
Mt. Pleasant, SC

Jodi Dodds-Kinner
Director of Elementary Reading
Chicago Public Schools, Chicago, IL

Dr. Ann Wild Evenson
District Instructional Coach
Osseo Area Schools, Maple Grove, MN

Stephanie Fascitelli
Principal
Apache Elementary, Albuquerque Public Schools, Albuquerque, NM

Alice Franklin
Elementary Coordinator, Language Arts & Reading
Spokane Public Schools, Spokane, WA

Laureen Fromberg
Assistant Principal
PS 100 Queens, NY

Kimberly Gibson
First Grade Teacher
Edgar B. Davis Community School
Brockton, MA

Kristen Gray
Lead Teacher
A.T. Allen Elementary School
Concord, NC

Mary Ellen Hazen
State Pre-K Teacher
Rockford Public Schools #205
Rockford, IL

Patrick M. Johnson
Elementary Instructional Director
Seattle Public Schools, Seattle, WA

Theresa Jaramillo Jones
Principal
Highland Elementary School
Las Cruces, NM

Sophie Kowzun
Program Supervisor, Reading/Language Arts, PreK–5
Montgomery County Public Schools
Rockville, MD

David W. Matthews
Sixth Grade Teacher
Easton Area Middle School
Easton, PA

Ana Nuncio
Editor and Independent Publisher
Salem, MA

Joseph Peila
Principal
Chappell Elementary School
Chicago, IL

Ivana Reimer
Literacy Coordinator
PS 100 Queens, NY

Sally Riley
Curriculum Coordinator
Rochester Public Schools
Rochester, NH

Dyan M. Smiley
Independent Educational Consultant

Michael J. Swiatowiec
Lead Literacy Teacher
Graham Elementary School
Chicago, IL

Dr. Helen Taylor
Director of English Education
Portsmouth City Public Schools
Portsmouth, VA

Carol Thompson
Teaching and Learning Coach
Independence School District
Independence, MO

Erinn Zeitlin
Kindergarten Teacher
Carderock Springs Elementary School
Bethesda, MD

Any Path, Any Pace

UNIT 5

Adventures by Land, Air, and Water

In this Teacher's Edition Unit 5, Volume 1

WEEK 1 · Smokejumpers

WEEK 2 · Lost City

WEEK 3 · Cliff Hanger

In the **First Stop** on Reading Street

- **Dear Fourth Grade Teacher**
- **Research into Practice on Reading Street**
- **Guide to Reading Street**
- **Assessment on Reading Street**
- **Customize Writing on Reading Street**
- **Differentiated Instruction on Reading Street**
- **ELL on Reading Street**
- **Customize Literacy on Reading Street**
- **Digital Products on Reading Street**
- **Teacher Resources for Grade 4**
- **Index**

GO Digital!

See It!
- **Big Question Video**
- **Concept Talk Video**
- **Envision It! Animations**

Hear It!
- **eSelections**
- **eReaders**
- **Grammar Jammer**
- **Leveled Reader Database**

Do It!
- **Vocabulary Activities**
- **Story Sort**
- **21st Century Skills Activities**
- **Online Assessment**
- **Letter Tile Drag and Drop**

Turning Points

Volume 1

Volume 2

UNIT **2**

Teamwork

Volume 1

Volume 2

UNIT 3

Patterns in Nature

Volume 1

Volume 2

Puzzles and Mysteries

Key
- **SI** Strategic Intervention
- **OL** On-Level
- **A** Advanced
- **ELL** ELL

Volume 1

Volume 2

UNIT 5

Adventures by Land, Air, and Water

Volume 1

Volume 2

UNIT 6

Reaching for Goals

Volume 1

Volume 2

Skills Overview

Key

T Tested Skill

Target Skill

	WEEK 1	WEEK 2
	Smokejumpers Expository Text pp. 178–191 **Camp with Care** Persuasive Essay pp. 196–197	**Lost City** Biography pp. 206–217 **Riding the Rails to Machu Picchu** Personal Essay pp. 222–225

Get Ready to Read

Question of the Week	How can we prepare for emergencies?	What surprises can happen on an expedition?
Amazing Words	generator, deserted, fire escape, medical, first aid, hurricane watch, dangerous, ignite, wildfires, gear	region, cultivate, gigantic, legend, century, highland, adobe, research, records, culture
Word Analysis	French Word Origins	Suffixes -ous , -able, -ible
Literary Terms	Word Choice	Sensory Words
Story Structure/ Text Features	Description/ Definition	Sequence

Read and Comprehend

Comprehension	T ⊙ **Skill** Author's Purpose ⊙ **Strategy** Important Ideas Review **Skill** Graphic Sources	T ⊙ **Skill** Compare and Contrast ⊙ **Strategy** Visualize Review **Skill** Literary Elements: Plot and Character
Vocabulary	T ⊙ **Skill** Homographs	T ⊙ **Skill** Greek and Latin Roots
Fluency	Rate and Accuracy	Appropriate Phrasing

Language Arts

Writing	Fantasy/Conventions	Legend/Sentences
Conventions	Adjectives and Articles	Adverbs
Spelling	Multisyllabic Words	Words with double consonants
Speaking/Listening	Dramatization	Media Literacy: Radio Announcement
Research Skills	Parts of a Book	Outline

The Big Question
What makes an adventure?

WEEK 3	WEEK 4	WEEK 5	WEEK 6

Cliff Hanger Realistic Fiction pp. 234–245 **Rock Climbing** Online Sources pp. 250–253	**Antarctic Journal** Autobiography pp. 262–277 **Swimming Towards Ice** Biography pp. 282–285	**Moonwalk** Science Fiction pp. 294–305 **A Walk on the Moon** Expository Text pp. 310–313	**Interactive Review**
What does it take to be a hero?	What does a person sacrifice to explore the unknown?	What are the risks when walking on the moon?	Connect the Question of the Week to the Big Question.
extraordinary, decency, secure, protect, flood, courage, valiant, generous, individual, admirable	survived, frigid, conquer, durable, obstacle, wily, supply, venture, confident, rugged	astronomers, crater, spacesuit, spacewalk, dusty, launch, probes, gravity, telescopes, geologists	**Review** Amazing Words for Unit 5
Related Words	Suffix -ion	Word Origins–German	
Imagery	Word Choice	Point of View	
Climax	Illustrations	Rising Action	
T Skill Literary Elements: Character, Plot, Theme **Strategy** Story Structure **Review Skill** Author's Purpose	**T Skill** Main Idea and Details **Strategy** Text Structure **Review Skill** Fact and Opinion	**T Skill** Draw Conclusions **Strategy** Monitor and Clarify **Review Skill** Literary Elements: Character, Plot, Theme	**Review** Unit 5 Target Comprehension Skills
T Skill Unfamiliar Words	**T Skill** Greek and Latin Affixes	**T Skill** Synonyms	**Review** Unit 5 Target Vocabulary Skills
Expression	Expression	Rate and Accuracy	**Review** Unit 5 Fluency Skills
Thank You Note/Word Choice	Persuasive Ad/Focus-Ideas	Writing for Tests: Personal Narrative/Sentences	Quick Write for Fluency
Comparative and Superlative Adjectives and Adverbs	Time Order Words	Prepositions and Prepositional Phrases	**Review** Conventions
Greek Word Parts	Latin Roots	Related Words	**Review** Spelling patterns
Demonstration (How-to)	Panel Discussion	Media Literacy: Talk Show	
Diagram/Scale Drawing	SPQ3R	Order Form/Application	

UNIT 5 Monitor Progress

SUCCESS PREDICTOR	WEEK 1	WEEK 2	WEEK 3	WEEK 4
Fluency (WCPM)	Rate and Accuracy 115–125 WCPM	Appropriate Phrasing 115–125 WCPM	Expression 115–125 WCPM	Expression 115–125 WCPM
Oral Vocabulary/ Concept Development (assessed informally) (Vocabulary)	generator deserted fire escape medical first aid hurricane watch dangerous ignite wildfires gear	region cultivate gigantic legend century highland adobe research records culture	extraordinary decency secure protect flood courage valiant generous individual admirable	survived frigid conquer durable obstacle wily supply venture confident rugged
Lesson Vocabulary	T parachute T steer T essential T underbrush T wind T concentrating T dedication T method	T curiosity T thickets T torrent T ruins T glorious T terraced T granite	T trekked T foresaw T rappel T ridge T coil T descent T void T shaft	T forbidding T continent T anticipation T depart T heaves T icebergs T convergence
Text Comprehension (Retelling)	T ⊙ **Skill** Author's Purpose ⊙ **Strategy** Important Ideas	T ⊙ **Skill** Compare and Contrast ⊙ **Strategy** Visualize	T ⊙ **Skill** Literary Elements: Character, Plot, Theme ⊙ **Strategy** Story Structure	T ⊙ **Skill** Main Idea and Details ⊙ **Strategy** Text Structure

Key

T Tested Skill

Target Skill

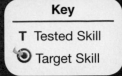

WEEK 5	WEEK 6
Rate and Accuracy 115–125 WCPM	R
astronomers	E
crater	V
spacesuit	
spacewalk	I
dusty	
launch	E
probes	
gravity	W
telescopes	
geologists	
T runt	
T taunted	
T summoning	
T loomed	
T rille	
T trench	
T trudged	
T staggered	
T **Skill** Draw Conclusions	
Strategy Monitor and Clarify	

Online Classroom

Manage Data

- Assign the Unit 5 Bench-mark Test for students to take online.

- Online Assessment records results and generates reports by school, grade, classroom, or student.

- Use reports to disaggregate and aggregate Unit 5 skills and standards data to monitor progress.

- Based on class lists created to support the categories important for AYP (gender, ethnicity, migrant education, English proficiency, disabilities, economic status), reports let you track adequate yearly progress every six weeks.

Group

- Use results from Unit 5 Benchmark Tests taken online through Online Assessment to measure whether students have mastered the English-Language Arts Content Standards taught in this unit.

- Reports in Online Assessment suggest whether students need Extra Support or Intervention.

Individualized Instruction

- Tests are correlated to Unit 5 tested skills and standards so that prescriptions for individual teaching and learning plans can be created.

- Individualized prescriptions target instruction and accelerate student progress toward learning outcome goals.

- Prescriptions include remediation activities and resources to reteach Unit 5 skills and standards.

Assessment and Grouping
for Data-Driven Instruction

4-Step Plan for Assessment
1 Diagnose and Differentiate
2 Monitor Progress
3 Assess and Regroup
4 Summative Assessment

STEP 1 Diagnose and Differentiate

Baseline Group Tests

Diagnose

To make initial grouping decisions, use the Baseline Group Test, the *Texas Primary Reading Inventory (TPRI),* or another initial placement test. Depending on student's ability levels, you may have more than one of each group.

Differentiate

If... student performance is **then...** use the regular instruction and the daily **Strategic Intervention** small group lessons.

If... student performance is **then...** use the regular instruction and the daily **On-Level** small group lessons.

If... student performance is **then...** use the regular instruction and the daily **Advanced** small group lessons.

Small Group Time

SI Strategic Intervention

- Daily small group lessons provide more intensive instruction, more scaffolding, more practice, and more opportunities to respond.
- Reteach lessons in the *First Stop on Reading Street* provide more instruction with target skills.
- Leveled readers build background and provide practice for target skills and vocabulary.

OL On-Level

- Explicit instructional routines teach core skills and strategies.
- Daily On-Level lessons provide more practice and more opportunities to respond.
- Independent activities provide practice for core skills and extension and enrichment options.
- Leveled readers provide additional reading and practice for core skills and vocabulary.

A Advanced

- Daily Advanced lessons provide instruction for accelerated learning.
- Advanced Leveled readers provide additional reading tied to lesson concepts and skills.

Additional Differentiated Learning Options

Reading Street Response to Intervention Kit

- Focused intervention lessons on the five critical areas of reading: phonemic awareness, phonics, vocabulary, comprehension, and fluency

My Sidewalks on Reading Street

- Intensive intervention for struggling readers

STEP 2 Monitor Progress

Don't Wait Until Friday

Use these tools during lesson teaching to **monitor student progress.**

- **Skill and Strategy** instruction during reading

- **Don't Wait Until Friday** boxes to check retelling, fluency, and oral vocabulary

- **Weekly Assessment** on Day 5 checks comprehension and fluency

- **Reader's and Writer's Notebook** pages at point of use

- **Weekly Tests** assess target skills for the week

- **Fresh Reads** for Fluency and Comprehension

Weekly Tests

Fresh Reads for Fluency and Comprehension

STEP 3 Assess and Regroup

Use these tools during lesson teaching to **assess and regroup.**

- **Weekly Tests** Record results of weekly assessments in retelling, comprehension, and fluency to track student progress.

- **Unit Benchmark Tests** Administer this assessment to check mastery of unit skills.

- **Regroup** We recommend the first regrouping to be at the end of Unit 2. Use weekly assessment information and Unit Benchmark Tests performance to inform regrouping decisions. Then regroup at the end of each subsequent unit.

Unit Assessment Chart in First Stop

Group

Baseline Group Test → **Regroup** Units 1 and 2 → **Regroup** Unit 3 → **Regroup** Unit 4 → **Regroup** Unit 5 → **End of Year**

| Weeks 1-6 | Weeks 7-12 | Weeks 13-18 | Weeks 19-24 | Weeks 25-30 | Weeks 31-36 |

Outside assessments, such as *TPRI, DRA,* and *DIBELS,* may recommend regrouping at other times during the year.

STEP 4 Summative Assessment

Use these tools after lesson teaching to **assess students.**

- **Unit Benchmark Test** Use to measure a student's mastery of each unit's skills.

- **End-of-Year Benchmark Test** Use to measure a student's mastery of program skills covered in all six units.

Unit and End-of-Year Benchmark Tests

Understanding By Design

Grant Wiggins, Ed. D.
Reading Street Author

"The big idea connects the dots for the learner by establishing learning priorities. As a teacher friend of ours observed, they serve as 'conceptual Velcro'—they help the facts and skills stick together and stick in our minds!"

Adventures
by Land, Air, and Water

Reading Street Online

www.ReadingStreet.com
• Big Question Video
• eSelections
• Envision It! Animations
• Story Sort

THE BIG ?Q

What makes an adventure?

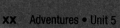

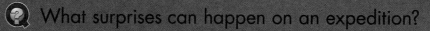

UNIT 5

Small Group Time
Flexible Pacing Plans

Key

- **SI** Strategic Intervention
- **OL** On-Level
- **A** Advanced
- **ELL** ELL

5 Day Plan

DAY 1	• Reinforce the Concept • Read Leveled Readers Concept Literacy Below Level
DAY 2	• Comprehension Skill • Comprehension Strategy • Read Main Selection
DAY 3	• Vocabulary Skill • Revisit Main Selection
DAY 4	• Practice Retelling • Read/Revisit Paired Selection
DAY 5	• Reread for Fluency • Reread Leveled Readers

4 Day Plan

DAY 1	• Reinforce the Concept • Read Leveled Readers Concept Literacy Below Level
DAY 2	• Comprehension Skill • Comprehension Strategy • Revisit Main Selection
DAY 3	• Vocabulary Skill • Read Main Selection
DAY 4	• Practice Retelling • Read/Revisit Paired Selection • Reread for Fluency • Reread Leveled Readers

3 Day Plan

DAY 1	• Reinforce the Concept • Read Leveled Readers Concept Literacy Below Level
DAY 2	• Comprehension Skill • Comprehension Strategy • Revisit Main Selection
DAY 3	• Practice Retelling • Read/Revisit Paired Selection • Reread for Fluency • Reread Leveled Readers

5 Day Plan

DAY 1	• Frontload Concept • Preteach Skills • Conventions/Writing
DAY 2	• Review Concept/Skills • Frontload and Read Main Selection • Conventions/Writing
DAY 3	• Review Concept/Skills • Reread Main Selection • Conventions/Writing
DAY 4	• Review Concept/Skills • Read ELL or ELD Reader • Conventions/Writing
DAY 5	• Review Concept/Skills • Reread ELL or ELD Reader • Conventions/Writing

4 Day Plan

DAY 1	• Frontload Concept • Preteach Skills • Conventions/Writing
DAY 2	• Review Concept/Skills • Frontload and Read Main Selection • Conventions/Writing
DAY 3	• Review Concept/Skills • Reread Main Selection • Conventions/Writing
DAY 4	• Review Concept/Skills • Read ELL or ELD Reader • Conventions/Writing

3 Day Plan

DAY 1	• Frontload Concept • Preteach Skills • Conventions/Writing
DAY 2	• Review Concept/Skills • Frontload and Read Main Selection • Conventions/Writing
DAY 3	• Review Concept/Skills • Read ELL or ELD Reader • Conventions/Writing

This Week on Reading Street!

Adventures

Question of the Week

How can we prepare for emergencies?

Daily Plan

Don't Wait Until Friday

Whole Group

- ◉ Author's Purpose
- ◉ Homographs
- • Fluency/Rate and Accuracy
- • Research and Inquiry

MONITOR PROGRESS	Success Predictor		
Day 1 Check Oral Vocabulary	Days 2–3 Check Retelling	Day 4 Check Fluency	Day 5 Check Oral Vocabulary

Small Group

Teacher Led

- • Reading Support
- • Skill Support
- • Fluency Practice

Practice Stations

Independent Activities

Customize Literacy More support for a balanced literacy approach, see pp. CL•1–CL•47

Customize Writing More support for a customized writing approach, see pp. CW•1–CW•10

Whole Group

- • Writing: Fantasy
- • Conventions: Adjectives and Articles
- • Spelling: Multisyllabic Words

Assessment

- • Weekly Tests
- • Day 5 Assessment
- • Fresh Reads

You Are Here! Unit 5 Week 1

This Week's Reading Selections

Leveled Readers

ELL and ELD Readers

Main Selection Genre: **Expository Text**

Paired Selection Genre: **Persuasive Essay**

Resources on Reading Street!

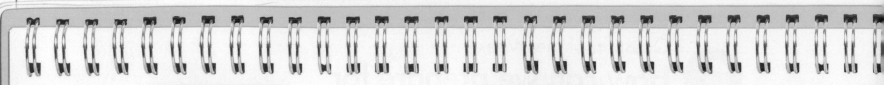

	Build Concepts	**Comprehension**
Whole Group	 Let's Talk About pp. 172–173	  Envision It! Skills/ Strategies — Comprehension Skills Lesson pp. 174–175
Go Digital	• Concept Talk Video	• Envision It! Animations • eSelections
Small Group and Independent Practice	 Smokejumpers pp. 178–179 ELL and ELD Readers Leveled Readers	 Smokejumpers pp. 178–179 ELL and ELD Readers Leveled Readers Envision It! Skills/ Strategies Reader's and Writer's Notebook Practice Station Flip Chart
Go Digital	• eReaders • eSelections	• Envision It! Animations • eSelections • eReaders
Customize Literacy	• Leveled Readers	• Envision It! Skills and Strategies Handbook • Leveled Readers
Go Digital	• Concept Talk Video • Big Question Video • eReaders	• Envision It! Animations • eReaders

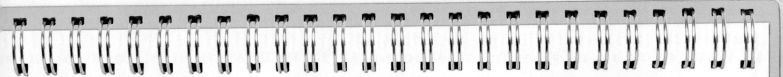

 Question of the Week
How can we prepare for emergencies?

Vocabulary

 Envision It! Vocabulary Cards

 Vocabulary Skill Lesson pp. 176–177

- Envision It! Vocabulary Cards
- Vocabulary Activities

 Envision It! Vocabulary Cards

Smokejumpers pp. 178–179

Practice Station Flip Chart

 Words! W•13

 Reader's and Writer's Notebook

- Envision It! Vocabulary Cards
- Vocabulary Activities
- eSelections

- Envision It! Vocabulary Cards

- Vocabulary Activities

Fluency

 Let's Learn It! pp. 198–199

- eSelections
- eReaders

 Smokejumpers pp. 178–179

 Practice Station Flip Chart

 Leveled Readers

 ELL and ELD Readers

- eSelections
- eReaders

- Leveled Readers

- eReaders

Conventions and Writing

 Let's Write It! pp. 194–195

- Grammar Jammer

 Reader's and Writer's Notebook

 Smokejumpers pp. 178–179

 Practice Station Flip Chart

- Grammar Jammer

- Reader's and Writer's Notebook

- Grammar Jammer

Week 1

 You Are Here! Unit 5 Week 1

My 5-Day Planner for Reading Street!

Don't Wait Until Friday
MONITOR PROGRESS

	Check Oral Vocabulary **Day 1** pages 172j–175f	Check Retelling **Day 2** pages 176a–185e

Get Ready to Read	**Concept Talk,** 172j
	Oral Vocabulary, 173a
	    generator, deserted, hurricane watch, dangerous
	Listening Comprehension, Read Aloud, 173b
		Concept Talk, 176a
		Oral Vocabulary, 176b fire escape, medical
		Word Analysis, 176c
		    French word origins
		Literary Terms, 176d
		    Word Choice
		Text Structure, 176d
		    Description/Definition

Read and Comprehend	**Comprehension Skill,**
	    ◉ Author's Purpose, 173c
	Comprehension Strategy,
	    ◉ Important Ideas, 173c
	READ Comprehension, 174–175
	Model Fluency, Rate and Accuracy, 174–175
	Introduce Lesson Vocabulary, 175a
	    parachute, steer, essential, underbrush, wind,
	    concentrating, dedication, method
		Vocabulary Skill, ◉ Homographs, 176e
		Vocabulary Strategy, Dictionary/Glossary, 176e
		Lesson Vocabulary, 176–177
		    parachute, steer, essential, underbrush, wind,
		    concentrating, dedication, method
		READ Vocabulary, 176–177
		Model Fluency, Rate and Accuracy, 176–177
		READ Main Selection, Smokejumpers, 178–185

Language Arts	**Research and Inquiry,** Identify Questions, 175b **Spelling,** Multisyllabic Words, 175c **Conventions,** Adjectives and Articles, 175d **Handwriting,** Cursive Letters Y and y, 175d **Writing,** Fantasy, 175e–175f	**Research and Inquiry,** Navigate/Search, 185b **Conventions,** Adjectives and Articles, 185c **Spelling,** Multisyllabic Words, 185c **Writing,** Fantasy, Story Sequence, 186d–185e

You Are Here!
Unit 5
Week 1

Check Retelling	**Check Fluency**	**Check Oral Vocabulary**
Day 3 pages 186a–195c	**Day 4** pages 196a–199e	**Day 5** pages 199f–199q

Concept Talk, 186a
Oral Vocabulary, 186b
  first aid, ignite
Comprehension Check, 186c
Check Retelling, 186d
	Concept Talk, 196a
	Oral Vocabulary, 196b
	  wildfires, gear
	Genre,
	  Persuasive Essay, 196c
		Concept Wrap Up, 199f
		Check Oral Vocabulary, 199g
		  generator, deserted, hurricane
		  watch, dangerous, fire escape,
		  medical, first aid, ignite, wildfires,
		  gear
		Amazing Ideas, 199g
		Review ◉ Author's Purpose, 199h
		Review ◉ Homographs, 199h
		Review Word Analysis, 199i
		Review Literary Terms, 199i

READ Main Selection, Smokejumpers,
  186–191
Retelling, 192–193
Think Critically, 193a
Model Fluency, Rate and Accuracy,
  193b
Research and Study Skills, Parts of a
  Book, 193c
	READ Paired Selection, "Camp
	  with Care," 196–197a
	Let's Learn It! 198–199a
	  Fluency: Rate and Accuracy
	  Vocabulary: Homographs
	  Listening and Speaking:
	  Dramatization
		Fluency Assessment,
		  WCPM, 199j–199k
		Comprehension Assessment,
		  ◉ Author's Purpose, 199l–199m

Research and Inquiry, Analyze, 193d
Conventions, Adjectives and Articles,
  193e
Spelling, Multisyllabic Words, 193e
Let's Write It! Fantasy, 194–195a
Writing, Fantasy, Complete
  Sentences, 195a–195c
	Research and Inquiry, Synthesize,
	  199b
	Conventions, Adjectives and
	  Articles, 199c
	Spelling, Multisyllabic Words,
	  199c
	Writing, Fantasy, Revising,
	  199d–199e
		Research and Inquiry, Communicate,
		  199n
		Conventions, Adjectives and Articles,
		  199o
		Spelling Test, Multisyllabic Words,
		  199o
		Writing, Fantasy, Adjectives and
		  Articles, 199p
		Quick Write for Fluency, 199q

Week 1

Grouping Options for Differentiated Instruction
Turn the page for the small group time lesson plan.

Planning Small Group Time on **Reading Street!**

SMALL GROUP TIME RESOURCES

Look for this Small Group Time box each day to help meet the individual needs of all your students. Differentiated Instruction lessons appear on the DI pages at the end of each week.

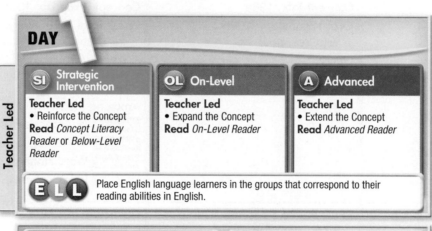

DAY 1

Teacher Led

SI Strategic Intervention	OL On-Level	A Advanced
Teacher Led • Reinforce the Concept **Read** *Concept Literacy Reader* or *Below-Level Reader*	**Teacher Led** • Expand the Concept **Read** *On-Level Reader*	**Teacher Led** • Extend the Concept **Read** *Advanced Reader*

ELL Place English language learners in the groups that correspond to their reading abilities in English.

Practice Stations
• Read for Meaning
• Get Fluent
• Word Work

Independent Activities
• Concept Talk Video
• *Reader's and Writer's Notebook*
• Research and Inquiry

ELL

When a Storm Comes
by Jennifer M. Johnson
ELL Reader
Advanced
Advanced High

When a Storm Comes
by Jennifer M. Johnson
ELD Reader
Beginning
Intermediate

ELL Poster

You Are Here!
Unit 5
Week 1

Day 1

SI Strategic Intervention	**Reinforce the Concept,** DI•1–DI•2 **Read Concept Literacy Reader** or **Below-Level Reader**
OL On-Level	**Expand the Concept,** DI•7 **Read On-Level Reader**
A Advanced	**Extend the Concept,** DI•12 **Read Advanced Reader**
ELL English Language Learners	DI•16–DI•25 **Frontload Concept** **Preteach Skills** **Writing**

Question of the Week
How can we prepare for emergencies?

SI Strategic Intervention

Putting a Stop to Wildfires
by Erin Cameron

Below-Level Reader

FIRE!
By Jeri Cipriano

Concept Literacy Reader

OL On-Level

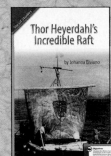
The Grizzly Bear Hotshots
by Kathleen Carey
Illustrated by Ben Shannon

On-Level Reader

A Advanced

Thor Heyerdahl's Incredible Raft
by Johanna Bisiano

Advanced Reader

Mark Beyer
SMOKEJUMPERS
Life Fighting Fires

Smokejumpers, pp. 178–179

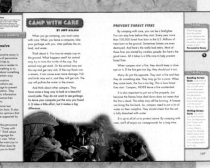

Camp with Care pp. 196–197

Week 1

Small Group Weekly Plan

Day 2	Day 3	Day 4	Day 5
Reinforce Comprehension, DI•3 **Revisit Main Selection**	**Reinforce Vocabulary,** DI•4 **Read/Revisit Main Selection**	**Reinforce Comprehension,** Practice Retelling, DI•5 Genre Focus **Read/Revisit Paired Selection**	**Practice Fluency,** DI•6 **Reread Concept Literacy Reader** or **Below-Level Reader**
Expand Comprehension, DI•8 **Revisit Main Selection**	**Expand Vocabulary,** DI•9 **Read/Revisit Main Selection**	**Expand Comprehension,** Practice Retelling, DI•10 Genre Focus **Read/Revisit Paired Selection**	**Practice Fluency,** DI•11 **Reread On-Level Reader**
Extend Comprehension, DI•13 **Revisit Main Selection**	**Extend Vocabulary,** DI•14 **Read/Revisit Main Selection**	**Extend Comprehension,** Genre Focus, DI•15 **Read/Revisit Paired Selection**	**Practice Fluency,** DI•15 **Reread Advanced Reader**
DI•16–DI•25 **Review Concept/Skills Frontload Main Selection Practice**	DI•16–DI•25 **Review Concept/Skills Reread Main Selection Practice**	DI•16–DI•25 **Review Concept Read ELL/ELD Readers Practice**	DI•16–DI•25 **Review Concept/Skills Reread ELL/ELD Readers Writing**

Practice Stations for Everyone on Reading Street!

Word Wise
Prefixes *un-*, *dis-*, and *in-*

Objectives
• Spell words with prefixes *un-*, *dis-*, and *in-*.

Materials
• *Word Wise* Flip Chart Activity 21
• Teacher-made word cards
• paper • pencil

Differentiated Activities

⬤ Choose two word cards with each prefix: *un-*, *dis-* and *in-*. Write the words. Write a sentence for each word. Think of other words with these prefixes. Add them to your list.

▲ Choose three word cards with each prefix: *un-*, *dis-* and *in-*. Write the words. Write sentences using each word. Add other words with these prefixes to your list.

■ Choose four word cards with prefixes *un-*, *dis-* and *in-*, and write the words. Write sentences using each word, and add other words with these prefixes to your list.

Technology
• Online Dictionary

Word Work
Prefixes *un-*, *dis-*, and *in-*

Objectives
• Identify, pronounce, and write words with prefixes *un-*, *dis-*, and *in-*.

Materials
• *Word Work* Flip Chart Activity 21
• Teacher-made word cards
• paper • pencil

Differentiated Activities

⬤ Choose three word cards with each prefix: *un-*, *dis-* and *in-*. Write the words. Say each word. Circle the base word in each word.

▲ Choose four word cards with each prefix: *un-*, *dis-* and *in-*, and write the words. Say each word. Circle the base word in each word.

■ Choose five word cards with each prefix: *un-*, *dis-* and *in-*, and write the words. Say each word, and circle the base word in each word.

Technology
• Modeled Pronunciation Audio CD

Words to Know
Synonyms and antonyms

Objectives
• Identify the meanings of synonyms and antonyms.

Materials
• *Words to Know* Flip Chart Activity 21
• Teacher-made word cards
• paper • pencil

Differentiated Activities

⬤ Choose four word cards. Think of a synonym and antonym for each word. Write a sentence for each word. Show similar meanings with synonyms, and opposite meanings with antonyms.

▲ Choose five word cards, and think of a synonym and antonym for each word. Write a sentence for each word. Show similar meanings with synonyms, and opposite meanings with antonyms.

■ Choose six word cards, and think of a synonym and antonym for each word. Write a sentence for each word. Show similar meanings with synonyms, and opposite meanings with antonyms.

Technology
• Online Dictionary

You Are Here!
Unit 5
Week 1

Use this week's materials from the Reading Street Leveled Practice Stations Kit to organize this week's stations.

Key
● Below-Level Activities
▲ On-Level Activities
■ Advanced Activities

Practice Station
Flip Chart

Let's Write!
Fictional adventure

Objectives
• Write a fictional adventure.

Materials
• *Let's Write!* Flip Chart Activity 21
• paper   • pencils

Differentiated Activities

● Imagine a character on an adventure that takes place in the past. Write about the character and his or her adventure. Give details about the adventure in the plot.

▲ Write about adventure that takes place in the past. Include a character in your adventure, and give details in the plot explaining what happens. Proofread your story for strong, active verbs.

■ Write an adventure story set in the past. Give details about the character and plot, and describe what happens to the character. Proofread to make sure you have used active, not passive, verbs.

Technology
• Online Graphic Organizers

Read for Meaning
Character and plot

Objectives
• Identify a story's characters and plot.

Materials
• *Read for Meaning* Flip Chart Activity 21
• Leveled Readers   • paper   • pencils

Differentiated Activities

● Read one of the books your teacher provides. Write one sentence describing a character in the story. Think about the story events. Write a sentence that explains the story's plot.

▲ Read one of the books your teacher provides, and think about the events that happen in the story. Write a sentence that tells the story's plot. Then, write sentences that describe two of the characters in the story.

■ Read one of the books your teacher provides. As you read, think about the plot of the story and its characters. Write two short paragraphs explaining the story's plot and characters.

Technology
• Leveled Reader Database

Get Fluent
Practice fluent reading.

Objectives
• Read aloud with expression.

Materials
• *Get Fluent* Flip Chart Activity 21
• Leveled Readers

Differentiated Activities

● Work with a partner. Choose a Concept Literacy Reader or Below-Level Reader. Take turns reading a page from the book. Use the readers to practice correct expression. Provide feedback as needed.

▲ Work with a partner. Choose an On-Level Reader. Take turns reading a page from the book. Use the reader to practice correct expression. Provide feedback as needed.

■ Work with a partner. Choose an Advanced Reader. Take turns reading a page from the book. Use the reader to practice correct expression. Provide feedback as needed.

Technology
• Leveled Reader Database
• Reading Street Readers CD-ROM

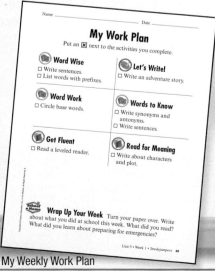

Name _____   Date _____

My Work Plan
Put an ☒ next to the activities you complete.

Word Wise
☐ Write sentences.
☐ List words with prefixes.

Let's Write!
☐ Write an adventure story.

Word Work
☐ Circle base words.

Words to Know
☐ Write synonyms and antonyms.
☐ Write sentences.

Get Fluent
☐ Read a leveled reader.

Read for Meaning
☐ Write about characters and plot.

Wrap Up Your Week Turn your paper over. Write about what you did at school this week. What did you read? What did you learn about preparing for emergencies?

My Weekly Work Plan

week 1

Objectives
- Introduce the weekly concept.
- Develop oral vocabulary.

Today at a Glance

Oral Vocabulary
generator, deserted, hurricane watch, dangerous

Comprehension
◉ Author's purpose
◉ Important ideas

Reading
"Parachutes All over the World"

Fluency
Rate and accuracy

Lesson Vocabulary
Tested vocabulary

Research and Inquiry
Identify questions

Spelling
Multisyllabic words

Conventions
Adjectives and articles

Handwriting
Cursive letters *Y* and *y*

Writing
Fantasy

Concept Talk

Question of the Week

How can we prepare for emergencies?

Introduce the concept

To further explore the unit concept of Adventures by Land, Air, and Water, this week students will read, write, and talk about how we can prepare for emergencies. Write the Question of the Week on the board.

> **ROUTINE** **Activate Prior Knowledge** **Team Talk**
>
> ① **Think** Have students think about the different ways people might react to emergencies.
>
> ② **Pair** Have pairs of students discuss the Question of the Week.
>
> ③ **Share** Call on a few students to share their ideas and comments with the group. Guide the discussion and encourage elaboration with prompts such as:
>
> - What objects do people keep handy to prepare for emergencies?
> - Who can we call to help during an emergency?

Routines Flip Chart

Anchored Talk

Develop oral vocabulary

Have students turn to pp. 172–173 in their Student Editions. Look at each of the photos. Then, use the prompts to guide discussion and create the *How we can prepare for emergencies* concept map. Remind students to ask and answer questions with appropriate detail.

- What type of emergency do you think the people are preparing for? (They might be preparing for a natural disaster, such as a flood.) Sometimes forces of nature can cause emergencies. Let's add *Nature* to our map.

- How do people use the stairs during an emergency? (They have a plan to escape from a fire using the stairs.) Let's add *Plan* to the map.

Oral Vocabulary

Objectives
• Speak clearly and to the point, give an opinion and support it with correct information. • Take part in discussions led by teachers or other students, ask and answer questions, and offer ideas that build on the ideas of other people.

Let's Talk About

Emergencies

● Share opinions about what an emergency is.

● Tell how to act, and include information in your description.

● Build upon the ideas of others.

READING STREET ONLINE
CONCEPT TALK VIDEO
www.ReadingStreet.com

You've learned
200
Amazing Words ★
so far this year!

173

Student Edition pp. 172–173

You've learned **200** words so far

You'll learn **010** words this week!

generator	medical
deserted	first aid
hurricane watch	ignite
dangerous	wildfires
fire escape	gear

 **Writing on Demand**

Writing Fluency
Ask students to respond to the photos on pp. 172–173 by writing as well as they can and as much as they can about how we can be prepared for emergencies.

• How might the person in the parachute be involved in an emergency? (The person might be involved in a rescue attempt or be arriving to help.) Let's add *Rescue* to our concept map.

• After discussing the photos, ask: How can we prepare for emergencies?

Connect to reading

Tell students that this week they will be reading about people who help to prepare for and respond to emergencies. Encourage students to add concept-related words to the concept map.

ELL **Preteach Concepts** Use the Day 1 instruction on ELL Poster 21 to assess and build background knowledge, develop concepts, and build oral vocabulary.

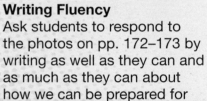 **ELL**

English Language Learners
ELL Support Additional ELL support and modified instruction is provided in the *ELL Handbook* and in the ELL Support lessons on pp. DI•16–DI•25.

Listening comprehension
English learners will benefit from additional visual support to understand the key terms in the concept map. Use the pictures on pp. 172–173 to scaffold understanding.

Frontload for Read Aloud Use the modified Read Aloud on p. DI•19 of the ELL Support lessons to prepare students to listen to "Coconuts" (p. 173b).

ELL Poster 21

Smokejumpers **172–173**

Oral Vocabulary
Amazing Words

Introduce Amazing Words

"Coconuts" on p. 173b is about preparing for a hurricane. Tell students to listen for this week's Amazing Words—*generator, deserted, hurricane watch,* and *dangerous*—as you read.

Model fluency

As you read "Coconuts," model appropriate rate by reading at a speed that is neither too slow nor too fast. Model accuracy with smooth, fluent reading.

Teach Amazing Words

Amazing Words Oral Vocabulary Routine

> generator
> deserted
> hurricane
>   watch
> dangerous

1 Introduce Write the word *generator* on the board. Have students say the word aloud with you. In "Coconuts," the boy's mother volunteers to check on the *generator* before a storm. Supply a student-friendly definition.

2 Demonstrate Have students answer questions to demonstrate understanding. Why would it be good to have a *generator* during a hurricane? Why is it important that a hospital have a *generator*?

3 Apply Have students apply understanding. If the power went out in a storm, what appliance would you use with the power from a *generator*?

See p. OV• 1 to teach *deserted, hurricane watch,* and *dangerous.*

Routines Flip Chart

Apply Amazing Words

To build oral language, lead the class in a discussion about the meanings of the Amazing Words. Remind students to listen attentively to speakers and to build on the ideas of others in the discussion.

MONITOR PROGRESS **Check Oral Vocabulary**

During discussion, listen for students' use of the Amazing Words.

If... students are unable to use the Amazing Words to discuss the concept,

then... use Oral Vocabulary Routine in the Routines Flip Chart to demonstrate words in different contexts.

Day 1	**Days 2–3**	**Day 4**	**Day 5**
Check Oral Vocabulary	Check Retelling	Check Fluency	Check Oral Vocabulary

Coconuts

by Dagmar Kost

This is how I learned about Calvin.

I came out of my room this morning, and found Mom and Dad standing in front of the TV. Something was happening. On the screen, Tony Verrazo said Calvin had turned west and was headed for land.

I didn't understand what was happening.

"I'm going to check on the generator," said Mom.

"I'm going to the grocery store," Dad said. He turned to my brother, Mike. "You can start by closing the shutters while I'm gone."

"You pick up coconuts, Jason," Dad said, pointing at me.

We had a bunch of palm trees and plenty of coconuts, but we'd never bothered with them before. Why pick them up now?

I found Mom and Mike in the utility room.

"Have I ever been in a hurricane?" I asked.

"Yes," Mom nodded. "Its name was Flora."

"You were little," said Mike. "You had a babysitter while we got ready."

I wanted to ask about the coconuts, but Mom shook her head.

"I'm sorry, Jason, but I don't have time for more questions," she said. "And you have a job to do."

I had no idea what was going on. I kicked a few coconuts and then walked down to the beach. I wanted to spot Calvin, but I wasn't really sure what to look for. The beach was deserted except for two men. One held a camera. The other was talking into a microphone. He was the same guy I'd seen on TV this morning.

"Folks," Tony Verrazo was saying, "we have a hurricane watch for Calvin. Stay tuned."

"Hi, kid," said Tony Verrazo. "Wazzup?"

"I'm just hanging out," I said.

"You're not helping your folks?"

"I'm taking a break from picking up coconuts."

"Coconuts," he said thoughtfully. "I forgot all about them."

He started writing while walking away. Then he said, "Hey, kid, stand over here and tell the camera who you are and what you're doing."

"Hi. My name is Jason. I'm picking up coconuts because Calvin is coming."

"Thanks, kid," Tony Verrazo said. "You better head home and finish your job!"

After hours of working, I'd filled every trash bag I could find. At last, Mike came to get me.

"It's coming," Mike said.

Continued on p. 199s

30–35 min

Objectives

◎ Identify author's purpose to aid comprehension.

◎ Use the important ideas strategy to aid comprehension.

• Read grade-level text with appropriate rate and accuracy.

Skills Trace

◉ Author's Purpose

Introduce U1W2D1; U1W4D1; U5W1D1

Practice U1W2D2; U1W2D3; U1W4D2; U1W4D3; U5W1D2; U5W1D3

Reteach/Review U1W2D5; U1W4D5; U1W5D2; U2W2D3; U5W1D5; U5W3D3

Assess/Test
Weekly Tests U1W2; U1W4; U5W1
Benchmark Tests U1; U5

KEY:
U=Unit   W=Week   D=Day

Skill ↔ Strategy
↻ Author's Purpose
↻ Important Ideas

Introduce author's purpose

Envision It!

The author's purpose for writing a certain text is to persuade, inform, express a feeling, or to entertain. Knowing the author's purpose for writing will help you adjust how you read that particular text. What are ways you might adjust your reading? (You might read more slowly and carefully if you know the author is trying to persuade or inform, and you'd read faster if the author is entertaining you.) Have students turn to p. EI•2 in the Student Edition to review author's purpose. Then read "Parachutes All over the World" with students.

Student Edition p. EI•2

Model the skill

 Think Aloud The first paragraph is about Leonardo da Vinci. From the way this paragraph is written, what do you think the author's purpose is? **(to inform)** The author doesn't directly state a purpose for writing, but there are many facts about da Vinci, so I think it is implied that the author's purpose is to inform. The author might also want readers to be amazed that da Vinci imagined parachutes long ago, so another implied purpose is to entertain.

Guide practice

Have students finish reading "Parachutes All over the World" on their own. After they have read, have them form small groups to explain what the author's implied purpose for writing is, and how this affected the way they read the selection. Have students write a sentence that the author could have included in the selection to state a purpose for writing.

Strategy check

Important Ideas Remind students that if they have difficulty understanding "Parachutes All over the World," they can use the strategy of important ideas. Model the strategy and have students summarize the important ideas and details in each paragraph in ways that maintain meaning.

Model the strategy

Envision It!

Think Aloud Focusing on the important ideas in an expository text helps me understand what I read. Often the most important idea of a paragraph is in the first sentence, and the rest of the paragraph contains details that give me more information about the important idea. Have students review the important ideas strategy on p. EI•17 of the Student Edition.

Student Edition p. EI•17

On their own

Use p. 316 in the *Reader's and Writer's Notebook* for additional practice with author's purpose.

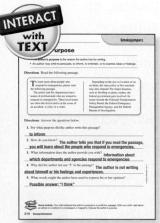

INTERACT with TEXT

Reader's and Writer's Notebook p. 316

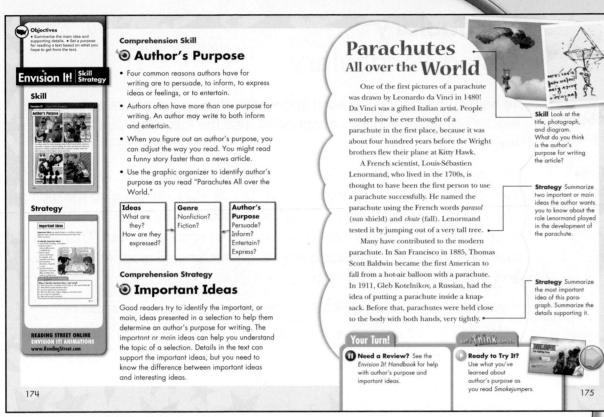

Student Edition pp. 174–175

Skill The purpose was to entertain and inform readers about how parachutes were developed.

Strategy 1. He was the first person to use a parachute successfully.
2. He gave the parachute its name.

Strategy Many people helped develop the modern parachute. One person tested the parachute, and another put the parachute in a knapsack

Academic Vocabulary

explicit purpose An author's explicit purpose is the stated purpose for writing a text. It is very clear for the reader to understand.

implicit purpose An author's implicit purpose for writing a text is implied in the way the author has put words together. The reader needs to infer the author's implicit purpose.

Model Fluency
Rate and Accuracy

Model fluent reading
Have students listen as you read the first paragraph of "Parachutes All over the World." Explain that you will read at a slightly slower rate that is appropriate for reading expository text. Explain that by slowing your reading speed, you are able to comprehend the text and to read fluently with accuracy.

 **Oral Rereading**

1. **Read** Have students read paragraph 2 orally.
2. **Reread** To achieve optimal fluency, students should reread the text three or four times with appropriate rate and accuracy.
3. **Corrective Feedback** Have students read aloud without you. Provide feedback about their rate and accuracy, and encourage them to adjust their rate to allow for accuracy and comprehension. To achieve optimal fluency, students should reread the text three or four times.

Routines Flip Chart

ELL

English Language Learners
Important ideas Draw a semantic map. Read aloud the selection as students follow along. Pause and ask questions about important ideas. Fill in the map with the important ideas.

Objectives
- Activate prior knowledge of words.
- Identify questions for research.

Vocabulary
Tested Vocabulary

Lesson vocabulary

To help students acquire word knowledge that improves reading, speaking, listening, and writing vocabularies, use the following Question and Answer activity.

Activate prior knowledge

Display the lesson words. Give students the opportunity to tell whatever they already know about these words. Guide students in using the dictionary or glossary to find the definition, syllabication, and pronunciation of each unknown word that fits with the topic of smokejumpers. Then ask oral questions such as those below. Students should respond *yes* or *no* and give reasons for their choice.

- Would lace or net be a good material to use to make a *parachute*?
- Will you get where you want to go if you *steer* a bike with a blindfold on?
- Is water *essential* to life?
- Does *underbrush* help put out a fire?
- Does *wind* have anything to do with a storm?
- If you are *concentrating* on something are you thinking hard about it?
- Do you have *dedication* to something if you don't care much about it?
- Does having a *method* help you do a better job brushing your teeth?

Compound words

Use the word *underbrush* to point out that some words are compound words. Have students identify the two words in *underbrush* (*under* and *brush*). Ask students if separating the two words helped them understand the meaning of the compound word.

By the end of the week, students should know the lesson words and should be able to add their definitions, pictures, or captions.

Preteach Academic Vocabulary

 Academic Vocabulary Write the following words on the board:

homographs	articles
multisyllabic words	adjectives
explicit purpose	implicit purpose

Have students share what they know about this week's Academic Vocabulary. Use the students' responses to assess their prior knowledge. Preteach the Academic Vocabulary by providing a student-friendly description, explanation, or example that clarifies the meaning of each term. Then ask students to restate the meaning of the Academic Vocabulary term in their own words.

Research and Inquiry
Identify Questions

Teach

Discuss the Question of the Week: *How can we prepare for emergencies?* Tell students they will research how carrying out emergency procedures can be like an adventure. They will present their findings to the class using a poster on Day 5.

Model

Think Aloud I'll start by brainstorming a list of emergency procedures. There's sandbagging for a flood, firefighting, helping free someone who is trapped, saving someone who is drowning, calling 911, helping stop bleeding. After I choose a topic, some questions might be *What is the process?* or *How is it done?*

Guide practice

After students have formulated open-ended inquiry questions, explain that tomorrow they will conduct online research using their questions. Help students identify keywords that will guide their search.

On their own

Have students work individually, in pairs, or in small groups to write an inquiry question.

INTERNET GUY
Don Leu

21st Century Skills

Weekly Inquiry Project

Day 1 Identify Questions

Day 2 Navigate/Search

Day 3 Analyze

Day 4 Synthesize

Day 5 Communicate

Differentiated Instruction

 Advanced

Have students think about possible sources that might contain useful information for their research about emergency procedures.

Small Group Time

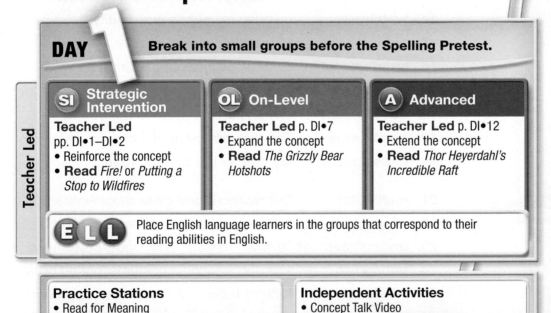

DAY 1

Break into small groups before the Spelling Pretest.

Teacher Led

SI Strategic Intervention	OL On-Level	A Advanced
Teacher Led pp. DI•1–DI•2 • Reinforce the concept • **Read** *Fire!* or *Putting a Stop to Wildfires*	**Teacher Led** p. DI•7 • Expand the concept • **Read** *The Grizzly Bear Hotshots*	**Teacher Led** p. DI•12 • Extend the concept • **Read** *Thor Heyerdahl's Incredible Raft*

ELL Place English language learners in the groups that correspond to their reading abilities in English.

Practice Stations
• Read for Meaning
• Get Fluent
• Word Work

Independent Activities
• Concept Talk Video
• *Reader's and Writer's Notebook*
• Vocabulary Activities

ELL

English Language Learners
Multilingual vocabulary
Students can apply knowledge of their home languages to acquire new English vocabulary by using Multilingual Vocabulary Lists (*ELL Handbook,* pp. 431-442).

Spelling Pretest
Multisyllabic Words

Introduce

Tell students to think of words that have three or more syllables *(interesting, terribly, excitable)*. This week we will spell multisyllabic words, or words with three or more syllables.

Pretest

Use these sentences to administer the spelling pretest. Say each word, read the sentence, and repeat the word.

1.	**reaction**	I had a **reaction** to the bee sting.
2.	**prerecorded**	I heard a **prerecorded** message.
3.	**incorrectly**	You spelled that word **incorrectly.**
4.	**incredibly**	It is **incredibly** cold outside.
5.	**disobedient**	My new puppy is **disobedient.**
6.	**disagreeable**	She was in a **disagreeable** mood.
7.	**refreshment**	I enjoy a cool **refreshment** on a hot day.
8.	**unbreakable**	The cups are **unbreakable.**
9.	**declaration**	The king is making a **declaration** today.
10.	**retirement**	My grandfather is ready for **retirement.**
11.	**misdialed**	I got a wrong number when I **misdialed** the phone.
12.	**undefined**	The faces in the painting are **undefined.**
13.	**unhappily**	**Unhappily,** our team lost the game.
14.	**watchfully**	I tended my puppy **watchfully.**
15.	**gleefully**	My puppy played **gleefully.**
16.	**sportsmanship**	Good **sportsmanship** is important.
17.	**repayment**	I will begin the **repayment** of my loan.
18.	**questionable**	The charge on my bill is **questionable.**
19.	**displacement**	The **displacement** of water caused flooding.
20.	**midshipman**	My brother is a **midshipman** in the navy.

Challenge words

21.	**multicultural**	Our **multicultural** class represents many countries.
22.	**universally**	A friendly person is **universally** liked.
23.	**understatement**	To say "I'm glad" is an **understatement.**
24.	**outlandish**	The dog wearing a costume looked **outlandish.**
25.	**inflammable**	**Inflammable** materials can easily catch fire.

Self-correct

After the pretest, you can either display the correctly spelled words or spell them orally. Have students self-correct their pretests by rewriting misspelled words correctly.

Let's Practice It!
TR DVD•245

On their own

Use *Let's Practice It!* page 245 on the *Teacher Resources DVD-ROM* for additional practice.

Conventions
Adjectives and Articles

Teach
Display Grammar Transparency 21, and read aloud the explanation and examples in the box. Point out the adjectives *careless, four,* and *that* as well as the questions they answer. Discuss the proper use of articles. Point out the proper adjectives, calling attention to their initial capital letter.

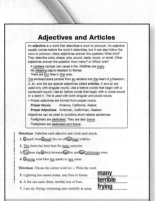

Grammar Transparency 21, TR DVD

Model
Model underlining each adjective and circling each article in numbers 1 and 2. Discuss how you decided on your answers.

Guide practice
Guide students to complete items 3 and 4. Remind them to look for articles and adjectives. Record the correct responses on the transparency.

Daily Fix-It
Use Daily Fix-It numbers 1 and 2 in the right margin.

Connect to oral language
Have students read sentences 5–7 on the transparency and choose the correct response.

Handwriting
Cursive Letters Y and y

Model letter formation
Display the capital cursive letter *Y* and the lower-case letter *y*. Follow the stroke instructions pictured to model letter formation.

Model letter shape
Explain that writing legibly means letters are the correct size, form, and slant. The writing has smoothness; the lines are not shaky or jagged. Model writing this sentence with attention to letter shape: *Yesterday, you were trying to fix the baby's tiny toy.* Point out the correct shape of the loops in both the lowercase *y* and the capital *Y.* Make sure the letters aren't too light, dark, or jagged.

Guide practice
Have students write these sentences. *Yuri bought a pretty hyacinth plant. You and Phyllis can play in the yard.* Circulate around the room, guiding students.

Academic Vocabulary

Adjectives are words that describe nouns.

Articles are the words *a, an,* and *the.*

Daily Fix-It

1. The men hapily volunteered to put out forest fires in the rocky mountains. *(happily; Rocky Mountains)*

2. Sometimes hed trac the forest fire from above in him airplane. *(he'd; track; his)*

English Language Learners
Language production: Writing and pronouncing the articles *a* and *an* Model writing and pronouncing *a* and *an*. Write and say *an apple, a boy, a car.* Point out that *a* is used before words that begin with a consonant and *an* is used before words that begin with a vowel. On separate pieces of paper, have students write *a* and *an* and pronounce each article. Say a noun and have students hold up the piece of paper with the correct article written on it. Then have them say the article and noun together.

Handwriting: Adjectives To provide practice in handwriting lowercase *y* and to extend language opportunities, have students write adjectives that include *y.* *(yellow, young, jolly)*

Objectives
- Understand and identify the features of a fantasy.

Writing—Fantasy
Introduce

MINI-LESSON

5-Day Planner
Guide to Mini-Lessons

DAY **1**	Read Like a Writer
DAY **2**	Developing a Story Sequence Chart
DAY **3**	Writing Complete Sentences
DAY **4**	Revising Strategy: Consolidating
DAY **5**	Proofread for Adjectives and Articles

MINI-LESSON

Read Like a Writer

■ **Introduce** This week you will write a narrative composition about an adventure by air. Your composition will be a fantasy, a make-believe story that never could happen in the real world.

Prompt	Write a fantasy story about fighting a fire.
Trait	Conventions
Mode	Narrative

Reader's and Writer's Notebook p. 317

■ **Examine Model Text** Let's read an example of a narrative that is a fantasy about an adventure in the air. Have students read "Hurricane Hunt" on p. 317 of their *Reader's and Writer's Notebook.*

■ **Key Features** Fantasies may have characters—people, animals, or objects—doing things they cannot do in the real world. Have students interact by underlining the sentences in the first paragraph that show an object doing things it could not do in the real world. Discuss how this information in the first paragraph helps the reader determine that this story is a fantasy.

A fantasy describes events that couldn't happen in the real world. Have students draw boxes around events in the story that couldn't happen in the real world.

A fantasy may have a setting that does not exist in the real world. Have students underline the setting at the beginning and end of the story. Discuss whether this setting could exist in the real world.

Review
Key features

Review the key features of fantasy with students. You may want to post the key features in the classroom for students to refer to as they work on their stories.

Key Features of Fantasy

- may have characters doing things they cannot do in the real world
- describes events that couldn't happen in the real world
- may have a setting that does not exist in the real world
- may be written to seem almost real
- may have a tone of happiness, nostalgia, or danger

Write Guy
Jeff Anderson

Let Me Check My List

Encourage students to keep lists of words they come across that are exciting or interesting to them. They can use their lists to increase their vocabulary and incorporate them in their own writing. This is a great way to improve vocabulary and word choice.

ROUTINE Quick Write for Fluency Team Talk

1) **Talk** Have partners take a few minutes to discuss the features of fantasy.

2) **Write** Each student writes a short paragraph that describes the setting of a fantasy story.

3) **Share** Partners read each other's paragraphs.

Routines Flip Chart

Wrap Up Your Day

✔ **Build Concepts** What did you learn about preparing for emergencies?

✔ **Oral Vocabulary** Have students use the Amazing Words they learned in context sentences.

✔ **Homework** Send home this week's Family Times newsletter in *Let's Practice It!* pp. 246–247 on the *Teacher Resources DVD-ROM.*

Let's Practice It
TR DVD•246–247

English Language Learners
Read the writing model aloud and help students understand it. Make sure students realize that fantasies should be as imaginative as possible and don't have to be realistic. Encourage them to brainstorm events that couldn't happen in the real world.

Preview DAY 2

Tell students that tomorrow they will read about how smokejumpers fight wildfires. This job involves a lot of risk!

Objectives
- Expand the weekly concept.
- Develop oral vocabulary.

Today at a Glance

Oral Vocabulary
fire escape, medical

Word Analysis
French word origins

Literary Terms
Word choice

Text Structure
Description/definition

Lesson Vocabulary
⊙ Homographs

Reading
"Remembering Firefighting Heroes"
Smokejumpers

Fluency
Rate and accuracy

Research and Inquiry
Navigate/search

Spelling
Multisyllabic words

Conventions
Adjectives and articles

Writing
Fantasy

Concept Talk

Question of the Week
How can we prepare for emergencies?

Expand the concept

Remind students of the Question of the Week. Tell students that today they will begin reading *Smokejumpers: Life Fighting Fires.* As they read, encourage students to think about how firefighters can prepare for emergencies.

Anchored Talk

Develop oral vocabulary

Use the photos on pp. 172–173 and the Read Aloud "Coconuts" to talk about the Amazing Words: *generator, deserted, hurricane watch,* and *dangerous.* Add these and other concept-related words to the concept map to develop students' knowledge of the topic. Discuss the following questions. Remind students to listen attentively to other students and to answer with appropriate detail. Encourage students to build on others' ideas when they answer.

- What are some *dangerous* emergencies that you can think of?

- A *generator* is a machine that can help in an emergency. What other tools and equipment can help people during or after an emergency?

- People prepare for emergencies in different ways. How do people prepare before a *hurricane watch* or other kinds of extreme weather such as a tornado or flood?

- Certain kinds of emergencies such as hurricanes or storms can leave places *deserted.* Explain why this might happen.

Oral Vocabulary
Amazing Words

Amazing Words

generator	medical
deserted	first aid
hurricane watch	ignite
	wildfires
dangerous	gear
fire escape	

Teach Amazing Words

Amazing Words Oral Vocabulary Routine

1 Introduce Write *fire escape* on the board. Have students say it with you. Relate *fire escape* to the photograph on p. 172 and to "Parachutes All over the World" on p. 175. How might a parachute accomplish the same goal as a *fire escape*? Have students determine the definition of the word. (metal stairway attached to the outside of a building)

2 Demonstrate Have students answer questions to demonstrate understanding. Why is a *fire escape* made of metal? Who might have difficulty using a *fire escape*?

3 Apply Have students apply their understanding. How would you get to a *fire escape* from inside a building?

See p. OV•1 to teach *medical*.

Routines Flip Chart

Apply Amazing Words

As students read "Remembering Firefighting Heroes" on p. 177, have them think about whether *fire escapes* would be helpful to smokejumpers and what kind of *medical* support smokejumpers need.

Connect to reading

Tell students that today they will read about people who parachute into remote areas to fight wildfires. As they read, they should think about how the Question of the Week and the Amazing Words *fire escape* and *medical* relate to the work of the smokejumpers.

ELL Reinforce Vocabulary Use the Day 2 instruction on ELL Poster 21 to teach lesson vocabulary and discuss the lesson concept.

 ELL Poster 21

Smokejumpers **176b**

Objectives

- Expand knowledge of words derived from French.
- Understand an author's choice of words.
- Analyze text structure to aid reading comprehension.

Word Analysis
French Word Origins

Teach word origins

Explain that many words we use come from other languages. Tell students that the word *parachute* comes from the French language. Explain that you can determine the meaning of unknown English words that are derived from other linguistic roots by looking up the origin of a word in dictionaries, etymology books, or on the Internet.

Model

 Think Aloud I looked up the origin of the word *parachute.* The word is from French, and it means "defense against falling."

Word from French	Meaning and History
parachute	*para* (defense against) + *chute* (fall) First use—1785
chapter	
continue	
deserted	
escape	
medical	
aid	

Guide practice

Have students choose a word from the first column and research its linguistic roots in a dictionary. Explain that *O.F.* means old French and *Fr.* means French. Then have students use the French root to explain the word's meaning.

On their own

Have students fill in the chart with their findings and cite their sources. Follow the Strategy for Multisyllabic Words to teach the word *parachute.*

ROUTINE **Strategy for Multisyllabic Words**

1. **Connect to sound spellings** Chunk the word into syllables. Circle each. When I say *parachute,* I can hear three syllables. I will circle the syllables *par, a,* and *chute.*

2. **Read the word** Read each syllable, and then read them together. This is how I read this word. First I read each syllable, and then I read the syllables together: *par / a / chute* becomes *parachute.*

Continue the routine with the words *chapter* and *continue.*

Routines Flip Chart

Literary Terms
Word Choice

Teach word choice

Tell students that authors of both fiction and expository text choose their words carefully. Authors revise their writing many times, searching for just the right words to get their point across.

Model word choice

Think Aloud Let's look at some of the words the author of "Parachutes All over the World" uses. Take the sentence *Lenormand tested his parachute by jumping out of a very tall tree.* The author uses the word *tested,* instead of *tried out.* I think the author chose this word deliberately because *tested* is more precise than *tried out.* It implies that Lenormand is putting something to a test or trying to prove something.

Guide practice

Have students locate the last sentence in the first paragraph of "Parachutes All over the World." Have them analyze why the author chose the word *wondered.*

On their own

Have students look for other instances of word choice in other selections of their Student Edition.

Text Structure
Description/Definition

Teach description/ definition

Expository nonfiction can be structured differently. *Smokejumpers* is written in the description/definition text structure. Information is listed and described.

Model the strategy

Think Aloud The first page of *Smokejumpers* describes where wildfires occur. The first paragraph has a good description of what hot shots do, and the second paragraph introduces smokejumpers. Knowing the text structure helps me set my purpose for reading—in this case, to read for information.

Guide practice

Work with students to find other examples of description/ definition text structure in *Smokejumpers.*

On their own

Have students skim the selection and choose one sentence to share as an example of the description/ definition text structure.

Academic Vocabulary

Multisyllabic words Words that have more than two syllables are multisyllabic words.

E L L

English Language Learners
Idioms Explain to students that an idiom is a phrase that means something other than the usual meaning of the individual words combined. Share some examples that could come in handy in emergencies: *All systems go* means "everything is ready." *He's asleep at the wheel* means "he's not paying attention." *It makes your blood run cold* means "it's horrifying." *Keep your head above water* means "stay out of trouble." Work with students to carry on a conversation using these idioms.

Objectives
- Use a dictionary or glossary to determine meaning and pronunciation of homographs.
- Read grade-level text accurately and at an appropriate rate.

Vocabulary Strategy for
Homographs

Student Edition p. W•10

Teach homographs

Envision It!

Explain that homographs are words that are spelled the same but have different meanings and sometimes different pronunciations. Tell students that when they encounter a homograph, they can use the strategy of checking a dictionary to find the word's different meanings and pronunciations, and then decide which meaning makes the most sense in the sentence. Refer students to *Words!* on p. W•10 in the Student Edition for additional practice. Then read "Remembering Firefighting Heroes" on p. 177 with students.

Model the strategy

Think Aloud I see the word steer in the first sentence. Write on the board: *Smokejumpers use the parachute to steer themselves near deadly fires.* I know that *steer* is a homograph that has more than one meaning. I can check a dictionary to see which meaning makes sense in the sentence. I see in the dictionary that this word is pronounced the same way and has the same number of syllables for each entry. *Steer* can mean "a young male cow" or "to guide." The second definition makes sense in the sentence, because the smokejumpers can use the parachutes to guide themselves near fires.

Guide practice

Write this sentence on the board: *The wind began blowing in the same direction*. Help students identify the homograph *wind* in the sentence. Then have students check the meanings, syllabication, and pronunciations of *wind* in a dictionary and determine which meaning and pronunciation applies to the sentence. For additional support, use *Envision It! Pictured Vocabulary Cards* or *Tested Vocabulary Cards*.

On their own

Read "Remembering Firefighting Heroes" on p. 177. Have students look for any additional homographs, such as *bolt*. Have them use the context of the sentence to guess the meaning of the word. Then have students check a dictionary to find other pronunciations and meanings for *bolt*. For additional practice, use *Reader's and Writer's Notebook* p. 318.

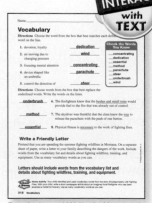

Reader's and Writer's Notebook
p. 318

Student Edition pp. 176–177

(Student Edition reproduction)

Objectives
• Determine the meanings of unfamiliar or multiple-meaning words by using the context of the sentence.
• Use a dictionary or glossary to find the meanings of unknown words, the syllable rules for these words, and how to pronounce them.

Envision It! | Words to Know

concentrating
parachute
underbrush
dedication
essential
method
steer
wind

READING STREET ONLINE VOCABULARY ACTIVITIES www.ReadingStreet.com

176

Vocabulary Strategy for
Homographs

Dictionary/Glossary Homographs are words that are spelled the same but have different meanings and sometimes different pronunciations. For example, *dove* is a homograph. *Dove* (duv) means "a kind of bird." *Dove* (long /o/ sound) means "jumped headfirst into water."

1. When you read a homograph, read the words and sentences around it.
2. Is there an example or definition of the word in the context? Put that meaning into the sentence and see if it makes sense.
3. If the word still doesn't make sense, use a dictionary or glossary to find the meaning.

As you read "Remembering Firefighting Heroes," use a dictionary or glossary to figure out the meanings of *wind* and *steer*.

Words to Write Reread "Remembering Firefighting Heroes." Figure out the meanings of the homographs in the passage. Write what you think each word means. Use a dictionary or glossary to check your work.

Remembering
Firefighting Heroes

Smokejumpers are firefighters who parachute into remote areas and use the parachute to steer themselves near deadly fires. The U.S. Forest Service began using smokejumpers in 1940. They have become an essential part of protecting our country's national forests.

On August 5, 1949, a wildfire raged at Mann Gulch in Montana. A bolt of lightning had probably set fire to some underbrush near the Missouri River. At the same time, the wind picked up, feeding the fire even more.

Smokejumpers began by concentrating their efforts in an area behind the fire. The foreman, Wagner Dodge, led his men to a lower part of the gulch. Smokejumpers faced the conflict with fierceness and dedication, but it still burned.

Dodge realized that his method wasn't working. The fire was getting worse, so he ordered his men to run up the slope of the gulch to escape. At about the same time, the wind began blowing in the same direction, essentially chasing the firefighters up the hill. Fifteen men lost their lives.

In 1999, a dedication ceremony was held on the fiftieth anniversary of the fire. Smokejumpers landed in Mann Gulch to remember the sacrifice of those who had died.

Your Turn!

Need a Review? For help with homographs, see *Words!*

Ready to Try It? Read *Smokejumpers: Life Fighting Fires* on pp. 178–191.

177

Reread for Fluency
Rate and Accuracy

Model fluent reading

Read the first paragraph of "Remembering Firefighting Heroes" aloud, keeping your rate slow and steady and pausing at natural places. Remind students that you are reading the passage at an appropriate speed so that you can understand the text.

 **Oral Rereading**

1. **Read** Have students read paragraph 1 of "Remembering Firefighting Heroes" orally.
2. **Reread** To achieve optimal fluency, students should reread the text three or four times.
3. **Corrective Feedback** Have students read aloud without you. Listen to ensure that students are reading accurately at an appropriate rate. Provide feedback about their rate and accuracy, and encourage students to adjust their rate in order to read more accurately and better comprehend the text.

Routines Flip Chart

Lesson Vocabulary

concentrating paying close attention; focusing the mind
dedication the act of giving time and energy to something
essential necessary
method a way of doing something
parachute umbrella-shaped device made of fabric; it allows people to fall slowly from an airplane
steer to guide
underbrush bushes and small trees growing under large trees
wind air that moves

Differentiated Instruction

SI Strategic Intervention
Homographs Have students work with a partner to identify the homographs from this week's lesson vocabulary. Have partners use a dictionary to find two meanings for each homograph. Then have partners come up with a sentence for each homograph.

ELL

English Language Learners
Build Academic Vocabulary
Use the lesson vocabulary pictured on p. 176 to teach the meanings of *concentrating*, *parachute*, and *underbrush*. Call on pairs to write the words on sticky notes and use them to label images of the words on the ELL Poster.

Objectives

- Understand the elements of expository text.
- Use text features to preview and predict.
- Set a purpose for reading.

Mark Beyer

SMOKEJUMPERS
Life Fighting Fires

Question of the Week
How can we prepare for emergencies?

Genre **Expository Text** gives information about real people and events. As you read, think about the skills needed to become a smokejumper.

178

Let's **Think** About Reading!

Student Edition pp. 178–179

Build Background

Discuss fighting fires

Team Talk Have students turn to a partner and discuss the Question of the Week and these questions about the work of smokejumpers. Remind students to ask and answer questions with appropriate detail and to give suggestions that build on the ideas of others.

- What are some of the dangers of fighting fires?
- What kind of training do you need to fight fires?
- How do you think a smokejumper might be different from a firefighter?

Connect to selection

Have students discuss their answers with the class. Remind students to listen to speakers and to make relevant, pertinent comments. Possible responses: Firefighters face many dangers, such as extreme heat, falling objects, and the possibility of getting burned or inhaling smoke. To fight fires, you need to be trained in using the equipment, how to be safe, and how to look for people who might need to be rescued. The word *jump* in the word *smokejumpers* makes me think that maybe a smokejumper's job involves jumping, while a firefighter's job does not. For additional opportunities to build background, use the Background Building Audio.

Prereading Strategies

Genre
Explain that **expository text** tells about real people, places, things, or events. Tell students that expository texts are often organized by text features, such as heads, subheads, charts, diagrams or illustrations, photos, and captions.

Preview and predict
Have students preview the selection by reading the title and subheads. Have them examine the photographs and read the captions and labels. Ask students to predict what they will learn as they read.

Set purpose
Prior to reading, have students set their own purposes for reading this selection. To help students set a purpose, ask them to think about how people who fight fires can prepare for emergencies.

Strategy Response Log

INTERACT
with
TEXT

Have students use p. 27 in the *Reader's and Writer's Notebook* to review and use the strategy of important ideas.

Small Group Time

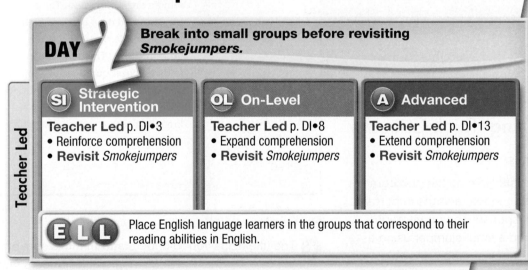

DAY 2

Break into small groups before revisiting *Smokejumpers*.

Teacher Led

(SI) Strategic Intervention
Teacher Led p. DI•3
• Reinforce comprehension
• **Revisit** *Smokejumpers*

(OL) On-Level
Teacher Led p. DI•8
• Expand comprehension
• **Revisit** *Smokejumpers*

(A) Advanced
Teacher Led p. DI•13
• Extend comprehension
• **Revisit** *Smokejumpers*

ELL Place English language learners in the groups that correspond to their reading abilities in English.

Practice Stations
• Words to Know
• Get Fluent
• Word Wise

Independent Activities
• Background Building Audio
• *Reader's and Writer's Notebook*
• Research and Inquiry

Differentiated Instruction

(A) Advanced
After students have previewed the selection, have them make a Venn diagram comparing the job of a firefighter to the job of a smokejumper.

Multidraft Reading

For **Whole Group** instruction, choose one of the reading options below. For each reading, have students set the purpose indicated.

Option 1
Day 2 Read the selection. Use Guide Comprehension to monitor and clarify understanding.
Day 3 Reread the selection. Use Extend Thinking to develop higher-order thinking skills.

Option 2
Day 2 Read the first half of the selection, using both Guide Comprehension and Extend Thinking instruction.
Day 3 Read the second half of the selection, using both Guide Comprehension and Extend Thinking instruction.

English Language Learners
Build background To build background, review the selection summary (*ELL Handbook*, p. 151). Use the Retelling Cards to provide visual support for the summary.

OPTION 1 Guide Comprehension Skills and Strategies

Teach Important Ideas

🔊 **Important Ideas** Tell students that understanding the important ideas in text helps a reader understand the text's message. Sometimes the most important ideas are stated in a topic sentence. Have students use topic sentences and supporting details to summarize the important ideas in paragraph 1 on p. 181.

Corrective Feedback

If... students are unable to determine the important ideas,

then... model how to identify important ideas.

Model the Strategy

Think Aloud The first sentence says that smokejumpers and hot shots are equally dedicated to their work. What details support this idea? (They have the same mission, which is to stop fires.) What other important idea does the paragraph contain?

Student Edition pp. 180–181

OPTION 2 Extend Thinking Think Critically

Higher-Order Thinking Skills

🔊 **Important Ideas • Analysis** How do the photographs on pages 180–181 help you to understand the important ideas in the text? Possible response: The photographs show a dangerous wildfire and a smokejumper using a parachute to get to the fire. These photographs help me to understand the important idea that fighting wildfires is a dangerous job that requires smokejumpers to jump from planes.

Let's Think About...

How can you figure out what the important idea of this section will be? Do the title and pictures help?

🔊 **Important Ideas**

①

Extreme Risk

Fighting forest wildfires is a dangerous business. Some wildfires, however, are easier to get to than others. They can begin to burn near roads, or they can move through low-lying forests, on flat ground or gentle slopes. These wildfires are fought bravely by ground crews of "hot shots." Hot shots can be a line of five, eighteen, or seventy men and women who are working very close to a blazing wall of fire.

Other wildfires burn in far-off, remote areas of a forest. These wildfires can start in a deep gulch or high on a mountainside. These places are often far from roads. The only way to get to these blazes quickly is by dropping firefighters from planes. So what do you get when you cross a wildfire firefighter with a parachutist? That's right: a smokejumper.

180

Let's Think About...

① The title helps you to understand that this section talks about the dangers that hot shots and smokejumpers face. The pictures support this idea by showing readers that fires can be large and out of control, so smokejumpers must use a parachute to get to the fire.

② I know that a firefighter uses special equipment to stop fires before they cause damage to homes or harm to people and animals. This helps me understand what smokejumpers do on the ground, because they also try to stop fires and use some of the same equipment.

(Smokejumpers also have to concentrate on jumping and landing.) I think the important idea from the first paragraph is that smokejumpers and hot shots have similar jobs and goals, but smokejumpers have the additional task of jumping from a plane.

When a wildfire occurs in a remote area, parachuting firefighters called smokejumpers are called in to battle the blaze.

Smokejumpers and hot shots are equally dedicated to putting out wildfires. Their mission is the same: stop wildfires before their destructive energy destroys the forest, kills the animals, or threatens human life. Smokejumpers have an added task, however. Before they even hit the ground, smokejumpers are hard at work tracking the fire, finding the right place to jump, and concentrating on landing safely.

Once on the ground, smokejumpers work the same way any forest firefighter does. They cut down trees and drag them from the wildfire's path. They dig up stumps. They chop away the underbrush. Then they turn the soil over and over until just dirt remains. All of this work is done while the fire creeps closer to them.

Let's Think About...

How does using what you know about firefighters help you understand what a smokejumper does when on the ground?
Background Knowledge

2
181

On Their Own

Have students reread the second paragraph on p. 181 and summarize the important ideas and the supporting details in ways that maintain meaning.

Word Choice • Analysis Why did the author choose to describe a wildfire as a *blazing wall of fire*? Possible response: The author wanted to create a vivid description of the intensity and size of a wildfire. This helps readers understand how dangerous it is for hot shots to fight wildfires.

Author's Purpose • Analysis Why does the author compare and contrast hot shots and smokejumpers on these two pages? Possible response: The author wants the reader to know that both hot shots and smokejumpers do the same kind of work for the same reason, but there are some differences in the ways they get to the fires.

Differentiated Instruction

 Strategic Intervention
Have students discuss the term "hot shot" and why they think it is used to refer to people who fight wildfires. Ask students to think of people in other jobs that might be called "hot shots."

English Language Learners
Activate prior knowledge Have students discuss what they know about firefighters and list important details on the board. Direct the discussion with questions such as: How do the firefighters get to the fire? What types of tools and equipment do they use? As students read the selection, revisit the list to monitor students' understanding of contexts that are familiar to unfamiliar. Add information that they have learned.

Objectives
◎ Identify author's purpose to enhance comprehension.

Let's Practice It!
TR DVD•248

OPTION 1 Skills and Strategies, continued

Teach Author's Purpose

Author's Purpose Ask students to reread pp. 182–183 to determine whether they think the author's implied purpose for writing was to entertain, express, persuade, or inform. Remind students that an author can have more than one purpose for writing.

Corrective Feedback

If... students are unable to determine the author's purpose,

then... model how to identify author's purpose.

Student Edition pp. 182–183

Model the Skill

Think Aloud As I read pages 182 and 183, I notice that the author includes facts about smokejumpers. What kind of information does the author include?

A firebreak is a wide dirt barrier created by firefighters to contain a forest fire.

The firefighters create a firebreak, a wide dirt barrier, which is essential in helping to stop the spread of a wildfire. Sometimes, though, even fifty feet of dirt is not enough to keep sparks from drifting over to another dry forest area. Little sparks can create raging fires. Smokejumpers can work for days against a large wildfire. They might work eighteen hours with only breaks for food. Their dedication has stopped the destruction of millions of acres of forests all over the world.

182

OPTION 2 Think Critically, continued

Higher-Order Thinking Skills

Author's Purpose • Analysis Explain how you can tell the difference between when an author's purpose is stated and when it is implied. Has the author's purpose for writing been stated in *Smokejumpers*? **Possible response:** When an author's purpose is stated in the text, the author directly explains why he or she wrote that selection. When an author's purpose is implied, the author does not directly explain his or her purpose for writing. Readers can infer the author's purpose by looking at the facts and opinions that are included in the text, and by thinking about the author's tone and word choice. The author has not directly stated his purpose for writing *Smokejumpers*.

Let's Think About...

❸ Smokejumpers use their training, special uniforms, equipment, tools, and teamwork to overcome the dangers of their jobs.

(The author includes facts about how wildfires start and spread, the steps smokejumpers take to fight the fires, and the dangers they face.) I think the author's implied purpose is to inform readers about smokejumpers, because he included important facts and interesting details about their jobs.

umping into a Fire

Every summer seems drier than the last up in the Rocky Mountains. Underbrush is like a tinderbox. A careless hiker or a flash of lightning could cause the area to quickly go up in flames. And then it happens. Lightning hits in the high gulch. Smoke is spotted from miles off. There are no roads nearby, and before long the wildfire may get out of control. This is a job for smokejumpers.

Danger lurks all around the smokejumpers. The airplane fights high winds caused by the rush of air from the blaze below. The plane must get the smokejumpers to the drop zone. There is no large clearing. Rocks line the mountainside. The area is remote. If the fire rages out of control, rescuing the smokejumpers will be difficult and dangerous. What is the plan?

Situations like this are almost a daily routine for smokejumpers. However, they trust that their training will help them overcome the obstacles that make fighting wildfires so difficult. Special uniforms, equipment, and tools also help smokejumpers fight wildfires as well as provide them with protection while they battle those blazes. Most of all, smokejumpers work together and help one another to make it through a long day—or days—of wildfire firefighting.

Let's **Think** About...

What are some of the ways smokejumpers overcome the dangers of their jobs?
⊙ **Important Ideas**

❸ 183

On Their Own
Have students reread p. 182 and explain an additional implied purpose the author might have had. (He might have written to express admiration for smokejumpers' accomplishments and dedication.) For additional practice, use *Let's Practice It!* page 248 on the *Teacher Resources DVD-ROM.*

Connect to Science
Lightning Lightning is the main cause of wildfires in the western United States. Dry lightning happens during thunderstorms that produce rain that never reaches the ground. During the summer, the air is so hot and dry that the rain evaporates before it even reaches the ground. When lightning strikes a dry forest, it can spark a blaze in seconds.

ELL

English Language Learners
Monitor comprehension Help students monitor understanding by visualizing the dangers smokejumpers face. Have students close their eyes as you read the first two paragraphs on p. 183 aloud. Then ask: What did you "see"? Have students share their responses in words or pictures.

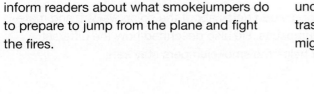

⊙ **Author's Purpose • Analysis** If the author had stated his purpose for writing the section "Jumping into a Fire," what might it have been? Possible response: I want to inform readers about what smokejumpers do to prepare to jump from the plane and fight the fires.

Inferring • Synthesis How could a careless hiker cause a wildfire to start? Possible responses: If a hiker is not careful when lighting a campfire, a spark could touch the dry underbrush and start a wildfire. If hikers leave trash or paper litter in the wilderness, that might add fuel to the fire.

Objectives
- Use graphic sources to clarify understanding.

OPTION 1 Skills and Strategies, continued

Teach Graphic Sources

Review **Graphic Sources** Have students read about smokejumpers' safety gear on p. 184. Then have students look at p. 185, identify the graphic sources, and explain what information they present.

Corrective Feedback

If... students cannot identify the graphic sources,
then... model how to explain information presented graphically.

Let's Practice It!
TR DVD•249

Model the Skill

Think Aloud The text on page 184 describes the different parts of a smokejumper's gear. What graphic sources appear on page 185? (a diagram containing a photograph, labels with arrows, and a caption)

Student Edition pp. 184–185

Let's **Think** About...

Use multiple text features to locate information and important ideas. How do the heading and the photo help you predict what this section will be about?
Predict

❹

Let's **Think** About...

Read the text and look at the photo. What details did the author provide about the smokejumpers' jumpsuits and safety gear?
 Important Ideas

❺

Jumpsuit and Safety Gear

You don't go to the beach without your swimsuit, do you? Of course not. Well, smokejumpers don't jump from an airplane into a firestorm without the right clothing either. Smokejumpers wear lightweight jumpsuits made of fire-retardant material. The jumpsuits help keep them cool during the long workday digging a firebreak. Jumpsuits are either bright orange, white, or yellow. These colors can be easily seen from the air and through the trees. If a smokejumper gets separated from his or her crew, or stick, during a jump or while fighting a blaze, a plane has a better chance of spotting the bright-colored suit.

Jumpsuits are padded to break the fall of a parachute jump. This is important in the rocky areas of a drop zone. Each jumpsuit has several large pockets for carrying small tools and the all-important safety line ladder. Smokejumpers also wear gloves while fighting wildfires. Gloves, however, are not worn during the jump because controlling a parachute is easier with bare hands.

A helmet and goggles are supplied to each smokejumper. The helmet is made of aluminum because this metal is lightweight and strong. Also, metal does not burn, so smokejumpers don't have to worry about burning embers floating around while they work. Attached to the helmet is a face mask, somewhat like the one on a football helmet. The face mask protects a smokejumper from branches when he or she lands in a tree. Goggles protect the eyes from wind, flying embers, branches, and smoke.

184

OPTION 2 Think Critically, continued

Higher-Order Thinking Skills

Review **Graphic Sources • Analysis** Do you think that a smokejumper's gear is heavy? Explain how the text on page 184 and the graphic sources on page 185 help you to draw this conclusion. Possible response: The text explains that the jumpsuit and helmet are lightweight, but the photograph and labels help readers understand how much additional gear a smokejumper carries, which altogether is probably very heavy.

Draw Conclusions • Analysis Why do smokejumpers need special jumpsuits? Possible response: Smokejumpers need jumpsuits that protect them from fire. The jumpsuits also need to be brightly colored and easy to see so that smokejumpers can keep track of each other.

Let's **Think** About...

❹ The heading tells me that I will read about what smokejumpers wear and use to stay safe. The photograph also helps me to understand about the gear and clothing.

❺ The author provided detail about the color, weight, and material of the jumpsuits. He also described how the different equipment helps the smokejumpers stay safe.

How does the diagram help readers understand the text on page 184? **(The diagram gives readers an idea about what the smokejumpers' gear looks like. The labels point out each individual piece so that readers can understand what each piece looks like.)** The photograph and labels help me to understand and visualize what a smokejumper wears and carries while fighting fires.

Helmet with face mask

Fire-retardant, bright-colored

Gloves

Reserve parachute

Smokejumpers' jumpsuits help protect them from extreme heat and are specially made to keep them cool.

185

On Their Own

Have students read the caption on p. 185 and explain the information presented. Ask students why they think this caption is included with the photograph. For additional practice, use *Let's Practice It!* page 249 on the *Teacher Resources DVD-ROM.*

Monitor and Clarify • Synthesis • Text to World What other types of jobs does the job of smokejumper remind you of, and why? Possible response: A smokejumper is like an astronaut or a deep sea scuba diver because they all go places most people don't go. They all use special equipment to keep them safe from the dangers they face.

Check Predictions Have students look back at the predictions they made earlier and discuss whether they were accurate. Then have students preview the rest of the selection and either adjust their predictions accordingly or make new predictions.

Differentiated Instruction

 Strategic Intervention

Graphic sources Have students use the photo on p. 185 to discuss what it might feel like to wear a smokejumper's jumpsuit and gear. Have students explain the positive and negative aspects of carrying so much gear.

A **Advanced**

Have students find out more about the materials used to make a smokejumper's gear light and fire-retardant.

E L L

English Language Learners

Graphic sources Help students review the photo on p. 185 to understand the vocabulary on p. 184. Have students point to and name each part of a smokejumper's gear and explain to a partner how each item protects the smokejumper.

 If you want to teach this selection in two sessions, stop here.

Objectives

- Find pertinent information from print and online sources.
- Recognize and correctly use adjectives and articles.
- Practice correctly spelling multisyllabic words.

Research and Inquiry
Navigate/Search

Teach Have students use their inquiry questions and keywords generated from those questions to search the Internet. Remind students that they can use those same keywords to look in the table of contents or index of print sources such as reference texts.

Model Think Aloud I used the keywords *stop bleeding* and the phrase *how to stop bleeding* to look in the table of contents in the front and indexes at the back of reference texts about medical emergencies that the librarian helped me find.

Guide practice Have students continue their review of print sources they identified. Have them skim and scan each source for information, looking in table of contents and indexes of print sources. Have them look for text features such as bold or italicized print to locate information on the page. As students find information, remind them that it is important to take notes, citing the title, author, publisher, publication date, and the page on which information was found for each source. Explain that if they need to check information or verify a source, they must know how to find it again.

On their own Have students take notes and write down the title, author, publisher, publication date, and the page on which information was found for each source to create a Works Cited page.

Conventions
Adjectives and Articles

Teach
Write these sentences on the board: *The smokejumper put on his face mask. He rushed toward the largest fire near the pole where the American flag hung.* Point out the article in the first sentence and the adjective that describes the mask. Explain that *A* in *American* is capitalized because it is a proper adjective.

Guide practice
Write these sentences on the board. Have students supply an article or adjective to complete each sentence.

> **There is _____ opening.**
>
> **Smokejumpers wear _____ jumpsuits.**
>
> **_____ firefighters create a firebreak.**

Daily Fix-It
Use Daily Fix-It numbers 3 and 4 in the right margin.

Connect to oral language
Have students look for and read aloud adjectives, proper adjectives, and articles in *Smokejumpers*. (*forest wildfires*, p. 180; *dangerous business*, p. 180; *little sparks*, p. 182; *raging fires*, p. 182; *eighteen hours*, p. 182)

On their own
For additional practice use *Reader's and Writer's Notebook* p. 319.

Spelling
Multisyllabic Words

Teach
Write *reaction* and *prerecorded* on the board and ask students to tell how to break each word into syllables *(re-ac-tion; pre-re-cord-ed)*. Remind students to break multisyllabic words into syllables before they begin to spell the words.

Guide practice
Write the remaining spelling words on the board. Have students write them and draw a line between the syllables. Remind them to refer to the dictionary if they are unsure how to divide a word.

On their own
For additional practice, use Reader's and Writer's Notebook p. 320.

Reader's and Writer's Notebook p. 320

Academic Vocabulary
Multisyllabic words are words with three or more syllables.

Daily Fix-It
3. A incredebly powerful fire blazed in this forest last year. *(An; incredibly)*
4. The childrens watched the terrible fire on television? *(children; television.)*

Reader's and Writer's Notebook p. 319

English Language Learners
Conventions To provide students with practice on adjectives and articles, use the modified grammar lessons in the *ELL Handbook* and Grammar Jammer online at www.ReadingStreet.com

Objectives
- Organize ideas to prepare for writing

Writing—Fantasy
Writer's Craft: Story Sequence

Introduce the prompt

Review the key features of fantasy. Remind students that they should think about these features as they begin their writing. Explain that they will begin the writing process for a fantasy today. Read aloud the writing prompt.

> **Writing Prompt**
> Write a fantasy story about fighting a fire.

Select a setting and make-believe twist

 Think Aloud To help plan a fantasy, let's make a chart showing story settings and some make-believe twists that might happen. Display a T-chart. In *Smokejumpers*, you read about real fires in the forest. I'm going to start the T-chart with that setting. Add the information to the T-chart. A few examples have been provided for you. Ask students to name other settings where fires might occur and suggest a make-believe twist that might happen in a fantasy set in that place. Fill in the chart as they give examples. Discuss with students what they know about the setting and the people and creatures that live there.

Remember to keep this chart as the students will refer back to it tomorrow as they draft.

Setting	Make-Believe Twist
forest	the trees reroute the river to put out fire
savannah	elephants squirt water from their trunks to put out fire
jungle	monkeys form a bucket brigade
ship on the ocean	whales spout water to put out fire

Corrective feedback

Circulate among the students as they use the chart to choose a setting for their fantasy about fighting a fire. Talk briefly with students who are having difficulty with making a choice. Ask each struggling student which setting or twist they find most interesting.

Developing a Story Sequence Chart

■ Display a story sequence chart. A story sequence chart helps you organize ideas for writing a story. Review the key features of a fantasy. I'm going to write about a boy who goes back in time and then returns to the present. I'll use a story sequence chart to plot my story. I'll skip the title for now.

■ Under *Characters,* write the story characters. I'll write *a boy*, a man named *Jake, the boy's family*. Under *Setting*, write the places where the story will be set. I'll write *Museum of History; Kansas, on the trail to California*. In the *Events* box, make some notes about the plot of the story. I'll write the first event: *A boy and his family visit the gold rush exhibit at the museum*. Have students begin their own story sequence chart using the form on p. 321 of their *Reader's and Writer's Notebook*. Explain that they will fill in their charts with details about the fantasy they are writing.

Differentiated Instruction

 Advanced

Create a graphic Challenge students to draw an illustration showing the setting of their fantasy.

Reader's and Writer's Notebook p. 321

Teacher Tip

Do a periodic check of students' Quick Writes to make sure they are on task and communicating effectively with their partners.

ROUTINE Quick Write for Fluency   **Team Talk**

① **Talk** Have pairs discuss details of their make-believe twist.

② **Write** Each student writes two sentences that describe the make-believe twist in his or her story.

③ **Share** Partners read their sentences and then ask each other one question about the make-believe twist.

Routines Flip Chart

Wrap Up Your Day

✔ **Build Concepts** What did you learn about being a smokejumper?

✔ **Author's Purpose** What do you think was the author's purpose for writing this selection?

✔ **Important Ideas** What was an important idea from today's reading?

Preview DAY 3

Tell students that tomorrow they will continue reading about how smokejumpers fight wildfires.

Objectives
- Expand the weekly concept.
- Develop oral vocabulary.

Today at a Glance

Oral Vocabulary
first aid, ignite

Comprehension Check/Retelling
Discuss questions

Reading
Smokejumpers: Life Fighting Fires

Think Critically
Retelling

Fluency
Rate and accuracy

Research and Study Skills
Parts of a book

Research and Inquiry
Analyze

Spelling
Multisyllabic words

Conventions
Adjectives and articles

Writing
Fantasy

Concept Talk

Question of the Week

 How can we prepare for emergencies?

Expand the concept

Remind students of the Question of the Week. Discuss how the question relates to how smokejumpers respond to a specific type of emergency: fighting wildfires. Tell students that today they will read about smokejumpers and how they prepare to put out wildfires. Encourage students to think about how smokejumpers are prepared to handle dangerous emergencies.

Anchored Talk

Develop oral vocabulary

Use text features—photos, captions, subheads, and diagrams—to review pp. 178–185 of *Smokejumpers: Life Fighting Fires*. Discuss the Amazing Words *fire escape* and *medical*. Add these and other concept-related words to the concept map. Use the following questions to develop students' understanding of the concept. Remind students to ask and answer questions with appropriate detail and to give suggestions based on the ideas of others.

- How does a *fire escape* help people during an emergency? What other kinds of preparations in building or automobile design are created to help if there is an emergency?

- What kinds of *medical* supplies and equipment would help to prepare for an emergency? What *medical* supplies might be especially useful for smokejumpers?

Oral Vocabulary
Amazing Words

Amazing Words

generator	medical
deserted	first aid
hurricane	ignite
watch	wildfires
dangerous	gear
fire escape	

Amazing Words Oral Vocabulary Routine

Teach Amazing Words

1 **Introduce** Write *first aid* on the board. Have students say it with you. Yesterday we learned about some of the dangers that smokejumpers face. What might cause a firefighter to need *first aid*? Have students determine a definition for *first aid.* (First aid is treatment given to a hurt or sick person before seeing a doctor.)

2 **Demonstrate** Have students answer questions to demonstrate understanding. When would you be most likely to need *first aid*? How is *first aid* different from medical treatment at a hospital?

3 **Apply** Have students apply their understanding. What supplies would you expect to find inside a *first aid* kit?

See p. OV•1 to teach *ignite.*

Routines Flip Chart

Apply Amazing Words

As students read pp. 186–191 of *Smokejumpers,* have them think how the Amazing Words *first aid* and *ignite* apply to dangers the smokejumpers face.

Connect to reading

Explain that today students will read more about how smoke-jumpers prepare to fight wildfires. As they read, students should think about how the Question of the Week and the Amazing Words *first aid* and *ignite* apply to being prepared for emergencies.

E L L **Expand Vocabulary** Use the Day 3 instruction on ELL Poster 21 to help students expand vocabulary.

E L L Poster 21

Comprehension Check

Have students discuss each question with a partner. Ask several pairs to share their responses.

☑ **Genre • Analysis**

Why do you think the author chose to include photos with captions? Possible response: The author wanted to help readers visualize what smokejumpers do. The photos and captions help readers understand how smokejumpers work and stay safe.

☑ **Author's purpose • Evaluation**

How can you tell whether the author's purpose for writing this selection is stated or implied? Explain how you are able to infer the author's purpose for writing this selection. Possible response: The author's purpose in writing this selection is implied because there is no single statement of purpose. I can infer that the author's purpose is to inform by thinking about the tone, word choice, text features, and facts that are included in the selection.

☑ **Important ideas • Synthesis**

Summarize an important idea and three supporting details from the "Jumpsuit and Safety Gear" section of the text in a way that maintains meaning and logical order. Possible response: Smokejumpers have special clothing and equipment to help them do their job safely. Three supporting details are that jumpsuits are fire-retardant; jumpsuits are padded to break falls; smokejumpers wear helmets that do not burn.

☑ **Homographs • Analysis**

Write on the board: *Smokejumpers wear special suits so the fire does not wound them.* How do you know how to pronounce the homograph *wound*? Use a dictionary to check the meaning and find the correct pronunciation. Possible response: Context clues tell me that the sentence *wound* is used here to mean "injure." The dictionary confirms this definition and pronunciation.

☑ **Connect text to world**

Why might firefighting be more or less difficult in different parts of the world? Possible response: Some areas are more difficult to reach, or have much less water to help put out the fire.

Strategy Response Log

INTERACT with TEXT

Have students list 2–3 important ideas presented in *Smokejumpers: Life Fighting Fires* on p. 27 in the *Reader's and Writer's Notebook.*

Check Retelling

Have students retell *Smokejumpers,* summarizing the information in the text in a logical order. Encourage students to use text features and maintain meaning in their retellings.

Corrective feedback

If... students leave out important details,
then... have students look back through the photographs, heads, and the diagram in the selection.

Small Group Time

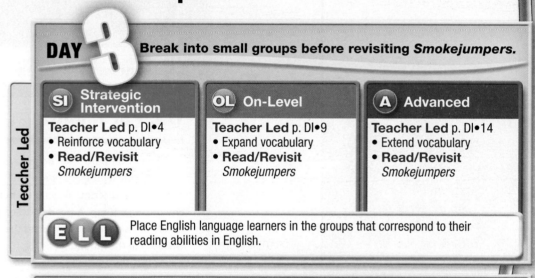

DAY 3 Break into small groups before revisiting *Smokejumpers.*

Teacher Led

SI Strategic Intervention	OL On-Level	A Advanced
Teacher Led p. DI•4	**Teacher Led** p. DI•9	**Teacher Led** p. DI•14
• Reinforce vocabulary	• Expand vocabulary	• Extend vocabulary
• **Read/Revisit** *Smokejumpers*	• **Read/Revisit** *Smokejumpers*	• **Read/Revisit** *Smokejumpers*

ELL Place English language learners in the groups that correspond to their reading abilities in English.

Practice Stations
• Let's Write
• Get Fluent
• Word work

Independent Activities
• AudioText: *Smokejumpers*
• *Reader's and Writer's Notebook*
• Research and Inquiry

English Language Learners
Check retelling To support retelling, review the multilingual summary for *Smokejumpers* with the appropriate Retelling Cards to scaffold understanding.

Objectives
◉ Summarize important ideas and supporting details to improve comprehension.

OPTION 1 Skills and Strategies, continued

Teach Important Ideas

◉ **Important Ideas** Ask students to summarize the most important idea in the first paragraph on p. 186. (Parachutes must be packed in a certain way.)

Corrective Feedback

If… students are unable to identify the important ideas,
then… model how to find the important ideas and supporting details.

Multidraft Reading

If you chose…

Option 1 Return to Extend Thinking instruction starting on p. 180–181.
Option 2 Read pp. 186–191. Use the Guide Comprehension and Extend Thinking instruction.

Student Edition pp. 186–187

OPTION 2 Think Critically, continued

Higher-Order Thinking Skills

◉ **Important Ideas • Synthesis** Summarize the most important idea on page 187. How do the photograph and details in the text support the important idea? The important idea on p. 187 is that a jumpmaster's job is to make sure that the conditions are right for smokejumpers to jump safely. The text gives details about the tasks a jumpmaster does. The photograph helps readers understand how a jumpmaster gives the signal to jump.

Model the Strategy

Think Aloud What is the first paragraph on page 186 about? (parachutes and how they are packed) After I read the first paragraph, how can I summarize the most important idea? (Look for details that support an important idea.)

Smokejumpers hook their parachutes to a static line, which causes their chutes to open automatically when they jump.

The Parachute

The master parachute rigger is in charge of packing each smokejumper's parachute. Parachutes must be packed in a certain way for them to unfold properly during a jump. A poorly packed parachute could tangle in its own ropes and send the smokejumper crashing to the ground.

As the plane carrying the smokejumpers nears the drop zone, the smokejumpers check their parachutes and gear. The parachute is attached to their backs by a harness. The harness is strapped around a jumper's shoulders, across the chest, and between the legs. The harness keeps the jumper attached to the parachute during the fall. An emergency parachute sits in a pack against the jumper's stomach.

Let's Think About…
What clues in the text help you infer what a "drop zone" is? **Inferring**

6

186

Let's Think About…

6 The text says that the smokejumpers check their parachutes and gear before they get to the drop zone. This must mean that they are getting ready to jump out of the plane. I think that a drop zone is the area where the smokejumpers leave the plane.

7 The jumpmaster spots safe places to land; the jumpmaster makes sure the plane is in the right position and checks the wind direction; the jumpmaster makes sure the smokejumpers are jumping from the right place in the air so they land safely.

I look at the facts and details and see that they explain the importance of having a parachute packed properly. One detail is that it is one person's job to pack the parachutes. Another sentence explains what can happen if a parachute is not packed right. These details support the important idea that parachutes must be packed properly.

The Jumpmaster

The jumpmaster does not jump with the smokejumpers. The jumpmaster's job is to make sure that the smokejumpers are jumping from the right place in the air so that they will land safely near the fire. The jumpmaster does this with the help of the airplane pilot. They both spot areas on the ground that could serve as the landing zone. Before the jumpmaster gives the signal to jump, however, he or she must be sure that the plane is in the right position. To do this, the jumpmaster drops crepe paper streamers out of the plane from 1,500 feet. This is the proper height for smokejumpers to jump from. The jumpmaster watches the streamers fall toward the ground, and their path tells the jumpmaster if the wind direction is right for the smokejumpers to drop safely to the ground.

The jumpmaster makes sure that smokejumpers are jumping from the right spot to land safely near a fire.

 Let's **Think** About...

What important idea have you learned about the jumpmaster's job?
◉ **Important Ideas**

 7

187

On Their Own

Have students read the second paragraph of "The Parachute." Ask them to summarize the most important idea and identify supporting details in a way that maintains meaning. Ask how they can identify the important idea.

Draw Conclusions • Analysis What do smokejumpers do if their parachute does not open? They use the emergency parachute that is located in a pack against their stomach.

Sequence • Synthesis Before the smokejumper can jump, what do the jumpmaster and pilot do? Possible response: They both make sure that the plane is in the right position and over a safe spot. The jumpmaster checks the wind direction and the pilot keeps the plane at the proper height.

Differentiated Instruction

 SI Strategic Intervention

Important ideas Have students work with a partner to explain the roles of the master parachute rigger and the jumpmaster. Have students discuss how the jobs are alike and different.

A Advanced

Have students write job descriptions for a master parachute rigger and for a jumpmaster. Have them think of questions they would ask people to determine if he or she would be suited for either one of these jobs.

Connect to Science

Gravity and weight The force that pulls all objects to the ground is called *gravity*. Every time you jump up, the force of gravity will pull you back to the ground. A smokejumper needs to weigh between 120 and 200 pounds. A person weighing over 200 pounds will fall too fast and too hard. Someone weighing less than 120 pounds will drift in the wind, far from the target spot.

 **ELL**

English Language Learners
Build Academic Vocabulary *Rig* can be both a noun and a verb. *Rig* can mean "special equipment or gear." Or to *rig* also means "to fit out with equipment." A *rigger* is a person who rigs. Ask: What does a parachute rigger do? Then have students name other occupations that end in *-er* and tell what these people do.

Objectives

◎ Use a dictionary or glossary to determine the pronunciation, syllabication, and meaning of homographs.

OPTION 1 Skills and Strategies, continued

Teach Homographs

Homographs Remind students that homographs are words that are spelled the same but have different meanings and sometimes different pronunciations. Have students use context clues and a dictionary to explain the meaning, syllabication, and pronunciation of *clearing* on p. 189.

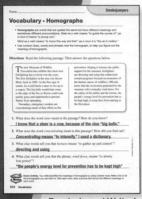

Reader's and Writer's Notebook p. 322

Corrective Feedback

If... students are unable to figure out the meaning of *clearing*,

then... model using context and a dictionary to figure out the meaning.

Student Edition pp. 188–189

Model the Strategy

Think Aloud I know that *clearing* is a homograph and has more than one meaning. How can I find the correct definition of *clearing* in this sentence? **(Look in a dictionary.)** The dictionary shows that there are many meanings for *clearing*.

During tower training, smokejumper recruits learn what it feels like to land with a parachute.

While the jumpmaster and the pilot spot for landing zones, the smokejumpers look out the window at the land below. They study the ground and the area near the fire. They need to know where clearings, rocky land, and the wildfire are located.

When the plane is positioned correctly, it circles the drop zone. The smokejumpers then prepare to jump. They hook their parachutes to a static line, which is a thick wire attached inside the plane that holds parachute release cords so that smokejumpers' chutes open automatically when they jump. When the chutes open, the smokejumpers don't just float down. Instead, they use the parachute "shroud lines" attached to the chute to steer toward the landing zone—and away from the fire. When the smokejumpers hit the ground,

Let's Think About...

How does the smokejumper steer with the "shroud lines"? **Questioning**

188 **8**

OPTION 2 Think Critically, continued

Higher-Order Thinking Skills

Homographs • Synthesis Look back at page 184 and find the homograph *wind.* Use a dictionary or glossary to find the pronunciations, syllabication, and meanings of *wind* and decide which meaning is being used in the sentence. Possible response: The dictionary says that two meanings of *wind* are "air that moves," which is pronounced with short *i,* and "to twist or turn something," which is pronounced with long *i.* Each word has the same number of syllables. Since the text talks about how goggles protect smokejumpers from the wind, I think the definition in the sentence is "air that moves."

Let's Think About...

8 The shroud lines are attached to the parachute, so the smokejumper pulls the shroud lines to steer the parachute away from the fire.

9 The heading says "Bundled Tools" and the photograph shows a pulaski, which is a tool used by smokejumpers. Both the heading and the photo tell readers that the text will be about tools.

It can be a noun that means "an open space of land." It is also a verb that means, among other things, "removing to leave a space free of debris." How can I tell which meaning is being used here? (context clues) Since the smokejumpers will aim for trees if there is no *clearing*, I think "an open space of land" is the right definition here.

they roll to absorb the hard impact. They quickly pull their chutes onto the ground and gather them to make sure no wind pulls the chutes and drags their bodies along the ground.

Sometimes smokejumpers actually aim for trees if there is no clearing. Once caught on a tree, they drop themselves to the ground with their safety line. Smoke-jumpers get out of trees quickly. They don't want to be caught dangling from a branch when fire is nearby.

Bundled Tools

Once the smokejumpers have gathered themselves on the ground, they need their tools. The plane circles the area and drops more parachutes. These chutes hold pack-ages containing tools, food supplies, or other equipment. If a stream, pond, or lake is near the fire, hoses and water pumps will be packed too.

The parachutes are colored to identify what they are carrying. A red parachute's bundle might include shovels and saws. A yellow parachute might carry food supplies. Color-coded supply parachutes save smokejumpers valuable time. The last thing a smokejumper needs is to find sandwiches when he or she is looking for a shovel!

The pulaski, a combination of an ax and a hoe, is the tool of choice for smokejumpers.

189

Let's Think About...

How do the heading and photo help predict what this section will be about? **Predict**

9

On Their Own

Have students write a sentence using each definition of *clearing* to demon-strate understanding. For additional practice, see *Reader's and Writer's Notebook* p. 322.

see *Reader's and Writer's Notebook* p. 322.

Differentiated Instruction

SI Strategic Intervention

Sequence Have partners retell in order what smokejumpers must do when they jump from the plane.

A Advanced

Have students explain what they think training to be a smokejumper would be like. Then have students use the Internet to find out more about smokejumpers' recruitment and training.

ELL

English Language Learners

Monitor understanding Explain that *static* means "having no motion, fixed in position." Direct students' attention back to the reference to a static line on p. 188. Explain how a static line works and ask students to explain why it is called *static*.

Formal and informal language Tell students: *Chute* is a casual way of saying *parachute*. A chute is also a steep hole for dropping things to a lower level, such as a mail chute or laundry chute. Ask: How are all these meanings of *chute* related? Have students say a sentence using *parachute* and another sentence using *chute*.

Inferring • Evaluation Are smokejumpers well prepared before a real jump? What evidence in the text supports this conclusion? Possible response: Smokejumpers are well prepared to jump because they spend time training and learning how to land with a para-chute. The photograph shows smokejumpers during tower training.

Monitor and Clarify • Analysis Reread the section "Bundled Tools" on page 189 aloud. How do the smokejumpers get supplies and how are these supplies organized? Possible response: Supplies are dropped to them by parachute. They are color-coded and bundled by type of supply: tools, food, other equipment.

Objectives

◎ Identify the author's purpose for an expository text.

OPTION 1 Skills and Strategies, continued

Teach Author's Purpose

Author's Purpose Have students reread "Getting Home Safely" on p. 190. Ask them to identify whether the author's purpose is stated or implied. Then have students explain the author's implied purpose for writing "Getting Home Safely."

Corrective Feedback

If... students have difficulty identifying the author's purpose,

then... model how to determine the author's purpose.

Model the Skill

Think Aloud I know that sometimes the author does not directly state his or her purpose for writing. I don't see one sentence that explains why the author wrote this section, but I can infer the author's purpose by looking at details, tone, and word choice.

Ready to Move Out

Once the supplies are gathered, the smoke-jumpers head toward the fire with all their gear on their backs. Now the real work begins. But before they can get to the fire's edge, the smokejumpers must determine where the fire is, where it might be heading, and the best way to tackle the blaze.

Getting Home Safely

Putting out a wildfire may be the job that smokejumpers are sent to do, but the first order of business is to keep everyone safe. Over the many years smokejumpers have been fighting wildfires, very few of them have died. This is because safety precautions are taken before, during, and after a fire is fought. As crazy as these men and women who work as smokejumpers may seem, they have no death wish. The opposite is true. They love the environment and want to help keep it safe for animals and humans. Their job is extremely dangerous, but they are professionals. They understand the risks, and know what to do to avoid death.

Let's **Think** About...

Do you understand why smokejumpers choose to do such a dangerous job? How has the author explained this idea?
◎ **Important Ideas**

10

190

Student Edition pp. 190–191

OPTION 2 Think Critically, continued

Higher-Order Thinking Skills

Author's Purpose • Synthesis What do you think is the author's purpose for writing "Ready to Move Out"? Explain how you can tell if the purpose is stated or implied. Possible response: The author's purpose for writing this section is to inform readers about the steps smokejumpers take to fight wildfires after they get their supplies. The purpose is implied because the author does not directly explain to readers what his purpose for writing is.

Important Ideas • Evaluation What details in "Getting Home Safely" support the idea that safety is important to smokejumpers? very few have died, smokejumpers are professionals

Let's **Think** About...

10 Smokejumpers love the environment and want to help keep it safe for animals and humans. The author supports this idea with details about smokejumpers.

11 You can go back and reread the sections about how smoke-jumpers use a parachute to jump from an airplane.

What facts and details does the author include in this paragraph? (Smokejumpers take precautions; they understand the risks of their job.) The author emphasizes the safety precautions that smokejumpers take while on the job. I think the author's purpose is to inform readers that safety is very important to smokejumpers.

On Their Own

Have students discuss other possible reasons the author may have had for writing. Then have students write a sentence that the author could have included in the text to directly state his purpose for writing.

Differentiated Instruction

 Strategic Intervention

Author's purpose Have students look at the photo at the bottom of p. 191. Have partners explain to each other why they think the author chose to include this photo here.

 Advanced

Author's purpose Have students generate a list of questions they would want to ask the author about the selection, and why he included certain facts and features.

When the fire has been smothered and all the work is done, it's time for the smokejumpers to return to base. But since they dropped from the skies into this remote area, how will they get out? Often by the same method they got in. The team radios its base and calls for a helicopter to come pick the smokejumpers up. Sometimes the team must walk a long way to get to a clearing where a helicopter can land. This walk is a victory march. The success the team has achieved by putting out a destructive fire is well worth the few hours that smokejumpers must hike to get to the rescue area. When all are aboard, a cheer goes up. They're going home.

Let's Think About...

If you are not clear on how the smokejumpers got into the remote areas, what can you do? **Monitor and Clarify**

⑪

191

Comprehension Check

Spiral Review

Draw Conclusions • Synthesis What kind of person would enjoy being a smokejumper? Possible response: Someone who loves nature; someone who is very brave.

Compare and Contrast • Analysis Compare and contrast the job of a smokejumper to another emergency worker. How are their jobs similar and different?

Possible response: A smokejumper is similar to a paramedic because they help during emergencies. A paramedic helps injured people. A smokejumper works to protect the environment.

Check Predictions Have students return to the predictions they made earlier and confirm whether they were accurate.

ELL

English Language Learners
Monitor comprehension Read the first sentence on p. 191. What does *smothered* mean here? Explain that to smother a fire means to extinguish or to put out the fire. Have students act out how they would smother or extinguish a fire.

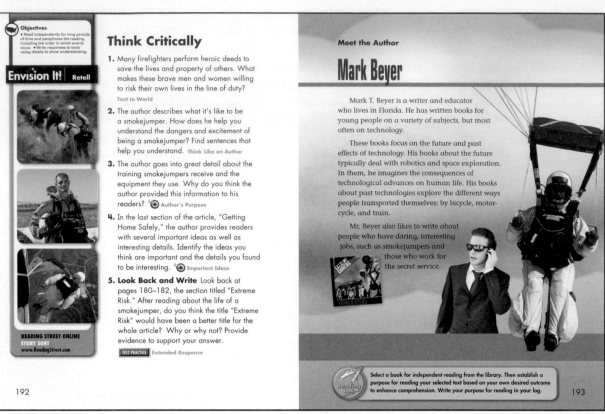

Student Edition pp. 192–193

Plan to Assess Retelling

☑ **This week assess Strategic Intervention students.**

☐ **Week 2** Assess Advanced students.

☐ **Week 3** Assess Strategic Intervention students.

☐ **Week 4** Assess On-Level students.

☐ **Week 5** Assess any students you have not yet checked during this unit.

Retelling

Envision It!

Have students work in pairs to retell the selection, using the Envision It! Retelling Cards as prompts. Remind students that they should accurately describe the main topic and important ideas in a logical order and use key vocabulary as they retell. Monitor students' retellings.

Scoring rubric

Top-Score Response A top-score response makes connections beyond the text, describes the main topic and important ideas using accurate information, and draws conclusions from the text.

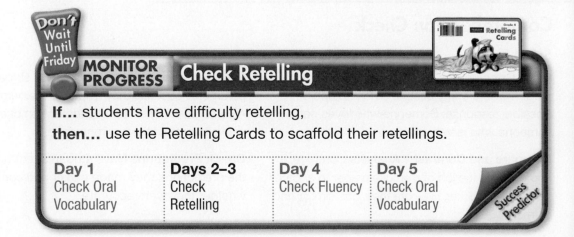

Don't Wait Until Friday

MONITOR PROGRESS **Check Retelling**

If... students have difficulty retelling,

then... use the Retelling Cards to scaffold their retellings.

| **Day 1** Check Oral Vocabulary | **Days 2–3** Check Retelling | **Day 4** Check Fluency | **Day 5** Check Oral Vocabulary |

Success Predictor

Think Critically

Text to world

1. I think firefighters are willing to risk their lives for others because they care about helping people in emergencies.

Think like an author

2. The author uses descriptive language and explains the obstacles that the smokejumpers face. One example is on p. 183, *The airplane fights high winds caused by the rush of air from the blaze below.*

◉ Author's purpose

3. I think the author wanted to show that there are many safety precautions designed to keep smokejumpers safe. Even though their job is risky, the author wanted readers to understand that smokejumpers are well-prepared for the risks involved.

◉ Important ideas

4. I think the important ideas are that smokejumpers care about safety and that they are professionals who understand the danger they face. One interesting detail is the way the author describes the smokejumpers' long walk back to be picked up by the helicopter as a victory march.

5. **Look Back and Write** To build writing fluency, assign a 10–15 minute time limit.

Suggest that students use a prewriting strategy, such as brainstorming or using a graphic organizer, to organize their ideas. Remind them to establish a topic sentence and support it with facts, details, or explanations. As students finish, encourage them to reread their responses, revise for organization and support, and proofread for errors in grammar and conventions.

Scoring rubric

> **Top-Score Response** A top-score response uses details from *Smokejumpers* to support or deny the argument that "Extreme Risk" would have been a better title for the selection.
>
> **A top-score response should include:**
>
> • Smokejumpers work in remote areas to fight dangerous wildfires.
>
> • Smokejumpers use special uniforms, equipment, and tools to avoid of injury.
>
> • Smokejumpers are part of a team of people who work together to stay safe.

Meet the Author

Have students read about author Mark Beyer on p. 193. Ask them how he expresses his interest in technology in *Smokejumpers*.

Independent Reading

Encourage students to gradually increase the period of time spent reading library books independently. To enhance comprehension, tell students to establish their own purposes for reading, based on their own desired outcome. After students read independently for a sustained 30-minute period of time, have them enter their independent reading information into their Reading Logs. Have students paraphrase a portion of the text they have just read. Tell them that when we paraphrase, we express the meaning of a passage, using other words and maintaining logical order.

E L L

English Language Learners
Retelling Have students use the Envision It! Retell pictures on p. 192 of the Student Edition and the vocabulary students have internalized in prior weeks to identify and describe the people, places, and objects shown in the photographs. Then have them use the same pictures to retell the main points and basic information from the story.

Objectives

- Read grade-level text with accuracy and at an appropriate rate.
- Reread for fluency.
- Analyze the formats and text features of a book.

Model Fluency
Rate and Accuracy

Model fluent reading

Have students turn to p. 187 of *Smokejumpers: Life Fighting Fires*. Have students follow along as you read this page. Tell them to listen to how you read smoothly and at the right speed for the type of text. Explain that you will adjust your rate in order not to read too quickly or too slowly.

Guide practice

Have students follow along as you read the page again. Then have them reread the page as a group without you until they read at an appropriate rate and with no mistakes. Ask questions to be sure students comprehend the text. Continue in the same way on p. 188.

Reread for Fluency

Corrective feedback

If... students are having difficulty reading with accuracy and at the correct rate,
then... prompt:

- Did you read every word? Where do you see difficult words?

- Read the sentence more quickly. Now read it more slowly. Which helps you read with better accuracy and understand what you are reading?

- Read me the sentence at the rate that would help me understand it. Make sure you read carefully and do not miss any words.

ROUTINE Choral Reading

 Read Have students read the first paragraph on p. 184 of *Smokejumpers: Life Fighting Fires* orally.

 Reread To achieve optimal fluency, students should reread the text three or four times.

 Corrective Feedback Have students read aloud without you. Provide feedback about their rate and accuracy, and encourage them to adjust their rate to allow for comprehension of this informational text. Listen to ensure that students are reading accurately at an appropriate rate.

Routines Flip Chart

Research and Study Skills
Parts of a Book

Teach

Demonstrate for students how to find information by looking at the parts of a book, both in the front of the book and in the back.

- A **title page** shows the book's title, author, and publisher. It can help students decide if a book is related to their topic.

- A **copyright page** shows the year the book was published and who the publisher is. This helps researchers decide whether the information in the book is recent enough for their purpose.

- A **table of contents** lists chapter titles or section headings and their page numbers. It gives an overview of the contents and allows readers to locate specific information more quickly.

- A **bibliography** lists sources the authors used to research or write the book. A **glossary** gives definitions of important words in the book. An **index** lists a book's topics in alphabetical order and shows where information can be found.

- **Captions**, **section heads**, and **topic and concluding sentences** are also helpful in locating and understanding information throughout the body of a book.

Guide practice

Provide groups of students with expository texts. Have students locate each of the parts of their book.

Discuss these questions:

What part of a book helps you find a chapter title? (**table of contents**)

What feature of a book would help you understand the meaning of a word you did not know? (**glossary**)

What parts of a book give you information about the publisher? (**copyright page and title page**)

On their own

Ask groups to use the features of their books to locate information and explain the content of the text. Then have students review p. 323 and complete p. 324 of the *Reader's and Writer's Notebook*.

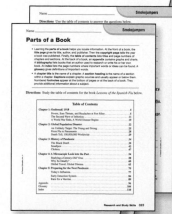

Reader's and Writer's Notebook pp. 323–324

English Language Learners
Language production Students can be given the option to tape record an oral reading passage. Students will improve in fluency as they rehearse the passage before recording their performance. Encourage students to share their opinion about the passage and suggest ways to practice rate and accuracy in oral reading.

Objectives

- Analyze data for usefulness.
- Identify and correctly use adjectives and articles.
- Spell frequently misspelled words.

Research and Inquiry
Analyze

Teach

Have students analyze their print and Internet sources for information that answers their questions and any new questions they formulated as a result of their research.

Model

Think Aloud When I began to research about how to stop bleeding, I had been thinking of cuts and mild bleeding. I soon realized that a lot of the information is about stopping traumatic bleeding. So I narrowed my search to learn about mild bleeding.

Guide practice

Have students analyze their findings. They may need to refocus their inquiry question to better fit the information they found, or collect more information to answer the question. Remind students that if they have difficulty improving their focus, they can ask a reference librarian for guidance. Remind students to use the table of contents and index in books, and to skim and scan for guide words in italics and bold print, if they conduct additional research.

On their own

Have students compile, summarize, and evaluate their research. Encourage them to consider the most important points to convey to their audience. Remind students to make note of their sources.

Conventions
Adjectives and Articles

Review

Remind students that this week they learned about adjectives and articles.

• An adjective describes a noun or pronoun.

• *A*, *an*, and *the* are special adjectives called articles.

• Proper adjectives are formed from proper nouns.

Daily Fix-It

Use Daily Fix-It numbers 5 and 6 in the right margin.

Connect to oral language

Have students use the following lists to choose an article, an adjective, and a noun to form a phrase to say aloud.

> **Articles: a, an, the**
>
> **Adjectives: giant, watering, Canadian, purple, seventy, unopened**
>
> **Nouns: spaceship, umbrella, can, flag, elephant, children**

On their own

For additional practice, use *Let's Practice It!* page 250 on the *Teacher Resources DVD-ROM.*

Let's Practice It!
TR DVD•250

Differentiated Instruction

SI Strategic Intervention

Brainstorming Working in small groups, have students take turns naming a noun and asking group members to brainstorm adjectives that describe how it looks, how it sounds, or how it smells. Students can take turns recording suggestions.

Daily Fix-It

5. What damage the wildfire costed the forest? *(cost; forest!)*

6. At one point the fire seem to stop then its flames swept through the forest again. *(seemed; stop. Then)*

Spelling
Multisyllabic Words

Frequently misspelled words

The words *I, I'm,* and *off* are words that seem simple, but students often misspell them. The words *reaction* and *unhappily* from your spelling list are also difficult to spell. I'm going to read a sentence. Choose the correct word to complete the sentence and then write it correctly.

> 1. He scowled _____, when our team lost.
>
> 2. I took _____ my wet shoes as soon as I got home.
>
> 3. _____ reading a very interesting book.
>
> 4. _____ can't wait to go on our class trip.

On their own

For additional support, use *Reader's and Writer's Notebook* p. 325.

Reader's and Writer's Notebook
p. 325

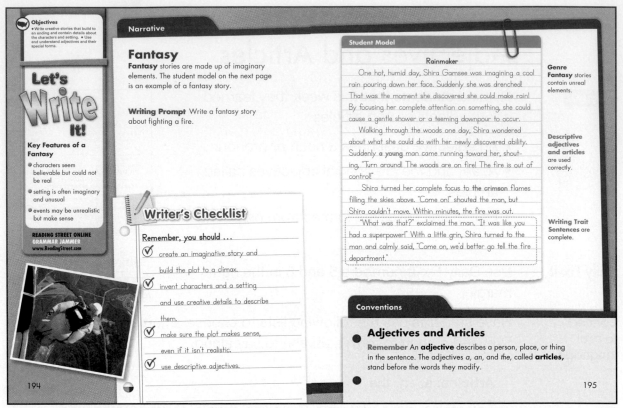

Student Edition pp. 194–195

Let's Write It!
Fantasy

Teach

Use pp. 194–195 in the Student Edition. Direct students to read the key features of fantasy which appear on p. 194. Remind students that they can refer to the information in the Writer's Checklist as they write their fantasy.

Read the student model on p. 195. Point out the imaginary elements in the model, as well as the descriptive adjectives and articles. Explain that these words create imagery, a picture in the reader's mind. Discuss the role of the narrator, the person who is telling the story. Help students determine whether the narrator is first person, someone in the story, or third person, someone outside of the story who knows about the characters and events.

Connect to conventions

Remind students that the writer used complete sentences. Also point out the correct placement of adjectives and articles in the model.

Writing—Fantasy
Writer's Craft: Complete Sentences

Display rubric

Display Scoring Rubric 21 from the *Teacher Resources DVD* and go over the criteria for each trait under each score. Then, using the model in the Student Edition, choose students to explain why the model should score a 4 for one of the traits. If a student suggests that the model should score below 4 for a particular trait, the student should offer support for that response. Remind students that this is the rubric that will be used to evaluate the fantasy they will begin writing today.

Scoring Rubric: Fantasy

	④	③	②	①
Focus/Ideas	Situation in fantasy clear; good supporting details	Situation in fantasy mostly clear; some details.	Situation in fantasy at times unclear; few details	Situation in fantasy not clear; no details
Organization	Organized in a logical pattern	Organized in a mostly logical pattern	Organizational pattern attempted, but not clear	No organizational pattern evident; hard to follow
Voice	Lively, original voice	Mostly original voice	Mostly impersonal voice	Flat writing with no personallty
Word Choice	Realistic dialogue; lively adjectives; language that creates imagery	Dialogue mostly realistic; some lively adjectives; some language that creates imagery	Dialogue and vocabulary mostly flat; limited use of adjectives or language that creates imagery	Dialogue unnatural; words vague and dull; no use of language that creates imagery
Sentences	Complete sentences throughout; a variety of sentence patterns; appropriate end punctuation	Mostly complete sentences; some variety in sentence patterns; mostly appropriate end punctuation	Many incomplete sentences; little variety of sentence patterns; some appropriate end punctuation	Mostly incomplete sentences; no variety of sentence patterns; mostly incorrect end punctuation
Conventions	Excellent use of adjectives; appropriate use of articles	Good use of adjectives; mostly appropriate use of articles	Sparse and incorrect use of adjectives; several incorrect uses of articles	Serious errors in use of adjectives; articles used inappropriately

Story sequence chart

Have students get out the story sequence charts they worked on yesterday. If their charts are not complete, have them complete them now.

Write

You will be using your story sequence chart as you write the paragraphs for the first draft of your fantasy. When you are drafting, don't worry if your story does not sound exactly as you want it. You will have a chance to revise tomorrow.

Differentiated Instruction

A **Advanced**

Shifting perspective Working in pairs, have students take turns telling parts of the fantasy on p. 195 in the Student Edition from a first-person point of view.

English Language Learners
Support recognizing kinds of sentences

Beginning Working with partners, students can choose a sentence from the model, identify the end punctuation, and tell the kind of sentence it is.

Intermediate Working with partners, students can choose a sentence from the model, identify the kind of sentence, and explain the reason it is that kind.

Advanced/Advanced High Working with a partner, have students take turns reading a sentence from the student model, identifying the kind of sentence and changing it to another kind of sentence. For example, students can change a statement to a question.

Objectives
- Write a first draft of a narrative story.
- Recognize and use complete sentences.
- Include adjectives that create imagery in writing.
- Incorporate elements of fantasy in writing.

Writing, continued
Writer's Craft: Complete Sentences

MINI-LESSON

Writing Complete Sentences

■ **Introduce** Explain to students that good writers write in complete sentences. Provide examples of and identify complete declarative sentences, interrogative sentences, imperative sentences, and exclamatory sentences. Review end punctuation for each kind of sentence. Then discuss how complete sentences express a complete thought and include both a subject and a predicate. Remind students that good writers include adjectives in their sentences to create imagery that helps the reader imagine how people, animals, or the setting in the story look, feel, or act. Display the Drafting Tips for students. Tell them that the focus of drafting is to get their ideas down in an organized way.

An Adventure to Remember

We got there quickly. My family and I had traveled to the city on a speed train. We wanted to spend the day at the Museum of History. We paid for Admission. We headed straight to the Gold rush exhibit. The first display showed an store. It was where gold-seekers bought supplies before heading west. I stared at the life-size figures of the prospectors. I studied the gold-digging tools. Wham. Suddenly, a gust of air transported me into the shop. I was standing right next to a guy from Boston. He was stopping in Kansas for a few days to buy things he needed for the trip to California. The bostonian introduced himself as Jake. He asked, Would you like to travel west with me. I hear there's gold everywhere out in California." I agreed. It sounded exciting.

We set out in a wagon pulled by mules. We camped outdoors, hunted for food, and built campfires. One windy day a campfire got out of control. Everyone grabbed buckets and raced to a nearby stream. I helped. Soon the fire was out. Life on the trail was very hard. This was like no other trip I'd ever taken. It was certainly a adventure. But I didn't like it much?

"I'm ready to turn back," I told Jake one morning.

"That's not a problem, he replied. Just think very hard about your family and before you know it, you'll be back at the museum."

I thought as hard as I could about my folks. As I concentrated, a gust of air, just like the one that had thrust me into the store, shoved me back into the museum. I was standing right next to my family, looking into the supply shop None of them seemed to have noticed that I'd been missing!

Unit 5: Smokejumpers   Writing: Model **21A**

Writing Transparency 21A,
TR DVD

Drafting Tips

✔ Review your story sequence chart.

✔ Don't worry about grammar and mechanics when drafting. You will concentrate on these things during the editing process.

✔ Write in a way that allows your imagination to shine through.

Think Aloud I'm going to write the first paragraph of my fantasy called "An Adventure to Remember." When I draft, I refer to my story sequence chart and develop my ideas. I include elements of fantasy, but also make sure my story has a plot that builds to a climax and characters that my readers can identify with. I write complete sentences, but I don't worry if my ideas are somewhat disconnected because I can clean them up during the next step in the writing process, revising.

Direct students to use the Drafting Tips to guide them in writing their drafts. Remind them to make sure that their draft includes complete sentences.

ROUTINE Quick Write for Fluency Team Talk

1 Talk Pairs talk about the main characters in their fantasy story.

2 Write Each student writes a brief paragraph about one of the characters they discussed, using adjectives to describe the character and create imagery.

3 Share Partners read each other's writing and check for inclusion of adjectives that help them imagine the character.

Routines Flip Chart

Differentiated Instruction

SI Strategic Intervention

Complete sentences Have groups of two or three students work together to write an example of a declarative sentence, an interrogative sentence, an exclamation, and a command. Each student in the group can make suggestions to ensure that each is a complete sentence.

Wrap Up Your Day

✔ **Build Concepts** Have students discuss how smokejumpers prepare for emergencies.

✔ **Author's Purpose** How did understanding the author's purpose help you understand the selection?

✔ **Important Ideas** What were two important ideas from today's reading?

Preview DAY 4

Tell students that tomorrow they will read a new selection about being careful when you go camping.

Objectives
- Expand the weekly concept.
- Develop oral vocabulary.

Today at a Glance

Oral Vocabulary
wildfires, gear

Genre
Persuasive Text

Reading
"Camp with Care"

Let's Learn It!
Fluency: Rate and accuracy
Vocabulary: Homographs
Listening/Speaking: Dramatization

Research and Inquiry
Synthesize

Spelling
Multisyllabic words

Conventions
Adjectives and articles

Writing
Fantasy

Concept Talk

Question of the Week

? **How can we prepare for emergencies?**

Expand the concept

Remind students that this week they have read about how people prepare for and handle emergencies such as hurricanes and wildfires. Tell students that today they will read an essay that persuades the reader to see the importance of protecting the environment when camping.

Anchored Talk

Develop oral vocabulary

Use text features—photos, captions, heads, and diagrams—to review pp. 186–191 of *Smokejumpers: Life Fighting Fires.* Discuss the Amazing Words *first aid* and *ignite.* Add these and other concept-related words to the concept map. Use the following questions to develop students' understanding of the concept. Remind students to ask and answer questions with appropriate detail and to build on other students' answers.

- Smokejumpers fight to put out wildfires. Other emergency workers administer *first aid.* In what kinds of emergencies might someone need *first aid*?

- The protective clothing worn by smokejumpers will not *ignite* even if it gets close to flames. What kinds of equipment and preparations would help you if something were to *ignite* in your home?

Strategy Response Log

INTERACT with TEXT

Have students complete p. 27 in *Reader's and Writers' Notebook.* Then have students summarize the important ideas that they found in the selection.

Oral Vocabulary
Amazing Words

Teach Amazing Words

Amazing Words Oral Vocabulary Routine

1 **Introduce** Write the word *wildfires* on the board. Have students say it aloud with you. We've read about how smokejumpers help put out *wildfires.* What do we know about *wildfires* from what we've read? (They are fires that are started by lightning or people that can move through the forest and underbrush very quickly.)

2 **Demonstrate** Have students answer questions to demonstrate understanding. Why are *wildfires* difficult to put out? How are *wildfires* different from fires in a town or city?

3 **Apply** Have students apply their understanding. How can people prevent *wildfires* when hiking or camping?

See p. OV•1 to teach *gear.*

Routines Flip Chart

Apply Amazing Words

As students read "Camp with Care" on pp. 196–197, have them think about how wildfires start, and what kind of gear smokejumpers need to fight them.

Connect to reading

As students read today's selection about how to protect the environment while camping, have them think about how the Question of the Week and the Amazing Words *wildfires* and *gear* apply to camping and preventing forest fires.

Amazing Words

generator	medical
deserted	first aid
hurricane	ignite
watch	wildfires
dangerous	gear
fire escape	

E L L **Produce Language** Use the Day 4 instruction on ELL Poster 21 to extend and enrich language.

E L L Poster 21

Let's Think About Genre

Persuasive Text: Persuasive Essay

Introduce the genre

Explain to students that what we read is structured according to the author's reasons for writing and the kind of information he or she wishes to convey. Different types of texts are called genres. Tell students that a persuasive essay is one type of genre.

Discuss the genre

Discuss what students know about persuasive text. Ask: When someone tries to persuade you, what is this person trying to do? (trying to convince you to think or act a certain way) Explain: In persuasive text, authors use language to present information that will influence their readers. One type of persuasive text is a persuasive essay. The author of a persuasive essay presents facts and opinions about a topic to try to convince readers to think or act in a certain way. Let's take a closer look at persuasive essays.

On the board, draw a Venn diagram like the one below. Label the sides *Expository Essay* and *Persuasive Essay.* Ask the following questions:

• What is the purpose of a persuasive essay? **Possible response: to persuade, to influence readers to think and act in a certain way**

• What is the purpose of an expository essay? **Possible response: to inform, to present facts**

• How does an author try to influence readers in a persuasive essay? **Possible response: authors use language to present information that will influence what readers think and do**

• How are persuasive essays and expository essays alike? **Possible responses: both give facts**

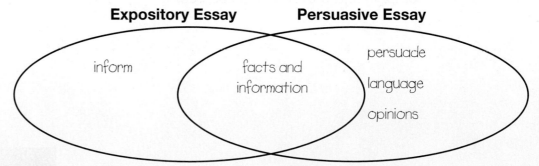

Expository Essay   **Persuasive Essay**

inform   facts and information   persuade / language / opinions

Guide practice

Have students work in pairs to discuss the kind of language an author might use to influence readers to think or do something. Have pairs list words that could be used to persuade readers and share the list with the class.

Connect to reading

Tell students that they will now read a persuasive essay about the proper way to camp safely. Have the class think about how the author uses language to influence the reader.

Small Group Time

DAY 4

Break into small groups before reading or revisiting "Camp with Care."

Teacher Led

 Strategic Intervention

Teacher Led p. DI•5
- Practice Retelling
- Genre Focus
- **Read/Revisit** "Camp with Care"

OL On-Level

Teacher Led p. DI•10
- Practice Retelling
- Genre Focus
- **Read/Revisit** "Camp with Care"

Ⓐ Advanced

Teacher Led p. DI•15
- Genre Focus
- **Read/Revisit** "Camp with Care"

ELL Place English language learners in the groups that correspond to their reading abilities in English.

Practice Stations
- Read for Meaning
- Get Fluent
- Words to Know

Independent Activities
- AudioText: "Camp with Care"
- *Reader's and Writer's Notebook*
- Research and Inquiry

English Language Learners
Cognates The Spanish word *persuadir* may be familiar to Spanish speakers as a cognate for *persuade*.

Objectives

- Identify persuasive language used to influence readers.
- Compare and contrast across texts.

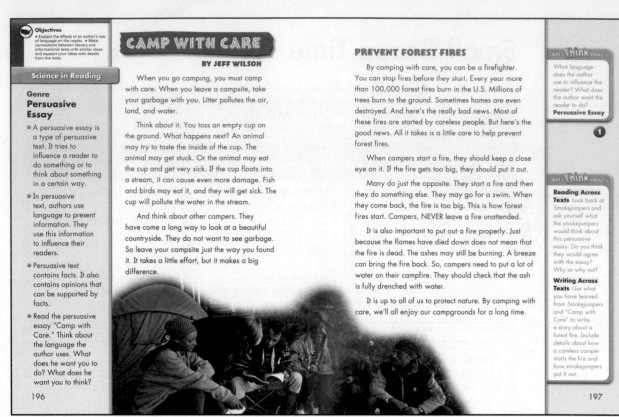

Student Edition pp. 196–197

Guide Comprehension

Teach the genre

Genre: Persuasive Essay Have students preview "Camp with Care" on pp. 196–197. Have them look at the title, photographs, and subhead in the essay. Then ask: What do you think this persuasive essay will try to convince readers to think or do?

Corrective feedback

If... students are unable to predict the purpose of the persuasive essay, **then...** guide students in predicting what the essay will be about.

Model the genre

Think Aloud

I see that this is a persuasive essay about camping. The essay is titled "Camp with Care." The photo shows campers at their campsite. The subhead is about preventing forest fires. I think the writer will use language to try and convince readers to take certain steps to be careful while camping. As I read, I'll look for persuasive language and opinions supported by facts to see how the author tries to influence readers to camp with care.

On their own

Have students work in pairs to discuss something they would like to convince others to do, such as recycling. Have them brainstorm details and persuasive language they would include to influence people.

Extend Thinking
Think Critically

Higher-order thinking skills

 Author's Purpose • Evaluation Why do you think the author wrote "Camp with Care"? Possible response: The author's purpose for writing is to persuade readers to be cautious when camping. The author wants to persuade readers to care for the environment.

Generalize • Synthesis What generalizations or inferences can you make about persuasive essays? Use examples from "Camp with Care" to support your generalization. Possible response: Persuasive essays use language to convince readers to do something or think a certain way. Authors who write persuasive essays give an opinion about a topic and use facts to support it. In this selection, the author tells readers not to litter and includes facts about what can happen to animals because of litter.

Let's Think About...

 The author uses strong words such as *NEVER* to urge people not to be careless. The author wants the reader to protect nature by not leaving trash or by doing something that could cause a forest fire when camping.

Reading Across Texts

Have students work in pairs to create a T-chart of reasons why smokejumpers would agree or disagree with this essay.

Writing Across Texts

Have students look back at "Camp with Care" and think of how a careless camper in the story might start a fire. Then have students look back at *Smokejumpers* to review how the smokejumpers put fires out. Encourage students to list details from each selection that they wish to include before writing their story. Remind students to think about similar ideas that are presented in each text when writing.

Differentiated Instruction

SI **Strategic Intervention**
Author's purpose Have students work with a partner to list the reasons the author gives for trying to get campers to camp with care.

A **Advanced**
Have students choose a safety topic that they feel strongly about and list several facts that they would use to support their opinions in a persuasive essay on the topic.

English Language Learners
Activate prior knowledge
Direct students to the photos of the campers on pp. 196–197. Ask: What do you know about going camping? What do people bring to a campsite? What do people do while camping? Create a web and list students' responses. Then discuss with students how campers' actions affect the environment.

Objectives

- Read with fluency and comprehension.
- Use a dictionary or glossary to determine the meaning, pronunciation, and syllabication of homographs.
- Present a dramatization.

Check Fluency WCPM

SUCCESS PREDICTOR

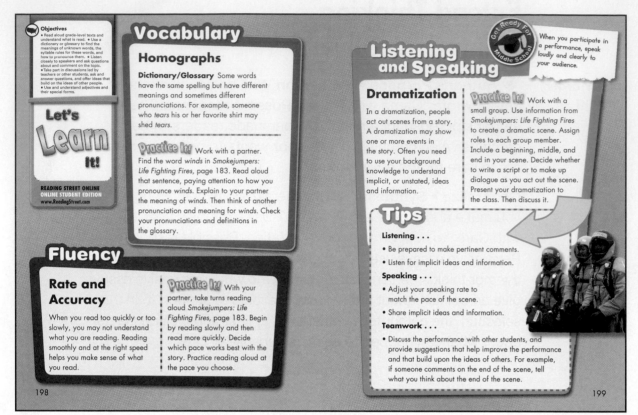

Student Edition pp. 198–199

Fluency
Rate and Accuracy

Guide practice

Use the Student Edition activity as an assessment tool. Make sure the reading passage is at least 200 words in length. As students read aloud with partners, walk around to make sure that students are reading at an appropriate speed for expository text and are reading with accuracy.

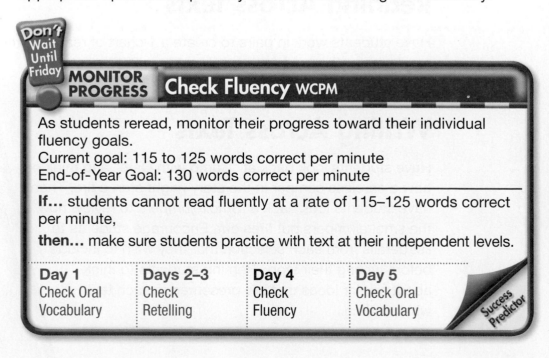

Don't Wait Until Friday

MONITOR PROGRESS **Check Fluency WCPM**

As students reread, monitor their progress toward their individual fluency goals.
Current goal: 115 to 125 words correct per minute
End-of-Year Goal: 130 words correct per minute

If... students cannot read fluently at a rate of 115–125 words correct per minute,

then... make sure students practice with text at their independent levels.

Day 1	Days 2–3	Day 4	Day 5
Check Oral Vocabulary	Check Retelling	Check Fluency	Check Oral Vocabulary

Success Predictor

Vocabulary
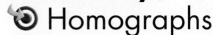
Homographs

Teach homographs

Dictionary/Glossary Write the following sentence on the board: *It is important to close the windows during a storm.* Circle *close* and have a volunteer read the sentence aloud, paying special attention to how he or she pronounces the circled word.

Guide practice

Have students use a dictionary to determine the meaning and pronunciation of *close* in the sentence, as well as its syllabication. Then have students read the other definitions of *close* and identify whether the pronunciation and number of syllables has changed.

On their own

Have partners complete the activity on p. 198 for *winds*. Walk around the room to make sure that students understand the correct pronunciation and meaning of *winds* in the sentence on p. 183. Ask volunteers to read the definitions and meanings aloud to the class.

Listening and Speaking
Dramatization

Teach

Tell students that in order for a dramatization to be successful, everyone must work together. Remind students that their dramatic scene should have a clear beginning, middle, and end and should use facts and information from *Smokejumpers*. Point out that students should use descriptive words and adjectives correctly in their dialogue.

Guide practice

As students practice their roles, remind them to speak and respond to each other as their characters would. Explain that the dialogue should seem natural and should be appropriate for the mood of the scene. If students are having trouble remembering dialogue, suggest that they use a script. Be sure that students pose questions and make suggestions that build on the ideas of others in their group as they practice their scenes.

On their own

Have students present their dramatization for the class. Remind students in the audience to listen attentively so that they are prepared to ask relevant questions and make comments at the end of the presentation.

Dramatization

Remind students that when they perform their role they should vary the rate, pitch, and volume of their voice as appropriate to the action in the scene. Tell students that it is important to be aware of the audience and to enunciate so the audience can understand exactly what is being said.

ELL

English Language Learners
Practice pronunciation Assist pairs of students by modeling how to read the pronunciation guide provided in a dictionary and then having students repeat after you. Pair students with mixed language proficiencies together to practice pronunciation and employ self-corrective techniques.

Objectives

- Use a poster to present information.
- Review adjectives and articles.
- Spell multisyllabic words.

Research and Inquiry
Synthesize

Teach Have students synthesize their research findings and results. Encourage students to organize their information by using a graphic organizer or including a diagram. Review how to choose relevant information from a number of sources and organize it logically.

Guide practice Have students use poster board and photographs, drawings, labels, diagrams, and heads to present their information on emergency procedures. Check to see that they used appropriate labels for all photographs, diagrams, and charts. Make sure that students have cited their sources on the back of their poster.

On their own Have students write a brief explanation of their research findings. Then have them organize and combine information for their poster presentation.

Conventions
Adjectives and Articles

Test practice

Remind students that grammar skills, such as adjectives and articles, are often assessed on important tests. Remind students that adjectives are words that describe nouns and that the words *a*, *an*, and *the* are special adjectives, called articles. Review that proper adjectives, such as *Mexican*, *Brazilian*, and *East Indian*, are formed from proper nouns and start with a capital letter.

Daily Fix-It

Use Daily Fix-It numbers 7 and 8 in the right margin.

On their own

For additional practice, use the *Reader's and Writer's Notebook* p. 326.

Spelling
Multisyllabic Words

Practice spelling strategy

Look at the spelling list. Find a word that is hard for you to spell.

Step 1: Say the word slowly. Listen for the syllables.

Step 2: Draw lines between the syllables.

Step 3: Focus on each syllable as you write the word.

On their own

For additional practice, use *Let's Practice It!* page 251 on the *Teacher Resources DVD-ROM*.

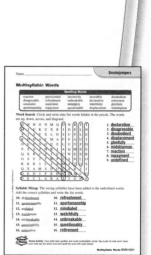

Let's Practice It!
TR DVD•251

Objectives
- Revise draft of a fantasy.
- Apply revising strategy: Consolidating.
- Include a variety of complete sentence types.

Writing—Fantasy
Revising Strategy

MINI-LESSON

Revising Strategy: Consolidating

■ Yesterday we wrote a fantasy about traveling back in time. Today we will revise our drafts. The goal is to make your writing clearer, more interesting, and more informative.

Writing Transparency 21B, TR DVD

■ Display Writing Transparency 21B. Remind students that revising does not include corrections of grammar and mechanics. Tell them that this will be done tomorrow as they proofread their work. Then introduce the revising strategy Consolidating.

When you revise, ask yourself *Where can I combine my sentences?* The revising strategy Consolidating is the strategy in which you combine sentences to make your writing smoother. Let's look at my introductory paragraph. There are several short, choppy sentences. I need to combine some of them into compound sentences to make the writing more interesting. **Combine the fourth and fifth sentences and read the consolidated sentence aloud.** Reread your composition for places where you might want to consolidate sentences for variety and to make the writing smoother.

Tell students that as they revise, they should look for places where they can consolidate sentences to make their writing smoother. They should also make sure they have included adjectives that describe the characters and the setting.

Revising Tips
✔ Combine sentences to make a more interesting sentence.

✔ Use a conjunction to combine sentences.

✔ Try to avoid using the same sentence pattern each time.

✔ Add adjectives that describe your characters and setting.

Peer conferencing

Peer Revision Have pairs of students exchange papers for peer revision. Students should write three questions about the partner's writing. Tell students that their questions should focus on where their partner could revise by consolidating to make the writing clearer and more informative. Refer to the *Reader's and Writer's Notebook* for more information about peer conferencing.

Have students revise their compositions using the questions their partners wrote during peer revision, as well as the key features of a fantasy to guide them. Be sure that students are using the revising strategy Consolidating.

Corrective feedback

Circulate around the room to monitor students and talk to them as they revise. Remind any student correcting errors that they will have time to edit tomorrow. They should be working on content and imagery today.

Quick Write for Fluency **Team Talk**

1. **Talk** Pairs discuss the elements of a fantasy.
2. **Write** Each student writes a paragraph describing what elements of an adventure can be found in a fantasy story.
3. **Share** Students read aloud their paragraphs to their partner. Partners read each other's writing for key features of fantasy.

Routines Flip Chart

Wrap Up Your Day

✔ **Build Concepts** What did you learn about camping with care?

✔ **Oral Vocabulary** Monitor students' use of oral vocabulary as they respond to this question: How can dangerous wildfires ignite from a deserted campfire?

✔ **Text Features** Discuss how text features helped students comprehend today's selection.

Write Guy
Jeff Anderson
Show Off In a Good Way

Post students' successful sentences or short paragraphs. Celebrate them as writers. Select a sentence of the week, and write it large! Display it as a poster inside or outside the classroom door. Students learn from each other's successes.

E L L

English Language Learners
Modify the prompt Allow beginning English speakers to work with a partner, dictating a portion of their composition as their partner records it. To revise, have the partner read aloud the composition and the partners can work together to revise sentences that can be combined.

Differentiated instruction If students have difficulty writing their compositions, suggest that they respond orally to the prompt.

Preview DAY 5

Remind students to keep thinking about how they can prepare for an emergency. Tell them that tomorrow they will read about calling 911.

Objectives
- Review the weekly concept.
- Review oral vocabulary.

Today at a Glance

Oral Vocabulary

Comprehension
- Author's purpose

Lesson Vocabulary
- Homographs

Word Analysis
French word origins

Literary Terms
Word choice

Assessment
Fluency
Comprehension

Research and Inquiry
Communicate

Spelling
Multisyllabic words

Conventions
Adjectives and articles

Writing
Fantasy

Check Oral Vocabulary
SUCCESS PREDICTOR

Concept Wrap Up

Question of the Week

How can we prepare for emergencies?

Review the concept

Have students look back at the reading selections to find examples that demonstrate how people can prepare for emergencies.

Review Amazing Words

Display and review this week's concept map. Remind students that this week they have learned ten Amazing Words related to emergencies. Have students use the Amazing Words and the concept map to answer the question *How can we prepare for emergencies?*

How people prepare for emergencies

Nature	Fires	Plan	Rescue	Tools and Equipment
hurricane	dangerous	hurricane watch	fire escape	generator
flood	wildfires	buy supplies	hot shots	medical
tornado	ignite	work together	smokejumpers	gear
deserted		training		first aid

ELL **Check Concepts and Language** Use the Day 5 instruction on ELL Poster 21 to monitor students' understanding of the lesson concept.

ELL Poster 21

Amazing Ideas

Connect to the Big Question

Have pairs of students discuss how the Question of the Week connects to the Big Question: *What makes an adventure?* Tell students to use the concept map and what they have learned from this week's Anchored Talks and reading selections to form an Amazing Idea—a realization or "big idea" about Adventures. Remind partners to pose and answer questions with appropriate detail and to give suggestions that build on each other's ideas. Then ask pairs to share their Amazing Idea with the class.

Amazing Ideas might include these key concepts:

- There are many ways to prepare for different kinds of emergencies.

- Workers that help out in emergencies often have risky and adventurous jobs.

- There are different kinds of tools and equipment that are helpful in emergencies and adventures.

Write about it

Have students write a few sentences about their Amazing Idea beginning with "This week I learned . . ."

 It's Friday

MONITOR PROGRESS | **Check Oral Vocabulary**

Have individuals use this week's Amazing Words to describe adventures. Monitor students' abilities to use the Amazing Words and note which words you need to reteach.

If... students have difficulty using the Amazing Words,

then... reteach using the Oral Vocabulary Routine, pp. 173a, 176b, 186b, 196b, OV•1.

Day 1	Days 2–3	Day 4	Day 5
Check Oral Vocabulary	Check Retelling	Check Fluency	Check Oral Vocabulary

Success Predictor

Amazing Words

generator	medical
deserted	first aid
hurricane watch	ignite
	wildfires
dangerous	gear
fire escape	

 E L L

English Language Learners
Concept map Work with students to discuss the meaning of any unfamiliar words on the concept map. Have students use words in oral sentences to check understanding.

Oral Vocabulary **Success Predictor**

Objectives

◎ Review author's purpose.
◎ Review homographs.
• Review French word origins.
• Review word choice.

Comprehension Review
🎯 Author's Purpose

Teach author's purpose

Envision It!

Review the definition of author's purpose on p. 174. Remind students that authors write to persuade, to inform, to express ideas or feelings, and to entertain. An author's purpose can be directly stated or implied. For additional support have students review p. EI•2 on author's purpose.

Student Edition p. EI•2

Guide practice

Have student pairs discuss whether the author's purpose for writing *Smokejumpers* is stated or implied, and explain how they know the difference. Have partners explain what they think is the author's purpose for writing *Smokejumpers* and use details from the text to support their answer.

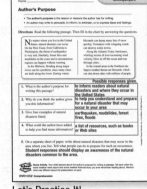

Let's Practice It!
TR DVD•252

On their own

For additional practice with author's purpose, use *Let's Practice It!* page 252 on the *Teacher Resources DVD-ROM*.

Vocabulary Review
🎯 Homographs

Teach homographs

Remind students to use a dictionary or glossary to check meanings and pronunciations of homographs.

Guide practice

Review with students the different pronunciations and meanings of the homograph *wind* they found by using a dictionary.

On their own

Have students write context sentences that show they understand the different meanings of the homographs *wind* and *steer.* Have students exchange sentences with a partner. Partners should read each other's sentences aloud for practice with pronouncing the homographs correctly. Then have students create a list of other homographs they know.

Word Analysis Review
French Word Origins

Teach French word origins

Review with students that a word origin explains the history of a word, including the language it comes from and any changes the word has undergone. Discuss the meaning of *parachute,* which comes from the French words *para* and *chute.*

Guide practice

Display the following words: *mayonnaise, rendezvous, dentist,* and *promenade.* Use the Strategy for Multisyllabic Words to teach *dentist.*

ROUTINE Strategy for Multisyllabic Words

1 Look for word parts Chunk the word into syllables. Circle each.
When I say *dentist,* I can hear two syllables. I will circle the syllables *dent* and *ist.*

2 Connect to meaning When I look up this word in a dictionary, I find that it comes from the French word *dent* which means "tooth." A dentist is a person who cares for the health of teeth.

3 Blend the word Blend the syllables together to read *dentist.*

Have students continue the routine to determine the meanings of *mayonnaise, rendezvous,* and *promenade.*

Routines Flip Chart

On their own

Have students see if they can think of other French-origin words.

Literary Terms Review
Word Choice

Teach word choice

Have students reread "Camp with Care" on pp. 196–197. Remind students that authors use specific words and phrases to communicate their meaning clearly.

Guide practice

Direct students to this sentence on p. 197, *And here's the really bad news.* Discuss why the author chose to include this sentence after describing the terrible effects of forest fires. Ask students how a different choice of words might have changed the tone of the sentence.

On their own

Have students find other examples in "Camp with Care" that demonstrate how the author's word choice affects meaning.

Lesson Vocabulary

concentrating paying close attention; focusing the mind

dedication the act of giving time and energy to something

essential necessary

method a way of doing something

parachute umbrella-shaped device made of fabric; it allows people to fall slowly from an airplane

steer to guide

underbrush bushes and small trees growing under large trees

wind air that moves

English Language Learners
Author's purpose If students have trouble understanding the different reasons why authors choose to write, compare and contrast the purposes behind *Smokejumpers* and "Camp with Care." Ask: Why did the author write *Smokejumpers*? Why did the author write "Camp with Care"? What kind of details and language did each author use to achieve this purpose?

Objectives
• Read grade-level text with fluency.

Plan to Assess Fluency

☑ **This week assess Advanced students.**

☐ **Week 2** Assess Strategic Intervention students.

☐ **Week 3** Assess On-Level students.

☐ **Week 4** Assess Strategic Intervention students.

☐ **Week 5** Assess any students you have not yet checked during this unit.

Set individual goals for students to enable them to reach the year-end goal.

• Current Goal: 115–125 WCPM

• Year-End Goal: 130 WCPM

Assessment

Check words correct per minute

Fluency Make two copies of the fluency passage on p. 199k. As the student reads the text aloud, mark mistakes on your copy. Also mark where the student is at the end of one minute. To check the student's comprehension of the passage, have him or her retell what was read. To figure words correct per minute (WCPM), subtract the number of mistakes from the total number of words read in one minute.

WCPM

Corrective feedback

If... students cannot read fluently at a rate of 115–125 WCPM,

then... make sure they practice with text at their independent reading level. Provide additional fluency practice by pairing nonfluent readers with fluent readers.

If... students already read at 130 WCPM,

then... have them read a book of their choice independently.

Small Group Time

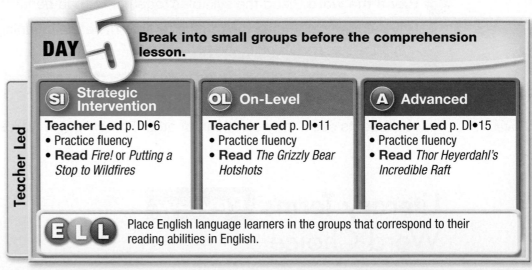

DAY 5 **Break into small groups before the comprehension lesson.**

Teacher Led

SI Strategic Intervention	**OL** On-Level	**A** Advanced
Teacher Led p. DI•6 • Practice fluency • **Read** *Fire!* or *Putting a Stop to Wildfires*	**Teacher Led** p. DI•11 • Practice fluency • **Read** *The Grizzly Bear Hotshots*	**Teacher Led** p. DI•15 • Practice fluency • **Read** *Thor Heyerdahl's Incredible Raft*

ELL Place English language learners in the groups that correspond to their reading abilities in English.

Practice Stations	**Independent Activities**
• Words to Know • Get Fluent • Read for Meaning	• Grammar Jammer • Concept Talk Video • Vocabulary Activities

Safe Rooms

Some parts of the country are often hit by hurricanes or tornadoes.   12

Many families living in these places are choosing to build safe rooms.   24

A safe room does what its name says. It keeps you safe, even in the   39

strongest winds.   41

Safe rooms are not very big. They usually can fit about eight   53

people who are sitting very closely together. Safe rooms can be in a   66

basement or on the first floor of a building. Safe rooms can also be   80

built underground, away from a building. The floor of a safe room is   93

anchored down. This way, the room cannot be turned over or lifted by   106

strong winds. The walls, ceiling, and door of a safe room are all built   120

in special ways. The wind cannot tear them up. Things blown against a   133

safe room by the wind will not hurt it. Where the parts of a safe room fit   150

together, very strong devices hold them tightly.   157

A safe room never has windows. It never shares the structure of the   170

building it is in. After a bad storm, you might see a safe room standing   185

by itself. The building around it has been destroyed. But the safe room   198

came through just fine!   202

MONITOR PROGRESS

• Check Fluency

Objectives
• Read grade-level text with comprehension.

Assessment

Check author's purpose

⊙ **Author's Purpose** Use "Calling 911" on p. 199m to check students' understanding of author's purpose.

1. Does the author state the purpose for writing this text? How can you tell whether the purpose is stated or implied? **Possible response: The author does not state the purpose for this text. If the author includes a statement explaining why the author wrote the text, the purpose is stated. If no statement is included, the purpose is implied.**

2. Why do you think the author included the details about the difference between cell phones and regular phones? **Possible response: The author wanted readers to understand why it is important to know exactly where you are when calling 911 from a cell phone.**

3. Why do you think the author chose to write this text? **Possible response: The author wanted to inform readers about what to do when calling 911.**

Corrective feedback

If... students are unable to answer the comprehension questions, **then...** use the Reteach lesson in the *First Stop* book.

Calling 911

Most of the time, life goes smoothly. However, if an emergency happens, you want to get help quickly. That is exactly what calling 911 is all about. Anyone can use this service. You just need to get to a safe place and make the call. By punching in these three numbers, you can reach the police, the fire department, or an ambulance.

When you dial 911, you are calling an emergency operator. This person is trained to connect you with the help you need. In order to do that, he or she must get some facts from you. You need to stay calm to answer the questions you are asked. Take a deep breath. Let the operator lead the talking.

All callers are asked many of the same questions. You will be asked to describe the emergency. You will be asked to give your name and to tell where you are. After that, the call will be about you and what is going on. The operator might tell you some things that you should do. Listen carefully. Do not hang up until you are told.

If you are calling on a cell phone, you might have to explain where you are in detail. When you call from a regular phone, the person on the other end of the call can see your address. The phone number and the address go together. With a cell phone, it is different. A cell phone is not hooked up at one place. That is why it is very important to know exactly where you are. Look for street signs or numbers on buildings.

Remember, call 911 only if a person is badly hurt or in danger. As soon as your call goes through, help will be on the way!

Objectives
- Communicate inquiry results.
- Administer spelling test.
- Review adjectives and articles.

Research and Inquiry
Communicate

Present ideas   Have students share their inquiry results by presenting their information and giving a brief talk on their research. Have students display the poster they created on Day 4, pointing out illustrations, photos, heads, labels, and also citing their list of sources on the back.

Listening and speaking   Remind students how to be good speakers and how to communicate effectively with their audience.

- Respond to relevant questions with appropriate details.
- Speak clearly and loudly.
- Keep eye contact with audience members.

Remind students of these tips for being a good listener.

- Listen attentively to speakers and wait until the speaker has finished before raising your hand to ask a relevant question or make a pertinent comment.
- Be polite, even if you disagree.

Spelling Test
Multisyllabic Words

Spelling test
To administer the spelling test, refer to the directions, words, and sentences on p. 175c.

Conventions
Extra Practice

Teach
Remind students that an adjective describes a noun or pronoun. Adjectives formed from the names of persons, places, or things are proper adjectives, and proper adjectives are written with a capital letter. Also review use and placement of the articles *a, an,* and *the.*

Guide practice
Have partners take turns naming objects in the room and supplying a sentence that includes an article and an adjective that describes the object. The other partner can add an adjective to each sentence. Ask students to use the following format.

> **Pencil**
> **The yellow pencil belongs to Tom.**
> **The shiny, yellow pencil belongs to Tom.**

Daily Fix-It
Use Daily Fix-It numbers 9 and 10 in the right margin.

On their own
Write these sentences. Have students look back in *Smokejumpers* to find the correct adjective to fill in the blanks. Remind students that adjectives describe a noun and often answer the questions *What kind? How many?* or *Which one?* For additional practice, use *Let's Practice It!* page 253 on the *Teacher Resources DVD-ROM.*

1. There is no _____ clearing. (large)

2. The _____ mask protects a smokejumper from branches when he or she lands in a tree. (face)

3. A _____ parachute's bundle might include shovels and saws. (red)

4. Fighting forest wildfires is a _____ business. (dangerous)

5. These wildfires can start in a _____ gulch or high on a mountainside. (deep)

Daily Fix-It
9. Their lifes were exciting. But sometimes dangerous. (*lives; exciting but*)
10. I'd like to help put out wild-fires, it would save forests from being destroyed. (*I'd; wildfires. It*)

Let's Practice It!
TR DVD•253

Writing—Fantasy
Writer's Craft: Adjectives and Articles

Review Revising

Remind students that yesterday they revised their fantasy stories, paying special attention to consolidating and combining sentences to make them more interesting and varied. Today they will proofread their fantasies.

MINI-LESSON

Proofread for Adjectives and Articles

■ **Teach** When we proofread, we look closely at our work, searching for errors in mechanics such as spelling, capitalization, punctuation, and grammar. Today we will focus on the adjectives and articles in our story.

■ **Model** Let's look at a paragraph from the fantasy we revised yesterday. Display Writing Transparency 21C. Explain that you will look for errors in the use of adjectives and articles. I see a problem in the second sentence. When a word is used as an adjective, it changes form. We need to add a *y* to *speed* to form an adjective. So I'll write *speedy*. In sentence 5, I see another error. The article should be *a* because the next word starts with a consonant sound. Point out that students should reread their fantasies several times, each time checking on different types of errors: spelling, punctuation, capitalization, and grammar.

Writing Transparency 21C, TR DVD

Proofread

Display the Proofreading Tips. Ask students to proofread their fantasies, using the Proofreading Tips and paying particular attention to adjectives and articles. Circulate around the room answering students' questions. When students have finished editing their own work, have pairs proofread one another's fantasy.

Proofreading Tips

✓ Use adjectives whenever possible to create imagery.

✓ Check the use of articles.

✓ If you use a computer, print out your story. It is easier to make corrections on paper than on a computer screen.

✓ Create a final draft only after you revise and edit.

Present

Have students incorporate revisions and proofreading edits into their fantasy to create a final draft.

Give students two options for presenting: A class fantasy book that will be shared with other classes or an oral presentation to the class. Have students who choose to do an oral presentation practice their presentation. Those who choose to contribute to the class book should create art to accompany their fantasy. When students have finished, have each complete the Writing Self-Evaluation Guide.

ROUTINE **Quick Write for Fluency** **Team Talk**

1. **Talk** Pairs discuss what they learned about fantasies.

2. **Write** Each student writes a paragraph summarizing his or her discussion.

3. **Share** Partners read their summaries to one another.

Routines Flip Chart

Teacher Note

Writing self-evaluation Make copies of the Writing Self-Evaluation Guide on p. 39 of the *Reader's and Writer's Notebook* and hand them out to students.

English Language Learners

Support editing Provide practice with adding adjectives to sentences. Beginning speakers may benefit from repeating a sentence you write on the board and adding an adjective to the sentence. Then have students read the new sentence.

Poster preview Prepare students for next week by using Week 2 ELL Poster 22. Read the Talk-Through to introduce the concept and vocabulary. Ask students to identify and describe actions in the art.

Selection summary Send home the summary of *Lost City* in English and the students' home languages, if available. They can read the summary with family members.

Preview NEXT WEEK

What surprises can happen on an expedition? Tell students that next week they will read about the adventure of discovering a lost city.

Weekly Assessment

Use pp. 154–161 of *Weekly Tests* to check:

✔ **Word Analysis** French Word Origins

✔ ◉ **Comprehension Skill** Author's Purpose

✔ Review **Comprehension Skill** Graphic Sources

✔ **Lesson Vocabulary**

concentrating	parachute
dedication	steer
essential	underbrush
method	wind

Weekly Tests

Advanced

On-Level

Strategic Intervention

Differentiated Assessment

Use pp. 121–126 of *Fresh Reads for Fluency and Comprehension* to check:

✔ ◉ **Comprehension Skill** Author's Purpose

✔ Review **Comprehension Skill** Graphic Sources

✔ **Fluency** Words Correct Per Minute

Fresh Reads for Fluency and Comprehension

Managing Assessment

Use *Assessment Handbook* for:

✔ **Weekly Assessment Blackline Masters for Monitoring Progress**

✔ **Observation Checklists**

✔ **Record-Keeping Forms**

✔ **Portfolio Assessment**

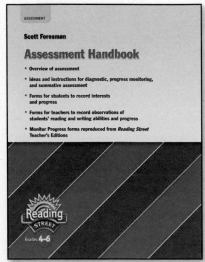

Assessment Handbook

Coconuts

Continued from p. 173b

Inside, Mom and Dad were standing in front of the TV, and Tony Verrazo was talking.

"Folks, you need to go pick up coconuts."

"See, [Mike said,] hurricane-force winds can make flying coconuts really dangerous!"

Tony Verrazo's face came back on the screen. "Folks, we want to give credit to the person who gave us the idea for this story."

And suddenly there I was saying, "Hi. My name is Jason. I'm picking up coconuts because Calvin is coming."

"Wow!" Mike grinned.

"All day, I thought I had to pick up coconuts just because I was little and had to stay out of everybody's way," [I said.]

"And yet you did it anyway?" asked Mom.

"I picked up every single one," I told her.

She nodded at the rest of us. "The generator is ready to run if the power goes out."

"The windows are O.K., and the shutters are locked tight," said Mike.

"We have plenty of food and drinking water," Dad said.

They turned to me.

"There are no coconuts on the ground," I said proudly.

"Then we're agreed," Dad said. "This family is ready!"

After hearing about Calvin all day, I was more than ready.

Small Group Time

5-Day Plan

DAY 1	• Reinforce the concept
	• Read Leveled Readers
	  Concept Literacy
	  Below Level

DAY 2	• ◉ Author's Purpose • ◉ Important Ideas • Revisit Student Edition pp. 178–185
DAY 3	• ◉ Homographs • Revisit Student Edition pp. 186–191
DAY 4	• Practice Retelling • Read/Revisit Student Edition pp. 196–197
DAY 5	• Reread for fluency • Reread Leveled Readers

3- or 4-Day Plan

DAY 1	• Reinforce the concept
	• Read Leveled Readers
	  Concept Literacy
	  Below Level

DAY 2	• ◉ Author's Purpose • ◉ Important Ideas • Revisit Student Edition pp. 178–185
DAY 3	• ◉ Homographs • Revisit Student Edition pp. 186–191

DAY 4	• Practice Retelling
	• Read/Revisit Student
	  Edition pp. 196–197
	• Reread for fluency
	• Reread Leveled
	  Readers

3-Day Plan: Eliminate the shaded box.

SI *Strategic Intervention*

DAY 1

Build Background

■ **Reinforce the Concept** Offer a sample answer to the weekly question *How can we prepare for emergencies?* One way we prepare for emergencies is by gathering the right equipment. For example, firefighters use special tools, protective clothing, and fireproof tents to fight fires and stay safe. Ask students to give you another example of how we prepare for emergencies. Discuss the words in the concept map.

■ **Connect to Reading** This week you will read about wildfires and the firefighters who risk their lives to put them out. What wildfires have you experienced, seen on the news, or read about? (*Students may have seen or read about the wildfires in California and the West Coast, or others.*) How can people help prevent forest fires before they begin? (*People can be careful to never leave a fire unattended and to make sure fires are completely put out with water before they leave. In addition, if a fire gets too big, it should also be put out.*)

Objectives
• Participate in teacher-led discussions by answering questions with appropriate detail.

 **SI** *Strategic Intervention*

DAY 1

For a complete literacy instructional plan and additional practice with this week's target skills and strategies, see the **Leveled Reader Teaching Guide.**

Concept Literacy Reader

- **Read** *Fire!*

- **Before Reading** Preview the book with students, focusing on key concepts and vocabulary. Then have them set a purpose for reading.

- **During Reading** Read the first two pages of the book aloud while students track the print. Then have students finish reading the book with a partner.

- **After Reading** After students finish reading the book, connect it to the weekly question *How can we prepare for emergencies?*

Below-Level Reader

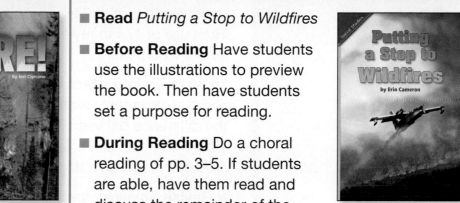

- **Read** *Putting a Stop to Wildfires*

- **Before Reading** Have students use the illustrations to preview the book. Then have students set a purpose for reading.

- **During Reading** Do a choral reading of pp. 3–5. If students are able, have them read and discuss the remainder of the book with a partner using these questions.

  - What started the fire in Colorado in 2005? (*lightning strikes on dry grasses and trees*)

  - What is the difference between hotshots and smokejumpers? (*Hotshots fight wildfires on the ground. Smokejumpers jump out of planes to fight fires in out-of-the-way places.*)

- **After Reading** Have students look at and discuss the concept map. Connect the Below-Level Reader to the weekly question *How can we prepare for emergencies?*

MONITOR PROGRESS

If... students have difficulty reading the selection with a partner,

then... have them follow along as they listen to the Leveled Readers DVD-ROM.

If... students have trouble understanding how smokejumpers can land safely,

then... reread pp. 13–14 and discuss the landing procedure together.

Objectives
- Participate in teacher-led discussions by answering questions with appropriate detail.

Reinforce Comprehension

Student Edition, p. EI•2

Skill Author's Purpose Review with students *Envision It!* p. EI•2 on Author's Purpose. Then use p. 174 to review the definition of author's purpose.

Strategy Important Ideas Review the definition of important ideas on p. 174. Discuss the difference between important ideas and supporting details. For additional support, refer students to *Envision It!* p. EI•17.

■ **Revisit** *Smokejumpers: Life Fighting Fires* on pp. 178–185. As students read, have them apply the comprehension skill and strategy to the selection.

- Why do you think the author wrote this article about smokejumpers? (*to inform the reader about the job smokejumpers do*)

- Why is the information organized in sections with headings? (*to guide readers and show the different topics related to smokejumpers*)

- Why is the photograph with labels included in the section "Jumpsuit and Safety Gear"? (*to show the information in the text in a visual way, to help readers understand each piece of safety gear smokejumpers wear*)

Use the During Reading Differentiated Instruction for additional support for struggling readers.

MONITOR PROGRESS

If... students have difficulty reading along with the group,

then... have them follow along as they listen to the AudioText.

More Reading

Use additional Leveled Readers or other texts at students' instructional levels to reinforce this week's skills and strategies. For text suggestions, see the Leveled Reader Database or the Leveled Readers Skills Chart on pp. CL 24–CL 29.

Objectives
- Explain the stated purpose for an expository text.
- Summarize the main idea in text in ways that maintain meaning.

SI *Strategic Intervention*  DAY 3

Reinforce Vocabulary

Student Edition, p. EI•10

Homographs/Dictionary/Glossary Say the word *close* (meaning "near") as you write it on the board. Then point to the word and say *close* (meaning "to shut"). Some words are spelled the same but have different meanings and pronunciations, such as *close* and *close*. Other words are spelled the same and pronounced the same but have different meanings, such as *fire,* which can mean "a blaze" or "to let someone go from a job." Words like these are called *homographs.* The Latin root *homo* means "same," and the Greek root *graph* means "write."

Look at the words *wind, can, flat,* and *ground* on p. 180. What are two meanings of each? (wind: *"movement of air" and "to twist or wrap";* can: *"able to" and "a tin to hold food";* flat: *"level" and "off-key, as in singing";* ground: *"the earth" and "crushed into small bits"*)

■ **Revisit** *Smokejumpers: Life Fighting Fires* on pp. 186–191. Review *Words!* on pp. W•10 and W•14. Encourage students to use a dictionary if they are unsure of the meaning of any homographs as they finish reading the selection with a partner.

• The picture on p. 185 shows a box labeled "Reserve Parachute." On p. 186, the words describe an "emergency parachute" in this position. What do you think the reserve, or emergency, parachute is for? (*to use in case the main parachute does not work*)

• What does the word *spot* mean on p. 187? (*look for*)

Use the During Reading Differentiated Instruction for additional support for struggling readers.

MONITOR PROGRESS

If... students need more practice with the lesson vocabulary,

then... use *Envision It! Pictured Vocabulary Cards*.

Objectives
• Use a dictionary or glossary to determine meanings of unknown words.

More Reading

Use additional Leveled Readers or other texts at students' instructional levels to reinforce this week's skills and strategies. For text suggestions, see the Leveled Reader Database or the Leveled Readers Skills Chart on pp. CL 24–CL 29.

SI Strategic Intervention

Practice Retelling

■ **Retell** Have students work in pairs and use the Retelling Cards to retell *Smokejumpers.* Monitor retelling and prompt students as needed. If students struggle, model a fluent retelling.

Genre Focus

■ **Before Reading or Revisiting** "Camp with Care" on pp. 196–197, read aloud the genre information about persuasive texts on p. 196. Explain to students that a persuasive text tries to influence a reader's thoughts or actions. In persuasive texts, authors use facts to provide information and to support their opinions. By including certain facts, authors try to convince readers to do or believe what they say.

Then have students preview "Camp with Care."

• What pictures, words, and features do you see? (*photographs, a title, and a subhead*)

• Look at the subhead on the second page. What do you predict the author will discuss on that page? (*the importance of preventing forest fires, methods of preventing forest fires*)

Ask students to set a purpose for reading based on their preview.

■ **During Reading or Revisiting** Have students read along with you while tracking the print. Stop to discuss any unfamiliar words, such as *pollute* and *drenched.*

■ **After Reading or Revisiting** Have students share their reactions to the article. Then guide them through the Reading Across Texts and Writing Across Texts activities. What mistakes might a camper make that would start a forest fire? (*leaving a fire unattended, forgetting to drench the ashes*)

MONITOR PROGRESS

If... students have difficulty retelling the selection,

then... have them review the selection using the photos and text features.

Objectives

• Explain how an author uses language to present information to influence what the reader thinks or does.

For a complete literacy instructional plan and additional practice with this week's target skills and strategies, see the **Leveled Reader Teaching Guide.**

Concept Literacy Reader

■ **Model** Demonstrate rate and accuracy for students. Ask students to listen carefully as you read aloud the first two pages of *Fire!* Have students note your accuracy and the rate at which you read, pausing appropriately at various marks of punctuation.

Fire!

■ **Fluency Routine**

1. Have students reread passages from *Fire!* with a partner.

2. For optimal fluency, students should reread three to four times.

3. As students read, monitor fluency and provide corrective feedback. Encourage them to slow down if they are skipping words or misreading words.

See *Routines Flip Chart* for more help with fluency.

■ **Retell** Have students retell *Fire!* Prompt as necessary.

Below-Level Reader

■ **Model** Ask students to listen carefully as you read aloud pp. 3–4 of *Putting a Stop to Wildfires,* emphasizing accuracy and appropriate rate.

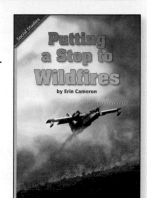

Putting a Stop to Wildfires

■ **Fluency Routine**

1. Have students reread passages from *Putting a Stop to Wildfires* with a partner or individually.

2. For optimal fluency, students should reread three to four times.

3. As students read, monitor fluency and provide corrective feedback. Discuss how adjusting the rate can help convey the tone and mood of the selection.

See *Routines Flip Chart* for more help with fluency.

■ **Retell** For additional practice, have students retell *Putting a Stop to Wildfires* page-by-page, using the illustrations. Prompt as necessary.

• What does this part explain?

• How does this picture relate to the text?

MONITOR PROGRESS

If... students have difficulty reading fluently,

then... provide additional fluency practice by pairing nonfluent readers with fluent ones.

Objectives
• Read aloud grade-level stories with fluency.

Small Group Time

Pacing Small Group Instruction

5-Day Plan

DAY 1	• Expand the concept • Read On-Level Reader
DAY 2	• Author's Purpose • Important Ideas • Revisit Student Edition pp. 178–185
DAY 3	• Homographs • Revisit Student Edition pp. 186–191
DAY 4	• Practice Retelling • Read/Revisit Student Edition pp. 196–197
DAY 5	• Reread for fluency • Reread On-Level Reader

3- or 4-Day Plan

DAY 1	• Expand the concept • Read On-Level Reader
DAY 2	• Author's Purpose • Important Ideas • Revisit Student Edition pp. 178–185
DAY 3	• Homographs • Revisit Student Edition pp. 186–191
DAY 4	• Practice Retelling • Read/Revisit Student Edition pp. 196–197 • Reread for fluency • Reread On-Level Reader

3-Day Plan: Eliminate the shaded box.

OL On-Level   DAY 1

Build Background

■ **Expand the Concept** Connect to the weekly question *How can we prepare for emergencies?* and expand the concept. How we prepare for an emergency depends on the type of emergency we face. Emergencies involving fires require special preparation because fires have unique dangers. What unique dangers do fires have? Add new words to the concept map.

On-Level Reader

For a complete literacy instructional plan and additional practice with this week's target skills and strategies, see the **Leveled Reader Teaching Guide.**

■ **Before Reading** *The Grizzly Bear Hotshots,* have students preview the reader by looking at the title, cover, and pictures in the book.

The Grizzly Bear Hotshots

• What is the topic of this book? (*a boy who has made the Grizzly Bear crew, a team of firefighters known as "hotshots"*)

• Based on the pictures in the book, what might be some of the pros of being a hotshot? What are some cons? (*Pros: excitement, the chance to help people; Cons: danger, difficult conditions*)

Have students create KWL charts based on this book.

In column 1, What I <u>K</u>now, write what you already know about hotshots. In column 2, What I <u>W</u>ant to Find Out, write what you hope to learn from this book. Fill out column 3, What I <u>L</u>earned, after you finish reading.

■ **During Reading** Read aloud the first three pages of the book as students follow along. Then have them finish reading the book on their own. Remind students to complete their KWL charts as they read.

■ **After Reading** Have partners compare their KWL charts.

• What new information did you learn from the story?

• How does the topic relate to the weekly question *How can we prepare for emergencies?*

Objectives

• Participate in teacher-led discussions by answering questions with appropriate detail.

On-Level

DAY 2

Expand Comprehension

Student Edition, p. EI•17

🎯 **Skill Author's Purpose** Use p. 174 to review the definition of author's purpose. For additional review, see Author's Purpose in *Envision It! Skill.* Authors often have more than one purpose for writing. Even in an essay that is intended to inform or persuade, an author might include passages that are entertaining or that express ideas or feelings.

🎯 **Strategy Important Ideas** Review the definition of important ideas. Encourage students to separate important ideas from supporting details as they read, and suggest that they use important ideas to help determine the author's purpose. For additional support, use the Extend Thinking questions and refer students to *Envision It! Strategy* p. EI•17.

■ **Revisit** *Smokejumpers: Life Fighting Fires* on pp. 178–185. As students read, have them apply the comprehension skill and strategy to the selection.

* How do the headings help the reader determine the author's purpose for the various sections of the selection? (*They tell the reader what the author plans to cover in each section.*)

* Why does the author include this sentence: "So what do you get when you cross a wildfire firefighter with a parachutist?" (*The author is trying to be entertaining—by using a common joke line—at the same time that he is being informative.*)

More Reading

Use additional Leveled Readers or other texts at students' instructional levels to reinforce this week's skills and strategies. For text suggestions, see the Leveled Reader Database or the Leveled Readers Skills Chart on pp. CL 24–CL 29.

Objectives
* Explain the stated purpose for an expository text.
* Summarize the main idea in text in ways that maintain meaning.

OL On-Level

DAY 3

Expand Vocabulary

Student Edition, p. W•10

More Reading

Use additional Leveled Readers or other texts at students' instructional levels to reinforce this week's skills and strategies. For text suggestions, see the Leveled Reader Database or the Leveled Readers Skills Chart on pp. CL 24–CL 29.

🔊 **Homographs/Dictionary/Glossary** Write the word *wind* on the board. Then ask:

- What are two ways to pronounce this word? (*with a short* i *and with a long* i)

- What does the word mean when pronounced with a short vowel sound? (*"fast-moving air"*)

- What does it mean when pronounced with a long vowel sound? (*"to twist or coil, as thread on a spool"*)

For more meanings, look it up in a dictionary. Words with the same spelling but different meanings are called *homographs.* Homographs can have the same or different pronunciations. What are two different meanings of the word *right*? (*"correct"* and *"in a direction the opposite of left"*)

- Find three homographs in the selection. (*Sample answers:* course, cool, break)

- What are two meanings for each of your homographs? (course: *"a track or path"* and *"rough"*; cool: *"cold"* and *"calm"*; break: *"rest"* and *"to cut or crack"*)

■ **Revisit** *Smokejumpers: Life Fighting Fires* on pp. 186–191. Encourage students to watch for homographs as they read.

- Why do smokejumpers use color-coded parachutes for their supplies? (*so they know exactly what is in each bundle without wasting time*)

- Why do smokejumpers often have to walk long distances after they put out fires? (*They need to walk to a clearing where a helicopter can land and pick them up.*)

- Find an example of an entertaining sentence included with the factual information in the selection. (*Possible answer: "The last thing a smokejumper needs is to find sandwiches when he or she is looking for a shovel!"*)

Objectives
- Use a dictionary or glossary to determine meanings of unknown words.

On-Level

DAY **4**

Practice Retelling

■ **Retell** To assess students' comprehension, use the Retelling Cards. Monitor retelling and prompt students as needed.

Genre Focus

■ **Before Reading or Revisiting** "Camp with Care" on pp. 196–197, read aloud the genre information about persuasive text on p. 196. Have students preview "Camp with Care" and set a purpose for reading.

* What do you think the author will try to persuade you to do? (*be a responsible camper*)

* Why do you think the author uses the heading *Prevent Forest Fires* on the second page? (*to alert the reader to the new topic he will focus on*)

■ **During Reading or Revisiting** Have students read along with you while tracking the print.

* What are some arguments that are used to persuade you to camp with care? (*Litter is dangerous to animals, litter pollutes streams, and other campers want to see a litter-free countryside.*)

* What are some tips the author gives for preventing forest fires? (*Never leave a fire unattended, and make sure a fire is completely out before you leave.*)

■ **After Reading or Revisiting** Have students share their reaction to the persuasive text. Then have them write a persuasive paragraph about an issue that concerns them, such as an environmental issue or an issue at school or in their community.

Objectives
* Explain how an author uses language to present information to influence what the reader thinks or does.

Small Group Time

On-Level Reader

■ **Model** Read aloud p. 3 of the On-Level Reader *The Grizzly Bear Hotshots,* emphasizing appropriate reading rate and accuracy. Demonstrate how to adjust your rate according to the speaker and mood of the text. Encourage students to avoid reading too quickly to maintain accuracy.

The Grizzly Bear Hotshots

■ **Fluency Routine**

1. Have students reread passages from *The Grizzly Bear Hotshots* with a partner.

2. For optimal fluency, students should reread passages three to four times.

3. As students read, monitor fluency and provide corrective feedback. Check that students adjust their rate as they read. For example, they might increase their rate during frightening or suspenseful moments and decrease their rate when the mood of the story becomes calm.

See *Routines Flip Chart* for more help with fluency.

■ **Retell** For additional practice, have students use headings and photographs as a guide to retell *The Grizzly Bear Hotshots.* Prompt as necessary.

- Who are the main characters in the story?

- What is the main problem in the story?

- How is the main problem resolved?

Objectives
• Read aloud grade-level stories with fluency.

A Advanced

DAY 1

Build Background

■ **Extend the Concept** Discuss the weekly question *How can we prepare for emergencies?* Think about how location affects how you would react in an emergency. For example, what would you do if you were at home during a severe storm? What would you do if you were in a car or at a park?

Advanced Reader

For a complete literacy instructional plan and additional practice with this week's target skills and strategies, see the **Leveled Reader Teaching Guide**.

■ **Before Reading** *Thor Heyerdahl's Incredible Raft,* prepare students to read the selection. Today you will read about a man who wanted to prove that it was possible to cross the Pacific Ocean in a raft. Have students look at the illustrations in the book and use them to predict what will happen in the text and set a purpose for reading.

Thor Heyerdahl's Incredible Raft

■ **During Reading** Have students read the Advanced Reader independently. Encourage them to think critically.

• How do you think the men on the Kon-Tiki felt during those first few stormy days at sea? (*worried, frightened, determined, tired*)

• Why do you think Thor Heyerdahl decided not to use modern navigation systems of his time, relying instead on celestial navigation? (*He wanted to prove that ancient peoples could have made the trip without modern navigational tools.*)

■ **After Reading** Have students review the concept map on p. 173 and explain how *Thor Heyerdahl's Incredible Raft* helps answer the weekly question How can we prepare for emergencies?

• What kinds of supplies did the men pack as preparation for emergencies? (*food, medical supplies, extra materials for the raft, fishing gear*)

• Did Heyerdahl's voyage prove that Polynesians came from South America? Explain. (*No, but it did prove that the journey was possible and that ancient Polynesians could have come from South America.*)

■ **Now Try This** Assign "Now Try This" at the end of the Advanced Reader.

Objectives
• Participate in teacher-led discussions by answering questions with appropriate detail.

Pacing Small Group Instruction

15–20 min

5-Day Plan	
DAY 1	• Extend the concept • Read Advanced Reader
DAY 2	• Author's Purpose • Important Ideas • Revisit Student Edition pp. 178–185
DAY 3	• Homographs • Revisit Student Edition pp. 186–191
DAY 4	• Genre Focus • Read/Revisit Student Edition pp. 196–197
DAY 5	• Reread for fluency • Reread Advanced Reader

3- or 4-Day Plan	
DAY 1	• Extend the concept • Read Advanced Reader
DAY 2	• Author's Purpose • Important Ideas • Revisit Student Edition pp. 178–185
DAY 3	• Homographs • Revisit Student Edition pp. 186–191
DAY 4	• Genre Focus • Read/Revisit Student Edition pp. 196–197 • Reread for fluency • Reread Advanced Reader

3-Day Plan: Eliminate the shaded box.

Small Group Time

Extend Comprehension

Skill Author's Purpose Review the definition of author's purpose. To broaden students' understanding of author's purpose, encourage them to reflect on the Advanced Reader. Explain that reflecting on how a book affects you can give you clues about what the author intended. Think of the book *Thor Heyerdahl's Incredible Raft* that you just read.

- How did it affect you?

- Based on your reactions, what do you think was the author's purpose or purposes for writing it? (*to inform, to express feelings of awe, and to entertain by telling an incredible story*)

Strategy Important Ideas Review the definition of the strategy of important ideas. Remind students to be aware of important ideas as they read *Smokejumpers.*

■ **Revisit** *Smokejumpers: Life Fighting Fires* on pp. 178–185. Have students apply the comprehension skill and strategy as they read. Why would an author write a text that not only informs but also entertains? (*Most likely, readers will find the topic more interesting and memorable if they are entertained as they are informed.*)

■ **Critical Thinking** Have students think about what they know about smokejumpers so far.

- How would you feel if a close friend of yours decided to become a smokejumper?

- Suppose the article was written from the perspective of a smokejumper who was injured on the job. How might the article be different? (*It might be more serious, perhaps with more emphasis on safety. It might also focus more on persuading readers of the risks involved with the job.*)

During reading, use the Extend Thinking questions and the During Reading Differentiated Instruction for additional support.

More Reading

Use additional Leveled Readers or other texts at students' instructional levels to reinforce this week's skills and strategies. For text suggestions, see the Leveled Reader Database or the Leveled Readers Skills Chart on pp. CL 24–CL 29.

Objectives
- Explain the stated purpose for an expository text.
- Summarize the main idea in text in ways that maintain meaning.

A Advanced

DAY **3**

Extend Vocabulary

◉ **Homographs/Dictionary/Glossary** Choose and read a sentence containing a homograph, such as this one from p. 7 of *Thor Heyerdahl's Incredible Raft*: "Heyerdahl imagined the mysterious bearded men of Peru floating on a current all the way to Easter Island, Fatu Hiva, and the other islands of Polynesia."

- The word *current* has several meanings. Look it up in a dictionary and name two meanings. (*"a flow of water or flow within a larger body of water or mass of air" and "now in progress"*)

- How can you know which meaning the author intended? (*by considering the context in which the word appears*)

- Which meaning of *current* makes the most sense in this sentence? (*a flow of water*)

Discuss how important it is to use a dictionary to verify which meaning of a homograph to use. Remind students to use the strategy as they read *Smokejumpers*.

■ **Revisit** *Smokejumpers: Life Fighting Fires* on pp. 186–191. Have students recall what they have learned so far and then finish reading on their own. Pause to check comprehension.

- What skills and qualities does a person need to qualify for a job as a smokejumper? (*strength, endurance, bravery, knowledge*)

- What are some uses a smokejumper might find for a pulaski? (*chopping down trees and shrubs, clearing away brush, digging trenches*)

■ **Critical Thinking** Encourage students to think critically and creatively about the selection. What challenges might a new smokejumper encounter? (*using the parachute correctly, avoiding the fire, breathing in a smoky atmosphere, preventing the fire, not getting lost*)

More Reading

Use additional Leveled Readers or other texts at students' instructional levels to reinforce this week's skills and strategies. For text suggestions, see the Leveled Reader Database or the Leveled Readers Skills Chart on pp. CL 24–CL 29.

Objectives
- Use a dictionary or glossary to determine meanings of unknown words.

A · Advanced

Genre Focus

■ **Before Reading or Revisiting** "Camp with Care" on pp. 196–197, read the genre information on persuasive text. Then have students use the text features to set a purpose for reading.

■ **During Reading or Revisiting** Have students read the selection independently. Ask them to share their reactions to "Camp with Care," and jot down a list on the board. The author gives several reasons to avoid littering around a campsite. What are three of them? (*It can be dangerous to animals, it can pollute water, and it is unsightly.*)

■ **After Reading or Revisiting** Have students discuss Reading Across Texts. Then have them do Writing Across Texts independently.

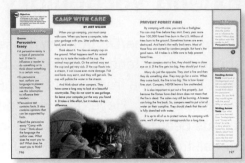

"Camp with Care"

Objectives
• Explain how an author uses language to present information to influence what the reader thinks or does.

A · Advanced

■ **Reread for Fluency** Have students silently reread passages from *Thor Heyerdahl's Incredible Raft.* Then have them reread aloud with a partner or individually. As students read, monitor fluency and provide corrective feedback. If students read fluently on the first reading, they do not need to reread three to four times. Assess the fluency of students in this group using p. 199j.

■ **Retell** Have students summarize the main idea and key details from *Thor Heyerdahl's Incredible Raft.*

■ **Now Try This** Have students complete their projects. You may wish to review their plans to see if they need additional ideas. Have them share their plans and Captain's Logs with classmates.

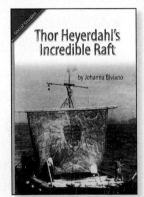

Thor Heyerdahl's Incredible Raft

Objectives
• Read aloud grade-level stories with fluency.

The ELL lessons are organized by strands. Use them to scaffold the weekly curriculum of lessons or during small group time instruction.

Academic Language

Students will hear or read the following academic language in this week's core instruction. As students encounter the vocabulary, provide a simple definition or concrete example. Then ask students to suggest an example or synonym of the word and identify available cognates.

Skill Words	adjective *(adjetivo)* definition *(definición)* description *(descripción)*	syllable author's purpose word choice
Concept Words	emergency *(emergencia)* rescuer	pilot flood

* Spanish cognates in parentheses

Concept Development

How can we prepare for emergencies?

■ Preteach Concept

- **Prior Knowledge** Have students turn to pp. 172–173 in the Student Edition. Call attention to the picture of the fire escapes and tap into students' prior knowledge of fire escapes. Why do buildings have fire escapes? How can fire escapes help us in an emergency?

- **Discuss Concept** Elicit students' prior knowledge and experience of preparing for emergencies. How does a parachute help people? What are some others things people use in emergencies? How can people prepare for emergencies? Supply background information as needed.

- **Poster Talk-Through** Read the Poster Talk-Through on ELL Poster 21 aloud and work through the Day 1 activities.

■ Daily Concept and Vocabulary Development Use the daily activities on ELL Poster 21 to build concept and vocabulary knowledge.

Objectives
- Use prior knowledge and experiences to understand meanings in English.

Content Objectives
- Use concept vocabulary related to preparing for emergencies.

Language Objectives
- Use prior knowledge and experiences to understand meanings.

Daily Planner

DAY 1	• **Frontload Concept** • **Preteach** Comprehension Skill, Vocabulary, Phonics/Spelling, Conventions • **Writing**
DAY 2	• **Review Concept,** Vocabulary, Comprehension Skill • **Frontload Main Selection** • **Practice** Phonics/Spelling, Conventions/Writing
DAY 3	• **Review Concept,** Comprehension Skill, Vocabulary, Conventions/Writing • **Reread Main Selection** • **Practice** Phonics/Spelling
DAY 4	• **Review Concept** • **Read ELL/ELD Readers** • **Practice** Phonics/Spelling Conventions/Writing
DAY 5	• **Review Concept,** Vocabulary, Comprehension Skill, Phonics/Spelling, Conventions • **Reread ELL/ELD Readers** • **Writing**

See the ELL Handbook for ELL Workshops with targeted instruction.

Concept Talk Video

Use the Concept Talk Video Routine (*ELL Handbook,* p. 477) to build background knowledge about emergencies. For more listening practice, see *Use Classroom Resources* (*ELL Handbook,* pp. 406–407).

ELL English Language Learners

Basic Vocabulary

■ **High-Frequency Words** Use the vocabulary routines and the high-frequency word list on p. 453 of the *ELL Handbook* to systematically teach newcomers the first 300 sight words in English. Students who began learning ten words per week at the beginning of the year are now learning words 201–210. The *ELL Handbook* (p. 446) contains a bank of strategies that you can use to ensure students' mastery of high-frequency words.

Lesson Vocabulary

■ **Preteach** Introduce the Lesson Vocabulary using this routine:

1. Distribute copies of this week's Word Cards (*ELL Handbook,* p. 149).

2. Display ELL Poster 21 and reread the Poster Talk-Through.

3. Using the poster illustrations, model how a word's meaning can be expressed with other similar words: The *parachute,* or sheet used to slow one's fall, opened right away and the smokejumper floated down.

4. Use these sentences to reveal the meaning of the other words.

- Smokejumpers can *steer* a parachute so they will land in a safe spot. (direct)

- A helmet is *essential* to protect a smokejumper's head when landing. (needed)

- When she cut the bush down, she saw a rabbit run out of the *underbrush*. (bushes)

- A strong *wind* can fan a small fire and make it quickly grow into a big one. (air blowing)

- Firefighters must *concentrate* or they may be hurt. (thinking, focus)

- He was on time every day because he had great *dedication* to his job. (caring, devotion)

- Their *method* was different from our way. (way, system)

Language Objectives
- Understand and use basic vocabulary.
- Learn meanings of grade-level vocabulary.

Cognates
For Spanish speakers, point out that the word for *concentration* is spelled *concentración* in Spanish. Reinforce the concept that these languages share many words that are the same or similar.

English Opportunity
Help students expand and internalize the high-frequency words. Read each word aloud. Then use each word to identify or describe people, places or objects, such as *The water is cold*. Then have students repeat the high-frequency word, using it in a sentence if possible.

ELL Workshop
Provide an opportunity for students to practice new basic and academic vocabulary by working with *Learn New Words* (*ELL Handbook,* pp. 402–403).

Objectives
- Expand and internalize initial English vocabulary by learning and using high-frequency English words necessary for identifying and describing people, places, and objects, by retelling simple stories and basic information represented or supported by pictures, and by learning and using routine language needed for classroom communication.

 ELL English Language Learners

Language Objectives

- Produce drawings, phrases, or short sentences to show understanding of Lesson Vocabulary.

ELL Teacher Tip

According to ELL experts Collier and Ovando, "Writing, whether in a home language or especially in a new language, is the most difficult mode of language use to master." By understanding the support English learners require, teachers can tailor instruction to fit individual needs.

English Opportunity

Write the following newly acquired vocabulary words on the board: *method, concentrating, essential*. Read the words aloud to students. Help students recognize elements of the English sound system by pointing to and underlining the *e* in each word. Have students practice pronouncing the sounds of the newly acquired vocabulary by saying each word aloud. Guide them to identify the short *e* sound in each word.

■ **Reteach** Distribute Word Cards and write sentences on the board. Read each sentence aloud and ask which vocabulary word belongs in the blank. Have students write the correct word in the blank.

- You need to have a _____ when you jump from a flying plane. **(parachute)**

- You turn the handlebars to _____ a bike. **(steer)**

- A _____ is a way to do something. **(method)**

- Air blowing outside is called _____. **(wind)**

- If you are thinking hard you are _____. **(concentrating)**

- To do a job well, you have to care about it or have _____. **(dedication)**

- A group of bushes is called _____. **(underbrush)**

- Something is _____ if you need it. **(essential)**

■ **Writing** Place students in small groups with others of different English language proficiency. Give two Word Cards to each group and tell them to write a fill-in-the-blank sentence for each word. Circulate and assist groups with sentence frames if needed. Have each group read their sentences. Tell the other groups to confer with their group's members and then write down their answer for each blank.

Leveled LS Support

Beginning Have students write the answer words for their group.

Intermediate Give students the job of reading their group's sentences.

Advanced/Advanced High Tell students to brainstorm with their group to create a fill-in-the-blank sentence for each word. Have them write the sentences or offer support to other writers.

Objectives
- Recognize elements of the English sound system in newly acquired vocabulary such as long and short vowels, silent letters, and consonant clusters.
- Expand and internalize initial English vocabulary by learning and using high-frequency English words necessary for identifying and describing people, places, and objects, by retelling simple stories and basic information represented or supported by pictures, and by learning and using routine language needed for classroom communication.

Content Objectives

- Monitor and adjust oral comprehension.

Language Objectives

- Discuss oral passages.
- Use linguistic support to enhance and confirm understanding.

Graphic Organizer

What Job to Do	Reason for Job

ELL Teacher Tip

Remind students that although this story has factual information about preparing for a hurricane, it is a fictional story. In real life, a boy should not go to the beach by himself and talk to strangers. In addition, the TV announcer would have to have permission from the boy's parents for him to be interviewed on TV.

ELL English Language Learners

Listening Comprehension

My Job

"Hurricane Calvin is coming," the man on TV said. "I'll check the power supply," said Mom. "I'll check the power supply," said Mom. "I'll go to the store and get food and water," said Dad. "I'll close the shutters," my brother Mike said. "Jason, you pick up coconuts," Dad told me. We had a bunch of palm trees and coconuts around our house. We never picked them up before. Why now I wondered?

I went outside to pick up coconuts. A TV reporter asked me what I was doing. "Picking up coconuts," I answered. "Coconuts!" the TV reporter said. "I forgot all about them." The TV reporter asked me to say, "My name is Jason. I am picking up coconuts because Calvin is coming." The TV reporter thanked me.

I picked up all the coconuts I could find. My family and I saw the reporter on TV. "Hurricane winds make flying coconuts dangerous," the TV reporter said. And there I was on TV. "My name is Jason. I am picking up coconuts because Calvin is coming." Well, I thought. We had food. The shutters were closed. And the coconuts were picked up. We were ready for Hurricane Calvin.

Prepare for the Read Aloud The modified Read Aloud above prepares students for listening to the oral reading "Coconuts" on p. 173b.

■ **First Listening: Listen to Understand** Write the title of the Read Aloud on the board. This is a fictional story about a family getting ready for a hurricane. Listen to find out how they prepare. What job does each person have to do? Give students linguistic support to enhance and confirm their understanding. Afterward, ask the question again and have students share their answers.

■ **Second Listening: Listen to Check Understanding** Draw a T-Chart on the board with the headings "What Job to Do" and "Reason for Job." Listen again to discover the jobs needed to prepare for the hurricane. Afterward, discuss the reasons and fill in the chart.

Objectives

- Use visual, contextual, and linguistic support to enhance and confirm understanding of increasingly complex and elaborated spoken language.

 English Language Learners

Phonics and Spelling

■ **Multisyllabic Words** Copy and distribute *ELL Handbook* p. 274.

• **Preteach** Write the word *dic/tion/ar/y* on the board, dividing it between syllables. Read the word blended together. Read it again pausing between syllables and holding up fingers for counting as you say each syllable. This word has four syllables. Listening for the syllables in words will help you spell and pronounce words.

• **Teach** Write the words *underbrush, essential, parachute, concentrate,* and *dedication* on the board. How many syllables are in the word *underbrush*? Have a student come to the board and divide the word into syllables. Repeat this routine for the other vocabulary words. Not all long words have many syllables. The word *straight* has eight letters and only one syllable. Some short words have many syllables. The word *Ohio* has only four letters, but it has three syllables.

Leveled LS Support

Beginning/Intermediate Tell students to find two words with four syllables in the Student Edition. Have them write the words on the board and divide them into syllables.

Advanced/Advanced High Pass out dictionaries and challenge students to find one of the following words: *disobedient, unbreakable, disagreeable, questionable.* Have them count the syllables and use the word in a sentence.

MINI-LESSON

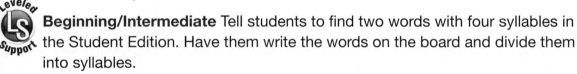

Homographs

Have students turn to p. 176 in the Student Edition. Read the page aloud to students. Then point out the word *wind* at the bottom of the page. To help students comprehend English language structures, tell them that *wind* is a homograph. When it is pronounced /w/ /i/ /n/ /d/ it means "blowing air." When it is pronounced /w/ /ī/ /n/ /d/ and it means "to wrap something around a center object." Have students explain the differences between these two meanings. Then to demonstrate their understanding, have them use each word in a sentence.

Content Objectives

• Identify syllables of multisyllabic words.

• Divide multisyllabic words between syllables.

Language Objectives

• Apply phonics and decoding skills to vocabulary.

• Explain details of the meanings of homographs.

ELL Teaching Routine

For more practice with multisyllabic words, use the Multisyllabic Word Strategy Routine *(ELL Handbook,* p. 473).

 Transfer Skills

Directionality The directionality of some languages is different from English. For example, Arabic and Hebrew read from right to left, and some Asian languages read from top to bottom. Students who speak these languages need more exposure to print concepts through oral reading activities of books and classroom materials.

Objectives
• Narrate, describe, and explain with increasing specificity and detail as more English is acquired.

Support for English Language Learners

Content Objectives
- Identify formal and informal language.
- Identify the author's purpose in grade-level text.

Language Objectives
- Discuss author's purpose and genre.
- Discuss usage of formal and informal language.

ELL Workshop
Encourage students to ask questions to monitor their understanding of instruction of comprehension skills. Use *Ask Clarifying Questions* (*ELL Handbook,* pp. 404–405) for practice.

ELL English Language Learners

Comprehension
Author's Purpose

- **Preteach** Authors have many reasons or purposes for writing. They inform, entertain, persuade, and express. Sometimes an author will have more than one purpose for writing. Have students turn to *Envision It!* on p. EI•2 in the Student Edition. Read aloud the text together. To have students use visual support to confirm understanding, have them use the pictures to identify each purpose.

- **Reteach** Distribute copies of the Picture It! (*ELL Handbook,* p. 150). Have students look at the image. Have the students read the passage aloud with a partner. Have the partners share what they learned about making a 9-1-1 call. Why do you think the author wrote this passage? (1. You should know where you live and your phone number. Call from a safe place. Do not hang up until the operator tells you to. 2. People should be able to provide any important information about the emergency.)

  Beginning/Intermediate Choral read the passage with the students. Discuss what the passage taught them to do. Have the students complete the sentence frame: *The author informed me _____.*

  Advanced/Advanced High Have students reread the passage. Have students work with a partner to discuss the author's purpose in writing this passage.

MINI-LESSON

Formal and Informal Language

Discuss with the class the differences between formal and informal language. Write on the board: *Hurricane winds can make flying coconuts very dangerous. Wow! Flying coconuts are really dangerous!* Have students orally identify the formal and informal sentences. Ask them to give reasons for their choices. Have students adapt the informal sentences into formal language for a formal audience. Have them identify some familiar situations in which they would use formal and informal language. For additional practice, write a list of informal expressions on the board, such as *Hi, ya!, Dude,* and *Awesome,* and have students work in pairs to provide and present the more formal equivalents for each.

Objectives
- Use visual, contextual, and linguistic support to enhance and confirm understanding of increasingly complex and elaborated spoken language.
- Adapt spoken language appropriately for formal and informal purposes.

 English Language Learners

Reading Comprehension
Smokejumpers

Student Edition pp. 178–179

■ **Frontloading** Read the title aloud and discuss what a smokejumper does, and the special equipment and training essential to prepare for the emergencies inherent in this dangerous occupation. I wonder how the smokejumpers get out of the woods after they finish fighting a fire. Let's look through the selection to find out. To have students use visual and contextual support to develop a grasp of language structure, guide them on a picture walk through *Smokejumpers.* Have students read aloud captions, subheads, and sidebar boxes. Ask students to predict what a smokejumper's job involves and record their predictions. Provide students with a Web chart to fill out as they read the selection.

Sheltered Reading Ask questions such as the following to guide students' comprehension of details:

• p. 180: Why is being a smokejumper a dangerous job? (they drop into the middle of fires)

• p. 182: How many hours may a smokejumper work? (eighteen hours with breaks for food)

• pp. 185–186: Where do smokejumpers carry their emergency or reserve parachute? (against their stomach)

• p. 189: What is the tool of choice for smokejumpers? (a Pulaski, a combination of an ax and a hoe)

• p. 191: How do smokejumpers get out of the woods when they are done fighting the fire? (they often radio for a helicopter to pick them up)

■ **Fluency: Improve Rate and Accuracy of Reading** Encourage students to reread several times to increase speed and reduce mispronunciations. Read the first paragraph on p. 183 twice. Model rate and accuracy improvement with the second reading. Have students demonstrate listening comprehension of increasing complex English by collaborating with peers to offer feedback on the rate and accuracy of their partner's oral reading.

After Reading Have students turn to p. 192 in the Student Edition. Read the page to them. Have students think critically about by answering the question at the bottom of the page. Encourage them use content-based vocabulary to express their opinions.

Content Objectives

• Monitor and adjust comprehension.

• Make and adjust predictions.

Language Objectives

• Improve rate and accuracy with grade-level text.

• Reinforce comprehension with visual and contextual support.

Graphic Organizer

Smokejumpers

Audio Support

Students can prepare for reading *Smokejumpers* by using the eSelection or the AudioText CD (*ELL Handbook,* p. 477).

Objectives

• Express opinions, ideas, and feelings ranging from communicating single words and short phrases to participating in extended discussions on a variety of social and grade-appropriate academic topics.

Support for English Language Learners

ELD Reader   ELL Reader

For additional leveled instruction, see the **ELL/ELD Reader Teaching Guide.**

Comprehension
When a Storm Comes

■ **Before Reading** Distribute copies of the ELL and ELD Readers, *When a Storm Comes,* to students at their reading level.

• **Preview** Read the title aloud with students: This is a nonfiction text about how people prepare for storms. Invite students to look through the pictures and name what they see. Have them predict how people prepare for storms based on the picture clues and their prior knowledge.

• **Set a Purpose for Reading** Let's read to find out how to get ready for a storm.

■ **During Reading** Follow the Reading Routine for both reading groups.

1. Read the entire Reader aloud slowly.

2. Reread pp. 1–5, pausing to build background or model comprehension. Use the questions in the chart to check students' comprehension.

3. Have students reread pp. 1–5 in pairs, taking turns reading alternate pages.

4. Repeat steps 2–3 above for pp. 6–8.

■ **After Reading** Use the exercises on the inside back cover of each Reader and invite students to share their writing. In a whole-group discussion, ask students What things can people do to get ready for storms? Record their answers on the board and invite them to point to pictures in the book to support their answers.

ELD Reader   Beginning/Intermediate

■ **p. 4** Where do students go when a hurricane is coming? (a place with no windows) Read aloud the sentence that gives you the answer.

■ **p. 7** Is a basement a safe place to be in a storm? Why or why not? Read aloud the sentence that gives you the answer.

Writing What do you do when a storm comes? Draw a picture of you and your family getting ready for a storm. Write a sentence about your picture.

ELL Reader   Advanced/Advanced High

■ **p. 4** What happens when the water in the ocean is too warm? (There might be a hurricane.)

■ **p. 6** What has faster winds, a tornado or a hurricane? (tornado)

Study Guide Distribute copies of the ELL Reader Study Guide *(ELL Handbook,* p. 154). Scaffold comprehension of determining the author's purpose by helping students look back through the Reader in order to complete the activity. Review their responses together. (See *ELL Handbook,* pp. 209–212.)

Objectives
• Use strategic learning techniques such as concept mapping, drawing, memorizing, comparing, contrasting, and reviewing to acquire basic and grade-level vocabulary.

 ELL **English Language Learners**

Conventions
Adjectives and Articles

■ **Teach/Model** Write these sentences on the board: *The family was ready for a storm. They had an emergency kit.* Read the sentences. Underline the articles as you refer to them. The words *a, an,* and *the* are called articles. They come before a noun. *A* is used before singular nouns (just one thing) that begin with a consonant sound. *An* is used before singular nouns that begin with a vowel sound. Write: *A hurricane is a bigger storm. A tornado has faster winds.* Underline the adjectives. *Bigger* and *faster* are words that tell more about the nouns *storm* and *winds.* They are called adjectives. They come before the noun. Adjectives tell what kind, how many, or what size.

■ **Practice** Write: *He has a blue shirt. I have two books. She has long hair.* Have students come to the board and underline the adjectives and articles. Then ask students to suggest other adjectives.

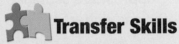 **Leveled LS Support**

Beginning Tell students to point to objects and give an adjective. Use their responses to write sentences on the board and have them underline the articles and adjectives.

Intermediate Have these students choose a sentence frame to complete with an adjective. *I have _____ sisters. I have _____ shoes. I have a _____ brother.* Remind them to point out the articles.

Advanced/Advanced High Tell students to create sentences with adjectives.

■ **Reteach** Draw the chart and direct attention to *Smokejumpers.*

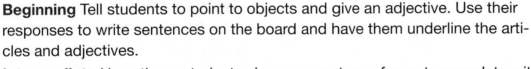

Article	Adjective	Noun

Read the first sentence and write *a, dangerous,* and *business* in the proper columns. Have students find adjectives to add to the chart.

Beginning Guide students to identify articles, adjectives, and nouns.

Intermediate Encourage students to find and read sentences with adjectives.

Advanced/Advanced High Have students read the first sentence on p. 183. Explain that *every* and *drier* are adjectives telling about the noun *summer.* Sometimes, an adjective is linked to a noun by a linking verb. Challenge students to find more examples.

Content Objectives
• Identify adjectives and articles.
• Correctly use adjectives and articles.

Language Objectives
• Write sentences with adjectives and articles.

Transfer Skills

Articles Spanish speakers may use the word *one* in place of the article *a* (or *an*) just as *un/una* is used in Spanish. English learners may use (or omit) the article *the* differently from native English speakers—*I like the science; My cousin is nurse.*

Adjectives Spanish adjectives have endings that match the gender and number of nouns they modify. Assure students that English adjectives do not have these endings.

Grammar Jammer

For more practice with adjectives, use the Grammar Jammer for this target skill. See the Grammar Jammer Routine (*ELL Handbook,* p. 478) for suggestions on using this learning tool.

Support for English Language Learners

ELL English Language Learners

Writing Complete Sentences

Content Objectives

- Identify complete sentences in a text.
- Identify that formal English is written and spoken in complete sentences.

Language Objectives

- Write complete sentences using appropriate sentence lengths and patterns.
- Share feedback for editing and revising.

English Opportunity

Write these sentences on the board: *Smokejumpers fight fires. Use water.* Have students distinguish which sentence is an example of formal language and which is informal. Have students tell why the one sentence is informal. (not a complete sentence) Then have students turn the informal sentence into formal language and tell when it is appropriate to use formal language like their example.

In small groups have students create a short talk using informal expressions and language and present it. Work with partners to adapt the speech.

■ **Introduce** Display the paragraph and read it aloud. Every complete sentence has two parts. One part tells who or what the sentence is about. It is called the subject. Look at the first sentence. It's about smokejumpers. The second part tells what the subject does or is. It is called the predicate. *Have dangerous jobs* is the predicate. Read each sentence and circle the subject and underline the predicate.

Writing Model

Smokejumpers have dangerous jobs. They work close to wildfires. These men and women have special equipment and training.

■ **Practice** Write this paragraph on the board and read it aloud. Some of these sentences may sound strange. They are missing parts and are not complete sentences. Work with students to identify and supply the missing parts to the sentences. (*Sample responses:* parachute, they, pick) Explain to students that good writing uses a variety of sentence lengths and patterns. When having students supply missing parts of sentences, help guide them to supply missing parts that would create sentences of varying length and pattern.

Smokejumpers into places close to fires. Fight wildfires. Helicopters them up.

■ **Write** Instruct students to write a paragraph about fighting a fire. Remind them to create complete sentences with subjects and predicates using appropriate sentence length and patterns. Have students use new content-area vocabulary from *Smokejumpers* in their writing. When they have finished, ask them to read at least three sentences containing these words.

Beginning Have students draw a picture of people fighting a fire. Ask them questions about their picture. Work together to create complete sentences. Write their sentences down and have them copy the sentences.

Intermediate Supply students with the beginning sentence: *The wind blew hard and the fire suddenly got bigger.* Have partners work together to write what happens next. Remind students to use complete sentences. Allow time for students to share their stories with the class.

Advanced/Advanced High Have students create stories independently. Then pair students to exchange stories and provide feedback for revising and editing. Ask students to read their stories to the class.

Objectives

- Demonstrate an increasing ability to distinguish between formal and informal English and an increasing knowledge of when to use each one commensurate with grade-level learning expectations.
- Write using a variety of grade-appropriate sentence lengths, patterns, and connecting words to combine phrases, clauses, and sentences in increasingly accurate ways as more English is acquired.

Align Instruction to Common Core Anchor Standards

- Introduce and explore this unit's weekly concepts through rich, structured conversations
- Develop complex content knowledge and vocabulary
- Expand on a single concept with engaging literature and nonfiction
- Build better readers in all content areas

What makes an adventure?

WEEK 1
QUESTION OF THE WEEK

How can we prepare for emergencies?

Concept Talk Guide students as they discuss questions such as:

- What objects do people keep handy to prepare for emergencies?
- Who can we call to help during an emergency?

Writing Write a fantasy story about fighting a fire.

YOU ARE HERE: WEEK 2
QUESTION OF THE WEEK   What surprises can happen on an expedition?

As students answer this unit's Big Question and this week's Question of the Week, they will address:

CCSS Reading 3. Analyze how and why individuals, events, and ideas develop and interact over the course of a text. **(Also CCSS Reading 6.)**

Concept Talk Guide students as they discuss questions such as:
- What kinds of expeditions can you think of?
- What movies or TV shows have you seen, or stories have you read, about an expedition?

As students answer this week's Concept Talk questions, they will address:

CCSS Language 3. Apply knowledge of language to understand how language functions in different contexts, to make effective choices for meaning or style, and to comprehend more fully when reading or listening. **(Also CCSS Speaking/Listening 1.)**

Writing Write a legend about Hiram Bingham and the discovery of Machu Picchu.

As students write about this week's prompt, they will address:

CCSS Writing 3. Write narratives to develop real or imagined experiences or events using effective technique, descriptive details, and clear event sequences. **(Also CCSS Writing 5.)**

Listening and Speaking On page 227, students learn that when they give a talk, they should speak clearly and provide details about the topic. They should also use adverbs correctly. By doing so, they address:

CCSS Speaking/Listening 4. Present information, findings, and supporting evidence such that listeners can follow the line of reasoning and the organization, development, and style are appropriate to task, purpose, and audience. **(Also CCSS Speaking/Listening 1.)**

WEEK 5
QUESTION OF THE WEEK

What are the risks when walking on the moon?

Concept Talk Guide students as they discuss questions such as:

- What would you expect to find on the moon?
- How would you prepare for walking on the moon?

Writing Write about a time you took a risk that paid off.

WEEK 4
QUESTION OF THE WEEK

What does a person sacrifice to explore the unknown?

Concept Talk Guide students as they discuss questions such as:

- What kind of shelter would you have?
- What kinds of things might you eat?

Writing Write an advertisement encouraging readers to take a trip to Antarctica.

WEEK 3
QUESTION OF THE WEEK

What does it take to be a hero?

Concept Talk Guide students as they discuss questions such as:

- What are some examples of heroism?
- Who are some heroes you know of?
- What kinds of qualities do heroes possess?

Writing Imagine that you, not Grits, were the one Axel saved in *Cliff Hanger*. Write a thank-you note to your friend for his help.

ISBN-13: 978-0-328-67819-8   ISBN-10: 0-328-67819-8

Skills Overview

Target Skills and Strategies	© Common Core State Standards for English Language Arts*
Comprehension ◉ **Skill:** Compare and Contrast	**CCSS Informational Text 6.** Compare and contrast a firsthand and secondhand account of the same event or topic; describe the differences in focus and the information provided.
Comprehension ◉ **Strategy:** Visualize	**CCSS Informational Text 1.** Refer to details and examples in a text when explaining what the text says explicitly and when drawing inferences from the text.
Vocabulary ◉ **Skill:** Greek and Latin Roots • **Strategy:** Word Structure	**CCSS Language 4.b.** Use common, grade-appropriate Greek and Latin affixes and roots as clues to the meaning of a word (e.g., *telegraph*, *photograph*, *autograph*).
Fluency • **Skill:** Appropriate Phrasing	**CCSS Foundational Skills 4.** Read with sufficient accuracy and fluency to support comprehension. **CCSS Foundational Skills 4.b.** Read grade-level prose and poetry orally with accuracy, appropriate rate, and expression.
Listening and Speaking • Media Literacy: Radio Announcement	**CCSS Speaking/Listening 4.** Report on a topic or text, tell a story, or recount an experience in an organized manner, using appropriate facts and relevant, descriptive details to support main ideas or themes; speak clearly at an understandable pace.
Six-Trait Writing • **Trait of the Week:** Sentences	**CCSS Language 1.f.** Produce complete sentences, recognizing and correcting inappropriate fragments and run-ons.
Writing • Legend	**CCSS Writing 3.a.** Orient the reader by establishing a situation and introducing a narrator and/or characters; organize an event sequence that unfolds naturally.
Conventions • **Skill:** Adverbs	**CCSS Language 1.** Demonstrate command of the conventions of standard English grammar and usage when writing or speaking.

Use with Conventions, TE p. 203d

Common Core State Standard: CCSS Language 1.

Write this sentence from *Lost City* on the board: "He placed his hands on the sun-warmed stones so beautifully carved, as if they had grown together." Underline the words *so, beautifully*, and *together*. Tell students that all three underlined adverbs tell how.

• Point out that the adverb *so* tells about another adverb, but the adverbs *beautifully* and *together* tell about verbs.

• Have students write two sentences with adverbs from the selection.

• Ask students to underline each adverb; identify whether it tells about a verb, an adjective, or another adverb; and tell whether the adverb tells how, to what extent, how often, where, or when.

Michigan
COMMON CORE EDITION

LOST CITY
The Discovery of Machu Picchu
BY TED LEWIN

This Week's Common Core/Michigan Skills Overview

This Week's Target Skills and Strategies

Target Skills and Strategies	Common Core State Standards for English Language Arts*	Michigan English Language Arts Grade Level Content Expectations
Comprehension Skill: Compare and Contrast	**CCSS Informational Text 6.** Compare and contrast a firsthand and secondhand account of the same event or topic; describe the differences in focus and the information provided.	MI R.MT.04.02 Plan, monitor, regulate, and evaluate skills, strategies, and processes to construct and convey meaning (e.g., decoding unknown words) and use graphic organizers to deepen their understanding of compare/contrast, and sequential organizational patterns.
Strategy: Visualize	**CCSS Informational Text 1.** Refer to details and examples in a text when explaining what the text says explicitly and when drawing inferences from the text.	MI R.MT.04.01 Self-monitor comprehension when reading or listening to text by automatically applying and discussing the strategies used by mature readers to increase comprehension including: predicting, constructing mental images, visually representing ideas in text, questioning, rereading or listening again if uncertain about meaning, inferring, summarizing, and engaging in interpretive discussions.
Vocabulary Skill: Greek and Latin Roots Strategy: Word Structure	**CCSS Language 4.b.** Use common, grade-appropriate Greek and Latin affixes and roots as clues to the meaning of a word (e.g., *telegraph, photograph, autograph*).	MI R.WS.04.02 Use structural, syntactic, and semantic cues including lettersound, rimes, base words, affixes, and syllabication to automatically read frequently encountered words, decode unknown words, and decide meanings including multiple meaning words.
Fluency Skill: Appropriate Phrasing	**CCSS Foundational Skills 4.** Read with sufficient accuracy and fluency to support comprehension. **(Also CCSS Foundational Skills 4.b.)**	MI R.WS.04.06 Fluently read beginning grade-level text and increasingly demanding text as the year proceeds.
Listening and Speaking Radio Advertisement	**CCSS Speaking/Listening 4.** Report on a topic or text, tell a story, or recount an experience in an organized manner, using appropriate facts and relevant, descriptive details to support main ideas or themes; speak clearly at an understandable pace.	MI S.CN.04.02 Adjust their use of language to communicate effectively with a variety of audiences and for different purposes including community-building, appreciation, invitations, and cross-curricular discussions.
Six-Trait Writing Trait of the Week: Sentences	**CCSS Language 1.f.** Produce complete sentences, recognizing and correcting inappropriate fragments and run-ons.	MI W.GR.04.01 In the context of writing, correctly use simple and compound sentences; direct and indirect objects; prepositional phrases; adjectives; common and proper nouns as subjects and objects; pronouns as antecedents; regular and irregular verbs; hyphens between syllables; apostrophes in contractions; and commas in salutations to set off words; phrases and dialogue; quotation marks or italics to identify titles or names.
Writing Legend	**CCSS Writing 3.a.** Orient the reader by establishing a situation and introducing a narrator and/or characters; organize an event sequence that unfolds naturally.	MI W.PR.04.01 Set a purpose, consider audience, and replicate authors' styles and patterns when writing a narrative or informational piece. **(Also** MI W.PR.04.02, MI W.PR.04.03, MI W.PR.04.04, MI W.PR.04.05)
Conventions Skill: Adverbs	**CCSS Language 1.** Demonstrate command of the conventions of standard English grammar and usage when writing or speaking.	MI W.GR.04.01 In the context of writing, correctly use simple and compound sentences; direct and indirect objects; prepositional phrases; adjectives; common and proper nouns as subjects and objects; pronouns as antecedents; regular and irregular verbs; hyphens between syllables; apostrophes in contractions; and commas in salutations to set off words; phrases and dialogue; quotation marks or italics to identify titles or names.

Grade 4 Skills Trace

Skills and Strategies   Looking Back   This Week's Selection   Looking Ahead

This Week on Reading Street!

Adventures

Question of the Week
What surprises can happen on an expedition?

Daily Plan

Don't Wait Until Friday

Whole Group
- ◉ Compare and Contrast
- ◉ Greek and Latin Roots
- • Fluency/Appropriate Phrasing
- • Research and Inquiry

MONITOR PROGRESS | Success Predictor

Day 1	Days 2–3	Day 4	Day 5
Check Oral Vocabulary	Check Retelling	Check Fluency	Check Oral Vocabulary

Small Group

Teacher Led

- • Reading Support
- • Skill Support
- • Fluency Practice

Practice Stations

Independent Activities

Customize Literacy More support for a balanced literacy approach, see pp. CL•1–CL•47

Customize Writing More support for a customized writing approach, see pp. CW•1–CW•10

Whole Group
- • Writing: Legend
- • Conventions: Adverbs
- • Spelling: Words with Double Consonants

Assessment
- • Weekly Tests
- • Day 5 Assessment
- • Fresh Reads

You Are Here!
Unit 5 Week 2

This Week's Reading Selections

Main Selection
Genre: **Biography**

Paired Selection
Genre: **Personal Essay**

Leveled Readers

ELL and ELD Readers

	Build Concepts			Comprehension			
Whole Group	 Let's Talk About pp. 200–201			 Envision It! Skills/ Strategies	 Comprehension Skills Lesson pp. 202–203		
Go Digital	• Concept Talk Video			• Envision It! Animations • eSelections			
Small Group and Independent Practice	 Lost City pp. 206–207	ELL and ELD Readers	Leveled Readers	 Lost City pp. 206–207	ELL and ELD Readers	Leveled Readers	 Envision It! Skills/ Strategies
				Reader's and Writer's Notebook	Practice Station Flip Chart		
Go Digital	• eReaders • eSelections			• Envision It! Animations • eSelections • eReaders			
Customize Literacy	• Leveled Readers			• Envision It! Skills and Strategies Handbook • Leveled Readers			
Go Digital	• Concept Talk Video • Big Question Video • eReaders			• Envision It! Animations • eReaders			

Question of the Week
What surprises can happen on an expedition?

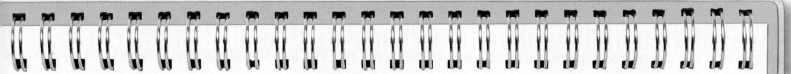

Vocabulary

Envision It!
Vocabulary
Cards

Vocabulary Skill Lesson
pp. 204–205

- Envision It! Vocabulary Cards
- Vocabulary Activities

Envision It!
Vocabulary
Cards

Lost City
pp. 206–207

Practice
Station
Flip Chart

Words! W•9

Reader's
and Writer's
Notebook

- Envision It! Vocabulary Cards
- Vocabulary Activities
- eSelections

- Envision It! Vocabulary Cards

- Vocabulary Activities

Fluency

Let's Learn It!
pp. 226–227

- eSelections
- eReaders

Lost City
pp. 206–207

Practice
Station
Flip Chart

Leveled
Readers

ELL and ELD
Readers

- eSelections
- eReaders

- Leveled Readers

- eReaders

Conventions and Writing

Let's Write It! pp. 220–221

- Grammar Jammer

Reader's
and Writer's
Notebook

Lost City
pp. 206–207

Practice
Station
Flip Chart

- Grammar Jammer

- Reader's and Writer's Notebook

- Grammar Jammer

You Are Here!
Unit 5
Week 2

My 5-Day Planner for Reading Street!

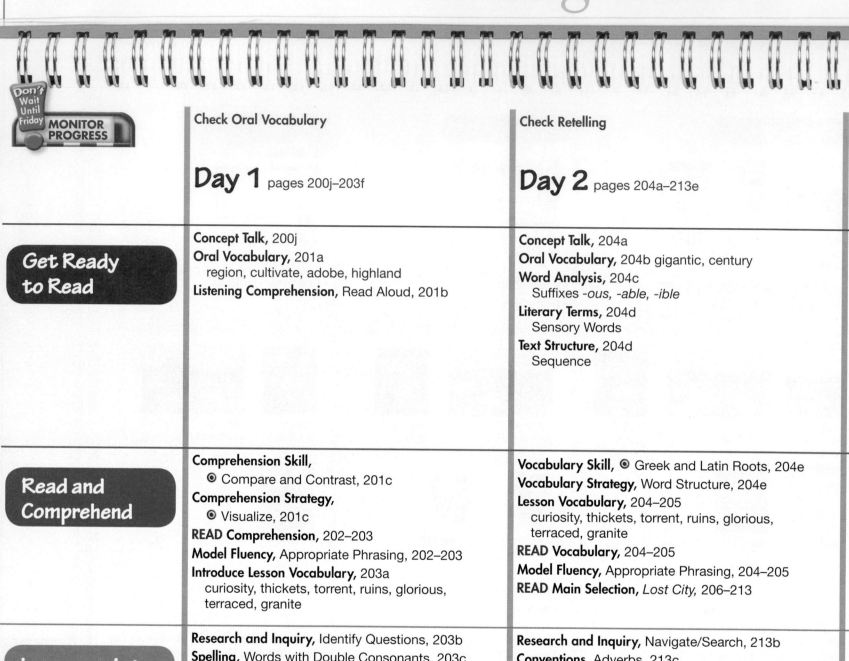

MONITOR PROGRESS — Don't Wait Until Friday

	Check Oral Vocabulary **Day 1** pages 200j–203f	Check Retelling **Day 2** pages 204a–213e
Get Ready to Read	**Concept Talk,** 200j **Oral Vocabulary,** 201a 　region, cultivate, adobe, highland **Listening Comprehension,** Read Aloud, 201b	**Concept Talk,** 204a **Oral Vocabulary,** 204b gigantic, century **Word Analysis,** 204c 　Suffixes *-ous, -able, -ible* **Literary Terms,** 204d 　Sensory Words **Text Structure,** 204d 　Sequence
Read and Comprehend	**Comprehension Skill,** 　◉ Compare and Contrast, 201c **Comprehension Strategy,** 　◉ Visualize, 201c **READ Comprehension,** 202–203 **Model Fluency,** Appropriate Phrasing, 202–203 **Introduce Lesson Vocabulary,** 203a 　curiosity, thickets, torrent, ruins, glorious, 　terraced, granite	**Vocabulary Skill,** ◉ Greek and Latin Roots, 204e **Vocabulary Strategy,** Word Structure, 204e **Lesson Vocabulary,** 204–205 　curiosity, thickets, torrent, ruins, glorious, 　terraced, granite **READ Vocabulary,** 204–205 **Model Fluency,** Appropriate Phrasing, 204–205 **READ Main Selection,** *Lost City,* 206–213
Language Arts	**Research and Inquiry,** Identify Questions, 203b **Spelling,** Words with Double Consonants, 203c **Conventions,** Adverbs, 203d **Handwriting,** Cursive Letters *Q* and *q,* 203d **Writing,** Legend, 203e–203f	**Research and Inquiry,** Navigate/Search, 213b **Conventions,** Adverbs, 213c **Spelling,** Words with Double Consonants, 213c **Writing,** Legend, Story Sequence, 213d–213e

You Are Here!
Unit 5
Week 2

What surprises can happen on an expedition?

Check Retelling	Check Fluency	Check Oral Vocabulary
Day 3 pages 214a–221c	**Day 4** pages 222a–227e	**Day 5** pages 227f–227q

Concept Talk, 214a
Oral Vocabulary, 214b
  culture, legend
Comprehension Check, 214c
Check Retelling, 214d
	Concept Talk, 222a
	Oral Vocabulary, 222b
	  research, records
	Genre, Personal Essay, 222c
		Concept Wrap Up, 227f
		Check Oral Vocabulary, 227g
		  region, cultivate, adobe, highland,
		  gigantic, century, culture, legend,
		  research, records
		Amazing Ideas, 227g
		Review ⊚ Compare and Contrast, 227h
		Review ⊚ Greek and Latin Roots, 227h
		Review **Word Analysis,** 227i
		Review **Literary Terms,** 227i

READ Main Selection, *Lost City,*
  214–217
Retelling, 218–219
Think Critically, 219a
Model Fluency, Appropriate Phrasing,
  219b
Research and Study Skills, Outline,
  219c
	READ Paired Selection, "Riding
	  the Rails to Machu Picchu,"
	  222–225
	Let's Learn It! 226–227a
	  Fluency: Appropriate Phrasing
	  Vocabulary: Greek and Latin
	  Roots
	  Media Literacy: Radio
	  Announcement
		Fluency Assessment,
		  WCPM, 227j–227k
		Comprehension Assessment,
		  ⊚ Compare and Contrast,
		  227l–227m

Research and Inquiry, Analyze, 219d
Conventions, Adverbs, 219e
Spelling, Words with Double
  Consonants, 219e
Let's Write It! Legend, 220–221a
Writing, Legend, Sentences,
  221a–221c
	Research and Inquiry, Synthesize,
	  227b
	Conventions, Adverbs, 227c
	Spelling, Words with Double
	  Consonants, 227c
	Writing, Legend, Revising
	  227d–227e
		Research and Inquiry, Communicate,
		  227n
		Conventions, Adverbs, 227o
		Spelling Test, Words with Double
		  Consonants, 227o
		Writing, Legend, Adverbs, 227p
		Quick Write for Fluency, 227q

Grouping Options for Differentiated Instruction
Turn the page for the small group time lesson plan.

Planning Small Group Time on Reading Street!

SMALL GROUP TIME RESOURCES

Look for this Small Group Time box each day to help meet the individual needs of all your students. Differentiated Instruction lessons appear on the DI pages at the end of each week.

DAY 1

Teacher Led

SI Strategic Intervention	**OL** On-Level	**A** Advanced
Teacher Led	**Teacher Led**	**Teacher Led**
• Reinforce the Concept	• Expand the Concept	• Extend the Concept
Read *Concept Literacy Reader* or *Below-Level Reader*	**Read** *On-Level Reader*	**Read** *Advanced Reader*

ELL Place English language learners in the groups that correspond to their reading abilities in English.

Practice Stations
• Read for Meaning
• Get Fluent
• Word Work

Independent Activities
• Concept Talk Video
• *Reader's and Writer's Notebook*
• Research and Inquiry

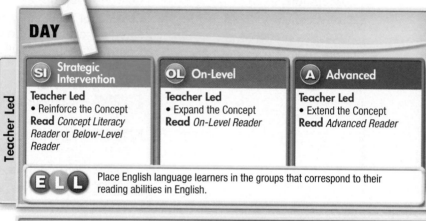

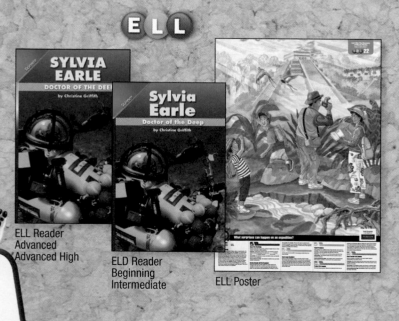

ELL Reader Advanced Advanced High

ELD Reader Beginning Intermediate

ELL Poster

You Are Here!
Unit 5
Week 2

Day 1

SI Strategic Intervention	**Reinforce the Concept,** DI•26–DI•27 **Read Concept Literacy Reader** or **Below-Level Reader**
OL On-Level	**Expand the Concept,** DI•32 **Read On-Level Reader**
A Advanced	**Extend the Concept,** DI•37 **Read Advanced Reader**
ELL English Language Learners	DI•41–DI•50 **Frontload Concept** **Preteach Skills** **Writing**

Reading Street Response
to Intervention Kit

Reading Street
Practice Stations Kit

Question of the Week
What surprises can happen on an expedition?

SI Strategic Intervention

Discovering
Machu Picchu
By Linda Cernak

OL On-Level

A Advanced

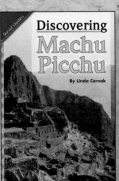

Let's Get to Know
the **Incas**
by Jennifer Coates-Conroy

Below-Level
Reader

Concept Literacy Reader

Pompeii,
The Lost City
by Patricia West

On-Level Reader

Meet
the Maya

Advanced
Reader

LOST CITY
The Discovery of Machu Picchu
BY TED LEWIN

Lost City, pp. 206–207

Riding the Rails
to Machu
Picchu
by Katanka Diaz

Riding the Rails to Machu Picchu
pp. 222–223

Small Group Weekly Plan

Day 2	Day 3	Day 4	Day 5
Reinforce Comprehension, DI•28 **Revisit Main Selection**	**Reinforce Vocabulary,** DI•29 **Read/Revisit Main Selection**	**Reinforce Comprehension,** Practice Retelling, DI•30 Genre Focus **Read/Revisit Paired Selection**	**Practice Fluency,** DI•31 **Reread Concept Literacy Reader** or **Below-Level Reader**
Expand Comprehension, DI•33 **Revisit Main Selection**	**Expand Vocabulary,** DI•34 **Read/Revisit Main Selection**	**Expand Comprehension,** Practice Retelling, DI•35 Genre Focus **Read/Revisit Paired Selection**	**Practice Fluency,** DI•36 **Reread On-Level Reader**
Extend Comprehension, DI•38 **Revisit Main Selection**	**Extend Vocabulary,** DI•39 **Read/Revisit Main Selection**	**Extend Comprehension,** Genre Focus, DI•40 **Read/Revisit Paired Selection**	**Practice Fluency,** DI•40 **Reread Advanced Reader**
DI•41–DI•50 **Review Concept/Skills** **Frontload Main Selection** **Practice**	DI•41–DI•50 **Review Concept/Skills** **Reread Main Selection** **Practice**	DI•41–DI•50 **Review Concept** **Read ELL/ELD Readers** **Practice**	DI•41–DI•50 **Review Concept/Skills** **Reread ELL/ELD Readers** **Writing**

Practice Stations for Everyone on Reading Street!

Word Wise
Multisyllabic words

Objectives
- Spell multisyllabic words.

Materials
- *Word Wise* Flip Chart Activity 22
- Teacher-made word cards
- paper   • pencils

Differentiated Activities

⬤ Choose four word cards. Write the words and the number of syllables in the words. Write sentences using each word.

🔺 Choose six word cards, and write the words. Write the number of syllables in each word. Write sentences using each word.

🟥 Choose eight word cards, and write the words. Next to each word, write the number of syllables in the word. Write sentences using each word.

Technology
- Online Dictionary

Word Work
Multisyllabic words

Objectives
- Identify, pronounce, and write multisyllabic words.

Materials
- *Word Work* Flip Chart Activity 22
- Teacher-made word cards
- paper   • pencils

Differentiated Activities

⬤ Choose six word cards. Write the words, and say each word. Think of other multisyllabic words you know. Add them to your list.

🔺 Choose nine word cards, and write the words. Say each word. Add other multisyllabic words you know to your list.

🟥 Choose twelve word cards and write the words. Say each word. Add other multisyllabic words you know to your list.

Technology
- Modeled Pronunciation Audio CD

Words to Know
Homographs

Objectives
- Identify and understand homographs.

Materials
- *Words to Know* Flip Chart Activity 22
- Teacher-made word cards
- dictionary   • paper   • pencils

Differentiated Activities

⬤ Choose three word cards. Write the words. Use a dictionary to find two meanings for each word. Write two sentences for each word to show its different meanings.

🔺 Choose four word cards, and write the words. Use a dictionary to find two meanings for each word. Write two sentences for each word to show its different meanings.

🟥 Choose six word cards, and write the words. Use a dictionary to find at least two meanings for each word. Write at least two sentences for each word to show its different meanings.

Technology
- Online Dictionary

You Are Here!
Unit 5
Week 2

Key

● Below-Level Activities
▲ On-Level Activities
■ Advanced Activities

Practice Station Flip Chart

Let's Write!
Fantasy

Objectives
• Write a fantasy narrative.

Materials
• *Let's Write!* Flip Chart Activity 22
• paper   • pencils

Differentiated Activities

● Imagine that you met a person from another planet. Write a short fantasy telling about the meeting. Explain why the person was visiting Earth. Proofread your work for complete sentences.

▲ Write a fantasy about meeting a person from another planet. Include details explaining the person's reasons for visiting Earth. Check punctuation, and use complete sentences.

■ Write a fantasy about meeting a person from another planet. Include details explaining what brought the person to Earth. Proofread for capitalization and punctuation.

Technology
• Online Graphic Organizers

Read for Meaning
Author's purpose

Objectives
• Identify an author's purpose for writing.

Materials
• *Read for Meaning* Flip Chart Activity 22
• Student Book   • paper   • pencils

Differentiated Activities

● Read one of the books your teacher provides. Think about the author's purpose for writing the selection. Write a sentence stating the author's purpose. Write a sentence with a detail from the selection to support your opinion.

▲ Read one of the books your teacher provides, and think about the author's purpose. Write one sentence stating the author's purpose. Write two sentences with details from the selection to support your opinion.

■ Read one of the books your teacher provides. As you read, think about the author's purpose for writing. Write a short paragraph stating the author's purpose. Include three details from the selection to support your opinion.

Technology
• Leveled Reader Database

Get Fluent
Practice fluent reading.

Objectives
• Read aloud with appropriate rate and accuracy.

Materials
• *Get Fluent* Flip Chart Activity 22
• Leveled Readers

Differentiated Activities

● Work with a partner. Choose a Concept Literacy Reader or Below-Level Reader. Take turns reading a page from the book. Use the readers to practice rate and accuracy. Provide feedback as needed.

▲ Work with a partner. Choose an On-Level Reader. Take turns reading a page from the book. Use the reader to practice rate and accuracy. Provide feedback as needed.

■ Work with a partner. Choose an Advanced Reader. Take turns reading a page from the book. Use the reader to practice rate and accuracy. Provide feedback as needed.

Technology
• Leveled Reader Database
• Reading Street Readers CD-ROM

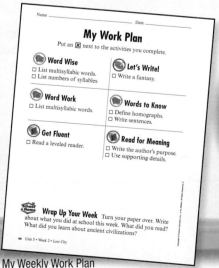

Name _____   Date _____

My Work Plan
Put an ☒ next to the activities you complete.

Word Wise
☐ List multisyllabic words.
☐ List numbers of syllables.

Let's Write!
☐ Write a fantasy.

Word Work
☐ List multisyllabic words.

Words to Know
☐ Define homographs.
☐ Write sentences.

Get Fluent
☐ Read a leveled reader.

Read for Meaning
☐ Write the author's purpose.
☐ Use supporting details.

Wrap Up Your Week Turn your paper over. Write about what you did at school this week. What did you read? What did you learn about ancient civilizations?

Unit 5 • Week 2 • *Lost City*

My Weekly Work Plan

Week 2

Objectives
- Introduce the weekly concept.
- Develop oral vocabulary.

Today at a Glance

Oral Vocabulary
region, cultivate, adobe, highland

Comprehension
◉ Compare and contrast
◉ Visualize

Reading
"Archaeology: Dig It"

Fluency
Appropriate phrasing

Lesson Vocabulary
Tested vocabulary

Research and Inquiry
Identify questions

Spelling
Words with double consonants

Conventions
Adverbs

Handwriting
Cursive letters *Q* and *q*

Writing
Legend

Concept Talk

Question of the Week

What surprises can happen on an expedition?

Introduce the concept

To further explore the unit concept of Adventures by Land, Water, and Air, this week students will read, write, and talk about what surprises can happen on an expedition. Write the Question of the Week on the board.

ROUTINE **Activate Prior Knowledge** **Team Talk**

 Think Have students think about what surprises could happen on an expedition or a trip that is organized for a specific purpose.

 Pair Have pairs of students discuss the Question of the Week.

Share Call on a few students to share their ideas with the group. Guide the discussion and encourage elaboration with prompts such as:

- What kinds of expeditions can you think of?
- What movies or TV shows have you seen, or stories have you read, about an expedition?

Routines Flip Chart

Anchored Talk

Develop oral vocabulary

Have students turn to pp. 200–201 in their Student Editions. Look at each of the photos. Then, use the prompts to guide discussion and create the *Surprises that can happen on an expedition* concept map. Remind students to answer questions with appropriate details, and provide suggestions that build upon the ideas of others.

- Look at the picture of the huge carved heads. Why do you think an ancient culture would carve huge statues like these? **(to worship or honor; for art and beauty)** Let's add *Ancient cultures* to our concept map.
- Look at the giant pyramid. What purpose do you think this ancient building served long ago? **(for worship; living; storage; burial)** Let's add *Ancient buildings* to our concept map.

Objectives
• Take part in discussions led by teachers or other students, ask and answer questions, and offer ideas that build on the ideas of other people.

Oral Vocabulary

Let's Talk About

Ancient Cities

• Tell what you would like about exploring an ancient city.

• Maintain eye contact when you speak.

• Answer questions with appropriate detail by including descriptions of size, color, and shape in your response.

READING STREET ONLINE
CONCEPT TALK VIDEO
www.ReadingStreet.com

You've learned
2 1 0
Amazing Words
so far this year!

Student Edition pp. 200–201

Amazing Words

You've learned **2 1 0** words so far

You'll learn **0 1 0** words this week!

region	century
cultivate	culture
adobe	legend
highland	research
gigantic	records

Writing on Demand

Writing Fluency
Ask students to respond to the photos on pp. 200–201 by writing as well as they can and as much as the can about what surprises can happen on an expedition.

• Look at the photo of the dinosaur skeleton. Why do you think museums display new findings that are centuries old? **(so people can learn more about the past)** Let's add *New findings* to our concept map.

• After discussing the photos, ask: What surprises can happen on an expedition?

Connect to reading

Tell students that this week they will be reading about an ancient civilization and the surprises that could happen on an expedition. Encourage students to add concept-related words to this week's concept map.

ELL Preteach Concepts Use the Day 1 instruction on ELL Poster 22 to assess and build background knowledge, develop concepts, and build oral vocabulary.

English Language Learners
ELL Support Additional ELL support and modified instruction is provided in the *ELL Handbook* and in the ELL Support lessons on pp. DI•41–DI•50.

Listening Comprehension
English learners will benefit from additional visual support to understand the key terms in the concept map. Use the pictures on pp. 200–201 to scaffold understanding.

Frontload for Read Aloud Use the modified Read Aloud on p. DI•36 in the ELL Support lessons to prepare students to listen to "The Incas." (p. 201b).

Oral Vocabulary
Amazing Words

Introduce Amazing Words

"The Incas" on p. 201b gives information about the lives of ancient Inca farmers and their way of life. Tell students to listen for this week's Amazing Words—*region*, *cultivate*, *adobe*, and *highland*—as they read.

Model fluency

As you read "The Incas," model appropriate phrasing by grouping words in a meaningful way and paying attention to punctuation cues.

Teach Amazing Words

Amazing Words Oral Vocabulary Routine

region
cultivate
adobe
highland

1. **Introduce** Write the word *region* on the board. Have students say the word aloud with you. In "The Incas," we learn about the *region* where the ancient Incas lived and farmed the land. What crops did they grow in their *region*? (cacao, beans, peanuts, pumpkins, potatoes). Supply a student-friendly definition.

2. **Demonstrate** Have students answer questions to demonstrate understanding. In what *region* of Texas do you live? (Possible responses: Panhandle, Gulf Coast, Piney Woods, Blackland Prairie)

3. **Apply** Have students give examples of types of *regions*.

See p. OV•2 to teach *cultivate, adobe,* and *highland*.

Routines Flip Chart

Apply Amazing Words

Lead the class in a discussion about the meanings of the Amazing Words. Remind students to answer questions with appropriate detail and to build on the ideas of others.

MONITOR PROGRESS Check Oral Vocabulary

During discussion, listen for students' use of the Amazing Words.

If... students are unable to use the Amazing Words to discuss the concept,

then... use Oral Vocabulary Routine in the Routine Flip Chart to demonstrate words.

Day 1	Days 2–3	Day 4	Day 5	
Check Oral Vocabulary	Check Retelling	Check Fluency	Check Oral Vocabulary	Success Predictor

The Incas

by Shirlee P. Newman

Most people ruled by the Great Incas were farmers. In some places, they cut terraces resembling steps on steep hillsides to create flat spaces on which to plant. Stones between the "steps" kept dirt from washing down when it rained. Farmers fed themselves and their families with whatever they could grow in their region. Cacao, used to make chocolate, flourished at the edge of the jungle where it was warm and damp. Beans, peanuts, and pumpkins grew in high Andes valleys. Fruits and vegetables grew in the lower valleys where the days were warm and the nights cool. Andean farmers experimented with potatoes and learned to cultivate many different kinds under various growing conditions. Potatoes were unknown in other parts of the world until the Spaniards arrived and found the Incas growing them.

Inca farmers had no machinery or animals to help them. Llamas could carry small loads, but they were too delicate for harder jobs such as plowing. Farmers used a simple digging stick, a pole with a sharp point, to turn over soil before planting.

A farmer's home was usually a one-room adobe hut, whether he lived in the warm coastal desert region or in the mountains. The hut had no chairs, tables, or beds. The family sat, ate, and slept on straw mats on the dirt floor. Highland nights were cold, but the hut had no stove or fireplace. The farmer's wife cooked in a shed apart from the house. The stove was made of clay and had three openings, so three neighbors could cook a one-pot meal at the same time. Dried llama dung and grass were used for fuel. Most people ate two meals a day. Breakfast was cereal or soup. Dinner was also soup, made of potatoes, corn, or quinoa, onions, squash, and any other grain or vegetable available. Meat was rarely eaten. If a llama or guinea pig was eaten for a special occasion, the leftover meat was dried in the sun to preserve it for another time. Dried meat was called charqui and is still eaten in Peru. The English word "jerky" comes from that Quechua word.

Inca farmers devised a way of freeze-drying potatoes so they could be stored for as long as five or six years without spoiling. They set the potatoes out in the freezing night air and defrosted them the next day in the warm noonday sun. The farmer's wife pressed out the moisture with her feet. This process was repeated until the potatoes dried into a thick white chunk that looked like plastic foam. When the family needed potatoes, the chunk was soaked in water and cooked. Chuno, freeze-dried potatoes, are eaten to this day in Peru.

Oral Vocabulary

Success Predictor

Objectives

◎ Compare and contrast to aid comprehension.

◎ Use the strategy of visualize to aid comprehension.

• Read grade-level text with appropriate phrasing.

Skills Trace

◉ **Compare and Contrast**

Introduce U4W1D1; U4W2D1; U5W2D1

Practice U4W1D2; U4W1D3; U4W2D2; U4W2D3; U5W2D2; U5W2D3

Reteach/Review U4W1D5; U4W2D5; U4W4D2; U4W5D3; U5W2D5; U6W3D3

Assess/Test
Weekly Tests U4W1; U4W2; U5W2
Benchmark Tests U4
KEY:
U=Unit   W=Week   D=Day

Skill ↔ Strategy
🎯 Compare and Contrast
🎯 Visualize

Student Edition p. EI•5

Introduce compare and contrast

Envision It!

When you compare and contrast, you tell how two or more things are alike and different. Authors use clue words that show how things are alike or different. What clue words show likenesses? (*like, as*) What clue words show differences? (*but, unlike, different*) Have students turn to p. EI•5 in the Student Edition to review compare and contrast. Then read "Archaeology: Dig It" with students.

Model the skill

Think Aloud As I look at page 203, I see the clue words *some* and *others* in the first paragraph. This helps me know that there may be comparisons and contrasts. As I read, I can use a graphic organizer like the one on page 202 to keep track of the similarities and differences I read about. Have students follow along as you read the first paragraph of "Archaeology: Dig It." Based on the first paragraph, what is different about the kinds of archaeologists? (Some study people who left behind written records while other archaeologists do not.)

Guide practice

Have students finish reading "Archaeology: Dig It" on their own. After they read, have them use a graphic organizer like the one on p. 202 and compare and contrast two or more things from the passage.

Strategy check

Visualize Remind students that if they have difficulty understanding "Archaeology: Dig It," they can use the strategy of visualize. Model the strategy of creating sensory images to monitor and assess comprehension.

Model the strategy

Envision It!

Think Aloud If I want to know more about digs, I can use the text in the second paragraph to visualize. I imagine a team of tired archaeologists digging up layers of dirt on a hot day. They are carefully uncovering pieces of broken pots and dusting them off to take with them. Have students use the strategy of visualize on p. EI•25 of the Student Edition.

Student Edition p. EI•25

On their own

Use p. 327 in the *Reader's and Writer's Notebook* for additional practice with compare and contrast.

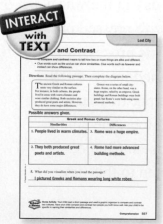

Reader's and Writer's Notebook, p. 327

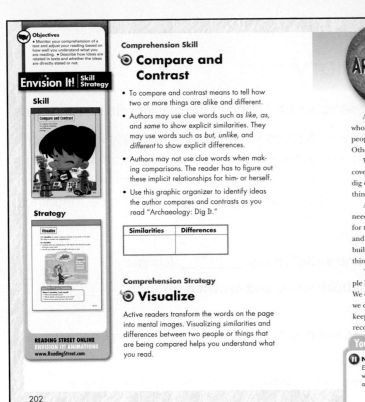

Objectives
• Monitor your comprehension of a text and adjust your reading based on how well you understand what you are reading. • Describe how ideas are related in texts and whether the ideas are directly stated or not.

Envision It! Skill Strategy

Skill

Compare and Contrast

Strategy

Visualize

READING STREET ONLINE
ENVISION IT! ANIMATIONS
www.ReadingStreet.com

Comprehension Skill
Compare and Contrast

• To compare and contrast means to tell how two or more things are alike and different.

• Authors may use clue words such as *like, as,* and *same* to show explicit similarities. They may use words such as *but, unlike,* and *different* to show explicit differences.

• Authors may not use clue words when making comparisons. The reader has to figure out these implicit relationships for him- or herself.

• Use this graphic organizer to identify ideas the author compares and contrasts as you read "Archaeology: Dig It."

Similarities	Differences

Comprehension Strategy
Visualize

Active readers transform the words on the page into mental images. Visualizing similarities and differences between two people or things that are being compared helps you understand what you read.

ARCHAEOLOGY: DIG IT

Archaeology is the study of things left by people who lived in the past. Some archaeologists study people who left behind things and written records. Others study people who had no written language.

With the passing of time, ancient places often are covered with layers of earth. The archaeologist has to dig down to find the things people left behind. These things give clues to how those people lived.

All people have certain things in common. We all need to eat and a place to live. So archaeologists look for things such as dishes, cooking pots, arrowheads, and hunting knives. They hope to find things people built, such as houses and roads. They study these things to understand how people lived in the past.

The way we live today is different from how people lived long ago. Most of us don't hunt our food. We don't make our own cooking pots or dishes. But we do live in homes and travel on roads, and we do keep written records. We will leave behind these records for other people to read in the future.

Skill What does one type of archaeologist do that the other does not? Is this an explicit or implicit comparison?

Strategy What might people in the future discover about the way we live today? Visualize and describe things they might find that will tell them about us.

Skill Compare and contrast the way people live today with how people lived long ago.

Your Turn!

Need a Review? See *Envision It! Handbook* for help with comparing and contrasting and visualizing.

Ready to Try It? Use what you've learned about comparing and contrasting as you read *Lost City.*

LOST CITY

202   203

Student Edition pp. 202–203

Skill Some study people who had written language; some study people who did not. This is an explicit comparison.

Strategy Answers will vary, but should include a description of what things people in the future might discover about the way we live today.

Skill We don't hunt our food or make our own cooking pots or dishes, like people did in the past. We do keep written records and will leave behind for other people in the future.

Model Fluency
Appropriate Phrasing

Model fluent reading

Have students listen as you read the last paragraph of "Archaeology: Dig It" with appropriate phrasing. Explain that you will use punctuation cues to indicate the pauses during reading. Tell students to also listen to how the rhythm and flow of your voice helps convey meaning.

ROUTINE Oral Rereading

1 **Read** Have students read the selection orally.

2 **Reread** To achieve optimal fluency, students should reread the text three or four times.

3 **Corrective Feedback** Have students read aloud without you. Listen use of appropriate phrasing. Provide feedback about using punc as clues for pausing and using pausing to convey meaning.

Routines Flip Chart

Objectives
- Activate prior knowledge of words.
- Identify questions for research.

Vocabulary
Tested Vocabulary

Lesson vocabulary

Have students complete sentences by filling in the blanks with lesson words.

Display the lesson words and discuss what students already know about these words. Then write incomplete sentences and have students identify the lesson word that completes each sentence and makes sense in context. Have students check a dictionary or glossary to determine meanings of unknown words.

Activate prior knowledge

- **I solved the puzzle and satisfied my _____.** (curiosity)
- **The explorer cut the thick vines and crawled through _____ in the jungle.** (thickets)
- **The symphony played the most _____ music I've ever heard!** (glorious)
- **The _____ sections of the mountain looked like lush, green steps.** (terraced)
- **A large _____ monument stood in the park.** (granite)
- **Have you explored the ancient _____ of the temple?** (ruins)
- **The _____ of rain poured down the cliff.** (torrent)

Related words

Ask students to list things they would describe as glorious. Ask how *glorious* and *glorify* are related in meaning.

At the end of the week, students can review these fill-in-the-blank sentences or create their own with a partner.

Preteach Academic Vocabulary

 Academic Vocabulary Write the following words on the board:

personal essay	double consonants
legend	journal entry
adverbs	radio announcement

Have students share what they know about this week's Academic Vocabulary. Use the students' responses to assess their prior knowledge. Preteach the Academic Vocabulary by providing a student-friendly description, explanation, or example that clarifies the meaning of each term. Then ask students to restate the meaning of the Academic Vocabulary term in their own words.

Research and Inquiry
Identify Questions

Teach

Discuss the Question of the Week: *What surprises can happen on an expedition?* Tell students they will conduct research to find out more about archaeological expeditions and the surprises that can sometimes occur. They will present their findings to the class on Day 5 in the form of a journal entry.

Model

Think Aloud I'll start by brainstorming a list of questions about archaeological expeditions. I know that there are often surprises, so I will ask myself questions about this: *What surprising discoveries might happen purely by accident? What surprises might happen to someone in an unfamiliar environment? What surprises might a person uncover while doing research?*

Guide practice

After students have formulated open-ended inquiry questions, explain that tomorrow they will conduct research using their questions. Help students generate a research plan by identifying topics that will guide their search.

On their own

Have students work individually, in pairs, or in small groups to write an inquiry question.

INTERNET GUY
Don Leu

21st Century Skills

Weekly Inquiry Project

Day 1 Identify Questions

Day 2 Navigate/Search

Day 3 Analyze

Day 4 Synthesize

Day 5 Communicate

Academic Vocabulary

journal entry a personal account of events, thoughts, and feelings kept by an individual

Small Group Time

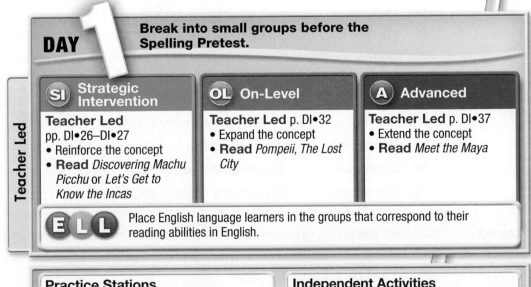

DAY 1

Break into small groups before the Spelling Pretest.

Teacher Led

(SI) Strategic Intervention	**(OL) On-Level**	**(A) Advanced**
Teacher Led pp. DI•26–DI•27 • Reinforce the concept • **Read** *Discovering Machu Picchu* or *Let's Get to Know the Incas*	**Teacher Led** p. DI•32 • Expand the concept • **Read** *Pompeii, The Lost City*	**Teacher Led** p. DI•37 • Extend the concept • **Read** *Meet the Maya*

ELL Place English language learners in the groups that correspond to their reading abilities in English.

Practice Stations
• Read for Meaning
• Get Fluent
• Word Work

Independent Activities
• Concept Talk Video
• *Reader's and Writer's Notebook*
• Vocabulary Activities

ELL

English Language Learners
Multilingual vocabulary
Students can apply knowledge of their home languages to acquire new English vocabulary by using Multilingual Vocabulary Lists (*ELL Handbook* pp. 431–442).

Objectives

- Spell words with double consonants.
- Use and understand adverbs.
- Write cursive capital letter *Q* and lowercase *q* in words.

Spelling Pretest
Words with Double Consonants

Introduce Some words are spelled with double consonants. Double consonants are two consonants that appear together in a word.

Pretest Use these sentences to administer the spelling pretest. Say each word, read the sentence, and repeat the word.

1.	**tomorrow**	It's late, so I'll finish **tomorrow**.
2.	**borrow**	If you need more, you can **borrow** some from me.
3.	**different**	I'd like to try a **different** kind of shampoo.
4.	**rabbit**	The **rabbit** jumped through the grass.
5.	**matter**	What's the **matter** with your friend?
6.	**written**	The book was **written** a long time ago.
7.	**bottle**	Store what's left in a glass **bottle**.
8.	**ridden**	She had **ridden** a camel across the desert.
9.	**odd**	Jim made an **odd** comment about his friend.
10.	**bubble**	You can blow a **bubble** under water.
11.	**offer**	I'll **offer** to take Jack to school.
12.	**suffer**	Anna will **suffer** if she gets a bee sting.
13.	**slippers**	Her new **slippers** kept her feet warm.
14.	**grasshopper**	The **grasshopper** ate the insects in the grass.
15.	**worry**	Mom will **worry** if we get home late.
16.	**current**	Ian read the most **current** issue of the magazine.
17.	**lettuce**	Lots of people like to eat a **lettuce** salad.
18.	**saddle**	Put the **saddle** on the horse first.
19.	**shudder**	Walking into a cold ocean makes me **shudder**.
20.	**hobby**	Greta's **hobby** is making stuffed animals.

Challenge words

21.	**Mississippi**	**Mississippi** is a state in the United States.
22.	**recess**	At **recess**, we play in the school yard.
23.	**impossible**	It's **impossible** to eat so much food at one time.
24.	**antennas**	Those **antennas** transmit cell phone signals.
25.	**allowance**	Save some of your **allowance** each week.

Self correct After the pretest, you can either display the correctly spelled words or spell them orally. Have students self-correct their pretests by rewriting misspelled words correctly.

Let's Practice It!
TR DVD•254

On their own Use *Let's Practice It!* page 254 on the *Teacher Resources DVD-ROM* for additional practice.

Conventions
Adverbs

Teach
Display Grammar Transparency 22, and read aloud the explanation and examples in the box. Point out the adverbs in the examples and discuss how they are used to describe or to combine two sentences

Model
Model writing the adverbs in sentences 1 and 2. Apply the rules for adverbs to show why you selected your answer.

Guide practice
Guide students to complete items 3–6. Remind them to think about the fact that an adverb can come before or after the word it describes. Record the correct responses on the transparency.

Daily Fix-It
Use Daily Fix-It numbers 1 and 2 in the right margin.

Connect to oral language
Have students read numbers 7 and 8 on the transparency and combine the sentences by adding an adverb.

Grammar Transparency 22, TR DVD

Handwriting
Cursive Letters Q and q

Model letter formation
Display the capital cursive letter *Q* and the lowercase letter *q*. Follow the stroke instructions pictured to model letter formation.

Model spacing
Explain that writing legibly means letters are the correct size, form, and slant. The letters have the proper space between them. Model writing this sentence with attention to spacing: Demonstrate how you leave a small amount of space between letters and a larger space between words. *Quincy had a question about the aquarium.* Make sure the letters aren't too tight or too loose.

Guide practice
Have students write these sentences. *There were many requests for rowboats in the Queens River. Qualified experts had a quarrel about the aqua quilt's history.* Circulate around the room, guiding students. Point out correct letter spacing.

Academic Vocabulary

Adverbs are words that usually describe verbs. An adverb can tell how, when, where, or how often an action happens.

When a **double consonant** appears at the end or in the middle of a word, usually only one consonant is heard.

Daily Fix-It

1. A locul farm boy guided Hiram Bingham to Machu pic-chu. *(local; Picchu)*

2. The cities location had been a secret to most people until then. *(city's; secret)*

English Language Learners

Language transfer: Point out to speakers of Spanish that the ending *-ly* is like the ending *-mente* in Spanish. Give a few examples with cognates such as *rapidly/rápidamente; probably/ probablemente; absolutely/ absolutamente.* Working with a partner, have students take turns naming a verb and saying the adverb that is formed by adding *-ly*. Have partners take turns writing the adverb.

Handwriting: Adverbs To provide practice in handwriting lowercase *q*, and to extend language opportunities, have students write the following adverbs in cursive: *frequently, quietly, quickly.*

Objectives
- Understand and identify the features of a legend.

Writing—A Legend
Introduce

MINI-LESSON

Read Like a Writer

■ **Introduce** This week you will write a legend. A legend is a story about a hero or heroes that may be based on historical events.

Prompt	Write a legend about Hiram Bingham and the discovery of Machu Picchu.
Trait	Sentences
Mode	Narrative

Reader's and Writer's Notebook p. 328

■ **Examine Model Text** Let's read an example of a legend that introduces us to a hero who performs amazing deeds. Have students read "The Legend of Pecos Bill and the Mountain Lion" on p. 328 of their *Reader's and Writer's Notebook.*

■ **Key Features** Legends often feature **historical elements.** Find the introductory paragraph in the model and circle it. Discuss how the first paragraph helps the reader understand the historic period in which the legend takes place—the time of westward expansion.

Legends are often **part true** and **part fiction.** Have students draw a box around parts of the story that might be true.

Legends often **exaggerate** the deeds of the hero. What are some of the exaggerated deeds you find in this legend? Have students underline the exaggerated deeds of Pecos Bill.

Review key features

Review the key features of legends with students. You may want to post the key features in the classroom for students to refer to as they work on their legends.

Key Features of Legends

- may be based on historical characters or events
- invents or exaggerates the great deeds of a hero
- uses details to describe the fictional traits of the hero
- is often part fact and part fiction

Write Guy
Jeff Anderson

What Do You Notice?

When students are examining the model text, ask, "What do you notice?" By giving students the responsibility of commenting on what they find effective in the text, they build self-confidence and often begin to notice features of the writing they might not have otherwise. Eventually they will start trying them in their writing. Relish students' movement toward correctness and beauty.

ROUTINE Quick Write for Fluency **Team Talk**

1. **Talk** Working with a partner, have students take a few minutes to discuss the features of legends.

2. **Write** Each student writes a few sentences that describe the key features of a legend.

3. **Share** Partners read their sentences to one another.

Routines Flip Chart

English Language Learners
Monitor Understanding Read the writing model aloud and help students understand it. Make sure students are aware of the westward expansion and the job of the cowboy. Discuss the hardships people faced on their journey. Ask students to tell how traveling today differs from the trip of the settlers. Encourage them to use complete sentences.

Wrap Up Your Day

✔ **Build Concepts** What did you learn about the surprises that can happen on an expedition?

✔ **Oral Vocabulary** Have students use the Amazing Words they learned in context sentences.

✔ **Homework** Send home this week's Family Times newsletter in *Let's Practice It!* pp. 255–256 on the *Teacher Resources DVD-ROM*.

Preview DAY 2

Tell students that tomorrow they will read about the discovery of an ancient Incan city in Peru.

Let's Practice It
TR DVD•255–256

Objectives
- Expand the weekly concept.
- Develop oral vocabulary.

Today at a Glance

Oral Vocabulary
gigantic, century

Word Analysis
Suffixes *-ous, -able, -ible*

Literary Terms
Sensory words

Text Features
Sequence

Lesson Vocabulary
⊙ Greek and Latin Roots

Reading
"Looking for the Past"

Lost City: The Discovery of Machu Picchu

Fluency
Appropriate phrasing

Research and Inquiry
Navigate/Search

Spelling
Words with double consonants

Conventions
Adverbs

Writing
Legend

Concept Talk

Question of the Week
What surprises can happen on an expedition?

Expand the concept

Remind students of the Question of the Week. Tell students that today they will begin reading *Lost City: The Discovery of Machu Picchu.* As they read, encourage students to think about what surprises can happen on an expedition.

Anchored Talk

Develop oral vocabulary

Use the photos on pp. 200–201 and the Read Aloud, "The Incas," to talk about the Amazing Words *region, cultivate, adobe,* and *highland.* Add these and other concept-related words to the concept map to develop students' knowledge of the topic. Discuss the following questions. Remind students to listen attentively to other students and to answer with appropriate detail. Encourage students to build on other's ideas when they answer.

- Why do you think it is important for farmers to *cultivate* crops that grow well in their *region*? (Possible response: It is easier to grow crops that are native to an area because the crops have a better chance of surviving.)

- What kinds of animals do you think can live in a *highland* area? (Possible responses: animals that can survive cold weather; animals with hooves or claws that can easily hold onto or grasp the rocky surface)

- Why do you think an *adobe* house is a good example of using available resources? (Possible response: The mud, straw, and twigs used to make the bricks are found in the area.)

Oral Vocabulary
Amazing Words

Amazing Words

region	century
cultivate	culture
adobe	legend
highland	research
gigantic	records

Teach Amazing Words

Amazing Words — Oral Vocabulary Routine

1 Introduce Write the Amazing Word *gigantic* on the board. Have students say it aloud with you. Relate *gigantic* to the photographs on pp. 200–201 and "The Incas." What do you think the girls in the photograph are thinking as they look up at the *gigantic* dinosaur skeleton? What do you think archaeologists must consider when they uncover a *gigantic* skeleton like this one? Have students determine the definition of the word. (*Gigantic* means "very large".)

2 Demonstrate Have students answer questions to demonstrate understanding. What *gigantic* things have you seen? (whales, mountains, skyscrapers) Why do you think scientists need *gigantic* amounts of money to fund their expeditions? (travel and salary expenses; equipment)

3 Apply Have students apply their understanding. What word is an antonym for *gigantic*? *(tiny, microscopic, miniature)*

See p. OV•2 to teach *century*.

Routines Flip Chart

Apply Amazing Words

As students read "Looking for the Past" on p. 205, have them think about *gigantic* findings that are *centuries* old.

Connect to reading

Explain that today students will read about the discovery of an ancient city in Peru called Machu Picchu. Help students establish a purpose for reading. As they read, they should think about how the Question of the Week and the Amazing Words *gigantic* and *century* apply to the events in Machu Picchu, the lost city of the Inca.

ELL Reinforce Vocabulary Use the Day 2 instruction on ELL Poster 22 to teach lesson vocabulary and the lesson concept.

Word Analysis
Suffixes -ous, -able, and -ible

Teach suffixes -ous, -able, and -ible

Tell students a suffix is a word part added to the end of a base word to change the word's meaning. Explain that when a suffix such as -ous is added to the end of a base word, the suffix changes the word's meaning and part of speech. Have them write the meaning of each base word. Then have them add the suffix -ous, -able, or -ible and write the new meaning.

Model

Think Aloud I will choose the word *glory* from the first column. I can look it up in the dictionary and write its meaning in the second column. The word *glory* means "magnificence." *Glory* is the base word of *glorious*. I know that -ous comes from Latin and means "full of," so *glorious* means "full of magnificence." I will write *glorious* and its meaning in the last two columns.

Base Word	Meaning	Base Word + Suffix	New Meaning
glory	magnificence	glory + ous = glorious	full of magnificence
move			
terror			
grace			
venom			

Guide practice

Have students write the meaning of each base word, add -ous, -able, or -ible to form the new word, and then write the meaning of the new word.

On their own

Have students use a dictionary to verify each word's spelling, meaning, and part of speech. Have students correct any mistakes in their charts. Follow the Strategy for Multisyllabic Words to teach *famous*.

ROUTINE Strategy for Multisyllabic Words

1. **Look for meaningful word parts** Circle the suffix -ous and underline the base word *fame*. Explain that the letter *e* must be dropped before the suffix -ous can be added.

2. **Connect to meaning** Define the word *fame* and add the suffix -ous to the end of the word. Then define the word *famous*.

3. **Blend** Blend the meaningful word parts together to read *famous*.

Continue the routine with *joyous* and *poisonous*.

Literary Terms
Sensory Words

Teach sensory words

Tell students that writers use sensory words to help the reader experience the way things look, sound, smell, taste, or feel. Explain that sensory words help readers create images in their minds and better visualize the events in the story.

Model sensory words

Think Aloud Let's look at "Looking for the Past" on p. 205. As I skim the selection looking for sensory words, I notice the phrase "cut their way through jungles." What do you think the author wants readers to visualize in their minds? (scientists cutting away thick vines so they can climb through the jungle)

Guide practice

Have students find sensory words and phrases in *Lost City: The Discovery of Machu Picchu.* Have students tell how the examples they chose make them see, hear, smell, taste or feel what the author is describing.

On their own

Have students look for sensory words in other selections in their Student Edition.

Text Structure
Sequence

Teach sequence

Expository nonfiction often uses text structures, such as sequence, to help readers better understand the topic.

Model sequence

Think Aloud I know that sequence organizes facts and events into their correct order in time. When I look at *Lost City: The Discovery of Machu Picchu,* I can skim the pages to look for specific dates. I can also look for signal words such as *now, when, until,* and *before* to help me follow the order of events.

Guide practice

Have students skim the selection and locate signal words or phrases that help them identify the explicit relationship among ideas organized by sequence.

On their own

Have students read the first paragraph of the selection. Ask them to describe the sequential way the ideas in the paragraph are organized. Then have students describe explicit and implicit relationships among ideas organized by sequence.

Objectives
◎ Use Greek and Latin roots to determine meanings of unknown words.
• Read grade-level text with appropriate phrasing.

Vocabulary Strategy for
↻ Greek and Latin Roots

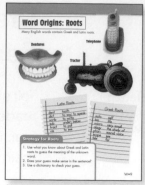

Student Edition p. W•9

Teach Greek and Latin roots

Envision It!

Explain that a *root* is a word or word part to which other word parts are added to form new words. Tell students that knowing the meaning of a Greek or Latin root may help them determine the meaning of a word. Explain how using the strategy of word structure and a dictionary or glossary can help students locate Greek and Latin roots and their meanings. Refer students to *Words!* on p. W•9 in the Student Edition for additional practice. Then read "Looking for the Past" on p. 205 with students.

Model the strategy

Think Aloud

Write on the board: *Machu Picchu is one of the most fascinating places to visit in the southern hemisphere.* I can't figure out the meaning of the word *hemisphere* by using context clues, so I will use word structure for help. *Hemisphere* is made up of two parts: *hemi* and *sphere.* When I look up the word in the dictionary, I find that *hemi-* has a Latin origin and means "half." *Sphere* comes from the Greek word *sphaira* and means "globe" or "ball." By combining the definitions, *hemisphere* means "half a globe."

Guide practice

Write this sentence on the board: *The rainbow was a glorious sight!* Have students determine the meaning of *glorious* using word structure and a dictionary or glossary to find out the root. (The Latin root *glori* means "praise.") For additional support, use *Envision It! Pictured Vocabulary Cards* or *Tested Vocabulary Cards.*

On their own

Read "Looking for the Past" on p. 205. Have students use word structure and a dictionary or glossary to find words with Greek and Latin roots. Have them write the words, circle the roots, and write the meaning for each word. For additional practice use the *Reader's and Writer's Notebook* p. 329.

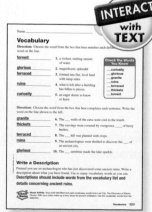

INTERACT with TEXT

Reader's and Writer's Notebook, p. 329

Objectives
• Determine the meaning of English words with roots from Greek, Latin, and other languages.

Envision It! Words to Know

ruins

terraced

thickets

curiosity
glorious
granite
torrent

READING STREET ONLINE
VOCABULARY ACTIVITIES
www.ReadingStreet.com

Vocabulary Strategy for

Greek and Latin Roots

Word Structure Many words, particularly academic vocabulary words, have Latin or Greek roots. The Latin root *terra* means "earth" or "land." It appears in *terrain* (surface of the ground) and *territory* (an area of land). The Greek root *graphikos* means "of writing" and *arkhaiologia* means "the study of ancient things." Knowing Latin and Greek roots can help you figure out unknown words.

1. Look at the unknown word. Try to identify a Greek or Latin root that you know.

2. Does the meaning of the Greek or Latin root give you a clue to the unknown word?

3. Try the meaning in the sentence to be sure it makes sense.

As you read "Looking for the Past," use what you know about Greek and Latin roots to help you figure out the meanings of *archaeologists, terraced,* and *graphics.*

Words to Write Reread "Looking for the Past." Imagine that you are a scientist looking for the past in a faraway land. Write a journal entry describing the sights you see and discoveries you make. Use words from the *Words to Know* list in your journal.

Looking for the Past

Some scientists called archaeologists study the past. They look at objects and buildings from past civilizations. They have curiosity about people who lived long ago. How did they live? What did they eat? What did they do every day? Did they read and write? Thanks to these scientists, we have learned a great deal about people who lived long ago.

These scientists have ventured into places that few others would go. They have cut their way through jungles with thickets full of dangerous animals. They have climbed steep mountains. They have crossed mountain rivers that fall in a raging torrent. They have found ruins of places people built long ago. These may look like nothing more than rocks to us, but they are glorious to these scientists.

Imagine a team of scientists as they discover terraced fields on the side of a mountain. These show that people long ago were clever farmers. Think of the scientists as they look at beautiful temples made of granite or marble. These show that people long ago had beliefs. Watch as the scientists carefully uncover clay pots decorated with unknown graphics. These show that people long ago were artistic and loved beauty.

Your Turn!

 Need a Review? For help with Greek and Latin roots, see *Words!*

 Ready to Try It? Read *Lost City: The Discovery of Machu Picchu* on pp. 206–217.

LOST CITY

204   205

Student Edition pp. 204–205

Reread for Fluency
Appropriate Phrasing

Model fluent reading

Read the first paragraph of "Looking for the Past" aloud, grouping words together in phrases. Tell students that even though each word has its own meaning, you are not reading each word by itself. You are grouping words together to help you read fluently and to comprehend what you are reading. Have students pay special attention to the new vocabulary within these phrases.

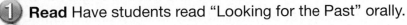

ROUTINE Oral Rereading

1 **Read** Have students read "Looking for the Past" orally.

2 **Reread** To achieve optimal fluency, students should reread the text three or four times.

3 **Corrective Feedback** Listen as students read aloud. Provide corrective feedback about their phrasing, and encourage them to pause to emphasize the most important phrases.

Routines Flip Chart

Lesson Vocabulary

curiosity a strong desire to know or learn something

glorious magnificent; splendid

granite a very hard, gray or pink rock that is used for buildings and monuments

ruins what is left after a building, wall, or other structure has fallen to pieces

terraced formed into a flat piece of land by cutting into a hillside; terraces are often made in hilly areas to create more space for raising crops

thickets bushes or small trees growing close together

torrent a violent, rushing stream of water

Differentiated Instruction

SI Strategic Intervention

Have volunteers reread the definitions from this week's lesson vocabulary. Have them use their own words to generate student-friendly definitions. With the group, brainstorm synonyms for each word.

A Advanced

Have students write a paragraph using all of this week's lesson vocabulary words.

ELL

English Language Learners
Build Academic Vocabulary
Use the lesson vocabulary pictured on p. 204 to teach the meanings of *ruins, terraced,* and *thickets.* Call on pairs to write the words on sticky notes and use them to label images of the words on the ELL poster.

Objectives
• Understand the elements of a personal narrative.
• Use text features to preview and predict.
• Set a purpose for reading.

LOST CITY
The Discovery of Machu Picchu
BY TED LEWIN

Genre A **biography** is a kind of literary nonfiction that tells about a real person and the events of his or her life. The details of these events are often presented in sequence. Look for the sequence of the events leading to the discovery of this lost city as you read.

Question of the Week
What surprises can happen on an expedition?

Student Edition pp. 206–207

Build Background

Discuss expeditions

Team Talk Have students turn to a partner and discuss the Question of the Week and these questions about expeditions. Remind students to ask and answer questions with appropriate details and to give suggestions that build on the ideas of others.

• What kinds of places might be fun to explore?

• What surprises do you think might happen on an expedition?

• What do you think makes someone want to go on an expedition?

• How do various types of expeditions seem similar or different?

Connect to selection

Have students discuss their answers with the class. Remind students to listen attentively to speakers and to make relevant, pertinent comments. Possible responses: Rainforests and oceans might be fun to explore. You might discover something you hadn't planned to find or meet new people. An adventurous person might go on an expedition to learn and see new things. Some expeditions might be scientific and research based, while others are for entertainment purposes. For additional opportunities to build background, use the Background Building Audio.

Prereading Strategies

Genre Explain that **literary nonfiction** tells about real people, places, and events in a story form. The details are often presented in sequence so that readers can follow the story. Literary nonfiction is often based on biographies and autobiographies; newspaper articles; and diaries and journals.

Preview and predict Have students preview the selection and predict what they will find out as they read. Remind them to look for text features such as illustrations and italicized text as they preview.

Set purpose Prior to reading, and to enhance comprehension, have students establish their own purposes for reading based upon their own desired outcomes. For example, they may want to learn about explorers, Peru, or Macchu Picchu.

Strategy Response Log

 INTERACT with TEXT

Have students use prior knowledge to visualize what *Lost City: The Discovery of Machu Picchu* will be about. Have them write their responses on p. 28 in the *Reader's and Writer's Notebook.*

Small Group Time

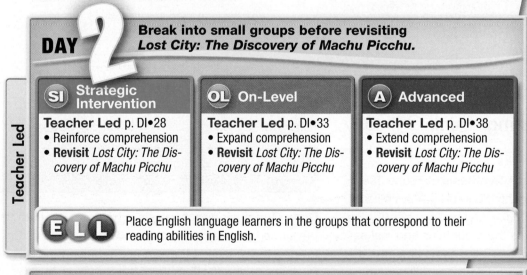

DAY 2 Break into small groups before revisiting *Lost City: The Discovery of Machu Picchu.*

Teacher Led

SI Strategic Intervention	OL On-Level	A Advanced
Teacher Led p. DI•28 • Reinforce comprehension • **Revisit** *Lost City: The Discovery of Machu Picchu*	**Teacher Led** p. DI•33 • Expand comprehension • **Revisit** *Lost City: The Discovery of Machu Picchu*	**Teacher Led** p. DI•38 • Extend comprehension • **Revisit** *Lost City: The Discovery of Machu Picchu*

ELL Place English language learners in the groups that correspond to their reading abilities in English.

Practice Stations
• Words to Know
• Get Fluent
• Word Wise

Independent Activities
• Background Building Audio
• *Reader's and Writer's Notebook*
• Research and Inquiry

Differentiated Instruction

 **A** **Advanced**

Investigate Have students look in books or on the Internet for information about an expedition and have them write a brief newspaper article as if they were there.

Double Day Read! Multidraft Reading

For **Whole Group** instruction, choose one of the reading options below. For each reading, have students set the purpose indicated.

Option 1
Day 2 Read the selection. Use Guide Comprehension to monitor and clarify understanding.
Day 3 Reread the selection. Use Extend Thinking to develop higher-order thinking skills.

Option 2
Day 2 Read the first half of the selection, using both Guide Comprehension and Extend Thinking instruction.
Day 3 Read the second half of the selection, using both Guide Comprehension and Extend Thinking instruction.

 **ELL**

English Language Learners
Build background To build background, review the selection summary in *English (ELL Handbook,* p. 157). Use the Retelling Cards to provide visual support for the summary.

Objectives

◎ Compare and contrast ideas in texts.

OPTION 1 Guide Comprehension Skills and Strategies

Teach Compare and Contrast

🔊 **Compare and Contrast** Ask students how the boy and Hiram Bingham are alike and different. (They are both looking at a beautiful sight and thinking about a mystery. The boy is young and lives on a farm. Bingham is a grown man visiting a city in Peru. The boy is looking at a landscape, while Bingham is looking at walls.)

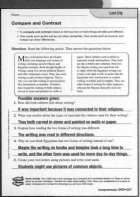

Let's Practice It!
TR DVD•257

Corrective Feedback

If... students cannot use text details to compare and contrast,

then... use the Model to help them compare and contrast as they read.

Model the Skill

Think Aloud I wonder why I am learning about both the boy and Hiram Bingham because they seem very different. I can see that they are alike because they are both looking at a beautiful site and thinking about mysteries.

In his first journey to South America, Yale professor Hiram Bingham longed to explore the hidden lands that lay beyond the snowcapped peaks of the Andes. Legend had it that the lost city of the Inca, Vilcapampa, lay there. Bingham was determined to discover it. So in 1910, the Yale Peruvian Expedition was organized. Finally, in July 1911, Bingham and his fellow adventurers arrived in Cusco, the first capital city of the Inca. What lay ahead for them was far from what they had expected. And more amazing. Our story begins high in the mountains of Peru. . . .

The boy looked out at the cloud-covered peaks all around him. Already his papa was working in the terraced fields. But last night he had dreamed of a tall stranger carrying a small black box. He could not get the dream out of his mind.

Suddenly, the clouds burned off and the mountains were bathed in glorious light. The dream foretold of something wonderful, he was sure.

Sixty miles south, in Cusco, Hiram Bingham gazed thoughtfully at the old Incan stone wall. He had come to Peru in search of Vilcapampa, the lost city of the Inca. But right here was the most beautiful stonework he had ever seen—huge stones cut so perfectly that not even a razor blade could be slipped between them.

208

Student Edition pp. 208–209

OPTION 2 Extend Thinking Think Critically

Higher-Order Thinking Skills

🔊 **Compare and Contrast • Synthesis** On page 208, infer how the appearance of the glorious light is similar to the foretold dream. Use textual evidence to support understanding. The light illuminates the mountains and makes the wonderful view easy to see. At the same time, the boy believes that his dream about the dark box will become more clear and wonderful.

Draw Conclusions • Analysis Why does Bingham think that the stones of the lost city would look the same as the beautifully carved stones of the famous Temple of the Sun? Both the lost city and the Temple of the Sun were built by the Inca. Bingham knew that the Inca created beautiful stonework architecture.

How are their thoughts about the mystery different? (The boy is wondering what his dream means, and Bingham is wondering about the lost city.) As I read, I can look for other ways the boy and Bingham are alike and different.

The Inca had no iron tools to carve them, no wheel or draft animals to move them. The wall had withstood time and earthquakes. How had the Inca built it?

It was a mystery.

He walked through the cobbled streets of the old capital. The Spanish had come to this city, conquered the Inca, taken their gold, and built churches over their temples. Suddenly, he stopped. Before him was the famous Temple of the Sun. He placed his hands on the sun-warmed stones so beautifully carved, as if they had grown together.

Hidden in the mountains, the lost city would be built of stones like these. Would it hold gold and fabulous riches like the Spanish had found in Cusco?

More than ever he was determined to find that city.

Draw Conclusions • Evaluation Do you think it is important to visit historical sites? Why? Possible response: Yes. We can learn about history and the people of the past by studying what they made and how they lived. We can learn about a period of time different from our own.

On Their Own

Have students use a Venn diagram to compare and contrast as they read. Have them explain the information they wrote. For additional practice, use *Let's Practice It!* p. 257 on the *Teacher Resources DVD-ROM*.

Differentiated Instruction

SI Strategic Intervention

Clarify text Read aloud the introduction on page 208. Explain that Yale is a university in Connecticut. Have students use their own words to retell what the introductory paragraph is about. Be sure they also include the names of important people and places mentioned in the paragraph.

Connect to Social Studies

The Inca Empire was a wealthy and highly developed civilization of South American people centered in the Andes Mountains of Peru. The Incas were technologically advanced and created beautiful architecture, irrigation systems, and a vast system of roads. They were also goldsmiths and silversmiths. The empire's reign abruptly ended when treasure-seeking Spanish explorers conquered the Incas in the 1500s. The Quechua (KE chwah) people living in Peru today are descendants of the Incas.

ELL

English Language Learners
Vocabulary: Illustrations Remind students to refer to the selection's illustrations to help them with unfamiliar words and phrases, such as *stonework* and *cobbled streets*. To make sure they understand, ask them to point to the portions of the illustrations that helped them know the meanings of the words.

OPTION 1 Skills and Strategies, continued

Teach Visualizing

Visualizing Remind students that visualizing what they read will help them monitor and adjust their comprehension. Ask students what they visualize when they read the third paragraph on p. 210 about a sleepy old village. (The village is a quiet little town with terraces stretching up into the clouds.)

Corrective Feedback

If... students cannot use text details to visualize,

then... use the Model to help them visualize as they read.

Model the Strategy

Think Aloud As I read about the old village, I imagine that the rocks of the ancient stone terraces are worn down smooth with age. I visualize small cracks and chips in the large blocks of stone requiring the members of the group to step carefully.

The next day Bingham began his search. He would look for ruins—that might be the key.

He and his party, accompanied by military escort Sergeant Carrasco, left by mule train for the sacred valley of the Urubamba River.

They came to the sleepy old village of Ollantaytambo, long ago an important city. Its ancient stone terraces stepped up into the clouds.

"Are there any ruins nearby?" Bingham asked. He went door to door. He sat for hours in the cantina. "Are there any ruins near here?" he asked anyone who came in. "Do you know of the lost city of Vilcapampa?" No one knew of it.

Traveling north, the adventurers came upon a remote and wild canyon. Granite cliffs rose thousands of feet above the roaring rapids of the Urubamba River. In the distance were snowcapped mountains over three miles high. Bingham's

Student Edition pp. 210–211

OPTION 2 Think Critically, continued

Higher-Order Thinking Skills

Visualize • Synthesis What images do you create in your mind when you read about the thundering rapids? I visualize rushing water tumbling over rocks. I imagine standing at the base of the waterfall and hearing the roar of the water falling over the cliff.

Inferring • Synthesis On page 210, the author says that Bingham and his party were accompanied by military escort Sergeant Carrasco. Why did the party need an escort? Why do you think the escort was a military escort? Use textual evidence to support understanding. The group was not familiar with the area, so they needed someone to show them the way. The city that they were visiting was an ancient city, so a government official probably needed to make sure that nobody ruined the historical city.

What else do you picture in your mind when you think of a sleepy village? (Possible response: I imagine a very small village with nobody in sight. Maybe it is abandoned or there are few people left. I picture a cold, isolated city because it is located high in the mountains.) As I read, I can use the author's words to visualize what is happening.

determination to find the lost city grew with each turn of the increasingly wild trail.

Meanwhile, high on one of these granite ridges, the boy tried to help his papa on the terraces. But he couldn't shake the dream from his mind. Who was this stranger with the black box? When would he come? What was in the black box? Anxiously, he searched the mountains for a sign.

Far below in the valley, Bingham's party camped on a sandy beach alongside the thundering rapids of the Urubamba. Days had gone by. He was tired and discouraged. No one knew of any ruins.

But now the travelers aroused the curiosity of a local farmer named Arteaga.

"Are there ruins nearby?" Bingham asked when Arteaga ventured into camp.

This time, through the interpreter, the farmer said, "Yes. There are very good ruins on top of the mountain called Machu Picchu."

The farmer pointed straight up.

211

Author's Purpose • Analysis The author's main purpose with this selection is to share true information with the reader. What additional purpose does he have? How do you know? An additional purpose is to tell a story. The author presents the facts as a narrative. The events are presented in chronological order. The story has a setting, characters, and a plot.

On Their Own

Have students read the last paragraph on page 210 and compare and contrast what they visualize now with the images they pictured when they read about the old village.

Have students read the last paragraph on page 210

Differentiated Instruction

A **Advanced**

Root search Point out that the Latin root *ven* means "to come." *Ventured* means "dared to come." Provide students with a list of familiar Greek and Latin roots. Then have pairs brainstorm a list of words that contain Greek or Latin roots and have them derive the meaning of each word based on its root.

Connect to Social Studies

In 1532, Spanish explorer Francisco Pizarro captured the Inca Emperor Atahualpa (a tuh WAL puh). Legend has it that the ransom Atahualpa's people paid was a room filled once with gold and twice with silver. However, the Spanish still executed the ruler. Then they installed his nephew, Manco Inca, as a ruler they thought they could control. Manco Inca later fled to a place called Vilcapampa, high in the rugged Andes Mountains. According to legend, he carried with him a great treasure of gold. Hiram Bingham was searching for Vilcapampa when he found Machu Picchu.

English Language Learners

Multiple-meaning words Explain to students that *party* is a multiple-meaning word. One meaning is "a festive gathering." Help students use context clues to figure out the meaning of *party* in *Bingham's party camped* on p. 211, paragraph 2. (group, friends, expedition, or companions) Have students restate the phrase, replacing the word *party* with one of those synonyms.

Objectives
◎ Compare and contrast ideas in texts.

OPTION 1 Skills and Strategies, continued

Teach Compare and Contrast

◉ **Compare and Contrast** Remind students to compare and contrast to monitor and adjust their comprehension about what they read. Ask what the three men were each thinking and feeling as they climbed. (Arteaga was imagining snakes, Carrasco was thinking about his shoes, and Bingham was picturing the lost city. All three were experiencing exhaustion and heat.)

Corrective Feedback

If… students cannot use text details to compare and contrast,

then… review the Teacher Note on p. 213a and then use the Model to help them compare and contrast and identify implicit relationships as they read.

Model the Skill

Think Aloud I can use details to help me compare and describe implicit (unstated) relationships about the three men and what they were thinking and feeling. Arteaga was concerned about danger because of snakes.

> "Can you take us there?" Bingham asked.
>
> "No," said Arteaga. "It is a very hard climb and there are many snakes." Bingham offered him coins. Arteaga nodded—he would show them the way.
>
> Arteaga led them down the river trail. Suddenly, he plunged into the jungle. Bingham and the sergeant followed Arteaga through dense undergrowth down to the very edge of the river to a flimsy bridge made of slim logs. What was he getting himself into!
>
> Sergeant Carrasco and Arteaga took off their shoes and crossed easily, gripping with their bare feet. Bingham was terrified—he crept across the bridge on hands and knees. One slip and he would be dashed to pieces in the roaring torrent below.
>
> They climbed the bank into dense jungle. Now the slopes were slippery and the heat terrible. Arteaga had warned them of the fer-de-lance, a very venomous snake. Bingham's eyes searched the jungle.
>
> Up and up they climbed. The wide river was now but a silver thread, far below. Arteaga could think of nothing but the fer-de-lance;

212

Student Edition pp. 212–213

OPTION 2 Think Critically, continued

Higher-Order Thinking Skills

◉ **Compare and Contrast • Analysis** How does Bingham's trip across the bridge differ from the two other men's? Why do you think so? Bingham is terrified and crawls across the bridge on his hands and knees. Carrasco and Arteaga remove their shoes and cross easily. Bingham is not used to the environment, but the other men are used to the region.

◉ **Visualize • Analysis** What do you visualize when the author uses the phrase "silver thread"? A silver thread is thin and difficult to see so I imagine the river below as a snaking, thin sliver of blue that slices through the dense green jungle.

Carrasco was probably thinking about his pain because he left his shoes behind. How do you think Bingham was feeling? (**excited and hopeful because he kept thinking about seeing the lost city**) As I read, I can look for other implicit relationships among ideas in the story.

On Their Own

Have students describe other implicit relationships among ideas in the story, as they make comparisons while reading.

Sergeant Carrasco thought about his good, sturdy shoes; Bingham thought of nothing but the lost city. They cut their way through tangled thickets. Up and up they climbed.

Had an hour passed? Two? Three? Now they crept on all fours. They slipped and slid. In some places, they held on by their fingertips.

Finally, thirsty and exhausted, they broke through the jungle into sunlight. Above them stood a little Quechua boy beside a stone hut. What could he be doing at the top of this mountain?

Background Knowledge • Synthesis • Text to World How is the bridge Bingham crossed similar and different to a bridge you have crossed or know about? Possible responses: The bridge I crossed was also unsteady and scary. The bridge in the story was made of slim logs, but the bridge I crossed was made of wooden planks.

Check Predictions Have students look back at the predictions they made earlier and discuss whether they were accurate. Then have students preview the rest of the section and either adjust their predictions accordingly or make new predictions.

Differentiated Instruction

 Strategic Intervention

Compare and contrast If students have difficulty comparing and contrasting, review similarities and differences as a group. Then, have students work in pairs to fill in a Venn diagram, with two similarities and two differences.

Teacher Note

Review implicit relationships among ideas in texts organized by comparison. Tell students that implicit relationships are unstated and that good readers use context clues and details to determine these unstated relationships.

ELL

English Language Learners

Vocabulary: Idioms The exclamation *What was he getting himself into!* (p. 212, paragraph 3) contains the idiom *getting himself into*. Restate the sentence as: *What was he doing? Why was he in that situation? What was going to happen next?* Have students describe unusual situations they have "gotten themselves into."

Visualizing Assist students with the visualizing strategy using the description "tangled thickets." Underline the word *thick* in *thicket*. Explain that a thicket is a thick area of vines and shrubs that grows in a jungle or forest. To help students visualize a thicket, tangle together pieces of string, cord, or ribbon.

 If you want to teach this selection in two sessions, stop here.

Objectives

• Find pertinent information from reference texts and online sources.

• Recognize and correctly use adverbs.

• Practice correctly spelling words with double consonants.

Research and Inquiry
Navigate/Search

Teach

Have students use their inquiry questions from Day 1 to find out more about what happens on archaeological digs. Help them to locate information about their topics using reference texts and the Internet. Remind them to use skimming and scanning techniques to identify useful data. Explain that they can also compose and e-mail questions to museums, university professors of archaeology, or other experts in the field. Remind students to take notes as they gather their information.

Model

Think Aloud As I look for information about archaeological expeditions, I will use only information that is relevant. Later on, I can include relevant facts and details to make the journal entry I write seem more authentic. The information I gather can also help me visualize an archaeological dig, as if I were really there.

Guide practice

Have students continue their review of sources they identified yesterday, gathering relevant information on their topics. Suggest that students also write down their reactions, thoughts, and feelings about what they have read about or seen in photographs. Point out that jotting down sensory words will help them to write an engaging journal entry.

On their own

Have students write down Web and e-mail addresses, book titles, and authors, so they can verify the accuracy of their notes.

Conventions
Adverbs

Teach

Write this sentence on the board: *Hiram Bingham gazed thoughtfully at the old Incan stone wall.* Point out that the adverb *thoughtfully* adds information about how Bingham gazed. Explain that many adverbs ending in *-ly* tell how something happened. Some, such as *sometimes* and *usually*, tell how often something happens. *Almost* and the adverb phrase *a lot* tell to what extent something happens.

Guide practice

Say these sentences. Have students supply an adverb to describe the verb in each sentence.

> **They crept on all fours.**
>
> **The clouds burned off.**

Daily Fix-It

Use Daily Fix-It numbers 3 and 4 in the right margin.

Connect to oral language

Have students look for and read aloud adverbs in *Lost City*. (*Suddenly*, p. 208; *Anxiously*, p. 211; *easily*, p. 212)

On their own

For additional practice use the *Reader's and Writer's Notebook* p. 330.

Spelling
Words with Double Consonants

Teach

Write *bottle* and *offer* on the board and ask students to tell how to break each word into syllables (*bot-tle; of-fer*). Point out that the syllable breaks occur between the double consonants, and that the consonants *f, l,* and *s* are often doubled at the end of a word, such as in *off*.

Guide practice

Write the remaining spelling words on the board. Have students write them and underline the double consonants in each word.

On their own

For additional practice, use the *Reader's and Writer's Notebook* p. 331.

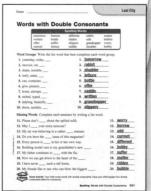

Reader's and Writer's Notebook p. 331

Academic Vocabulary

Adverbs tell about a verb, an adjective, or another adverb. An adverb can appear before or after the word it describes.

Double consonants are consonants that appear twice together in a word.

Daily Fix-It

3. After an long climb Bingham came across the city. *(a; climb, Bingham)*

4. The ruins were the better he had ever seed. *(best; seen)*

Reader's and Writer's Notebook p. 330

English Language Learners

Conventions To provide students with practice on adverbs, use the modified grammar lessons in the *ELL Handbook* and Grammar Jammer online at www.ReadingStreet.com.

Vocabulary: Adverbs Use gestures and classroom examples to demonstrate the meaning of adverbs such as *thoughtfully, suddenly,* and *anxiously*. Model demonstrating the meaning of the adverb and have students guess the word. Then have students work with partners to demonstrate and tell the meaning of these and other adverbs.

Writing—A Legend
Writer's Craft: Story Sequence

Introduce the prompt

Review the key features of legends. Remind students that they should think about these features as they begin their writing. Explain that they will begin the writing process for a legend today. Read aloud the writing prompt.

> **Writing Prompt**
>
> Write a legend about Hiram Bingham and the discovery of Machu Picchu.

Choose a deed

 Think Aloud To help choose a deed for our legendary hero Hiram Bingham, let's make a web of possible deeds he could have done. **Display a web.** First let's practice with our legend from yesterday, "The Legend of Pecos Bill and the Mountain Lion." We'll write the hero's name in the middle and his deeds in the outer ovals. We learned that Bill could outrun an antelope and fight a mountain lion. What were some of his other deeds? **Add the information to the web.** Now let's make a web for Hiram Bingham. Again we'll write the hero's name in the middle and his deeds in the outer ovals. In *Lost City,* we read that Hiram Bingham crept across a flimsy bridge in bare feet. I'll write that in an outer oval. **Add the information to the web.** Ask students to suggest other deeds from the selection, or those they make up, to generate ideas for an outline and first draft.

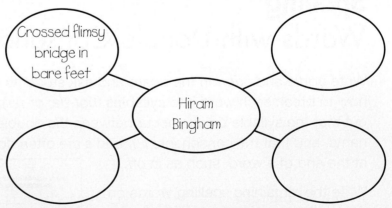

Gather Information

Remind students that they can do research to find more information about the deeds of Hiram Bingham. Remember to keep this web as the students will refer back to it tomorrow as they draft.

Corrective feedback

Circulate among the students as they identify character traits and deeds for their hero. Talk briefly with students who are having difficulty with making a choice and ask them which of the deeds they will focus on in their legend.

MINI-LESSON

Develop a Story Sequence Chart

▪ **Review the key features of a legend.** I'm going to write a legend about a hero named Stormalong. I'll use a story sequence chart to plan. A chart helps you organize ideas for writing.

▪ **Under *Characters*, write the story characters.** In the second box, I'll list my characters: Stormalong, sailors, a sea monster.

Under *Setting*, write where the story will be set. Next I'll write my settings: Cape Cod in the 1800s, on a ship in the ocean.

Under *Events*, make notes about the plot. Under *Events,* I'll write some of my hero's deeds: fights a sea monster, saves the ship.

Have students begin their own chart using *Reader's and Writer's Notebook* p. 332. They will fill in their charts with information about their chosen legend.

ROUTINE — Quick Write for Fluency — Team Talk

1. **Talk** Discuss the exaggerated deeds pairs will use in their stories.
2. **Write** Each student writes a few sentences about one deed.
3. **Share** Each pair shares their writing with other groups.

Routines Flip Chart

Wrap Up Your Day

✔ **Build Concepts** What did you learn about people like Hiram Bingham who go on such difficult adventures?

✔ **Compare and Contrast** How are the ancient city of Cusco and the legendary city of Vilcapampa alike? How are they different?

✔ **Visualize** Imagine how Hiram Bingham, Arteaga, and Sergeant Carrasco probably felt and looked crossing the river.

Differentiated Instruction

 Advanced

Include dramatic details Challenge students to include dramatic details when describing the character's deed in their legend. Tell them that dramatic details will help make exaggerated deeds more vivid.

Reader's and Writer's Notebook p. 332

Academic Vocabulary

Legends are stories that may be about historical periods or events that feature characters who perform great deeds and have exaggerated character traits.

Preview DAY 3

Tell students that tomorrow they will continue reading about the discovery of Machu Picchu.

Objectives
- Expand the weekly concept.
- Develop oral vocabulary.

Concept Talk

Question of the Week

What surprises can happen on an expedition?

Expand the concept

Remind students of the Question of the Week. Discuss how the question relates to the discovery of Machu Picchu. Tell students that today they will read about one of the most gigantic discoveries of the twentieth century. Encourage students to think about Hiram Bingham's expedition and the surprises that happen to him along the way.

Anchored Talk

Develop oral vocabulary

Use text features—illustrations and italicized text—to review pp. 206–213 of *Lost City: The Discovery of Machu Picchu*. Discuss the Amazing Words *gigantic* and *century*. Add these words to the concept map. Use the following questions to develop students' understanding of the concept. Remind students to answer questions with appropriate detail and to give suggestions based upon the ideas of others.

- Museums are full of ancient findings that we can study. What can we learn about the past by studying objects that are *centuries* old?

- Think about the small objects scientists discover on an expedition. How can even the smallest findings turn out to be *gigantic* discoveries?

Oral Vocabulary
Amazing Words

Teach Amazing Words

Amazing Words **Oral Vocabulary Routine**

1 Introduce Write the Amazing Word *culture* on the board. Have students say it with you. Yesterday, we learned about how the Incas lived and what their *culture* was like by looking at their ancient buildings and cities. Have students use the context of the sentence to determine a definition of *culture*. (*Culture* is the ways of a nation or people during a given time.)

2 Demonstrate Have students answer questions to demonstrate understanding. Based on what we learned yesterday about the Inca *culture*, why is their stonework so amazing? (In the Inca *culture*, there was no advanced technology to cut, move, and set large stones. The Incas used ropes, simple tools, and large animals to do the work.)

3 Apply Have students apply their understanding. Have them generate a list of questions, such as the following: What holidays or customs are common in our *culture*?

See p. OV•2 to teach *legend*.

Routines Flip Chart

Apply Amazing Words

As students read pp. 214–217 of *Lost City: The Discovery of Machu Picchu,* have students think about how the Amazing Words *culture* and *legend* apply to the discovery of Machu Picchu.

Connect to reading

Explain that today students will read more about Hiram Bingham's expedition in Peru. Help students establish a purpose for reading. As they read, students should think about how the Question of the Week and the Amazing Words *culture* and *legend* apply to Bingham's expedition and his discovery of a lost city.

E L L Expand Vocabulary Use the Day 3 instruction on ELL Poster 22 to help students expand vocabulary.

Amazing Words

region	century
cultivate	culture
adobe	legend
highland	research
gigantic	records

Academic Vocabulary

legend a story coming down from the past, which may be based on actual people or events

E L L Poster 22   *Lost City: The Discovery of Machu Picchu* **214b**

Objectives

◉ Compare and contrast to aid comprehension.

◉ Use the visualizing strategy to aid comprehension.

◉ Use Greek and Latin roots to determine the meanings of unknown words.

Comprehension Check

Have students discuss each question with a partner, monitoring and adjusting their comprehension. Ask several pairs to share their responses.

☑ **Genre • Analysis**

Why do you think the author chose not to include headings, charts, or maps? Possible response: The author presents facts in a narrative way. Headings, charts, and maps would not fit with the characters and plot of the selection.

☑ **Compare and Contrast • Synthesis**

How was Bingham's conversation with Arteaga similar to and different from his conversation with the villagers? Possible response: Bingham asked Arteaga and the villagers for the same information. He wanted to know if there were ruins nearby. Arteaga said that he knew of ruins nearby, while the villagers told Bingham that they did not.

☑ **Visualize • Evaluation**

Which sensory images on page 208 helped you visualize what the boy saw? Possible response: The phrase *cloud-covered peaks* helps me picture the boy standing really high up with mountains all around him. Later, the sun burned away the clouds, and there was a *glorious light*. This helps me "see" that the mountain peaks are now visible.

☑ **Greek and Latin Roots • Analysis**

Based on what you've read about the landscape of Peru, what is the meaning of the word *terraces*? Use your knowledge of Greek and Latin roots to determine the meaning of this English word. Possible response: The Latin root *terra* means "earth" or "land." I also know that a terrace is a high patio or deck and that it is flat. In this story, I think that a terrace is a high, flat surface of land.

☑ **Connect Text to World**

Why do you think people enjoy climbing high mountains, such as the mountains in Peru? Possible response: Climbing high mountains is challenging, but the view from the top of a mountain is beautiful and rewarding.

Strategy Response Log

INTERACT with TEXT

Have students use p. 28 in the *Reader's and Writer's Notebook* to revise and refine their mental pictures of *Lost City: The Discovery of Machu Picchu* based on what they have read so far.

Check Retelling

Have students retell the section of *Lost City: The Discovery of Machu Picchu* that they read on Day 2, summarizing information in the text in a logical order. Encourage students to use text features and sensory images in their retellings.

Corrective feedback

If... students leave out important details,
then... have students look back through the illustrations in the selection.

Small Group Time

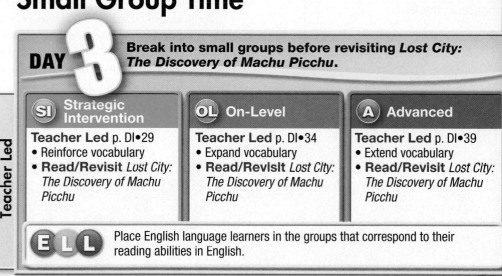

DAY 3

Break into small groups before revisiting *Lost City: The Discovery of Machu Picchu*.

Teacher Led

SI Strategic Intervention	**OL** On-Level	**A** Advanced
Teacher Led p. DI•29 • Reinforce vocabulary • **Read/Revisit** *Lost City: The Discovery of Machu Picchu*	**Teacher Led** p. DI•34 • Expand vocabulary • **Read/Revisit** *Lost City: The Discovery of Machu Picchu*	**Teacher Led** p. DI•39 • Extend vocabulary • **Read/Revisit** *Lost City: The Discovery of Machu Picchu*

ELL Place English language learners in the groups that correspond to their reading abilities in English.

Practice Stations
• Let's Write
• Get Fluent
• Word Work

Independent Activities
• AudioText of *Lost City*
• *Reader's and Writer's Notebook*
• Research and Inquiry

ELL

English Language Learners
Check retelling To support retelling, review the multilingual summary for *Lost City: The Discovery of Machu Picchu* with the appropriate Retelling Cards to scaffold understanding.

Objectives

- Describe how characters affect the plot's main events.

Let's Practice It!
TR DVD•258

OPTION 1 Skills and Strategies, continued

Teach Literary Elements

Review **Literary Elements: Character and Plot** Ask students to identify the characters in the story. (Hiram Bingham, Bingham's party, the boy, the boy's papa, Sergeant Carrasco, Arteaga) Ask them to summarize in logical order what happened just after Bingham saw the boy at the top of the mountain. (The boy greets them and sees the black box.)

Corrective Feedback

If... students have difficulty summarizing the events in logical order,
then... model how to identify important information in the text.

Multidraft Reading

If you chose...

Option 1 Return to Extend Thinking instruction starting on p. 208–209.
Option 2 Read pp. 214–217. Use the Guide Comprehension and Extend Thinking instruction.

OPTION 2 Think Critically, continued

Higher-Order Thinking Skills

Review Literary Elements: Character and Plot •
Evaluation Think about the characters in the story. Which character do you think is the bravest? Why? Possible response: Bingham. He is not familiar with the new surroundings and is afraid to cross the bridge. He conquers his fears and keeps looking for the ruins. He does not let anything stop him from reaching his goal.

Model the Skill

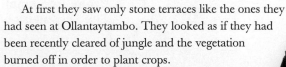

Think Aloud I know that if I pay attention to the order of events in the plot, I can better comprehend what is going on. What happens after Bingham asks the boy and his family about the ruins?

> "*Ama llulla, ama quella, ama su'a*" (Don't lie, don't be lazy, don't steal), the boy called out in the traditional Quechua greeting.
>
> It was the tall stranger from his dream. Carrying the black box!
>
> The boy's whole family crowded around to greet the exhausted travelers, then brought gourds of cool water and boiled sweet potatoes.
>
> Bingham, still gasping for breath, asked, "Where are the ruins?" The boy said, "*Amuy, amuy!*" (Come, come!)
>
> Bingham and the sergeant left Arteaga behind and followed at the boy's urging. "*Amuy, amuy!*" he kept saying.
>
> At first they saw only stone terraces like the ones they had seen at Ollantaytambo. They looked as if they had been recently cleared of jungle and the vegetation burned off in order to plant crops.

Student Edition pp. 214–215

Draw Conclusions • Evaluation Why do you think the boy's family greets the explorers so warmly? Would you have greeted them in the same way? Possible response: Perhaps they are welcoming, friendly people, or perhaps it is the custom where they live. Yes, I would also have greeted them warmly.

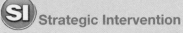

(Bingham follows the boy and sees stone terraces but no ruins. Then, in the jungle, he sees beautiful walls, a staircase, and finally, a stone temple.) I think this is an important point in the story since this might be the city Bingham has been looking for.

But there were no ruins. Just more jungle beyond. Bingham had climbed this mountain and found—no lost city.

"*Amuy, amuy!*" Still, the boy beckoned him into the jungle beyond. Weary and discouraged, Bingham followed. At first all he saw were bamboo thickets and more tangled vines. Then he looked closer. Through the vines, he saw—stones. Inca stones. Then walls, beautiful stone walls! They were covered with mosses. And trees.

"*Jaway, jaway!*" (See, see!) the boy whispered, pointing ahead to a curved stone wall. Bingham pushed his way to it and placed his hands on the fine granite stones. A sun temple. More beautiful even than the one in Cusco.

They came to a grand stone staircase. Where could this lead? What else was here?

"*Jaway, jaway,*" the boy called.

At the top of the staircase was a clearing. A small vegetable garden, and then . . . a temple built of enormous stones. Grander than any Bingham had ever seen. It stole his breath away.

Something was going on here, he could sense it.

Something just beyond his eyes. What was it?

215

Sensory Words • Analysis What sensory words does the author use to help you visualize Bingham's journey with the boy? The author says that Bingham is gasping for breath and that he is weary and discouraged. The author uses exclamations to show that the boy is excited to show Bingham the way to the ruins.

On Their Own

Have students use a chart to summarize the events in the text in logical order and explain why each event is important. For additional practice, use *Let's Practice It!* page 258 on the *Teacher Resources DVD-ROM*.

Differentiated Instruction

SI Strategic Intervention

Clarify Direct students' attention to the first sentence on p. 214. Explain that the boy's words show that he is afraid of strangers. The boy has most likely met travelers who do not work hard or who lie and steal from his people. Point out that the boy's attitude changes once his family welcomes Bingham and his party.

Connect to Social Studies

Hiram Bingham believed that his discovery at Machu Picchu was the legendary Vilcapampa, the lost city of the Incas. After Bingham's death in 1956, American archaeologist Gene Savoy excavated Espiritu Pampa, another site Bingham discovered in the region. Savoy and others were convinced this site was more likely to be the legendary Inca city than Machu Picchu.

English Language Learners

Figurative language Explain that the phrases in italics are what the boy says in his native language. The meanings follow in parentheses the first time each phrase appears. To make sure students understand, have them read the sentences with the English phrases in place of the boy's native language.

Objectives

◎ Identify Greek and Latin roots of words.

OPTION 1 Skills and Strategies, continued

Teach Greek and Latin Roots

🔊 **Greek and Latin Roots** Have students use Greek and Latin roots to determine the meaning of the word *perspiration* on p. 217.

Corrective Feedback

If... students are unable to figure out the meaning of *perspiration,*

then... model using Greek and Latin roots to figure out its meaning.

Reader's and Writer's
Notebook p. 333

Model the Skill

Think Aloud I'm not sure I remember the meaning of the word *perspiration*. I think the word *perspire* is the base word. The Latin prefix *per* means "through," and the Latin root *spir* means "to breathe."

He followed the boy to another temple. As magnificent. This one had three windows. But now he looked across the countryside. He looked past the thickets, past the vines. He began to see the outlines of stone streets and stone cottages. He began to see the outlines of a city!

"Here, boy," he said as he opened the black box that he had been carrying, extended the bellows and focused his camera.

The first picture would be of the boy. The boy who had led him to Vilcapampa, lost city of the Inca.

But about this Bingham was wrong. When the vines were removed and the tales told, he had discovered not Vilcapampa, but a place even more amazing.

He had stumbled on Machu Picchu, a city lost in time, a city lost in the clouds.

216

Student Edition pp. 216–217

OPTION 2 Think Critically, continued

Higher-Order Thinking Skills

🔊 **Greek and Latin Roots • Analysis** Based on what you know about Greek and Latin roots, what do you think the word *photograph* means? Possible response: I know that *photo* comes from an ancient Greek word meaning "light" and *graph* comes from a Greek word meaning "to write." If I combine the two meanings, then *photograph* must mean "written with light." I will look up the word in my dictionary to see if I am right. (A photograph is a picture made with a camera by exposing film or plates to the action of light rays.)

🔊 **Compare and Contrast • Synthesis** How does your knowledge of expeditions from this selection compare with fictional books or movies you know? Were you surprised by what you learned? Possible response: I was surprised at the physical work and the dangers Bingham and his crew went through as they hiked through jungles and climbed up mountains. I was also surprised that an entire city could be "lost." Expeditions seem easy and fun in the movies, and the scientists never seem to struggle.

If I combine the two meanings, then *perspire* means "to breathe through." What do you think you breathe through? Why? (the skin; the text says that the Quechua boy was dripping with perspiration after he ran down the mountain) What word can you think of that means the same as *perspiration*? *(sweat)*

On Their Own

Have students use Greek and Latin roots to figure out the meaning of the word *extended* on p. 216, paragraph 2. (*extend* means "to stretch out"; in Latin, *ex* means "out"; *tendere* means "to stretch") For additional practice, use *Reader's and Writer's Notebook* p. 333.

Differentiated Instruction

 Strategic Intervention

Figurative language Students may be unfamiliar with the expression *lost in the clouds* (p. 216, last sentence). Explain that Machu Picchu is on the top of a mountain, where clouds are close to the peak. Point out that Machu Picchu is hard to see because it is covered by the clouds, or *lost in the clouds,* making it difficult for Bingham to find. Have volunteers restate the expression; for example, *hidden by the clouds, hard to see,* or *foggy.*

 Advanced

Shifting perspective Discuss with students what they think is the author's point of view about his subject and what he wants his readers to think. Have students support their positions with examples from the selection. Ask them how a different point of view would affect the presentation of information in the selection.

AUTHOR'S NOTE

To research this book on the discovery of Machu Picchu, I first read Hiram Bingham's journal. In it he tells how a little Quechua boy led him to the site in the jungle. Then I traveled to Peru and followed in Hiram's footsteps as closely as I could.

I traveled to Ollantaytambo, as Hiram did, climbed the ancient terraces there, and sat in a little cantina, maybe the very one in which Hiram sat. I walked part of the rugged Inca trail to Pisac, and finally arrived at the Sun Gate above Machu Picchu.

I also journeyed through the sacred valley of the Urubamba River to Machu Picchu, and spent a week exploring and photographing the site and its surrounding cloud forest. And from the high pastures, I witnessed the magical sunset that I tried to capture on the jacket painting.

But the day the story began to come alive in my mind was the day I saw a young Quechua boy who raced our bus 2,500 feet down the mountain from Machu Picchu to the valley below—and won. As he stood, dripping with perspiration and chest heaving with exertion, I thought that Hiram's young guide must have looked just like this boy.

The most exciting part of working on the paintings was re-creating the way Machu Picchu must have looked when Hiram Bingham discovered it, hidden by five hundred years of jungle growth.

—Ted Lewin

217

Comprehension Check

Spiral Review

Cause and Effect • Analysis What effect did the sight of the young Quechua boy racing the bus have on Ted Lewin? It caused the story of Hiram's adventure to begin to come alive in his mind.

Author's Purpose • Analysis How do the author's beliefs about expeditions affect his purpose for writing this selection? Possible response: He believes that teams who work on expeditions discover ancient secrets and that their work is important for us to learn about people of the past. He thinks that exploring is hard work but that it is filled with excitement and surprises. He tells an exciting story so that the reader will also feel the same way about expeditions and discovering the past.

Check Predictions Have students return to the predictions they made earlier and confirm whether they were accurate.

 English Language Learners
Language transfer: Cognates Students literate in Spanish may recognize the cognates *fotografia* (photography), *magnifico* (magnificent), *explorar* (explore), and *magico* (magical).

Objectives

◎ Compare and contrast to aid in comprehension.

◎ Visualize to check understanding.

Check Retelling
SUCCESS PREDICTOR

Think Critically

1. In several ways, this selection is similar to the Unit 4 selection, *Encantado: Pink Dolphin of the Amazon*. Skim the earlier selection found on pages 58–71 in this book. Then discuss what the two selections have in common. **Text to Text**

2. The illustrations in this selection are big and bold, and run across two pages. Why do you think the author used the illustrations in this way? **Think Like an Author**

3. In what ways were Hiram Bingham and the stranger in the boy's dream alike? **Compare and Contrast**

4. The author describes the moment Hiram Bingham first sees Machu Picchu on page 215. Visualize as you reread that part of the selection. Describe what you see, hear, smell, and feel. **Visualize**

5. **Look Back and Write** Look back at pages 208–209. Why do you think Hiram Bingham considered the old stone wall in Cusco to be such a mystery? Provide evidence to support your answer. **TEST PRACTICE** Extended Response

Meet the Author

TED LEWIN

Ted Lewin loves to travel. He writes and illustrates books about his trips. For *Lost City*, he hiked the jungle trail to Machu Picchu in Peru. He has also photographed gorillas in Uganda and rhinos in Nepal. He has watched a tiger from an elephant's back in India. And he has been much too close to grizzly bears, rattlesnakes, and bison.

When he travels, Mr. Lewin uses a journal, a sketchbook, photographs, and recordings to help him remember what he sees. His wife, Betsy, comes with him. She is also an artist, and they sometimes write books together.

Mr. Lewin grew up in Buffalo, New York, where he says he had "two brothers, one sister, two parents, a lion, an iguana, a chimpanzee, and an assortment of more conventional pets." The lion stayed only a short time—his mother donated it to the Buffalo Zoo.

Here are other books by Ted and Betsy Lewin.

Student Edition pp. 218–219

Plan to Assess Retelling

☑ **Week 1** Assess Strategic Intervention students.

☑ **This week assess Advanced students.**

☐ **Week 3** Assess Strategic Intervention students.

☐ **Week 4** Assess On-Level students.

☐ **Week 5** Assess any students you have not yet checked during this unit.

Retelling

Have students work in pairs to retell the selection, using the Envision It! Retelling Cards as prompts. Remind students that they should accurately describe the main topic and important ideas and use key vocabulary as they retell. Monitor students' retellings.

Scoring rubric

Top-Score Response A top-score response makes connections beyond the text, describes the main topic and important ideas using accurate information, evaluates facts and opinions, and draws conclusions from the text.

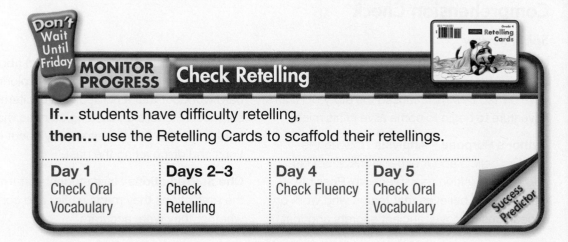

Don't Wait Until Friday

MONITOR PROGRESS Check Retelling

If... students have difficulty retelling,

then... use the Retelling Cards to scaffold their retellings.

Day 1	Days 2–3	Day 4	Day 5
Check Oral Vocabulary	Check Retelling	Check Fluency	Check Oral Vocabulary

Success Predictor

Think Critically

Text to text

1. Both selections discuss mysteries. Both have tropical settings in other countries. Both authors use words and pictures to help the reader visualize what is happening in the selection.

Think like an author

2. By looking at the illustrations, I can infer that the author may have wanted to show how big the landscape is. He may have wanted to show the reader what it really looked like to Hiram Bingham.

◉ Compare and Contrast

3. Both were tall and carried a small black box.

◉ Visualize

4. Possible responses: I see cobbled streets and buildings of a city, but they are covered in vines; I hear animals in the jungle and footsteps on rock as people climb the temple stairs; I smell the damp jungle and the flowers that grow there.

 **Writing on Demand**

5. **Look Back and Write** To build writing fluency, assign a 10–15 minute time limit.

Suggest that students use a prewriting strategy, such as brainstorming or using a graphic organizer, to organize their ideas. Remind them to establish a topic sentence and support it with facts, details, or explanations. As students finish, encourage them to reread their compositions, revise for organization and support, and proofread for errors in grammar and conventions.

Scoring rubric

> **Top-Score Response** A top-score response uses details to tell about why the old stone wall in Cusco was a mystery.
>
> **A top-score response should include:**
>
> - The stonework was amazing because the stones were cut perfectly and fit tightly with no large cracks between them.
>
> - It is a wonder that the Inca could do such amazing stonework because they did not have iron tools to carve the stones, nor a wheel or animals to move them.
>
> - The wall lasted for a long time through many earthquakes.

Differentiated Instruction

SI **Strategic Intervention**
Have pairs fill in a web with details about what Hiram saw and how the structure of the wall is described in the narrative.

Meet the Author

Have students read about author Ted Lewin on p. 219. Ask them how he uses a narrative style and illustrations to tell readers about Hiram Bingham's search for the lost city in *Lost City: The Discovery of Machu Picchu*.

Independent Reading

After students enter their independent reading information into their Reading Logs, have them take turns giving book talks about books they are reading now or have read.

 ELL

English Language Learners
Retelling Use the Retelling Cards to summarize the selection with students. Display the cards out of sequence. Prompt students by asking: What happens next? and Then what happens in the story? Have volunteers place the cards in the proper sequence. Once the cards are placed in their proper sequence, have pairs retell the story to one another.

Model Fluency
Phrasing

Model fluent reading

Have students turn to p. 215 of *Lost City: The Discovery of Machu Picchu*. Have students follow along as you read this page. Tell them to listen to your phrasing as you group words together and pause at punctuation while you read about the discovery of Machu Picchu.

Guide practice

Have students follow along as you read the page again. Then have them reread the page as a group without you until they read with correct phrasing and with no mistakes. Ask questions to be sure students comprehend the text. Continue in the same way on p. 216.

Reread for Fluency

Corrective feedback

If... students are having difficulty reading with correct phrasing, **then...** prompt:

• Where can we break up this sentence? Which words are related?
• Read the sentence again. Pause after each group of words.
• Tell me the sentence. Now read it with pauses after each group of words.

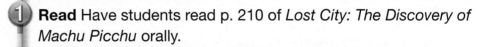

ROUTINE Oral Rereading

1. **Read** Have students read p. 210 of *Lost City: The Discovery of Machu Picchu* orally.

2. **Reread** To achieve optimal fluency, students should reread the text three or four times.

3. **Corrective Feedback** Have students read aloud without you. Provide feedback about their phrasing and encourage them to adjust their voice level to stress important words and to group words together into phrases. Listen for correct phrasing.

Routines Flip Chart

Research and Study Skills
Outline

Teach

Explain that chapter headings and subheadings can be used to locate information in a text. Ask students what information can be organized in an outline. Show an outline from a science or a social studies text and use it to review these terms:

- An **outline** is an organized overview of information, sometimes taken as notes from a reference book. The title is at the top.

- **Topics** are the most important ideas. They are labeled with Roman numerals. **Subtopics**, or secondary topics, are listed under a topic and tell more about it. They are labeled with capital letters.

- **Details**, or specific information, are listed under a subtopic and tell more about it. They are labeled with numbers.

Have students break into groups, and have each group create a short outline that summarizes a page or a short section of a reference text. Encourage students to use the topic sentences and concluding sentences in the text to write their outlines.

Guide practice

Discuss these questions:

How do you know what information an outline shows? (The title of the outline is listed at the top.)

What text features help you locate information? (Look for the topic next to each Roman numeral.)

What do all outlines have in common? (They organize information from important or general to very specific.)

On their own

Have students complete pp. 334–335 of the *Reader's and Writer's Notebook*.

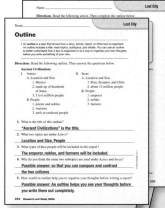

Reader's and Writer's Notebook pp. 334–335

ELL

English Language Learners
Outlines Have partners create outlines that tell about an indoor activity and an outdoor activity they like to do. After they have written down these topics, have them list subtopics and details that tell more about the two topics. Have them share their outlines with the class.

Objectives
- Analyze data for usefulness.
- Identify and correctly use adverbs.
- Spell frequently misspelled words.

Research and Inquiry
Analyze

Teach

Tell students that today they will analyze their findings and may need to change the focus of their original inquiry question before writing their journal entry.

Model

 Think Aloud Originally I thought an archaeological expedition was carried out pretty much as planned, with an occasional surprise. But when I received answers to the questions I e-mailed to an archaeologist, I found out that expeditions always have a few surprises. My research helped me realize that archaeologists must be flexible. I will refocus my inquiry question to include information about what happens after the unexpected things occur on an expedition. Now my inquiry question is *What happens when surprises, accidents, or mistakes occur during an archaeological expedition?*

Guide practice

Have students analyze their findings and draw conclusions. They may need to refocus their inquiry question to better fit the information they found. Remind students that if they have difficulty improving the focus of their research plan, they can ask a reference librarian or a local expert for guidance.

Remind students that they can use an outline to help them organize their data by topics, subtopics, and details. Point out that an outline is a useful tool for organizing information and drawing conclusions through brief written explanations.

On their own

Have pairs make an outline of the information they would like to include in their journal entries. Then have them write a brief paragraph, drawing conclusions about their findings.

Conventions
Adverbs

Review

Remind students that this week they learned about adverbs.

- An adverb tells how, where, or when an action happens, or how frequently or how much.
- Adverbs can be used to combine two sentences.

Daily Fix-It

Use Daily Fix-It numbers 5 and 6.

Connect to oral language

Have students combine the following sentences by adding an adverb from sentence B to sentence A.

> **A.** The library opened. **B.** Recently, it opened.
>
> **A.** He played the piano. **B.** Yesterday, he played it.

On their own

For additional practice, use *Let's Practice It!* page 259 on the *Teacher Resources DVD-ROM*.

Let's Practice It!
TR DVD•259

Differentiated Instruction

SI Strategic Intervention

Small group Working with a small group, create a T-Chart. On the chart, write a verb. Ask group members to suggest an adverb that tells how, when or where about the verb. Record their suggestions.

Daily Fix-It

5. What an amazing place this were for a city. *(was/is; city!)*

6. How do people centuries ago build anything so high in the mountains. *(did; mountains?)*

Spelling
Words with Double Consonants

Frequently misspelled words

The words *again, different, were,* and *want* are words that seem simple, but that students often misspell. The words *tomorrow* and *grasshopper* from your spelling list are also difficult to spell. I'm going to read a sentence. Choose the correct word to complete the sentence and then write it correctly.

> **1.** Get more practice by doing it _____.
>
> **2.** _____ I'll finish the chores I don't get to today.
>
> **3.** Mike will _____ to go to the amusement park.
>
> **4.** The _____ is hard to see in the tall, green grass.
>
> **5.** We like to play _____ sports.
>
> **6.** We _____ trying to win the game.

On their own

For additional practice, use the *Reader's and Writer's Notebook* p. 336.

Reader's and Writer's
Notebook p. 336

Objectives

- Understand the criteria for writing an effective legend.
- Write the draft of a legend that builds the plot to a climax.
- Include details about character and setting while drafting.

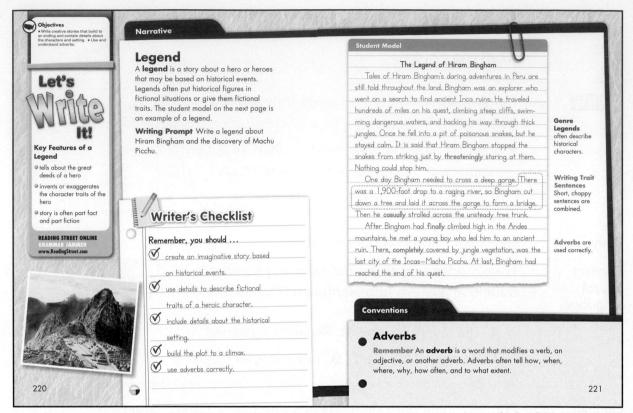

Student Edition pp. 220–221

Let's Write It!
A Legend

Teach

Use pp. 220–221 in the Student Edition. Direct students to read the key features of a legend which appear on p. 220. Then have students read the remainder of p. 220. Remind students that they can refer to the information in the Writer's Checklist as they write their legend.

Read the student model on p. 221. Point out the great deeds and exaggerated traits in the model, as well as the descriptive adverbs.

Connect to conventions

Point out that adverbs tell more about verbs and add interest and information to a story. Talk about the correct use of adverbs in the model.

Writing—Legend
Writer's Craft: Sentences

Display rubric

Display Scoring Rubric 22 from the *Let's Practice It! DVD* and go over the criteria for each trait under each score. Then, using the model in the Student Edition, choose students to explain why the model should score a 4 for one of the traits. If a student offers that the model should score below 4 for a particular trait, the student should offer support for that response. Remind students that this is the rubric that will be used to evaluate the legend they write.

Scoring Rubric: Legend

	4	3	2	1
Focus/Ideas	Vivid picture of character; many great deeds and exaggerated traits described; realistic details included	Fairly vivid picture of character; some great deeds and exaggerated traits described; some realistic details included	Few details about character's great deeds and exaggerated traits; few realistic details included	No great deeds or exaggerated traits described; story is completely unrealistic
Organization	Organized with clear beginning, middle, and end	Organized with beginning, middle, and end	Lacks clear beginning, middle, and end	Lacks organization
Voice	Lively, engaging	Mostly lively, somewhat engaging	Sometimes dull, uninvolved	Writer entirely uninvolved
Word Choice	Uses specific, vivid words, especially descriptive adverbs	Uses clear language; uses some descriptive adverbs	Uses some vague or repetitive words; no descriptive adverbs	Inaccurate, limited word choice
Sentences	Correct and varied sentences; few short choppy sentences	Most sentences correct; some variety; several short, choppy sentences	Some sentences incorrect; little variety; many short, choppy sentences	Incorrect sentences; no variety; mostly short, choppy sentences
Conventions	Few, if any errors; excellent use of adverbs	Several minor errors; good use of adverbs	Many errors; sparse and incorrect use of adverbs	Numerous errors; few adverbs; adverbs used incorrectly

Story Sequence Chart

Have students get out the story sequence charts they worked on yesterday. If their charts are not complete, have them complete them now.

Write

You will be using your story sequence chart as you write the paragraphs for the first draft of your legend. When you are drafting, don't worry if your story does not sound exactly as you want it. You will have a chance to revise it tomorrow.

Objectives

- Write a first draft of a legend.
- Recognize and use a variety of sentences.
- Incorporate elements of a legend.

Writing, continued
Writer's Craft: Sentences

MINI-LESSON

Write a Variety of Sentences

■ **Introduce** Explain to students that good writers include a variety of sentence types in their writing. They avoid short, choppy sentences. On the board, write an example of a simple sentence with a single subject, one with a compound subject, and one with a compound predicate. Point out the features of each. Then write a compound sentence. Discuss with students the difference between a simple and a compound sentence. Then write a complex sentence and discuss independent and dependent clauses. Display the Drafting Tips for students. Remind them that the focus of drafting is to get ideas down in an organized way. Then display Writing Transparency 22A.

The Legend of Stormalong

On a stormy night in the 1800s, a huge wave smacked loudly against the beach at Cape Cod. Its noise was drowned out by a baby crying louder than the sound of the wave. People rushed to the beech. A baby twelve feet tall sat there and looked around curiously. The local folks called him Stormalong and took care of him while he grew up.

Stormalong liked the ocean. When he was eighteen, he became a sailor. He wanted to explore the world. One day when Stormalong was aboard Ship, the sea began bubbling and boiling violent, and the ship began to shake. stormalong dived under the ship to see what the problem was

A tremendus Sea monster with ten tentacles was trying to drag the ship to the ocean bottom. Stormalong was determined to stop him. He grabbed two of the tentacles and tied them together in a sailor's knot. On the fourth day, the monster hurled Stormalong out of the water. Now stormalong was big. He was thirty feet tall by now. but this monster was bigger. The two fought furiouser for three days. Stormalong landed far away. The sea monster swam to the bottom of the ocean.

His shipmates searched for Stormalong. When they found him, they thanked him for saving their lives and there ship. But Stormalong hung his head as he boarded the ship He was ashamed that the monster had escaped. He was so ashamed that he gave up being a sailor and walked all the way to Kansas, where he became a farmer. There, he grew the tallest corn anyone ever saw?

Unit 5 Lost City   Writing: Model **22A**

Writing Transparency 22A, TR DVD

Drafting Tips

✓ Organize your ideas into a beginning, middle, and end.

✓ Show events in sequence.

✓ Think about how to describe the characters and their deeds.

✓ Don't worry about grammar and mechanics when drafting. You will concentrate on these things during the editing process.

Think Aloud I'm going to write the first paragraph of my legend, *The Legend of Stormalong.* I want to introduce my hero and my setting. When I draft, I develop my ideas. I don't worry about revising or proofreading because that will come later. I will refer to my story sequence chart to make sure I include the great deeds of my hero.

Direct students to use the drafting tips to guide them in writing their drafts. Remind them to make sure that their draft includes a variety of sentences.

ROUTINE **Quick Write for Fluency** **Team Talk**

1. **Talk** Pairs talk about the kinds of sentences they'll include in their writing.

2. **Write** Each person writes a few different kinds of sentences.

3. **Share** Partners read each other's writing and identify the kinds of sentences.

Routines Flip Chart

Differentiated Instruction

 A Advanced

Summarize Working in pairs, have students summarize the differences between a simple and a compound sentence. Have each pair write an example of each kind of sentence. Have pairs share their examples and discuss the characteristics of each.

Wrap Up Your Day

✔ **Build Concepts** What surprises did Hiram Bingham have on his expedition to Peru?

✔ **Compare and Contrast** How is the boy in the story like the boy Ted Lewin saw? How is he different?

✔ **Visualize** What details in the selection helped you visualize what the jungle looked like?

 **Preview DAY 4**

Tell students that tomorrow they will read a new selection about a trip to Machu Picchu.

Objectives
- Expand the weekly concept.
- Build oral vocabulary.

Today at a Glance

Oral Vocabulary
research, records

Genre
Literary Nonfiction: Personal Essay

Reading
Riding the Rails to Machu Picchu

Let's Learn It!
Fluency: Appropriate phrasing
Vocabulary: Greek and Latin roots
Media Literacy: Radio announcement

Research and Inquiry
Synthesize

Spelling
Words with double consonants

Conventions
Adverbs

Writing
Legend

Concept Talk

Question of the Week

What surprises can happen on an expedition?

Expand the concept

Remind students that this week they have read about surprising discoveries and expeditions. Tell students that today they will read an author's personal narrative about her adventurous trip to Machu Picchu.

Anchored Talk

Develop oral vocabulary

Use text features—illustrations and italicized text—to review pp. 214–217 of *Lost City: The Discovery of Machu Picchu.* Discuss the Amazing Words *culture* and *legend.* Add these and other concept-related words to the concept map. Use the following questions to develop students' understanding of the concept. Remind students to ask and answer questions with appropriate detail and to build on other students' answers.

- Think about the daily life and *culture* of the Incas. How is our daily life and *culture* similar? How is it different? (They ate, slept, worked, and lived together in cities, just like we do today. They farmed and built things like we do today. They used simpler tools, while we use advanced technology.)

- What inferences can you make about why people enjoy telling and listening to *legends*? (Possible response: People enjoy legends because the legends are stories that come from the past. People like hearing stories based on people and places from long ago.)

Strategy Response Log

INTERACT with TEXT

Have students continue to monitor and clarify their comprehension. If students are successful in comprehending the text, have them write a brief summary of the selection.

Oral Vocabulary
Amazing Words

Amazing Words

region	century
cultivate	culture
adobe	legend
highland	research
gigantic	records

Teach Amazing Words

Amazing Words Oral Vocabulary Routine

1 Introduce Write the word *research* on the board. Have students say it aloud with you. We read about how Bingham's *research* and knowledge of the Incas led him to discover the lost city of Machu Picchu. How do you think *research* can make an expedition more successful? (Possible response: Research helps scientists know where and what to look for.) Have students determine the definition of the word. *Research* is to study or investigate something.

2 Demonstrate Have students answer questions to demonstrate understanding. What tools do we use today to conduct *research*? (Possible responses: the Internet; scientific experiments; journals; books)

3 Apply Have students apply their understanding. Have them list several *research* topics they would like to learn more about.

See p. OV•2 to teach *records*.

Routines Flip Chart

Apply Amazing Words

As students read "Riding the Rails to Machu Picchu" on pp. 222–225, have them think about how *research* and *records* have helped people learn more about Machu Picchu.

Connect to reading

As students read today's selection about a present day trip to Machu Picchu, have them think about how the Question of the Week and the Amazing Words *research* and *records* apply to ancient civilizations. Have them also think about what questions they might want answered as they read.

ELL **Produce Oral Language** Use the Day 4 instruction on ELL Poster 22 to extend and enrich language.

ELL Poster 22

Lost City: The Discovery of Machu Picchu **222b**

Let's Think About Genre
Literary Nonfiction: Personal Essay

Introduce the genre

Explain to students that different types of texts are called genres. Ask students what they know about the different genres of writing. Then ask them what purposes an author may have for writing a personal essay. (to inform or entertain)

Discuss the genre

Explain that a personal essay is one type of literary nonfiction. Point out that a personal essay is an author's account of his or her own experience written to inform and/or entertain readers. It gives facts and details about actual events that the author experiences. Then say: Because a personal essay is written in the first-person point of view, it also reveals the thoughts, feelings, and opinions of the author. In *Lost City: The Discovery of Machu Picchu,* an author writes about Hiram Bingham's experiences and the thoughts and feelings that the author imagines Bingham had. When you read a personal essay, you are introduced to the author's personality and opinions directly. The author tells the reader what he or she thinks and feels as the actual events unfold. Think of some experiences you have had. What were you feeling at the time? What do you think and feel now about what happened? **Possible responses: a trip, witnessing an exciting event, a celebration**

On the board, draw a T-chart. Label the columns *Facts* and *Feelings*. Write *A Trip to the Zoo* above. Use the following prompts:

• Let's talk about a trip to the zoo. If you've never been to the zoo, imagine what it would be like. What did you see and hear at the zoo? **Possible responses: different animals, noises, and smells; people; exhibits.** List items that students volunteer under *Facts.*

• What feelings or thoughts did you have as you experienced these things? List students' responses under *Feelings.* Elicit different viewpoints about how they felt about what they experienced.

Guide practice

Have students sit in pairs and tell each other about a trip they took to the zoo or to visit someone. Have them tell the facts and then their feelings about their experience. Point out that these details might be included in a personal essay about the trip.

Connect to reading

Tell students that they will now read a personal essay about a trip to Machu Picchu. Help students establish a purpose for reading. As they read, ask them to notice whether the author is stating a fact or an opinion about what she was experiencing.

Small Group Time

DAY 4 Break into small groups before reading or revisiting "Riding the Rails to Machu Picchu."

Teacher Led

SI Strategic Intervention

Teacher Led p. DI•30
• Practice Retelling
• Genre focus
• **Read/Revisit** "Riding the Rails to Machu Picchu"

OL On-Level

Teacher Led p. DI•35
• Practice Retelling
• Genre focus
• **Read/Revisit** "Riding the Rails to Machu Picchu"

A Advanced

Teacher Led p. DI•40
• Genre focus
• **Read/Revisit** "Riding the Rails to Machu Picchu"

ELL Place English language learners in the groups that correspond to their reading abilities in English.

Practice Stations
• Read for Meaning
• Get Fluent
• Words to Know

Independent Activities
• Audio Text: "Riding the Rails to Machu Picchu"
• *Reader's and Writer's Notebook*
• Research and Inquiry

Academic Vocabulary

personal essay a true account written by an author that reflects his or her experiences, thoughts, and feelings

English Language Learners

Cognates The Spanish words *ficción, narrativo,* and *literario* may be familiar to Spanish speakers as the cognates for *fiction, narrative,* and *literary*.

Objectives

- Identify features of a personal essay.
- Identify the author's purpose.

Student Edition pp. 222–223

Guide Comprehension

Teach the genre

Genre: Personal Essay Have students preview "Riding the Rails to Machu Picchu" on pp. 222–223. Point out that a personal essay is mainly written to inform the reader, but it can also entertain. Explain that an author's purpose is not usually stated in the text. Instead, the reader must figure out the purpose, adjusting their comprehension as needed. Have students read "Riding the Rails to Machu Picchu." Ask: What is the author's implied purpose for writing this essay?

Corrective feedback

If... students are unable to identify the author's implied purpose, **then...** use the model to guide students in identifying the author's purpose.

Model the genre

Think Aloud A personal essay can read like fiction, but I know that it is still based on actual events and experiences described by the author. I see that the author uses the words *I, me,* and *my* to describe her journey. These words are clues that the author is writing to inform the reader about actual events and her own experiences.

On their own

Have students write a short paragraph about an important personal experience. Point out that just like the writer of "Riding the Rails to Machu Picchu," their personal essays are autobiographical because they are writing about their own personal experiences.

Extend Thinking
Think Critically

Higher-order thinking skills

 Compare and Contrast • Evaluation Compare and contrast the three methods of getting to Machu Picchu. Which method do you think is the best? Possible responses: the hiking trail because it is the most challenging; helicopter because it is the fastest; train because it is a quick way to see the scenery by land.

 Visualize • Synthesis What do you visualize when the author says that you can whisk to Machu Picchu by helicopter? Possible response: I visualize in my mind the whirring of the helicopter, and I look down and see the rooftops in Cusco. Everything is a blur as the helicopter takes me high in the sky. I imagine that I am a bird soaring above the mountains.

Let's Think About...

I I think the author's purpose for writing was to inform readers about Machu Picchu by sharing her personal experiences. The author includes facts about Machu Picchu and how to travel there, as well as details about her own train ride.

Differentiated Instruction

SI Strategic Intervention
Clarify text Explain that the twelfth century was during the 1100s, so the Incas lived in Machu Picchu for about 400 years before they were conquered by the Spanish in 1533.

A Advanced
Inquiry Have students search the Internet to find out about other people, places, and cultures that existed during the twelfth century.

ELL
English Language Learners
Apply meaning Explain that the word *whisk* means "to move quickly." Have students demonstrate meaning by whisking their pencils and other materials off of their desks.

Objectives

- Use text features to aid comprehension.
- Compare and contrast across texts.

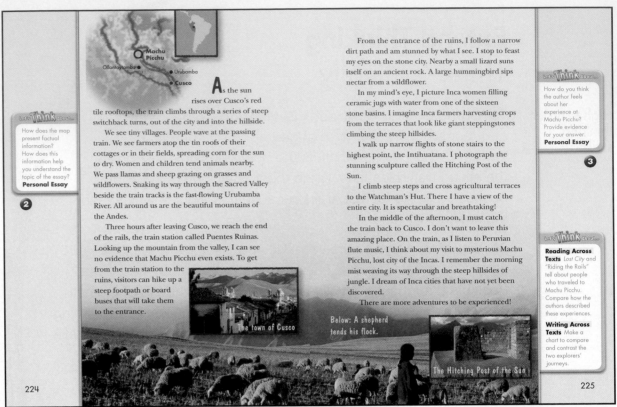

Let's **Think** *About...*

How does the map present factual information? How does this information help you understand the topic of the essay? **Personal Essay**

❷

As the sun rises over Cusco's red tile rooftops, the train climbs through a series of steep switchback turns, out of the city and into the hillside.

We see tiny villages. People wave at the passing train. We see farmers atop the tin roofs of their cottages or in their fields, spreading corn for the sun to dry. Women and children tend animals nearby. We pass llamas and sheep grazing on grasses and wildflowers. Snaking its way through the Sacred Valley beside the train tracks is the fast-flowing Urubamba River. All around us are the beautiful mountains of the Andes.

Three hours after leaving Cusco, we reach the end of the rails, the train station called Puentes Ruinas. Looking up the mountain from the valley, I can see no evidence that Machu Picchu even exists. To get from the train station to the ruins, visitors can hike up a steep footpath or board buses that will take them to the entrance.

The town of Cusco

From the entrance of the ruins, I follow a narrow dirt path and am stunned by what I see. I stop to feast my eyes on the stone city. Nearby a small lizard suns itself on an ancient rock. A large hummingbird sips nectar from a wildflower.

In my mind's eye, I picture Inca women filling ceramic jugs with water from one of the sixteen stone basins. I imagine Inca farmers harvesting crops from the terraces that look like giant steppingstones climbing the steep hillsides.

I walk up narrow flights of stone stairs to the highest point, the Intihuatana. I photograph the stunning sculpture called the Hitching Post of the Sun.

I climb steep steps and cross agricultural terraces to the Watchman's Hut. There I have a view of the entire city. It is spectacular and breathtaking!

In the middle of the afternoon, I must catch the train back to Cusco. I don't want to leave this amazing place. On the train, as I listen to Peruvian flute music, I think about my visit to mysterious Machu Picchu, lost city of the Incas. I remember the morning mist weaving its way through the steep hillsides of jungle. I dream of Inca cities that have not yet been discovered.

There are more adventures to be experienced!

Below: A shepherd tends his flock.

The Hitching Post of the Sun

Let's **Think** *About...*

How do you think the author feels about her experience at Machu Picchu? Provide evidence for your answer. **Personal Essay**

❸

Let's **Think** *About...*

Reading Across Texts *Lost City* and "Riding the Rails" tell about people who traveled to Machu Picchu. Compare how the authors described these experiences.

Writing Across Texts Make a chart to compare and contrast the two explorers' journeys.

Student Edition pp. 224–225

Guide Comprehension

Teach the genre

Genre: Personal Essay Explain that a personal essay can have elements to help readers understand the author's information. Have students identify text features on p. 224 and explain how the map gives additional information.

Corrective feedback

If... students are unable to identify the text features and explain the purpose of the map,

then... use the model to guide students in identifying text features and the map's purpose.

Model the genre

 Think Aloud As I read about riding the train out of the city, I will use the text features to imagine what the landscape is like and to understand where the train is going. The photos show what I might see from the window, but how can I know the train's route to Machu Picchu? **(The red path on the map between Cusco and Machu Picchu shows the train's route.)** The map inset shows the location of Machu Picchu in South America. The photos, map, and inset map support the text and help me understand author's description of her trip.

On their own

Have student pairs draw a map of the school and sketch a path from the classroom to another destination. Ask them to share their maps and briefly describe one or two things they would pass along the way.

Extend Thinking
Think Critically

Higher-order thinking skills

Inferring • Analysis When the author looks up the mountain from the valley, why can she see no evidence that Machu Picchu exists? Possible response: Because the mountain is so steep and Machu Picchu is so high up, we can infer that she wouldn't be able to see it from below.

Author's Purpose • Evaluation How do you think the selection would be different if the author did not write the selection as a personal essay? Which way do you think is best? Possible response: If the author presented facts and details but not her experiences, readers would have a harder time feeling as if they were there. I think the personal essay genre is best because I can better relate to the author's experiences and I feel as if I am going along on the journey.

Let's Think About...

2 The map shows places located in Peru. The reader can easily follow the graphic representation of the train route and the order of things that the author sees along the way.

3 She thought it was a fascinating adventure because she says that she doesn't want to leave this amazing place.

Reading Across Texts

Have students create a two-column chart comparing the description of Machu Picchu in each selection.

Writing Across Texts

Have students use details from their charts to explain how Hiram Bingham's expedition to Machu Picchu was similar to and different from Katacha Díaz's trip. Remind students to discuss the way the authors described these experiences.

Objectives
- Read with fluency and comprehension.
- Use Greek and Latin roots.
- Conduct a radio announcement.

Check Fluency WCPM
SUCCESS PREDICTOR

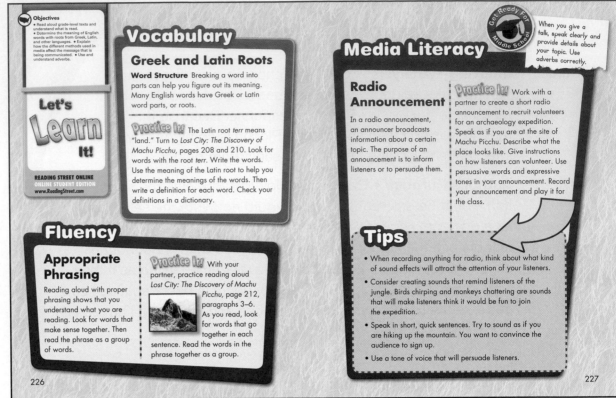

Objectives
- Read aloud grade-level texts and understand what is read.
- Determine the meaning of English words with roots from Greek, Latin, and other languages.
- Explain how the different methods used in media affect the message that is being communicated.
- Use and understand adverbs.

Let's
Learn
It!

READING STREET ONLINE
ONLINE STUDENT EDITION
www.ReadingStreet.com

Vocabulary

Greek and Latin Roots

Word Structure Breaking a word into parts can help you figure out its meaning. Many English words have Greek or Latin word parts, or roots.

Practice It! The Latin root *terr* means "land." Turn to *Lost City: The Discovery of Machu Picchu*, pages 208 and 210. Look for words with the root *terr*. Write the words. Use the meaning of the Latin root to help you determine the meanings of the words. Then write a definition for each word. Check your definitions in a dictionary.

Fluency

Appropriate Phrasing

Reading aloud with proper phrasing shows that you understand what you are reading. Look for words that make sense together. Then read the phrase as a group of words.

Practice It! With your partner, practice reading aloud *Lost City: The Discovery of Machu Picchu*, page 212, paragraphs 3–6. As you read, look for words that go together in each sentence. Read the words in the phrase together as a group.

Media Literacy

Get Ready For Middle School

When you give a talk, speak clearly and provide details about your topic. Use adverbs correctly.

Radio Announcement

In a radio announcement, an announcer broadcasts information about a certain topic. The purpose of an announcement is to inform listeners or to persuade them.

Practice It! Work with a partner to create a short radio announcement to recruit volunteers for an archaeology expedition. Speak as if you are at the site of Machu Picchu. Describe what the place looks like. Give instructions on how listeners can volunteer. Use persuasive words and expressive tones in your announcement. Record your announcement and play it for the class.

Tips

- When recording anything for radio, think about what kind of sound effects will attract the attention of your listeners.
- Consider creating sounds that remind listeners of the jungle. Birds chirping and monkeys chattering are sounds that will make listeners think it would be fun to join the expedition.
- Speak in short, quick sentences. Try to sound as if you are hiking up the mountain. You want to convince the audience to sign up.
- Use a tone of voice that will persuade listeners.

226
227

Student Edition pp. 226–227

Fluency
Phrasing

Guide practice

Use the Student Edition activity as an assessment tool. Make sure the reading passage is at least 200 words in length. As students read aloud with partners, walk around to make sure their phrasing is appropriate.

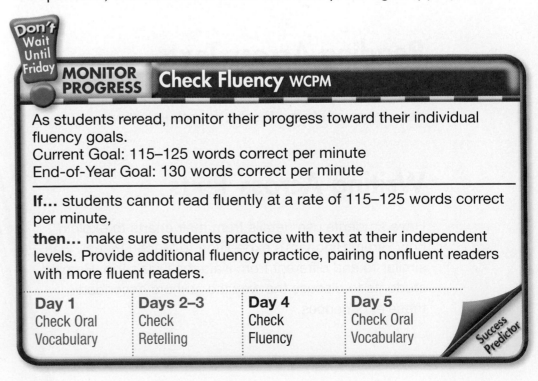

Don't Wait Until Friday

MONITOR PROGRESS **Check Fluency** WCPM

As students reread, monitor their progress toward their individual fluency goals.
Current Goal: 115–125 words correct per minute
End-of-Year Goal: 130 words correct per minute

If... students cannot read fluently at a rate of 115–125 words correct per minute,

then... make sure students practice with text at their independent levels. Provide additional fluency practice, pairing nonfluent readers with more fluent readers.

Day 1	**Days 2–3**	**Day 4**	**Day 5**
Check Oral Vocabulary	Check Retelling	Check Fluency	Check Oral Vocabulary

Success Predictor

Vocabulary
◉ Greek and Latin Roots

Teach Greek and Latin roots

Word Structure Write the following words on the board:

conquer	quest	conquistador	query

Many English words have Greek or Latin word parts. Explain that breaking a word into parts can help students determine its meaning. Point out that the four words above have the same Latin word part, or root, and that it means "to seek or to look."

Guide practice

Have students determine the meaning of each word by using their knowledge of its word structure and Latin root.

On their own

Have students work in pairs as you monitor their progress to make sure their definitions are correct. Have pairs consult a dictionary or a glossary to confirm the meanings.

Media Literacy
Radio Announcement

Teach

Explain that expressing an opinion is an advertising technique that can affect all kinds of media, such as radio announcements. Point out that opinions can have both positive and negative impacts on people.

Guide practice

Have partners create a radio announcement to convince volunteers to join the expedition site at Machu Picchu. Tell students to use persuasive words and to support their opinions with accurate information about the site.

On their own

Have partners take turns performing the radio announcement for each other and explaining the positive and negative impacts of advertisement techniques. Remind them to listen attentively when they are listening to the announcer and speak clearly, adjusting their speaking rate, when they are making the announcement.

Presenting

Remind students that when they give a presentation, they should present strong opinions and speak clearly to influence the thinking of others. Tell students to vary their speaking rate to emphasize key words in their radio announcements.

Academic Vocabulary

radio announcement A radio announcer broadcasts information about a certain topic.

ELL

English Language Learners
Practice pronunciation Assist pairs of students by modeling the correct pronunciation of the words from the Glossary, then having students repeat after you. Pair students with mixed language proficiencies together to practice pronunciation and employ self-corrective techniques.

Fluency

Success Predictor

Objectives
- Synthesize information.
- Review adverbs.
- Spell words with double consonants.

Research and Inquiry
Synthesize

Teach

Have students synthesize their research findings and results. Suggest that students skip lines as they jot down their journal entries. Remind them to write down what they visualize might happen on the expedition based on their research. Using the skipped lines, have them go back and jot down pertinent facts and details where they belong in the entry.

Guide practice

Have students use a word processing program to write the final copy of their journal entries. Have them use poster board or a computer graphics program to include visuals for their presentations on Day 5. Check to see that students are drawing conclusions through their writings, including their thoughts, feelings, and reactions to the archaeological expedition as well as the relevant facts and details of what is occurring.

On their own

Have students write a brief explanation of their research findings. Then have them organize and combine information and plan their presentations.

Conventions
Adverbs

Test practice Remind students that grammar skills, such as adverbs, are often assessed on important tests. Remind students that adverbs tell when, where, and how something happens. Adverbs can be also be used to combine two sentences to get rid of words that repeat.

Daily Fix-It Use Daily Fix-It numbers 7 and 8 in the right margin.

On their own For additional practice, use the *Reader's and Writer's Notebook* p. 337.

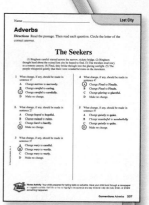
Reader's and Writer's Notebook p. 337

Daily Fix-It

7. Machu Picchu is famouser than this inca city. *(more famous; Inca)*

8. Thousands of tourists visits every year, they bring money to the local economy. *(visit; year. They)*

Spelling
Words with Double Consonants

Practice spelling strategy Review the rules for spelling words with double consonants. Then have each student write individual spelling words on note cards or slips of paper. Students should then work with a partner, placing the cards or papers face down on a desk, turning them over, saying the word aloud, and telling where each word has a double consonant.

On their own For additional practice, use *Let's Practice It!* page 260 on the *Teacher Resources DVD-ROM*.

Let's Practice It!
TR DVD•260

Objectives
- Revise draft of a legend.
- Include a variety of sentence structures.
- Include strong adverbs to add details.

Writing—Legend
Revising Strategy

MINI-LESSON

Clarifying

▪ Yesterday we wrote a legend about a hero that does great deeds. Today we will revise our drafts. The goal is to make your writing clearer, more interesting, and more informative.

▪ Display Writing Transparency 22B. Remind students that revising does not include corrections of grammar and mechanics. Tell them that this will be done tomorrow.

When you revise, ask yourself *How can I make my story clearer?* With the revising strategy Clarifying, you make sure the story's sequence, setting, characters, and events are easy for readers to understand. Let's look at the sentence that begins *On the fourth day*. It seems to be out of order because the next few sentences tell about what happened before the fourth day. I'll move the sentence to clarify the order of events. Insert the revising mark for *move* and read the sentences in the corrected order. Reread your composition for places you might want to clarify and model how to edit.

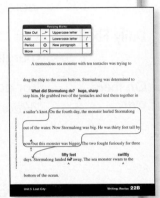

Writing Transparency 22B,
TR DVD

Tell students that as they revise, they should look for places where they can make their compositions clearer.

Revising Tips
✔ Review writing to be sure it has a beginning, middle, and an end.

✔ Check to be sure that events are presented in the right order.

✔ Include descriptive language to help readers picture what you're writing about.

Peer conferencing

Peer Revision Have pairs of students exchange papers for peer revision. Using sticky notes, partners should mark three places where the writing could be clearer and more informative and suggest ways to clarify. Refer to the *Let's Practice It! DVD* for more information about peer conferencing.

Have students revise their compositions using the notes placed on them during Peer Revision as well as the key features of legends to guide them. Be sure that students are using the revising strategy Clarifying.

Corrective feedback

Circulate around the room to monitor students and conference with them as they revise. Remind any students correcting errors that they will have time to edit tomorrow. They should be working on content and organization today.

ROUTINE **Quick Write for Fluency** **Team Talk**

1 **Talk** Have students discuss why *Lost City: The Discovery of Machu Picchu* is an adventure.

2 **Write** Each student writes a paragraph that summarizes their discussion.

3 **Share** Have students read their writing to their partner and have the partner check to see if the writing includes the key features of an legend.

Routines Flip Chart

Wrap Up Your Day

✔ **Build Concepts** Discuss the Inca civilization.

✔ **Oral Vocabulary** Monitor students' use of oral vocabulary as they respond: What kinds of legends are found in different regions and cultures?

✔ **Text Features** Discuss how photographs and maps help you understand the text as you read.

ELL

English Language Learners Revising

Beginning Students who share the same home language can work together or with a student with advanced language skills to revise their work.

Intermediate Working in pairs, students can revise their drafts.

Advanced/Advanced High In pairs, students can discuss and give reasons for their revisions.

Support vocabulary Have students translate an adverb into their native language and brainstorm synonyms. Have them translate those synonyms into English with the aid of a bilingual dictionary. Suggest that students begin a bilingual list of strong adverbs.

Preview DAY 5

Tell students that tomorrow they will read about another explorer and another expedition.

Objectives
• Review the weekly concept.
• Review oral vocabulary.

Today at a Glance

Oral Vocabulary

Comprehension
⊙ Compare and contrast

Lesson Vocabulary
⊙ Greek and Latin roots

Word Analysis
Suffixes *-ous, -able, -ible*

Literary Terms
Sensory words

Assessment
Fluency:
"The Arlington Springs Woman"

Comprehension:
"A Life-Saving Island"

Research and Inquiry
Communicate

Spelling
Words with double consonants

Conventions
Adverbs

Writing
Legend

Check Oral Vocabulary
SUCCESS PREDICTOR

Concept Wrap Up

Question of the Week
What surprises can happen on an expedition?

Review the concept

Have students look back at the reading selections to find examples that demonstrate surprises that can happen on an expedition.

Review Amazing Words

Display and review this week's concept map. Remind students that this week they have learned ten Amazing Words related to surprises that can happen on an expedition. Have students use the Amazing Words and the concept map to answer the Question of the Week, *What surprises can happen on an expedition?*

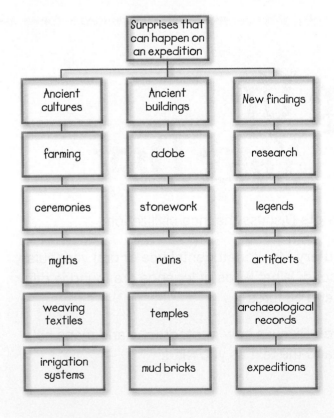

Surprises that can happen on an expedition

Ancient cultures	Ancient buildings	New findings
farming	adobe	research
ceremonies	stonework	legends
myths	ruins	artifacts
weaving textiles	temples	archaeological records
irrigation systems	mud bricks	expeditions

ELL Check Concepts and Language
Use the Day 5 instruction on ELL Poster 22 to monitor students' understanding of the lesson concept.

ELL Poster 22

Amazing Ideas

Connect to the Big Question

Have pairs of students discuss how the Question of the Week connects to the Big Question: *What makes an adventure?* Tell students to use the concept map and what they have learned from this week's Anchored Talks and reading selections to form an Amazing Idea—a realization or "big idea" about Land, Air, and Water. Remind partners to pose and answer questions with appropriate details and to give suggestions that build on each other's ideas. Then ask pairs to share their Amazing Idea with the class.

Amazing Ideas might include these key concepts:

- Expeditions can happen anywhere—on land, in air, or on water.
- Archaeologists can carefully research and plan expeditions, but they never know what they might discover.
- Ancient civilizations were suprisingly advanced.

Write about it

Have students write a few sentences about their Amazing Idea, beginning with "This week I learned . . ."

Amazing Words

region	century
cultivate	culture
adobe	legend
highland	research
gigantic	records

It's Friday

MONITOR PROGRESS | **Check Oral Vocabulary**

Have individuals use this week's Amazing Words to describe surprises on expeditions. Monitor students' abilities to use the Amazing Words and note which words you need to reteach.

If... students have difficulty using the Amazing Words,

then... reteach using the Oral Vocabulary Routine, pp. 201a, 204b, 214b, 222b, OV•2.

Day 1	Days 2–3	Day 4	Day 5
Check Oral Vocabulary	Check Retelling	Check Fluency	Check Oral Vocabulary

Success Predictor

ELL

English Language Learners
Concept map Work with students to add new words to the concept map.

227g

Oral Vocabulary

Success Predictor

Objectives
◎ Review compare and contrast.
◎ Review words with Greek and Latin roots.
• Review words with the Latin suffixes -ous, -able, and -ible.
• Review sensory words.

Comprehension Review
Compare and Contrast

Teach compare and contrast

Envision It!

Review the definitions of compare and contrast on p. 202. Remind students that a comparison tells how two or more things are alike, and a contrast tells how two or more things are different. For additional support, have students review p. EI•5 on compare and contrast.

Student Edition EI•5

Guide practice

Have student pairs find an example of compare or contrast in *Lost City: The Discovery of Machu Picchu.* Remind them that the comparison or the contrast can be implicit or explicit. Once they have located or figured out their examples, have pairs describe the explicit or implicit relationships, telling how the things or ideas are alike or different.

On their own

For additional practice with compare and contrast, use the *Let's Practice It! DVD.*

Let's Practice It!
TR DVD•261

Vocabulary Review
Greek and Latin Roots

Teach Greek and Latin roots

Remind students to use word structure to help them understand the meanings of words that have Greek and Latin roots.

Guide practice

Review with students how to find the correct meaning of words that come from Greek or Latin roots. Point out that the Greek root *log* means "word" or "speech," as in *catalog* and *dialogue*. Explain that the Latin root *cent* means "one hundred." Have students use these roots to find the meanings of *dialogue* and *century*.

On their own

Have students use a dictionary to determine which of this week's Amazing Words have Greek or Latin roots and what the meaning of those roots are.

Word Analysis `Review`

Teach suffixes -ous, -able, and -ible

Review the meaning of the Latin suffixes *-ous, -able,* and *-ible*. Discuss the meanings of *vicious, enjoyable,* and *sensible.*

Guide practice

Display *irritable, harmonious, lovable, anxious,* and *terrible.* Use the Strategy for Meaningful Word Parts to teach the word *adjustable.*

ROUTINE Strategy for Meaningful Word Parts

1 **Introduce word parts** Circle the Latin suffix *-able* and underline the base word *adjust.*

2 **Connect to meaning** Define the word *adjust* and add the suffix *-able* to the end of the word. Then define the word *adjustable.*

3 **Blend** Blend the meaningful word parts together to read *adjustable.* Continue the routine with *strenuous* and *responsible.*

Routines Flip Chart

On their own

Have students work in pairs to circle the suffix and underline the base word in each word. Encourage students to use a dictionary to confirm their definitions of unknown words.

Literary Terms `Review`
Sensory Words

Teach

Have students reread "Riding the Rails to Machu Picchu" on pp. 222–225. Remind students that authors use sensory words to help readers touch, taste, hear, smell, and see things in their minds.

Guide practice

Find a phrase in "Riding the Rails to Machu Picchu" in which the author uses sensory words. Discuss why the author included these words. Have students find and discuss other sensory words in this selection.

On their own

Have students select a person, place, or thing that they have learned about this week. Have them create a word web about that person, place, or thing, using words that appeal to the senses.

Lesson Vocabulary

curiosity a strong desire to know or learn something

glorious magnificent; splendid

granite a very hard, gray or pink rock that is used for buildings and monuments

ruins what is left after a building, wall, or other structure has fallen to pieces

terraced formed into a flat piece of land that is cut into a hillside; terraces are often made in hilly areas to create more space for raising crops

thickets bushes or small trees growing close together

torrent a violent, rushing stream of water

 ELL

English Language Learners
Word analysis Have students demonstrate the meaning of words that end in *-ous, -able,* and *-ible* through movement and facial expressions. Examples: acting in ways that are irritable, joyous, adorable, flexible, curious, vicious, or horrible. Have students say each word aloud as they demonstrate the movement.

ELL Professional Development
Language production Pair and group work naturally provides a low-anxiety environment that is conducive to language acquisition. When students are in a small group, everyone gets a chance to contribute to the discussion and production is increased.

Objectives
- Read grade-level text with fluency.

Assessment

Check words correct per minute

Fluency Make two copies of the fluency passage on p. 227k. As the student reads the text aloud, mark mistakes on your copy. Also mark where the student is at the end of one minute. To check the student's comprehension of the passage, have him or her retell you what was read. To figure words correct per minute (WCPM), subtract the number of mistakes from the total number of words read in one minute.

WCPM

Corrective feedback

If… students cannot read fluently at a rate of 115–125 WCPM,
then… make sure they practice with text at their independent reading level. Provide additional fluency practice by pairing nonfluent readers with fluent readers.

If… students already read at 130 WCPM,
then… have them read a book of their choice independently.

Plan to Assess Fluency

☑ **Week 1** Assess Advanced students.

☑ **This week assess Strategic Intervention students.**

☐ **Week 3** Assess On-Level students.

☐ **Week 4** Assess Strategic Intervention students.

☐ **Week 5** Assess any students you have not yet checked during this unit.

Set individual goals for students to enable them to reach the year-end goal.

- Current Goal: 115–125 WCPM
- Year-End Goal: 130 WCPM

Small Group Time

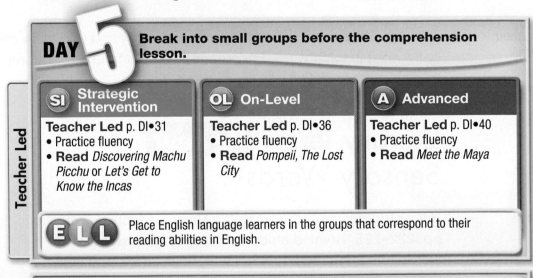

DAY 5 **Break into small groups before the comprehension lesson.**

Teacher Led

SI Strategic Intervention	**OL On-Level**	**A Advanced**
Teacher Led p. DI•31 • Practice fluency • **Read** *Discovering Machu Picchu* or *Let's Get to Know the Incas*	**Teacher Led** p. DI•36 • Practice fluency • **Read** *Pompeii, The Lost City*	**Teacher Led** p. DI•40 • Practice fluency • **Read** *Meet the Maya*

ELL Place English language learners in the groups that correspond to their reading abilities in English.

Practice Stations
- Words to Know
- Get Fluent
- Read for Meaning

Independent Activities
- Grammar Jammer
- Concept Talk Video
- Vocabulary Activities

The Arlington Springs Woman

In 1959, on Santa Rosa Island, a scientist named Phil Orr was   12

looking for signs of life from long ago. Orr found something important   24

buried 30 feet deep in a canyon. He found three human bones. Right   37

away, Orr knew the find was very important. He asked experts to help   50

him figure out how old the bones were.   58

Tests showed that the bones were 10,000 years old. This made   69

them the oldest remains ever found in North America. Still, Orr knew   81

that better ways of figuring out the age of remains were coming. He cut   95

out a block of earth where the bones were found. He wrapped it and   109

put it in a safe place. He named the bones "Arlington Springs Man."   122

Thirty years later, two scientists decided to test the bones again.   133

Amazing new methods for testing were then in use. The results showed   145

two new facts. First, the bones belonged to a woman, not a man.   158

Second, the bones were more than 13,000 years old! This meant   169

that humans could build boats and travel to islands much earlier than   181

we had thought. The remains of Arlington Springs Woman have led   192

to whole new ideas about when and how the first people reached   204

California.   205

MONITOR PROGRESS   • Check Fluency

Assessment

Check compare and contrast

⊙ **Compare and Contrast** Use "A Life-Saving Island" on p. 227m to check students' understanding of compare and contrast.

1. What was Vitus Bering's great discovery? Possible response: He found an island that is known today as Bering Island.

2. How were Bering's two trips from Kamchatka alike? Possible response: On both trips, he discovered an island. On both trips, he sailed on the Bering Strait.

3. How were the animals on Bering Island different from animals in other places? Possible response: They were not afraid of people.

Corrective feedback

If... students are unable to answer the comprehension questions, **then...** use the Reteach lesson in the *First Stop* book.

A Life-Saving Island

Vitus Bering was born in Denmark around 1680. At age 23, he joined the Russian Navy. He became a great explorer. In 1724, the ruler of Russia wanted Bering to find the distance between Asia and North America. The ruler asked Bering to go east across Russia to a place called Kamchatka. There he was to build a ship and set sail in search of North America.

On his first trip, Bering found a large island. He realized that the two continents were not far apart. They were divided by a strait, not a sea. On his second trip, in 1741, Bering discovered Alaska. Since the weather was very rough and many men on the ship were ill, Bering did not explore it. Instead, he set sail back to Kamchatka. A terrible storm blew the ship all around what is now called the Bering Strait. More men became sick, and the ship's sails were ripped by the winds. Finally, someone saw land. The men wanted it to be Kamchatka. Yet, the man sent ashore soon knew it was not. This land was a small island, and no humans lived there. The man knew this because the animals did not fear him. He returned to the ship with the news.

Bering himself was dying. He gave orders for everyone to leave the ship and go to the island. He and half of his men would die there. Yet, the rest of the crew made it through the winter. They built a small ship and sailed to Kamchatka. Even in death, Bering had made a great discovery. He had discovered an island that offered food and water to save his men. That island today is known as Bering Island.

MONITOR PROGRESS

• Compare and Contrast

Objectives
- Communicate inquiry results.
- Administer spelling test.
- Review adverbs.

Research and Inquiry
Communicate

Present ideas

Have students share their inquiry results by presenting their journal entries and sharing conclusions they've drawn about their research. Have students display any visuals they created on Day 4 to accompany their journal entries.

Listening and speaking

Remind students how to be good speakers and how to communicate effectively with their audience.

- Respond to relevant questions with appropriate details.
- Speak clearly, slowly, and loudly.
- Keep eye contact with audience members.

Remind students of these tips for being a good listener.

- Listen attentively to the speaker.
- Wait until the speaker has finished before raising your hand to ask a relevant question.
- Make positive, pertinent comments, if time allows.
- Be polite, even if you disagree.

Spelling Test
Words with Double Consonants

Spelling test To administer the spelling test, refer to the directions, words, and sentences on p. 203c.

Conventions
Extra Practice

Teach Remind students that an adverb can tell about a verb, an adjective, or another adverb. Adverbs may tell how, when, or where something happens and can come before or after a verb. Explain that many adverbs end in -*ly* and tell how something is done. Remind students that by using an adverb you can combine two sentences to get rid of words that repeat. Review that the phrase *a lot* is an adverb phrase.

Guide practice Have partners take turns performing an action and saying a sentence that names the action and includes an adverb that describes how, when, or where the action is performed.

Daily Fix-It Use Daily Fix-It numbers 9 and 10.

On their own Write these sentences. Have students look back in *Lost City* to find the correct adverb to fill in the blanks. For additional practice, use *Let's Practice It!* page 262 on the *Teacher Resources DVD-ROM*.

Let's Practice It!
TR DVD•262

1. _____, the clouds burned off and the mountains were bathed in glorious light. (Suddenly)

2. He placed his hands on the sun-warmed stones so _____ carved, as if they had grown together. (beautifully)

3. _____ he searched the mountains for a sign. (Anxiously)

4. Sergeant Carrasco and Arteaga took off their shoes and crossed _____, gripping with their bare feet. (easily)

5. They looked as if they had been _____ cleared of jungle and the vegetation burned off in order to plant crops. (recently)

6. _____, in July 1911, Bingham and his fellow adventurers arrived in Cusco, the first capital city of the Inca. (Finally)

Writing—Legends
Writer's Craft: Adverbs

Review revising

Remind students that yesterday they revised their legends, paying special attention to clarifying, making sure their story would be clear to a reader. Today they will proofread their legends.

MINI-LESSON

Proofread for Adverbs

■ **Teach** When we proofread, we look closely at our work, searching for errors in mechanics such as spelling, capitalization, punctuation, and grammar. Today we will focus on the adverbs in our story.

■ **Model** Let's look at a paragraph from the legend we revised yesterday. Display Writing Transparency 22C. Explain that you will look for errors in the use of adverbs, as well as places where adverbs would make the story more interesting. In the first sentence of the second paragraph, I see a place where I should add an adverb. I'll add the adverb phrase *a lot* to let the reader know how much Stormalong liked the ocean. In the second sentence of that paragraph, I see an error. Adverbs that tell how often end in *-ly*. Instead of violent, I'll write violently. Point out that students should read their legends several times, each time checking on different types of errors: spelling, punctuation, capitalization, and grammar.

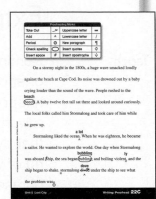
Writing Transparency 22C, TR DVD

Proofread

Display the Proofreading Tips. Ask students to proofread their legends, using the Proofreading Tips and paying particular attention to adverbs. Circulate around the room answering students' questions. When students have finished editing their own work, have pairs proofread one another's legend.

Proofreading Tips

✓ Use adverbs whenever possible to create a picture of an action.

✓ If your computer has a print preview feature, use it when you are finished typing. It will show how your work appears on the page.

✓ Draft, revise, and edit before you postwrite.

Present Have students incorporate revisions and proofreading edits, including feedback from their peers, into their legends to create a final draft.

Give students two options for presenting: A bound booklet or a display of their stories on a school bulletin board. Have students create art to accompany their writing. Students creating a bound book should create a cover page for their legend. When students have finished, have each complete the Writing Self-Evaluation Guide.

ROUTINE Write for Fluency Team Talk

1. **Talk** Pairs discuss what they learned about Hiram Bingham's discovery of Machu Picchu.

2. **Write** Each student writes a paragraph about one thing he or she discussed.

3. **Share** Partners read one another's writing.

Routines Flip Chart

Teacher Note

Writing Self-Evaluation Make copies of the Writing Self-Evaluation Guide on p. 39 of the *Reader's and Writer's Notebook* and hand out to students.

ELL

English Language Learners

Poster preview Prepare students for next week by using Week 3 ELL Poster 23. Read the Talk-Through to introduce the concept and vocabulary. Ask students to identify and describe actions in the art.

Selection summary Send home the summary of *Cliff Hanger* in English and the students' home languages, if available. They can read the summary with family members.

Preview NEXT WEEK

What does it take to be a hero? Tell students that next week they will read about a boy who has an adventure on a mountain and learn what it takes to be a hero.

Weekly Assessment

Use pp. 162–169 of *Weekly Tests* to check:

✔ **Word Analysis** Suffixes *-ous, -able, -ible*

✔ **Comprehension Skill** Compare and Contrast

✔ Review **Comprehension Skill** Literary Elements: Character and Plot

✔ **Lesson Vocabulary**

curiosity	terraced
glorious	thickets
granite	torrent
ruins	

Weekly Tests

Advanced

On-Level

Strategic Intervention

Differentiated Assessment

Use pp. 127–132 of *Fresh Reads for Fluency and Comprehension* to check:

✔ **Comprehension Skill** Compare and Contrast

✔ Review **Comprehension Skill** Literary Elements: Character and Plot

✔ **Fluency** Words Correct Per Minute

Fresh Reads for Fluency and Comprehension

Managing Assessment

Use *Assessment Handbook* for:

✔ **Weekly Assessment Blackline Masters for Monitoring Progress**

✔ **Observation Checklists**

✔ **Record-Keeping Forms**

✔ **Portfolio Assessment**

Assessment Handbook

Teacher Notes

Small Group Time

Pacing Small Group Instruction

15–20 min

5-Day Plan

DAY 1	• Reinforce the concept • Read Leveled Readers Concept Literacy Below Level
DAY 2	• ◉ Compare and Contrast • ◉ Visualize • Revisit Student Edition pp. 206–213
DAY 3	• ◉ Greek and Latin Roots • Revisit Student Edition pp. 214–217
DAY 4	• Practice Retelling • Read/Revisit Student Edition pp. 222–225
DAY 5	• Reread for fluency • Reread Leveled Readers

3- or 4-Day Plan

DAY 1	• Reinforce the concept • Read Leveled Readers
DAY 2	• ◉ Compare and Contrast • ◉ Visualize • Revisit Student Edition pp. 206–213
DAY 3	• ◉ Greek and Latin Roots • Revisit Student Edition pp. 214–217
DAY 4	• Practice Retelling • Read/Revisit Student Edition pp. 222–225 • Reread for fluency • Reread Leveled Readers

3-Day Plan: Eliminate the shaded box.

SI *Strategic Intervention*

DAY 1

Build Background

■ **Reinforce the Concept** Help students understand the weekly question *What surprises can happen on an expedition?* An *expedition* is a trip that people make for a reason. For example, your family might make an expedition to a museum to learn about history. One surprise that can happen on an expedition is that you might find evidence of the past. For instance, if you explore ancient ruins, you might find everyday items, such as combs and pitchers, or parts of buildings that are hundreds—or even thousands—of years old. As we study ancient civilizations, we learn how people lived many years ago. When we compare people's past adventures with the present, we understand our own lives better. **Discuss the words in the concept map.**

■ **Connect to Reading** This week you will read about ancient civilizations, or people who lived long ago. Each selection will provide you with details about how people in past civilizations lived. What do you already know about ancient civilizations such as the ancient Egyptians, Incas, or Aztecs? Think about the Read Aloud "The Incas." What new details did you learn about the Inca civilization? Encourage students to use their prior knowledge about ancient civilizations to connect this week's selections.

Objectives
• Participate in teacher-led discussions by answering questions with appropriate detail.

For a complete literacy instructional plan and additional practice with this week's target skills and strategies, see the **Leveled Reader Teaching Guide.**

Concept Literacy Reader

■ **Read** *Discovering Machu Picchu*

■ **Before Reading** Preview the book with students, focusing on key vocabulary. Then have them set a purpose for reading.

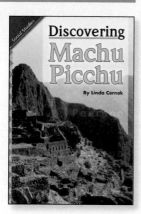

■ **During Reading** Read the first two pages aloud while students track the print. If students are able, have them finish reading with a partner.

■ **After Reading** After students finish reading the book, connect it to the weekly question *What surprises can happen on an expedition?*

Below-Level Reader

■ **Read** *Let's Get to Know the Incas*

■ **Before Reading** Have students use the illustrations to preview the selection. Then have students set a purpose for reading.

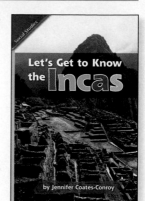

■ **During Reading** Do a choral reading of pp. 3–6. Have students read and discuss the remainder of the book with a partner.

● What was unusual about Inca farmland and farming methods? (*The farmland was on steep, terraced hillsides. Incas irrigated crops with rainwater and melted snow, which they collected in canals dug into the land.*)

● How did the Inca people support the emperors? (*They paid tribute of food, goods, and labor.*)

■ **After Reading** Have students look at and discuss the concept map. Connect the reader to the weekly question. What surprises might you find on an expedition to Machu Picchu? (*You might find treasures the ancient Incas hid from the Spaniards.*)

MONITOR PROGRESS

If... students have difficulty reading the selection with a partner,

then... have them follow along as they listen to the Leveled Readers DVD-ROM.

If... students have trouble understanding how Francisco Pizarro was able to defeat the mighty Inca Empire,

then... reread pp. 14–15 and discuss the details together.

Objectives
• Participate in teacher-led discussions by answering questions with appropriate detail.

Small Group Time

Student Edition, p. EI•5

More Reading

Use additional Leveled Readers or other texts at students' instructional levels to reinforce this week's skills and strategies. For text suggestions, see the Leveled Reader Database or the Leveled Readers Skills Chart on pp. CL 24–CL 29.

Reinforce Comprehension

Skill Compare and Contrast Review with students the information in *Envision It!* p. EI•5 on Compare and Contrast. Then use p. 202 to review the definitions of compare and contrast.

Strategy Visualize Review the definition of visualize. Remind students to picture scenes as they read. For additional support, refer to *Envision It!* p. EI•25.

■ **Revisit** *Lost City: The Discovery of Machu Picchu* on pp. 206–213. As students read, have them apply the comprehension skill and strategy.

• Compare and contrast the description of the boy and Hiram Bingham on the first page. How are they alike? How are they different? (*Alike: Both are looking at a beautiful sight and thinking about a mystery. Different: The boy is young and lives on a farm. Bingham is an adult visiting a city in Peru. The boy is looking at a landscape. Bingham is looking at walls.*)

• On p. 209, Bingham realizes something about the lost city. What is it? (*that its walls were probably built with the same kind of stones as the walls he is studying*)

Use the During Reading Differentiated Instruction for additional support for struggling readers.

MONITOR PROGRESS

If... students have difficulty reading along with the group,
then... have them follow along as they listen to the AudioText.

Objectives
• Compare and contrast ideas and information.
• Monitor comprehension.

SI Strategic Intervention

DAY 3

Reinforce Vocabulary

👁 **Greek and Latin Roots/Word Structure** Say the word *ventured* as you write it on the board. Read this sentence from the selection: " 'Are there ruins nearby?' Bingham asked when Arteaga ventured into camp." I know that *ven* is a root that means "to come" in Latin. The selection says Arteaga *ventured* into camp, so he must have come into camp. I happen to know that *ventured* means "dared to come," but if I didn't, I could still understand what is happening just by knowing the root *ven*. Point out the word *discouraged* on p. 211. I know that the Latin root *cor* means "heart." I also know that *dis-* is a prefix that means "not." What is another way to say that someone is discouraged? (*He or she has lost heart.*)

Student Edition, p. W•9

■ **Revisit** *Lost City: The Discovery of Machu Picchu* on pp. 214–217. Review *Words!* on p. W•9. Encourage students to use Greek and Latin roots to figure out the meaning of any unfamiliar words.

• Point out the word *exhausted* on p. 213. It is based on a Latin root, *haurire*, meaning "to draw, to drain." *Ex-* is a prefix that means "out." What does *exhausted* mean? (*"drawn out" or "drained out"*)

• Compare and contrast the trail right after the bridge and the trail near the top of the mountain. (*Both trails are thick with vegetation, but the top trail is much steeper and more slippery.*)

Use the During Reading Differentiated Instruction for additional support for struggling readers.

More Reading

Use additional Leveled Readers or other texts at students' instructional levels to reinforce this week's skills and strategies. For text suggestions, see the Leveled Reader Database or the Leveled Readers Skills Chart on pp. CL 24–CL 29.

MONITOR PROGRESS

If... students need more practice with the lesson vocabulary,
then... use *Envision It! Pictured Vocabulary Cards*.

Objectives
• Determine meaning of grade-level academic English words derived from Latin roots.
• Use word structure to analyze and decode new words.

Practice Retelling

■ **Retell** Have pairs of students use the Retelling Cards to retell *Lost City: The Discovery of Machu Picchu.* Monitor retelling and prompt students as needed.

- • What is the main character trying to accomplish?

- • How does the main character get help in accomplishing his goal?

If students struggle, model a fluent retelling.

Genre Focus

■ **Before Reading or Revisiting** "Riding the Rails to Machu Picchu" on pp. 222–225, read aloud the genre information about personal essays on p. 222. Personal essays describe the author's personal experiences and reactions. A personal essay gives the author the chance to express his or her personality and thoughts.

Then have students preview "Riding the Rails to Machu Picchu."

- • What text features do you see? (*photographs, a map, captions*)

- • Look at the photographs. How do they prepare you for reading the essay? (*They give you an idea about the content.*)

Help students set a purpose for reading based on their preview.

■ **During Reading or Revisiting** Have students read along with you while tracking the print. Stop to discuss any unfamiliar words, such as *conquered* and *whisk*.

■ **After Reading or Revisiting** Have students share their reactions to the essay. Then guide them through the Reading Across Texts and Writing Across Texts activities. Ask: How is this personal essay like *Lost City: The Discovery of Machu Picchu?* (*Both are about a trip to Machu Picchu.*) How are they different? (*One is a personal essay, and the other is a biography.*)

MONITOR PROGRESS

If... students have difficulty retelling the selection,

then... have them review the story using the illustrations.

Objectives
• Explain factual information presented graphically.

For a complete literacy instructional plan and additional practice with this week's target skills and strategies, see the **Leveled Reader Teaching Guide.**

Concept Literacy Reader

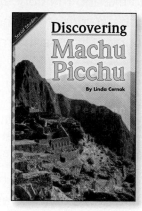

- **Model** Illustrate appropriate phrasing for students. Ask students to listen carefully as you read aloud the first two pages of *Discovering Machu Picchu.* Have students note the grouping of your words and the way you use punctuation cues.

- **Fluency Routine**

1. Have students reread passages from *Discovering Machu Picchu* with a partner.

2. For optimal fluency, students should reread three to four times.

3. As students read, monitor fluency and provide corrective feedback. Encourage students to monitor how they group words as they read.

See *Routines Flip Chart* for more help with fluency.

- **Retell** Have students retell *Discovering Machu Picchu.* Prompt as necessary.

Below-Level Reader

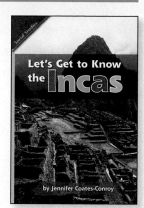

- **Model** Ask students to listen carefully as you read aloud pp. 3–4 of *Let's Get to Know the Incas,* emphasizing appropriate phrasing.

- **Fluency Routine**

1. Have students reread passages from *Let's Get to Know the Incas* with a partner or individually.

2. For optimal fluency, students should reread three to four times.

3. As students read, monitor fluency and provide corrective feedback. Point out that related words, such as those in prepositional phrases and clauses, should be read together.

See *Routines Flip Chart* for more help with fluency.

- **Retell** For additional practice, have students retell *Let's Get to Know the Incas* page-by-page, using the illustrations. Prompt as necessary. How does the picture help you remember this part?

MONITOR PROGRESS

If... students have difficulty reading fluently,

then... provide additional fluency practice by pairing nonfluent readers with fluent ones.

Objectives
• Read aloud grade-level stories with fluency.

Pacing Small Group Instruction

15–20 min

5-Day Plan

DAY 1	• Expand the concept • Read On-Level Reader
DAY 2	• ◉ Compare and Contrast • ◉ Visualize • Revisit Student Edition pp. 206–213
DAY 3	• ◉ Greek and Latin Roots • Revisit Student Edition pp. 214–217
DAY 4	• Practice Retelling • Read/Revisit Student Edition pp. 222–225
DAY 5	• Reread for fluency • Reread On-Level Reader

3- or 4-Day Plan

DAY 1	• Expand the concept • Read On-Level Reader
DAY 2	• ◉ Compare and Contrast • ◉ Visualize • Revisit Student Edition pp. 206–213
DAY 3	• ◉ Greek and Latin Roots • Revisit Student Edition pp. 214–217
DAY 4	• Practice Retelling • Read/Revisit Student Edition pp. 222–225 • Reread for fluency • Reread On-Level Reader

3-Day Plan: Eliminate the shaded box.

OL On-Level · DAY 1

Build Background

■ **Expand the Concept** Connect the weekly question (*What surprises can happen on an expedition?*) and expand the concept. When we go on an expedition to a historic place, we may be surprised at what we see. Ruins can reveal the everyday lives of ancient people. Discuss the meanings of the words on the concept map.

On-Level Reader

For a complete literacy instructional plan and additional practice with this week's target skills and strategies, see the **Leveled Reader Teaching Guide.**

■ **Before Reading** *Pompeii, The Lost City,* have students preview the book by looking at the title, cover, and pictures.

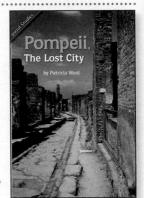

Pompeii, The Lost City

• What is the topic of this book? (*the history and remains of the lost city of Pompeii*)

• What might it have been like to excavate the ruins of Pompeii? Why? (*It would have been exciting because the ruins showed, in great detail, how people lived almost 2,000 years ago. It might also be dangerous and sad to see so many lives lost.*)

Have students create a Venn diagram with circles labeled *Where I Live* and *Pompeii* and the intersection of the circles labeled *Both.* This book tells about Pompeii. As you read, look for ways in which Pompeii and where you live are different and alike. Write those ways in the correct circles in the diagram.

■ **During Reading** Read aloud the first three pages of the book as students follow along. Then have them finish reading the book on their own. Remind students to add details to their Venn diagrams as they read.

■ **After Reading** Have partners compare their Venn diagrams. Point out that their comparisons will help them as they read about another lost city in tomorrow's selection, *Lost City: The Discovery of Machu Picchu.* How does the topic relate to the weekly question *What surprises can happen on an expedition?*

Objectives
• Participate in teacher-led discussions by answering questions with appropriate detail.

OL On-Level

DAY 2

Expand Comprehension

⊙ **Skill Compare and Contrast** Use p. 202 to review the definitions of compare and contrast. For additional review, see Compare and Contrast in *Envision It! Skill* p. EI•5. When you compare, you show what is similar about two or more things. Clue words such as *like* or *as* show comparisons. When you contrast, you show what is different about two or more things. Clue words such as *but* or *unlike* show contrasts, or differences.

⊙ **Strategy Visualize** Review the definition of visualize. Encourage students to visualize as they read. Note that visualizing can help them compare and contrast. For additional support, use the Extend Thinking questions and refer students to *Envision It!* p. EI•25.

■ **Revisit** *Lost City: The Discovery of Machu Picchu* on pp. 206–213. As students read, have them apply the comprehension skill and strategy to the selection.

- How does the city of Cusco contrast with the village of Ollantaytambo? (*Cusco is a modern city, and Ollantaytambo is a sleepy old village.*)

- How would you compare and contrast the two people introduced at the beginning of the biography? (*They seem very different. The boy is young, and Bingham is an adult. The boy lives on his father's farm, and Bingham is in the city of Cusco. They are alike in that both are looking at a beautiful sight—the mountains and the stonework. And they are both thinking about mysteries. The boy is wondering what his dream means, and Bingham is wondering about the lost city.*)

Student Edition, p. EI•5

More Reading

Use additional Leveled Readers or other texts at students' instructional levels to reinforce this week's skills and strategies. For text suggestions, see the Leveled Reader Database or the Leveled Readers Skills Chart on pp. CL 24–CL 29.

Objectives
- Compare and contrast ideas and information.
- Monitor comprehension.

Expand Vocabulary

Student Edition, p. W•9

Greek and Latin Roots/Word Structure Point out the passage "What was it? He followed the boy to another temple. As magnificent." Write the word *magnificent* as you say it aloud. Then model using Latin roots to determine the meaning.

I know that the root *magnus* means "great." The selection describes the temple ruins as "magnificent." Based on the Latin root, I know these temples looked quite impressive. Then point out the word *terraced* in the following sentence: "Already his papa was working in the terraced fields." The root of *terraced* is Latin, meaning "earth." Terraced fields are cut into the earth, such as into a hillside. What other words with the root *terra* do you know? (*territory, terrain, terrace*)

More Reading

Use additional Leveled Readers or other texts at students' instructional levels to reinforce this week's skills and strategies. For text suggestions, see the Leveled Reader Database or the Leveled Readers Skills Chart on pp. CL 24–CL 29.

■ **Revisit** *Lost City: The Discovery of Machu Picchu* on pp. 214–217. Encourage students to think about Greek and Latin roots as they read.

• What is the black box? (*a camera*)

• Why might it be mysterious to the boy? (*Because he lives in such a remote area in the early 1900s, the boy probably hasn't seen many cameras before.*)

• How are the three men who climb the mountain alike and different? (*All three are determined to climb the same difficult trail, yet they all have different things on their minds. Arteaga is fearful of snakes. The sergeant is pleased he has good shoes for climbing. Bingham is focused on his search for the ruins.*)

Objectives
• Determine meaning of grade-level academic English words derived from Latin roots.
• Use word structure to analyze and decode new words.

 **DAY 4**

Practice Retelling

■ **Retell** To assess students' comprehension, use the Retelling Cards. Monitor retelling and prompt students as needed.

Genre Focus

■ **Before Reading or Revisiting** "Riding the Rails to Machu Picchu" on pp. 222–225, read aloud the genre information about personal essays on p. 222. Have students preview "Riding the Rails to Machu Picchu" and set a purpose for reading.

- Why would the author include a map in the essay? (*to show the places she discusses in her essay*)

- How do the photographs help you understand the essay? (*They help the reader visualize the ruins as well as the countryside.*)

■ **During Reading or Revisiting** Have students read along with you while tracking the print.

- How do you know this is a personal essay? (*The author speaks in the first person and describes a personal experience.*)

- Based on this personal essay, what do you learn about the author's personality? (*The author is adventurous, curious, and observant.*)

- In what ways are this essay and *Lost City: The Discovery of Machu Picchu* alike and different? How are the visuals different? (*Both are about the same topic, a visit to Machu Picchu. Both describe Machu Picchu in detail. However, one is a personal essay, which means that the author is writing about her own experience. The other is a biography, which means the author is writing about someone else's experience. The personal essay uses photos and a map to tell the story. The biography uses drawings.*)

■ **After Reading or Revisiting** Have students share their reactions to the personal essay. Then have them write a paragraph about an interesting place they have visited.

Objectives
- Explain factual information presented graphically.

Small Group Time

On-Level Reader

■ **Model** Read aloud p. 3 of the On-Level Reader *Pompeii, The Lost City* twice. First, read in a monotone voice without pausing for punctuation. Then, read the page again, this time emphasizing appropriate phrasing. Ask students which reading was more effective and why. Discuss how phrasing helps make a text easier to understand.

■ **Fluency Routine**

1. Have students reread passages from *Pompeii, The Lost City* with a partner.

2. For optimal fluency, students should reread passages three to four times.

3. As students read, monitor fluency and provide corrective feedback. Have students note the grouping of your words into phrases and the rise and fall of your voice. Discuss how reading with a natural rhythm is much more pleasing than reading word by word.

See *Routines Flip Chart* for more help with fluency.

■ **Retell** For additional practice, have students use headings and photographs as a guide to retell *Pompeii, The Lost City.* Prompt as necessary.

• What is this section mostly about?

• What did you learn from reading this section?

Pompeii, The Lost City

Objectives
• Read aloud grade-level stories with fluency.

A Advanced

DAY 1

Build Background

■ **Extend the Concept** Discuss the weekly question *What surprises can happen on an expedition?* In history, what surprises have various explorers had as they went on expeditions? For example, what did the first archaeologist at King Tut's tomb find? (*artifacts that revealed truths about the ancient Egyptians*) Why is it important to research ancient civilizations?

Advanced Reader

For a complete literacy instructional plan and additional practice with this week's target skills and strategies, see the **Leveled Reader Teaching Guide.**

■ **Before Reading** *Meet the Maya,* have students look at the illustrations and use them to predict what will happen in the book. Then have students set a purpose for reading.

■ **During Reading** Have students read independently.

Meet the Maya

• Why do you think the Maya pyramids are terraced, rather than smooth like Egyptian pyramids? (*The Maya used the top of the pyramid for religious ceremonies, so they had to be able to climb to the top. The Egyptians used only the insides of the pyramids as tombs.*)

• Why is so much of the Maya writing based on government and religion, rather than on everyday affairs? (*Common people did not know how to read and write—only the ruler and priests did.*)

• Why do you think the Maya abandoned their cities? (*The land could no longer support agriculture because of drought and destruction of the rain forests.*)

■ **After Reading** Have students review the concept map on p. 201 and explain how *Meet the Maya* helps answer the weekly question *What surprises can happen on an expedition?*

• What did archaeologists find when they discovered the abandoned cities of the Maya? (*evidence of a great civilization*)

• What advantages did the Spanish conquerors have over the Maya? (*superior weapons and resistance to the diseases they brought with them*)

■ **Now Try This** Assign "Now Try This" at the end of the Advanced Reader.

Objectives
• Participate in teacher-led discussions by answering questions with appropriate detail.

Pacing Small Group Instruction

15–20 min

5-Day Plan

DAY 1	• Extend the concept • Read Advanced Reader
DAY 2	• ⊙ Compare and Contrast • ⊙ Visualize • Revisit Student Edition pp. 206–213
DAY 3	• ⊙ Greek and Latin Roots • Revisit Student Edition pp. 214–217
DAY 4	• Genre Focus • Read/Revisit Student Edition pp. 222–225
DAY 5	• Reread for fluency • Reread Advanced Reader

3- or 4-Day Plan

DAY 1	• Extend the concept • Read Advanced Reader
DAY 2	• ⊙ Compare and Contrast • ⊙ Visualize • Revisit Student Edition pp. 206–213
DAY 3	• ⊙ Greek and Latin Roots • Revisit Student Edition pp. 214–217
DAY 4	• Genre Focus • Read/Revisit Student Edition pp. 222–225 • Reread for fluency • Reread Advanced Reader

3-Day Plan: Eliminate the shaded box.

A **Advanced**   **DAY 2**

Extend Comprehension

◉ **Skill Compare and Contrast** Review the definitions of compare and contrast. Point out that writers may use comparisons and contrasts to develop their stories. Call attention to this sentence about the lost city on p. 209: "Would it hold gold and fabulous riches like the Spanish had found in Cusco? By remembering the Spanish experience in Cusco, Bingham wonders if the lost city will be similar. This develops the story by making me wonder what he will find. Will it be like Cusco? Or will it be different?

◉ **Strategy Visualize** Review the definition of the strategy. Remind students to visualize as they read *Lost City: The Discovery of Machu Picchu.*

■ **Revisit** *Lost City: The Discovery of Machu Picchu* on pp. 206–213. Tell students to compare and contrast the experiences of Bingham and the boy. Also have them visualize as they read. Visualize Bingham's experience as the farmer Arteaga answered his question "Are there ruins nearby?" How do you picture this scene? (*Bingham probably looks excited when he hears a positive response but shocked when Arteaga points straight up.*)

■ **Critical Thinking** Encourage students to think critically about what they have read so far. Why might Bingham and other explorers risk their lives to find ancient ruins? (*to learn about lost civilizations and people, to find riches, to gain fame, to find truth behind a legend*)

During reading, use the Extend Thinking questions and the During Reading Differentiated Instruction for additional support.

More Reading

Use additional Leveled Readers or other texts at students' instructional levels to reinforce this week's skills and strategies. For text suggestions, see the Leveled Reader Database or the Leveled Readers Skills Chart on pp. CL 24–CL 29.

Objectives
• Compare and contrast ideas and information.
• Monitor comprehension.

DAY **3**

Extend Vocabulary

◉ **Greek and Latin Roots/Word Structure**
Write a passage containing a word with a
Greek or Latin root, such as this one from p. 12
of *Meet the Maya*: "Maya astronomers tracked
the sun's position. . . ." The Greek root *astro*
means "star." So what does *astronomer* mean?
(*someone who studies the stars*) Discuss how
understanding Greek and Latin roots can be
helpful. Remind students to use the strategy as
they read *Lost City: The Discovery of Machu Picchu.*

■ **Revisit** *Lost City: The Discovery of Machu Picchu* on pp. 214–217. As students
finish reading, prompt them to use comparisons and contrasts to understand
the biography.

- Carrasco and Arteaga cross the flimsy bridge easily, but Bingham is terrified.
  What is the reason for this difference? (*Carrasco and Arteaga have probably
  crossed such bridges before.*)

- What does Bingham have in common with the other two men who climb the
  mountain with him? (*All are determined to reach their destination despite the
  hardships and dangers of the trail.*)

■ **Critical Thinking** After students finish reading the selection, encourage them to
think critically and creatively about what they have read.

- Why do you think Arteaga might have been so afraid of snakes, whereas
  Bingham hardly thought about them? (*Arteaga probably has personal experience with snakes in the area, so he knows how dangerous they can be.
  Bingham doesn't realize the danger, and he is too focused on finding the city
  to think of anything else.*)

- How could Bingham have persuaded Arteaga to guide him without offering
  money? (*He could have given him gifts or offered to take his picture for this
  historic moment.*)

More Reading

Use additional Leveled
Readers or other texts at students' instructional levels to
reinforce this week's skills and
strategies. For text suggestions, see the Leveled Reader
Database or the Leveled
Readers Skills Chart on
pp. CL 24–CL 29.

Objectives
- Determine meaning of grade-level academic English words derived from Latin roots.
- Use word structure to analyze and decode new words.

Genre Focus

- **Before Reading or Revisiting** "Riding the Rails to Machu Picchu" on pp. 222–225, read the panel information on personal essays. Then have students use the text features to set a purpose for reading.

- **During Reading or Revisiting** Have students read the selection on their own. Ask students to share their reactions to the personal essay.

  - If you were in the author's place, would you have done the four-day hike on the old Inca Trail, taken the helicopter ride, or taken the three-hour train ride to Machu Picchu? Why? (*Answers will vary. Students should give specific reasons for their opinions.*)

Riding the Rails to Machu Picchu

- **After Reading or Revisiting** Have students discuss Reading Across Texts. Then have them do Writing Across Texts independently.

Objectives
- Explain factual information presented graphically.

- **Reread for Fluency** Have students silently reread passages from the Advanced Reader *Meet the Maya.* Then have them reread aloud with a partner or individually. As students read, monitor fluency and provide corrective feedback. If students read fluently on the first reading, they do not need to reread three to four times. Assess the fluency of students in this group using p. 227j.

- **Retell** Have students summarize the main idea and key details from the Advanced Reader *Meet the Maya.*

- **Now Try This** Have students complete their syllabograms. You may wish to review their work to see if they need additional ideas. Have volunteers display their work in class.

Meet the Maya

Objectives
- Read aloud grade-level stories with fluency.

ELL English Language Learners

The ELL lessons are organized by strands. Use them to scaffold the weekly curriculum of lessons or during small group time instruction.

Academic Language

Students will hear or read the following academic language in this week's core instruction. As students encounter the vocabulary, provide a simple definition or concrete example. Then ask students to suggest an example or synonym of the word and identify available cognates.

Skill Words	compare (*comparar*)	visualize (*visualizar*)
	contrast (*contrastar*)	adverb (*adverbio*)
	suffix (*sufijo*)	base word
Concept Words	explore (*explorar*)	expedition (*expedición*)
	dive	

* *Spanish cognates in parentheses*

Concept Development

What surprises can happen on an expedition?

■ **Preteach Concept**

• **Prior Knowledge** Have students turn to pp. 200–201 in the Student Edition. Call attention to the picture of the Easter Island and have students share their knowledge of ancient statues. Have you ever seen a picture of these statues before? Do you know where they are? Were built recently or a long time ago? Can you think of other places where you might find ancient statues?

• **Discuss Concept** Elicit students' prior knowledge and experience of surprises that can happen on an expedition. How do you think people felt the first time they came upon these statues? What are some other surprises people might find if they explore new places? Supply background information as needed.

• **Poster Talk-Through** Read the Poster Talk-Through on ELL Poster 22 aloud and work through the Day 1 activities.

■ **Daily Concept and Vocabulary Development** Use the daily activities on ELL Poster 22 to build concept and vocabulary knowledge.

Objectives
• Use prior knowledge and experiences to understand meanings in English.

Content Objectives

• Use concept vocabulary related to traveling.

Language Objectives

• Use prior knowledge to understand meanings.

Daily Planner

DAY 1	• **Frontload Concept** • **Preteach** Comprehension Skill, Vocabulary, Phonics/ Spelling, Conventions • **Writing**
DAY 2	• **Review Concept,** Vocabulary, Comprehension Skill • **Frontload Main Selection** • **Practice** Phonics/ Spelling, Conventions/ Writing
DAY 3	• **Review Concept,** Comprehension Skill, Vocabulary, Conventions/ Writing • **Reread Main Selection** • **Practice** Phonics/ Spelling
DAY 4	• **Review Concept** • **Read ELL/ELD Readers** • **Practice** Phonics/ Spelling, Conventions/ Writing
DAY 5	• **Review Concept,** Vocabulary, Comprehension Skill, Phonics/Spelling, Conventions • **Read ELL/ELD Readers** • **Writing**

*See the ELL Handbook for ELL Workshops with targeted instruction.

Concept Talk Video

Have students use the Concept Talk Video Routine (*ELL Handbook* p. 477) to build content attainment about expeditions. For listening practice, see *Use Classroom Resources* (*ELL Handbook*, pp. 406–407).

Support for English Language Learners

Basic Vocabulary

- **High-Frequency Words** Use the ELL Vocabulary Words Routine on p. 471 of the *ELL Handbook* to systematically teach newcomers the first 300 sight words in English. Have the students expand and internalize high-frequency words by using three of the words to describe a person or place they know in pairs. Students who began learning ten words per week at the beginning of the year are now learning words 211–220 (*ELL Handbook*, p. 454). P. 446 of the handbook contains a bank of strategies that you can use to ensure students' mastery of high-frequency words.

Lesson Vocabulary

- **Preteach** Introduce the Lesson Vocabulary using this routine:

  1. Distribute copies of this week's Word Cards (*ELL Handbook*, p. 155).

  2. Display ELL Poster 22 and reread the Poster Talk-Through.

  3. Using the poster illustrations, model how a word's meaning can be expressed with other similar words: The family visited the *ruins*, or what is left of buildings from ancient civilizations.

  4. Use these sentences to reveal the meaning of the other words.

     - The pyramid looks as though it is made of *granite*. (a type of hard rock)

     - They have a lot of *curiosity* about the ancient city. (interest in something)

     - The ancient civilization has *glorious* monuments. (having great beauty)

     - The Mayans still grow their food in *terraced* gardens on the mountainside. (having steps carved into mountains for farming)

     - The boy can hardly see into the jungle through the *thickets*. (dense growth of plants)

     - The waterfall has the force of a *torrent*. (rush of water)

Objectives
- Expand and internalize initial English vocabulary by learning and using high-frequency English words necessary for identifying and describing people, places, and objects, by retelling simple stories and basic information represented or supported by pictures, and by learning and using routine language needed for classroom communication.

ELL English Language Learners

- **Reteach** Distribute a copy of the Word Cards to each student. Ask questions to check and reinforce students' understanding of the content-based vocabulary.

  - Were *ruins* built recently or long ago? (long ago)

  - What is another word for showing interest? (curiosity)

  - How does a *torrent* move? (very fast)

  - What is another word for thick bushes or plants? (thickets)

  - Which word describes flat parts of mountains where people farm? (terraced)

  - What kind of material is *granite*? (rock)

  - If something is amazing, how else might it be described? (glorious)

- **Writing** Distribute fourteen blank cards to each student. Have students write a clue for each content-based vocabulary word on a separate card and then have students write the vocabulary word on another card. Then have partners trade clue cards and try to match each card. Model the activity using the word *granite* and the clue *rock*. Circulate to provide assistance as needed.

  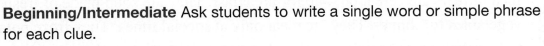

  Beginning/Intermediate Ask students to write a single word or simple phrase for each clue.

  Advanced/Advanced High Encourage students to write longer phrases or complete sentences for each clue.

Language Objectives

- Produce drawings, phrases, or short sentences to show understanding of content-based Lesson Vocabulary.

ELL Teacher Tip

According to ELL consultant Georgia Earnest García, English language learners "benefit when teachers shelter, or make comprehensible, their literacy instruction." One sheltering technique is to use gestures, photos, drawings, or physical actions to illustrate vocabulary. Engage students with this week's vocabulary by having them choose a vocabulary word and draw a picture to illustrate it.

ELL Workshop

As students speak using new vocabulary, they may need assistance knowing how to adapt spoken English for informal purposes. Use *Informal English* (*ELL Handbook*, pp. 390–391) provides extra support.

Objectives
- Internalize new basic and academic language by using and reusing it in meaningful ways in speaking and writing activities that build concept and language attainment.

Support for English Language Learners

Content Objectives
- Monitor and adjust oral comprehension.

Language Objectives
- Discuss oral passages.
- Use a graphic organizer to take notes.

Graphic Organizer

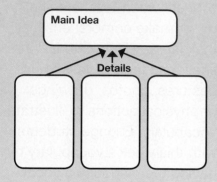

ELL Teacher Tip
Scaffold instruction by using a Think Aloud to model finding the main idea. I know that the main idea is what a text is mostly about. This text is mostly about Inca farmers and the foods they grew and stored.

ELL Workshop
Encourage students to demonstrate listening comprehension of the Read Aloud and other spoken messages. Provide *Retell or Summarize* (*ELL Handbook*, pp. 408–409) for practice.

ELL *English Language Learners*

Listening Comprehension

Inca Farmers

Incas had special ways to grow, cook, and keep their food. Inca farmers lived and worked in areas with steep mountains. They cut terraces into the hillsides. Terraces are large, flat steps. Farmers could plant crops on the flat terraces.

Inca farmers grew different foods in different areas. They grew cocao, which makes chocolate, near the jungle. They grew beans, peanuts, and pumpkins in the high mountain valleys. They grew fruits and vegetables in the lower valleys.

Inca farmers lived in small, simple huts made of adobe. Adobe is a kind of mud. They had no furniture inside their huts.

Inca farmers ate cereal or soup for breakfast. They ate soup made of fresh vegetables for dinner. They ate meat only at special times. They froze potatoes in the cold mountain air. Then Inca women walked on the potatoes to press out the water inside. These potatoes could be stored for years.

Prepare for the Read Aloud The modified Read Aloud above prepares students for listening to the oral reading "The Incas" on p. 201b.

- **First Listening: Listen to Understand** Write the title of the Read Aloud on the board. This is about how Inca farmers lived. Listen to find out about their daily lives. What kinds of foods did they grow and eat? Have students share their answers.

- **Second Listening: Listen to Check Understanding** Have students use contextual support to enhance listening comprehension and understanding by creating a Main Idea graphic organizer to take notes as they listen. Work with students to identify the main idea and details. Now listen again to find the main idea and to find details that tell more about the main idea. Record the main idea in the organizer. Then fill in the details together.

Objectives
- Learn new language structures, expressions, and basic and academic vocabulary heard during classroom instruction and interactions.

ELL English Language Learners

Phonics and Spelling

■ **Words with Double Consonants** Use Sound-Spelling Cards 14, 121, and 127 to teach the sounds, pronunciations, and spellings of words with double consonants.

- Display card 14. This is *ladder*. We spell *ladder* with two *d*s. **Point to the two ds.** Many words in English have double consonants. Pronounce the word *ladder*.

- Display card 121. This is *flipped*. We spell *flipped* with two *p*s, but we spell *flip* with just one *p*. **Cover the last three letters on the card.** When we add the *-ed* ending to *flip*, we have to double the consonant.

- Display card 127. This is *swimming*. We spell *swimming* with two *m*s, but we spell *swim* with just one *m*. **Cover the last four letters on the card.** When we add the *-ing* ending to words like *swim*, we have to double the consonant. **Sound out the word *swimming*.**

Word Analysis: Suffixes *-ous, -able, -ible*

■ **Teach/Model** Write the following words on the board: *walkable, sensible, glorious*. Each of these words is made up of a base or root word and a suffix. **Circle the suffix *-able*.** These letters are a suffix. A suffix is a word part added to the end of a word. **Ask volunteers to identify the other suffixes.** The suffixes *-able* and *-ible* mean "can be." The suffix *-ous* means "full of." **Model, using each word in a sentence.**

■ **Practice** Write these words on the board: *joyous, nervous, reversible, collectible, dependable, lovable*. Provide practice for students at their language proficiency level.

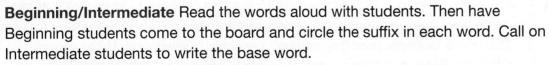

Beginning/Intermediate Read the words aloud with students. Then have Beginning students come to the board and circle the suffix in each word. Call on Intermediate students to write the base word.

Advanced/Advanced High Challenge students to work in pairs to use each word in a sentence.

Content Objectives

- Identify and use the suffixes *-ous, -able, -ible*.

- Review words with double consonants.

Language Objectives

- Apply phonics and decoding skills to vocabulary.

- Discuss the meaning of suffixes *-ous, -able, -ible*.

 Transfer Skills

Some English prefixes and suffixes have equivalent forms in the Romance languages. Students who are literate in these languages may be able to transfer their understanding of prefixes and suffixes by using parallel examples in the home language and in English.

Content Objectives

- Compare and contrast information in a text.

Language Objectives

- Compare two or more things in a text.
- Contrast two or more things in a text.

ELL Workshop

Encourage students to ask questions to monitor their understanding of instruction of comprehension skills. Use *Ask Clarifying Questions* (*ELL Handbook*, pp. 404–405) for practice.

ELL *English Language Learners*

Comprehension
Character and Plot

■ **Preteach** When you compare two things, you decide how they are alike. When you contrast two things, you think about how they are different. Have students turn to Envision It! on p. EI•5 in the Student Edition. Read aloud the signs and prices and discuss the environment print found on the picture. Have students talk about what the boy can compare and contrast before deciding which robot to buy. Why might the environmental print, the price tags, effect his decision?

■ **Reteach** Distribute copies of the Picture It! (*ELL Handbook*, p. 156). Tell students to describe the illustration. Then have students listen to the text as you read it aloud. Have students listen for how Pompeii and Herculaneum are alike and different. Have them underline sentences that tell how the places are alike and write the information in the center part of the Venn diagram. Then have students write the differences in the appropriate sections. (*Pompeii*: busy important city, buried by ash and rock; *Both*: ancient cities in Italy, located at the bottom of a mountain, buried by volcano erupting, dug up in 1700s, tourists visit today; *Herculaneum*: small rich town, buried by mud)

 Beginning/Intermediate Have students circle the word *both* and use it to identify information for the center area of the Venn diagram.

Advanced/Advanced High Have students reread the paragraph, looking at the Venn diagram as they read. Have them circle the word *both* where it appears. Then have them complete the Venn diagram listing how the places are different.

MINI-LESSON

Social Language

Explain that people often compare and contrast things while making everyday choices. For example, a person choosing what to have for lunch might say, The fish and the salad both look good. But the salad costs less. To ensure that students have comprehended this vocabulary, turn to p. 202 in the Student Edition. Then have students read the material presented. .Give students the topics *Clothing*, *Food*, and *Games*. Ask students to choose a category and think of two items they have compared and contrasted. Have pairs practice comparing using the frame *Both* _____ and _____ are _____.

Objectives

- Develop basic sight vocabulary, derive meaning of environmental print, and comprehend English vocabulary and language structures used routinely in written classroom materials.

ELL English Language Learners

Reading Comprehension
Lost City: The Discovery of Machu Picchu

Student Edition pp. 206–207

■ **Frontloading** Have students look through *Lost City: The Discovery of Machu Picchu*, pp. 206–217 in the Student Edition, and tell what they think makes it look like a biography. Distribute copies of the English summary of *Lost City: The Discovery of Machu Picchu* (*ELL Handbook*, p. 157). Have students read the summary aloud with you. Give students support to help them develop language structures needed to comprehend by encouraging them to ask questions about any unfamiliar words. Preview the selection by having students look at the pictures. Have students work to fill in the K-W-L graphic organizer as they read.

Sheltered Reading Ask questions such as the following to guide students' comprehension:

- p. 208: Who was Hiram Bingham? (a professor looking for Inca ruins)

- p. 211: Why did the farmer point straight up? (The ruins were up the steep mountain.)

- p. 215: Why couldn't Bingham see the ruins of the city at first? (The stones were covered by bamboo, vines, mosses, and trees.)

- p. 216: Do you think Bingham found what he was looking for? Explain. (Sample response: No, he was looking for Vilcapampa, but he found something much better (Machu Picchu) instead.)

■ **Fluency: Appropriate Phrasing** Remind students that reading with appropriate phrasing means grouping words together and using punctuation when you read. Read the last paragraph on p. 208. Model attention to phrasing. Point out that exclamation points give a clue how to read expressively. Have pairs choose a paragraph on p. 216. Have students read with attention to phrasing as their partners listen and offer feedback.

After Reading Have students turn to p. 218 of the Student Edition. Have students demonstrate their listening and reading comprehension of the story by using the pictures on the page to retell the story. Then have students further demonstrate their comprehension by answering the questions on the page.

Content Objectives

- Monitor and adjust comprehension.

- Make and adjust predictions.

Language Objectives

- Develop understanding of language structures to comprehend English.

- Summarize text using visual support.

Graphic Organizer

K What We Know	W What We Want to Know	L What We Learned

Audio Support

Students can prepare for reading *Lost City* by using the eSelection or the AudioText CD. See the AudioText CD Routine (*ELL Handbook*, p. 477).

Objectives
- Use visual and contextual support and support from peers and teachers to read grade-appropriate content area text, enhance and confirm understanding, and develop vocabulary, grasp of language structures, and background knowledge needed to comprehend increasingly challenging language.

Support for English Language Learners

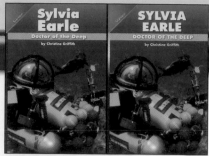

ELD Reader   ELL Reader

For additional leveled instruction, see the **ELL/ELD Reader Teaching Guide.**

Comprehension
Sylvia Earle: Doctor of the Deep

■ **Before Reading** Distribute copies of the ELL and ELD Readers, *Sylvia Earle: Doctor of the Deep*, to students at their reading level.

• Preview Read the title aloud with students: This is a nonfiction text about an ocean scientist named Sylvia Earle. Invite students to look through the pictures and name what they see. Have them predict how Sylvia Earle studies the oceans based on the picture clues and their prior knowledge.

• **Set a Purpose for Reading** Let's read to learn about how Sylvia Earle studies the ocean.

■ **During Reading** Follow this Reading Routine for both reading groups.

1. Read the entire Reader aloud slowly.

2. Reread pp. 1–4, pausing to build background or model comprehension. Have Beginning students finger-point as you read. Use the questions in the chart to check students' comprehension.

3. Have students reread pp. 1–4 independently.

4. Repeat steps 2–3 above for pp. 5–8 of the Reader.

■ **After Reading** Use the exercises on the inside back cover of each Reader and invite students to share their writing. In a whole-group discussion, ask students: What are the different ways Sylvia Earle explored the oceans? Record their answers on the board and invite them to point to pictures in the book to support their answers.

ELD Reader Beginning/Intermediate

■ **p. 4** How long did Sylvia stay underwater in Tektite? (two weeks) Read aloud the sentence that gives you the answer. (p. 4)

■ **p. 6** Why did scientists at Aquarius study coral? (They wanted to learn why it was dying.)

Writing What did Sylvia's company make? Find a sentence in the book that tells about what the company made. Copy the sentence. Read it to your partner.

ELL Reader Advanced/Advanced High

■ **p. 3** Why do divers use snorkels? (Snorkels help divers breathe so they can see underwater.)

■ **p. 8** What can hurt the ocean? (putting trash in it, taking out too many fish)

Study Guide Distribute copies of the ELL Reader Study Guide (*ELL Handbook*, p. 160). Scaffold comprehension of comparing and contrasting by helping students look back through the Reader in order to fill in the graphic organizer. Review their responses together. (See *ELL Handbook*, pp. 209–212.)

Objectives
• Express opinions, ideas, and feelings ranging from communicating single words and short phrases to participating in extended discussions on a variety of social and grade-appropriate academic topics.

 **ELL** English Language Learners

Conventions
Adverbs

■ **Teach/Model** Remind students that adverbs tell when, where, and how something happens. Write these sentences with adverbs on the board:

how: He drove <u>slowly</u>.

when: We went to the movies <u>yesterday</u>.

where: I like to sit <u>outside</u>.

As a class, brainstorm a list of adverbs for each category. As students say adverbs, write them on the board. For example: how: *fast, very, a lot, easily*; when: *early, late, tomorrow, sometimes*; where: *above, below, upstairs, everywhere.*

■ **Practice** Have students make up narrative sentences using the adverbs from the board such as: *They drive fast. We read upstairs.*

 Beginning/Intermediate Have students say, then write adverbs or adverb phrases. Monitor and edit phrases for correct use of adverbs.

Advanced/Advanced High Have students say, write simple sentences using adverbs or adverb phrases. Monitor and edit sentences for correct use of adverbs.

■ **Reteach** Show students how to use the correct adverb by writing these sentences, asking questions, and having students answer with adverbs. Remind students that their adverbs will change the meaning of the sentences.

Zhou walked _____. How did he walk?

Zhou _____ drives. When does he drive?

He likes to read _____. Where does he like to read?

Reread the sentences using the adverbs students provided.

■ **Practice** Tell students they are going to write a narrative story using adverbs.

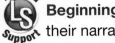 **Beginning** Have students brainstorm verbs and adverbs that they can use in their narrative story.

Intermediate Have students write simple sentences using adverbs in a narrative story.

Advanced/Advanced High Have students write the first paragraph of the story and include adverbs.

Content Objectives
• Identify adverbs.
• Correctly use adverbs.

Language Objectives
• Write sentences with adverbs.

 ## Transfer Skills

Adverbs English learners may use adjectives as adverbs. Help students use adverbs.

Adverbs Point out to Spanish speakers that the adverb suffix *-ly* is like the ending *-mente* in Spanish. Give examples with cognates such as *rapidly/ rápidamente.*

Grammar Jammer

For more practice with adverbs, use the Grammar Jammer for this target skill. See the Grammar Jammer Routine (*ELL Handbook*, p. 478) for suggestions on using this learning tool.

Content Objectives

- Analyze the structure of sentences.
- Recognize short, choppy sentence patterns.

Language Objectives

- Combine short, choppy sentences.
- Share feedback for editing and revising.

ELL Teaching Routine

For practice spelling words related to expeditions, use the Spelling Routine (*ELL Handbook*, p. 476).

ELL Workshop

Students may use classroom resources to respond to questions they have about their writing. *Use Classroom Resources (ELL Handbook, pp. 406–407) provides extra support.*

ELL English Language Learners

Strong Verbs

■ **Introduce** Display the paragraph model and read it aloud. Review that an author uses many different kinds of sentence patterns to make his or her writing more interesting. Which sentence is a simple sentence with one subject and one verb? (the first sentence) Which sentences have two verbs? (the second and fourth sentences). The writer used different types of sentence patterns to make this paragraph more interesting. Explain that the writing model uses formal language or language that is business like.

Writing Model

The Inca built their cities on top of steep mountains. They could see enemies and protect themselves. Although the Inca did not have wheels, they had a system of paved roads. The roads connected villages and were paved with flat stones.

■ **Practice** Write the short, choppy sentences below on the board. These sentences are short and choppy. We can combine them into one sentence to make our writing more interesting. Have students discuss different ways to create sentence patterns using formal language as they speak.

Potatoes were an important crop. Peanuts were an important crop.

■ **Write** Have students write a paragraph using a variety of sentence patterns about a place they would like to explore or an expedition they would like to go on using formal language. For ideas, they can refer to *Lost City* or *Sylvia Earle: Doctor of the Deep*. Have students check their sentence variety.

Beginning Have students draw a picture of a place they want to explore. Ask students to label their drawing. Provide assistance with labels as necessary.

Intermediate Have students use the sentence frames *I want to explore _____. _____ is interesting because _____.* Encourage students to add additional sentences to their paragraph.

Advanced/Advanced High Have students write their paragraph independently. Then have pairs exchange paragraphs and provide feedback for revising and editing.

Objectives

- Write using a variety of grade-appropriate sentence lengths, patterns, and connecting words to combine phrases, clauses, and sentences in increasingly accurate ways as more English is acquired.

Align Instruction to Common Core Anchor Standards

- Introduce and explore this unit's weekly concepts through rich, structured conversations
- Develop complex content knowledge and vocabulary
- Expand on a single concept with engaging literature and nonfiction
- Build better readers in all content areas

What makes an adventure?

WEEK 1
QUESTION OF THE WEEK

How can we prepare for emergencies?

Concept Talk Guide students as they discuss questions such as:

- What objects do people keep handy to prepare for emergencies?
- Who can we call to help during an emergency?

Writing Write a fantasy story about fighting a fire.

WEEK 2
QUESTION OF THE WEEK

What surprises can happen on an expedition?

Concept Talk Guide students as they discuss questions such as:

- What kinds of expeditions can you think of?
- What movies or TV shows have you seen, or stories have you read, about an expedition?

Writing Write a legend about Hiram Bingham and the discovery of Machu Picchu.

WEEK 5
QUESTION OF THE WEEK

What are the risks when walking on the moon?

Concept Talk Guide students as they discuss questions such as:

- What would you expect to find on the moon?
- How would you prepare for walking on the moon?

Writing Write about a time you took a risk that paid off.

WEEK 4
QUESTION OF THE WEEK

What does a person sacrifice to explore the unknown?

Concept Talk Guide students as they discuss questions such as:

- What kind of shelter would you have?
- What kinds of things might you eat?

Writing Write an advertisement encouraging readers to take a trip to Antarctica.

YOU ARE HERE: WEEK 3
QUESTION OF THE WEEK   What does it take to be a hero?

As students answer this unit's Big Question and this week's Question of the Week, they will address:

CCSS Reading 2. Determine central ideas or themes of a text and analyze their development; summarize the key supporting details and ideas. **(Also CCSS Reading 3.)**

Concept Talk Guide students as they discuss questions such as:
- What are some examples of heroism?
- Who are some heroes you know of?
- What kinds of qualities do heroes possess?

As students answer this week's Concept Talk questions, they will address:

CCSS Language 3. Apply knowledge of language to understand how language functions in different contexts, to make effective choices for meaning or style, and to comprehend more fully when reading or listening. **(Also CCSS Speaking/Listening 2.)**

Writing Imagine that you, not Grits, were the one Axel saved in *Cliff Hanger*. Write a thank-you note to your friend for his help.

As students write about this week's prompt, they will address:

CCSS Writing 4. Produce clear and coherent writing in which the development, organization, and style are appropriate to task, purpose, and audience. **(Also CCSS Writing 3.)**

Listening and Speaking On page 255, students learn that when they listen to a presentation, they should ask thoughtful questions. By doing so, they address:

CCSS Speaking/Listening 1. Prepare for and participate effectively in a range of conversations and collaborations with diverse partners, building on others' ideas and expressing their own clearly and persuasively. **(Also CCSS Speaking/Listening 2.)**

ISBN-13: 978-0-328-67819-8   ISBN-10: 0-328-67819-8

Skills Overview

Target Skills and Strategies	© Common Core State Standards for English Language Arts*
Comprehension ◉ **Skill:** Literary Elements: Character, Plot, Theme	**CCSS Literature 3.** Describe in depth a character, setting, or event in a story or drama, drawing on specific details in the text (e.g., a character's thoughts, words, or actions).
Comprehension ◉ **Strategy:** Story Structure	**CCSS Literature 2.** Determine a theme of a story, drama, or poem from details in the text; summarize the text.
Vocabulary ◉ **Skill:** Unfamiliar Words • **Strategy:** Context Clues	**CCSS Language 4.** Determine or clarify the meaning of unknown and multiple-meaning words and phrases *based on grade 4 reading and content*, choosing flexibly from a range of strategies. <line break> **CCSS Language 4.a.** Use context (e.g., definitions, examples, or restatements in text) as a clue to the meaning of a word or phrase.
Fluency • **Skill:** Expression	**CCSS Foundational Skills 4.b.** Read grade-level prose and poetry orally with accuracy, appropriate rate, and expression.
Listening and Speaking • Demonstration (How-To)	**CCSS Speaking/Listening 4.** Report on a topic or text, tell a story, or recount an experience in an organized manner, using appropriate facts and relevant, descriptive details to support main ideas or themes; speak clearly at an understandable pace.
Six-Trait Writing • **Trait of the Week:** Word Choice	**CCSS Writing 3.c.** Use a variety of transitional words and phrases to manage the sequence of events. **CCSS Writing 3.d.** Use concrete words and phrases and sensory details to convey experiences and events precisely.
Writing • Thank-You Note	**CCSS Writing 4.** Produce clear and coherent writing in which the development and organization are appropriate to task, purpose, and audience.
Conventions • **Skill:** Comparative and Superlative Adjectives and Adverbs	**CCSS Language 1.** Demonstrate command of the conventions of standard English grammar and usage when writing or speaking.

Use with Literary Terms, TE p. 232d

Common Core State Standard: CCSS Literature 2.

Write the words *See, Hear, Touch, Smell, Taste* in a five-column chart on the board. Discuss with students that imagery uses sensory details, or words that appeal to the senses, to make stories seem realistic.

- Ask students to review *Cliff Hanger* and to find sensory words and phrases they can put in the appropriate columns of the chart.
- Have students refer to the details to tell how they enhance the story.
- Help students identify the theme of the story. Ask them to explain how the story's imagery and other details support its theme.

Michigan
COMMON CORE EDITION

This Week's Common Core/Michigan Skills Overview

This Week's Target Skills and Strategies

Target Skills and Strategies	Common Core State Standards for English Language Arts*	Michigan English Language Arts Grade Level Content Expectations
Comprehension Skill: Literary Elements: Character, Plot, Theme	**CCSS Literature 3.** Describe in depth a character, setting, or event in a story or drama, drawing on specific details in the text (e.g., a character's thoughts, words, or actions).	MI R.MT.04.01 Self-monitor comprehension when reading or listening to text by automatically applying and discussing the strategies used by mature readers to increase comprehension including: predicting, constructing mental images, visually representing ideas in text, questioning, rereading or listening again if uncertain about meaning, inferring, summarizing, and engaging in interpretive discussions.
Strategy: Story Structure	**CCSS Literature 2.** Determine a theme of a story, drama, or poem from details in the text; summarize the text.	MI R.NT.04.02 Identify and describe the structure, elements, and purpose of a variety of narrative genre including poetry, myths, legends, fantasy, and adventure.
Vocabulary Skill: Unfamiliar Words Strategy: Context Clues	**CCSS Language 4.** Determine or clarify the meaning of unknown and multiple-meaning words and phrases *based on grade 4 reading and content*, choosing flexibly from a range of strategies. **(Also CCSS Language 4.a.)**	MI R.WS.04.07 In context, determine the meaning of words and phrases including similes, metaphors, content vocabulary, and literary terms using strategies and resources including context clues, semantic feature analysis, and a thesaurus.
Fluency Skill: Expression	**CCSS Foundational Skills 4.b.** Read grade-level prose and poetry orally with accuracy, appropriate rate, and expression.	MI R.WS.04.06 Fluently read beginning grade-level text and increasingly demanding text as the year proceeds.
Listening and Speaking Give a Demonstration	**CCSS Speaking/Listening 4.** Report on a topic or text, tell a story, or recount an experience in an organized manner, using appropriate facts and relevant, descriptive details to support main ideas or themes; speak clearly at an understandable pace.	MI S.CN.04.03 Speak effectively using facial expressions, hand gestures, and body language in narrative and informational presentations.
Six-Trait Writing Trait of the Week: Word Choice	**CCSS Writing 3.c.** Use a variety of transitional words and phrases to manage the sequence of events. **(Also CCSS Writing 3.d.)**	MI W.PS.04.01 Exhibit personal style and voice to enhance the written message in both narrative (e.g., strong verbs, figurative language, sensory images) and informational writing (e.g., precision, established importance, transitions).
Writing Thank-You Note	**CCSS Writing 4.** Produce clear and coherent writing in which the development and organization are appropriate to task, purpose, and audience.	MI W.PR.04.01 Set a purpose, consider audience, and replicate authors' styles and patterns when writing a narrative or informational piece. **(Also** MI W.GR.04.02, MI W.GR.04.03, MI W.GR.04.04, MI W.GR.04.05)
Conventions Skill: Comparative and Superlative Adjectives and Adverbs	**CCSS Language 1.** Demonstrate command of the conventions of standard English grammar and usage when writing or speaking.	MI W.GR.04.01 In the context of writing, correctly use simple and compound sentences; direct and indirect objects; prepositional phrases; adjectives; common and proper nouns as subjects and objects; pronouns as antecedents; regular and irregular verbs; hyphens between syllables; apostrophes in contractions; and commas in salutations to set off words; phrases and dialogue; quotation marks or italics to identify titles or names.

Grade 4 Skills Trace

Skills and Strategies	Looking Back	This Week's Selection	Looking Ahead
Comprehension Skill: Literary Elements:	Unit 1 79c, 80–81, 90–91, 91a, 94c, 95a, 96–97 **Unit 4** 141c, 142–143, 148–149,	229c, 230–231, 232c, 236–239, 241a, 242c, 242–247, 250–255, 255h, 255i	Unit 5 IR34–IR35

This Week on Reading Street!

 Question of the Week

What does it take to be a hero?

Daily Plan

Don't Wait Until Friday

Whole Group
- ◉ Literary Elements: Character, Plot, Theme
- ◉ Unfamiliar Words
- • Fluency/Expression
- • Research and Inquiry

MONITOR PROGRESS	Success Predictor		
Day 1 Check Oral Vocabulary	Days 2–3 Check Retelling	Day 4 Check Fluency	Day 5 Check Oral Vocabulary

Small Group

Teacher Led

- • Reading Support
- • Skill Support
- • Fluency Practice

Practice Stations

Independent Activities

Customize Literacy More support for a balanced literacy approach, see pp. CL•1–CL•47

Customize Writing More support for a customized writing approach, see pp. CW•1–CW•10

Whole Group
- • Writing: Thank-You Note
- • Conventions: Comparative and Superlative Adjectives and Adverbs
- • Spelling: Greek Word Parts

Assessment
- • Weekly Tests
- • Day 5 Assessment
- • Fresh Reads

You Are Here! Unit 5 Week 3

This Week's Reading Selections

Main Selection Genre: **Realistic Fiction**

Paired Selection **21st Century Skills**

Leveled Readers

ELL and ELD Readers

Resources on Reading Street!

	Build Concepts	**Comprehension**
Whole Group	 Let's Talk About pp. 228–229	  Envision It! Skills/ Comprehension Skills Strategies Lesson pp. 230–231
Go Digital	• Concept Talk Video	• Envision It! Animations • eSelections
Small Group and Independent Practice	 Cliff Hanger ELL and Leveled pp. 234–235 ELD Readers Readers	  Cliff Hanger ELL and Leveled Envision It! Skills/ pp. 234–235 ELD Readers Readers Strategies Reader's Practice and Writer's Station Notebook Flip Chart
Go Digital	• eReaders • eSelections	• Envision It! Animations • eSelections • eReaders
Customize Literacy	• Leveled Readers	• Envision It! Skills and Strategies Handbook • Leveled Readers
Go Digital	• Concept Talk Video • Big Question Video • eReaders	• Envision It! Animations • eReaders

Vocabulary

Envision It! Vocabulary Cards

Vocabulary Skill Lesson pp. 232–233

- Envision It! Vocabulary Cards
- Vocabulary Activities

Fluency

Let's Learn It! pp. 254–255

- eSelections
- eReaders

Conventions and Writing

Let's Write It! pp. 248–249

- Grammar Jammer

Envision It! Vocabulary Cards

Cliff Hanger pp. 234–235

Practice Station Flip Chart

Words! W•7

Reader's and Writer's Notebook

Cliff Hanger pp. 234–235

Practice Station Flip Chart

Leveled Readers

ELL and ELD Readers

Reader's and Writer's Notebook

Cliff Hanger pp. 234–235

Practice Station Flip Chart

- Envision It! Vocabulary Cards
- Vocabulary Activities
- eSelections

- eSelections
- eReaders

- Grammar Jammer

- Envision It! Vocabulary Cards

- Leveled Readers

- Reader's and Writer's Notebook

- Vocabulary Activities

- eReaders

- Grammar Jammer

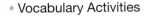

You Are Here!
Unit 5
Week 3

My 5-Day Planner for Reading Street!

MONITOR PROGRESS *Don't Wait Until Friday*

	Check Oral Vocabulary **Day 1** pages 228j–231f	Check Retelling **Day 2** pages 232a–241e
Get Ready to Read	**Concept Talk,** 228j **Oral Vocabulary,** 229a extraordinary, decency, courage, valiant **Listening Comprehension,** Read Aloud, 229b	**Concept Talk,** 232a **Oral Vocabulary,** 232b admirable, individual **Word Analysis,** 232c Related Words **Literary Terms,** 232d Imagery **Story Structure,** 232d Climax
Read and Comprehend	**Comprehension Skill,** ◉ Literary Elements: Character, Plot, Theme, 229c **Comprehension Strategy,** ◉ Story Structure, 229c **READ Comprehension,** 230–231 **Model Fluency,** Expression, 230–231 **Introduce Lesson Vocabulary,** 231a trekked, foresaw, rappel, ridge, coil, descent, void, shaft	**Vocabulary Skill,** ◉ Unfamiliar Words, 232e **Vocabulary Strategy,** Context Clues, 232e **Lesson Vocabulary,** 232–233 trekked, foresaw, rappel, ridge, coil, descent, void, shaft **READ Vocabulary,** 232–233 **Model Fluency,** Expression, 232–233 **READ Main Selection,** *Cliff Hanger,* 234–241
Language Arts	**Research and Inquiry,** Identify Questions, 231b **Spelling,** Greek Word Parts, 231c **Conventions,** Comparative and Superlative Adjectives and Adverbs, 231d **Handwriting,** Cursive Letters *O* and *o,* 231d **Writing,** Thank-You Note, 231e–231f	**Research and Inquiry,** Navigate/Search, 241b **Conventions,** Comparative and Superlative Adjectives and Adverbs, 241c **Spelling,** Greek Word Parts, 241c **Writing,** Thank-You Note, Word Choice, 241d–241e

You Are Here! Unit 5 Week 3

What does it take to be a hero?

Check Retelling	Check Fluency	Check Oral Vocabulary
Day 3 pages 242a–249c	**Day 4** pages 250a–255e	**Day 5** pages 255f–255q
Concept Talk, 242a **Oral Vocabulary,** 242b protect, secure **Comprehension Check,** 242c **Check Retelling,** 242d	**Concept Talk,** 250a **Oral Vocabulary,** 250b generous, flood **21st Century Skills,** Online Sources, 250c	**Concept Wrap Up,** 255f **Check Oral Vocabulary,** 255g extraordinary, decency, courage, valiant, admirable, individual, protect, secure, generous, flood **Amazing Ideas,** 283g Review ◉ Literary Elements: Character, Plot, Theme, 255h Review ◉ Unfamiliar Words, 255h Review **Word Analysis,** 255i Review **Literary Terms,** 255i
READ Main Selection, *Cliff Hanger,* 242–245 **Retelling,** 246–247 **Think Critically,** 247a **Model Fluency,** Expression, 247b **Research and Study Skills,** Diagram/Scale Drawing, 247c	**READ Paired Selection,** "Rock Climbing," 250–253 **Let's Learn It!** 254–255a Fluency: Expression Vocabulary: Unfamiliar Words Listening and Speaking: How-to Demonstration	**Fluency Assessment,** wcpm, 255j–255k **Comprehension Assessment,** ◉ Literary Elements: Character, Plot, Theme, 255l–255m
Research and Inquiry, Analyze, 247d **Conventions,** Comparative and Superlative Adjectives and Adverbs, 247e **Spelling,** Greek Word Parts, 247e **Let's Write It!** Thank-You Note, 248–249a **Writing,** Thank-You Note, Word Choice, 249a–249c	**Research and Inquiry,** Synthesize, 255b **Conventions,** Comparative and Superlative Adjectives and Adverbs, 255c **Spelling,** Greek Word Parts, 255c **Writing,** Thank-You Note, Revising, 255d–255e	**Research and Inquiry,** Communicate, 255n **Conventions,** Comparative and Superlative Adjectives and Adverbs, 255o **Spelling Test,** Greek Word Parts, 255o **Writing,** Thank-You Note, Comparative and Superlative Adjectives and Adverbs, 255p **Quick Write for Fluency,** 255q

Grouping Options for Differentiated Instruction
Turn the page for the small group time lesson plan.

Planning Small Group Time on Reading Street!

SMALL GROUP TIME RESOURCES

Look for this Small Group Time box each day to help meet the individual needs of all your students. Differentiated Instruction lessons appear on the DI pages at the end of each week.

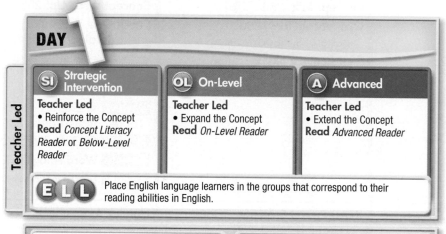

DAY 1

Teacher Led

(SI) Strategic Intervention

Teacher Led
• Reinforce the Concept
Read *Concept Literacy Reader* or *Below-Level Reader*

(OL) On-Level

Teacher Led
• Expand the Concept
Read *On-Level Reader*

(A) Advanced

Teacher Led
• Extend the Concept
Read *Advanced Reader*

(ELL) Place English language learners in the groups that correspond to their reading abilities in English.

Practice Stations
• Read for Meaning
• Get Fluent
• Word Work

Independent Activities
• Concept Talk Video
• *Reader's and Writer's Notebook*
• Research and Inquiry

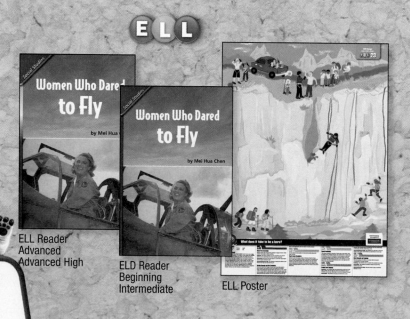

ELL Reader
Advanced
Advanced High

ELD Reader
Beginning
Intermediate

ELL Poster

	Day 1
(SI) Strategic Intervention	**Reinforce the Concept,** DI•51–DI•52 **Read Concept Literacy Reader** or **Below-Level Reader**
(OL) On-Level	**Expand the Concept,** DI•57 **Read On-Level Reader**
(A) Advanced	**Extend the Concept,** DI•62 **Read Advanced Reader**
(ELL) English Language Learners	DI•66–DI•75 **Frontload Concept** **Preteach Skills** **Writing**

You Are Here!
Unit 5
Week 3

Question of the Week
What does it take to be a hero?

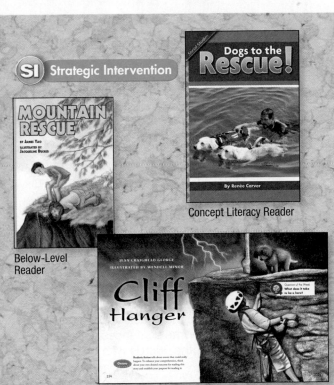

SI Strategic Intervention

MOUNTAIN RESCUE
Below-Level Reader

Dogs to the Rescue!
By Renée Carver
Concept Literacy Reader

Cliff Hanger
JEAN CRAIGHEAD GEORGE
ILLUSTRATED BY WENDELL MINOR
Cliff Hanger, pp. 234–235

OL On-Level

Bessie Coleman: Queen of the Skies
by Sharon Franklin
On-Level Reader

A Advanced

A BOOK OF THEIR OWN
by Barbara A. Donovan
illustrated by Dana Regan
Advanced Reader

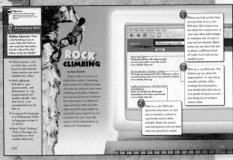

Rock Climbing pp. 250–251

Small Group Weekly Plan

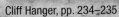

Day 2	Day 3	Day 4	Day 5
Reinforce Comprehension, DI•53 **Revisit Main Selection**	**Reinforce Vocabulary,** DI•54 **Read/Revisit Main Selection**	**Reinforce Comprehension,** Practice Retelling, DI•55 Genre Focus **Read/Revisit Paired Selection**	**Practice Fluency,** DI•56 **Reread Concept Literacy Reader** or **Below-Level Reader**
Expand Comprehension, DI•58 **Revisit Main Selection**	**Expand Vocabulary,** DI•59 **Read/Revisit Main Selection**	**Expand Comprehension,** Practice Retelling, DI•60 Genre Focus **Read/Revisit Paired Selection**	**Practice Fluency,** DI•61 **Reread On-Level Reader**
Extend Comprehension, DI•63 **Revisit Main Selection**	**Extend Vocabulary,** DI•64 **Read/Revisit Main Selection**	**Extend Comprehension,** Genre Focus, DI•65 **Read/Revisit Paired Selection**	**Practice Fluency,** DI•65 **Reread Advanced Reader**
DI•66–DI•75 **Review Concept/Skills** **Frontload Main Selection** **Practice**	DI•66–DI•75 **Review Concept/Skills** **Reread Main Selection** **Practice**	DI•66–DI•75 **Review Concept** **Read ELL/ELD Readers** **Practice**	DI•66–DI•75 **Review Concept/Skills** **Reread ELL/ELD Readers** **Writing**

Practice Stations for Everyone on Reading Street!

Word Wise
Double consonants

Objectives
• Spell words with double consonants.

Materials
• *Word Wise* Flip Chart Activity 23
• Teacher-made word cards
• paper   • pencils

Differentiated Activities

🔵 Choose five word cards. Write the words. Circle the double consonants in each word. Write a sentence for each word.

🔺 Choose seven word cards, and write the words. Circle the double consonants in each word, and then write a sentence for each word.

🟥 Choose nine word cards, and write the words. Circle the double consonants in each word, and write sentences using the word.

Technology
• Online Dictionary

Word Work
Double consonants

Objectives
• Pronounce and write words with double consonants.

Materials
• *Word Work* Flip Chart Activity 23
• Teacher-made word cards
• paper   • pencils

Differentiated Activities

🔵 Choose six word cards. Write the words, and say each word. Think of other words with double consonants. Add the words to your list.

🔺 Choose ten word cards, and write the words. Say each word. Add other words with double consonants to your list. Write a funny, four- or eight-line poem using some of the words.

🟥 Choose twelve word cards, and write the words. Say each word. Add other double consonant words to your list. Use the words in a funny, eight-line poem.

Technology
• Modeled Pronunciation Audio CD

Words to Know
Greek and Latin roots

Objectives
• Identify the meaning of words with Greek and Latin roots.

Materials
• *Words to Know* Flip Chart Activity 23
• Teacher-made word cards
• paper   • pencils

Differentiated Activities

🔵 Choose six word cards. Write the words. Circle the Greek or Latin root in each word. Write sentences using each word. Add other words with these roots to your list.

🔺 Choose eight word cards, and write the words. Circle the Greek or Latin root in each word. Write sentences using each word. Add other words with these roots.

🟥 Choose ten word cards, and write the words. Circle the Greek or Latin root in each word. Write sentences using each word, and add other words with these roots to your list.

Technology
• Online Dictionary

You Are Here!
Unit 5
Week 3

Use this week's materials from the Reading Street Leveled Practice Stations Kit to organize this week's stations.

Practice Station Flip Chart

Let's Write!
Legend

Objectives
• Write a legend.

Materials
• *Let's Write!* Flip Chart Activity 23
• paper • pencils

Differentiated Activities

 Think about a famous person from history. Write a legend about this person. Include interesting facts that tell about this person. Proofread your legend.

△ Think about a famous person from history. Write a legend about this person that gives interesting facts and details. Proofread and combine short sentences.

■ Think of a famous person from history. Write a legend about this person's life. Include interesting details, and explain the reason the person is famous. Combine short, choppy sentences.

Technology
• Online Graphic Organizers

Read for Meaning
Compare and contrast

Objectives
• Compare and contrast two settings.

Materials
• *Read for Meaning* Flip Chart Activity 23
• Leveled Readers • paper • pencils

Differentiated Activities

 Read one of the books your teacher provides. How does the setting of the selection compare to the setting in another story you have read? Write one sentence comparing the settings. Write one sentence contrasting them.

△ Read one of the books your teacher provides, and think about how the setting compares to the setting in another story you have read. Write two sentences comparing the settings. Write two sentences contrasting them.

■ Read one of the books your teacher provides. Compare and contrast the setting of the selection to the setting in another story you have read. Write a short paragraph comparing the settings. Write a short paragraph contrasting the settings.

Technology
• Leveled Reader Database

Get Fluent
Practice fluent reading.

Objectives
• Read aloud using appropriate phrasing.

Materials
• *Get Fluent* Flip Chart Activity 23
• Leveled Readers

Differentiated Activities

 Work with a partner. Choose a Concept Literacy Reader or Below-Level Reader. Take turns reading a page from the book. Use the readers to practice appropriate phrasing. Provide feedback as needed.

△ Work with a partner. Choose an On-Level Reader. Take turns reading a page from the book. Use the reader to practice appropriate phrasing. Provide feedback as needed.

■ Work with a partner. Choose an Advanced Reader. Take turns reading a page from the book. Use the reader to practice appropriate phrasing. Provide feedback as needed.

Technology
• Leveled Reader Database
• Reading Street Readers CD-ROM

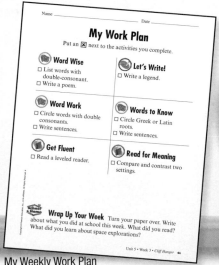

My Weekly Work Plan

week 3

Objectives
- Introduce the weekly concept.
- Develop oral vocabulary.

Today at a Glance

Oral Vocabulary
extraordinary, decency, courage, valiant

Comprehension
- Literary elements: character, plot, theme
- Story structure: climax

Reading
"A Family Just Like Ours"

Fluency
Expression

Lesson Vocabulary
Tested vocabulary

Research and Inquiry
Identify questions

Spelling
Greek word parts

Conventions
Comparative and superlative adjectives and adverbs

Handwriting
Cursive letters *O* and *o*

Writing
Thank-you note

Concept Talk

Question of the Week

What does it take to be a hero?

Introduce the concept

To further explore the unit concept of Adventures by Land, Air and Water, this week students will read, write, and talk about what it takes to be a hero. Write the Question of the Week on the board.

> **ROUTINE** **Activate Prior Knowledge** **Team Talk**
>
> **Think** Have students think about what heroism is and what it takes to be a hero.
>
> **Pair** Have students discuss the question by posing questions with appropriate detail and making pertinent comments.
>
> **Share** Call on a few students to share their ideas with the group. Guide discussion and encourage elaboration with prompts such as:
>
> - What are some examples of heroism?
> - Who are some heroes you know of?
> - What kinds of qualities do heroes possess?

Routines Flip Chart

Anchored Talk

Develop oral vocabulary

Have students turn to pp. 228–229 in their Student Editions. Look at each of the photos. Then use the prompts to guide discussion and create the *What it takes to be a hero* concept map. Remind students to ask and answer questions with appropriate details.

- What job does the man in front of the building have? (He is a police officer.) What do the police officer, firefighter, and mother have in common? (They are all heroes; they help others.) Let's add *Heroic People* and *Heroic Acts* to our concept map.

- In what ways do heroes act? In what ways are they *extraordinary*? (They act with bravery; put others first; save lives.) Let's add *Heroic Qualities* to our concept map and list *extraordinary* below it.

Objectives
• Listen closely to speakers and ask questions about and comment on the topic. • Speak clearly and to the point, give an opinion and support it with correct information.

Oral Vocabulary

Let's Talk About

Heroism
• Share opinions about what a hero is.
• Express opinions with appropriate speaking rate.
• Add comments to others' ideas.

READING STREET ONLINE
CONCEPT TALK VIDEO
www.ReadingStreet.com

You've learned `2 2 0`
Amazing Words ⭐ **so far this year!**

228
229

Student Edition pp. 228–229

 Amazing Words

You've learned `2 2 0` words so far

You'll learn `0 1 0` words this week!

extraordinary	individual
decency	protect
courage	secure
valiant	generous
admirable	flood

Writing on Demand ⏱

Writing Fluency
Ask students to respond to the photos on pp. 228–229 by writing as well as they can about what it takes to be a hero.

• After discussing the photos, ask: What does it take to be a hero?

What it takes to be a hero
- Heroic People
- Heroic Acts
- Heroic Qualities

Connect to reading

Tell students that this week they will be reading about different kinds of heroes. Encourage students to add concept-related words to this week's concept map.

ELL

English Language Learners
Extra support Additional ELL support and modified instruction is provided in the *ELL Handbook* and in the ELL Support lessons on pp. DI•66–DI•75.

Listening comprehension
English learners will benefit from additional visual support to understand the key terms in the concept map. Use the pictures on pp. 228–229 to scaffold understanding.

Frontload for Read Aloud
Use the modified Read Aloud in the ELL Support Lessons to prepare students to listen to "Heroes and She-roes" on p. 229b.

ELL **Preteach Concepts** Use the Day 1 instruction on ELL Poster 23 to assess and build background knowledge, develop concepts, and build oral vocabulary.

ELL Poster 23

Oral Vocabulary
Amazing Words

Introduce Amazing Words

"Heroes and She-roes" on p. 229b describes the qualities heroes have. Tell students to listen for this week's Amazing Words—*extraordinary*, *decency*, *courage*, and *valiant*—as you read.

Model fluency

As you read "Heroes and She-roes," model appropriate expression by adjusting your voice to demonstrate a lively, fluent reader.

Teach Amazing Words

Amazing Words Oral Vocabulary Routine

> extraordinary
> decency
> courage
> valiant

1 **Introduce** Write the word *extraordinary* on the board. Have students say the word aloud with you. The poem "Heroes and She-roes" describes heroes as *extraordinary* people. Supply a student-friendly definition. *Extraordinary* describes something that is very unusual or remarkable.

2 **Demonstrate** Have students answer questions to demonstrate understanding. Why are heroes *extraordinary*? (They do more than what's expected of them; they show *extraordinary* bravery.)

3 **Apply** Ask students to give a personal example of *extraordinary*.

See p. OV•3 to teach *decency, courage,* and *valiant*.

Routines Flip Chart

Apply Amazing Words

To build oral language, lead the class in a discussion about the meanings of the Amazing Words. Remind students to listen attentively to speakers and to build on the ideas of others in a discussion.

MONITOR PROGRESS Check Oral Vocabulary

During discussion, listen for students' use of the Amazing Words.

If... students are unable to use the Amazing Words to discuss the concept,

then... use Oral Vocabulary Routine on the Routines Flip Chart to demonstrate words in different contexts.

Day 1	**Days 2–3**	**Day 4**	**Day 5**
Check Oral Vocabulary	Check Retelling	Check Fluency	Check Oral Vocabulary

Read Aloud

Heroes and She-roes

by J. Patrick Lewis

Heroes [and she-roes] set aside their fear

To lend a hand or lend an ear,

To face the night or save the day

And never look the other way.

They do not, with a single bound,

Leap up tall buildings from the ground.

But from a sense of decency,

They share themselves with you and me.

No matter what or where or who,

When something must be done,

They do.

Give thanks to the he- and she-roes

Who will turn upon a dime

When occasion calls for action—

And be there in half the time.

Roll red carpets out for she-roes

And to heroes raise a toast

For extraordinary courage—

Yet you'll never hear them boast.

Lend your hand to he- and she-roes,

To the valiant and the brave,

To those simple people known by

Two simple words: *They gave.*

Oral Vocabulary

Success Predictor

Objectives

◎ Understand and use literary elements to aid comprehension.

◎ Use story structure to aid comprehension.

• Read grade-level text with expression.

Skills Trace

◎ **Literary Elements**

Introduce U1W3D1; U4W5D1; U5W3D1

Practice U1W3D2; U1W3D3; U4W5D2; U4W5D3; U5W3D2; U5W3D3

Reteach/Review U1W3D5; U1W4D2; U1W4D3; U2W1D3; U4W5D3; U5W5D2; U5W5D3; U5W3D5

Assess/Test Weekly Tests U1W3; U4W5; U5W3

Benchmark Tests U5

KEY:
U=Unit   W=Week   D=Day

Skill ↔ Strategy

◉ Literary Elements: Character, Plot, Theme
◉ Story Structure

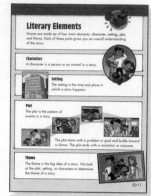

Student Edition p. EI•11

Introduce literary elements

Envision It!

When you read, it is important to pay attention to the character, plot, and theme of a story. What is the plot? (sequence of events in the story) Who are the characters in a story? (the people in the story) What is the theme of a story? (main idea, lesson, or message) Have students turn to pp. EI•10–EI•11 in the Student Edition to review the literary elements character, plot, and theme. Then read "A Family Just Like Ours" with students.

Model the skill

 Think Aloud The main characters in this story are Maddy and her mother. Characters affect the plot in the story. If the characters changed in the story, so would the plot. While on a camping trip, they encounter a moose family. The characters and plot of the story influence the theme, or main idea or central meaning, of the story.

Guide practice

Have students finish reading "A Family Just Like Ours" on their own. After they read, have them use a graphic organizer like the one on p. 230 to describe the interaction of the characters, to sequence the plot's main events, and to summarize the lesson or message of the story as its theme.

Strategy check

Story Structure Remind students that if they have difficulty understanding "A Family Just Like Ours," they can use the structure of the story to improve comprehension. Model the strategy by discussing the events at the beginning, middle, and end of the story. Have students explain how the plot's main events influence future events.

Model the strategy

Envision It!

 Think Aloud At the beginning of the story, Maddy and her mother wake up and take a walk. They see a mother moose and her baby near a stream. The baby splashes and Maddy laughs. Maddy's laughter influences future plot events by causing the father moose to nudge the family along. Understanding the sequence of events in the story helps me understand how the story is put together. Have students find additional examples of how the plot's main events influence future events.

Student Edition p. EI•22

On their own

Use p. 338 in the *Reader's and Writer's Notebook* for additional practice with character, plot, and theme.

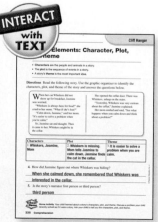

Reader's and Writer's Notebook p. 338

Objectives
- Understand that a story's theme is its central message or lesson.
- Tell the order of events in a story, summarize the events, and explain how they will influence future events in the story.

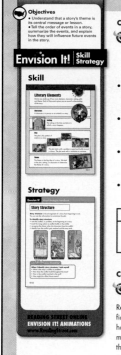

Envision It! | Skill Strategy

Skill

Literary Elements

Strategy

Story Structure

READING STREET ONLINE
ENVISION IT! ANIMATIONS
www.ReadingStreet.com

Comprehension Skill
Literary Elements: Character, Plot, and Theme

- **Characters** are the people in a story. Readers learn about characters by what they say and how they act.
- A **plot** is the sequence of events in a story. Events that happen in the story move the plot forward.
- A story's **theme** is the most important idea. When you finish reading, ask yourself *What does this story mean? What is it all about?*
- Use the graphic to identify the characters, plot, and theme of "A Family Just Like Ours."

Character	Plot	Theme

Comprehension Strategy
Story Structure

Readers pay attention to story structure, or how a fictional story is put together. As you read, notice how the story begins, how it builds through the middle, and how it ends. Events that take place throughout the story move the plot to its logical conclusion.

230

A Family Just Like Ours

Madeline rolled over in her sleeping bag. Blinking, she looked at her mom, wide awake and curled up in a sleeping bag in their tent. "Good morning, Maddy."

"Morning, Mom."

Maddy and her mother left their tent in Grand Teton National Park, Wyoming. Maddy peeked into her dad and brother's tent. She could hear snoring.

"Let's let them sleep. How about a walk?" Mom whispered, handing Maddy a water bottle.

They trekked past the edge of the campsite. Suddenly, Mom stopped. She touched Maddy lightly on the shoulder, put her finger against her lips as a sign for quiet, and pointed toward the stream.

There stood a huge bull moose with a giant rack of antlers, a smaller female moose, and a baby moose. The mother moose walked into the stream, nudging the baby moose along with her. The baby moose splashed in the water, just like Maddy's little brother might have done.

The mother moose must have heard Maddy laugh. Turning her head, the moose looked in their direction. The father moose began herding his family away.

Skill Describe the interactions of the characters and their relationships.

Strategy What events have happened so far? Explain how the mother's sign for quiet results in the next event in the plot.

Skill What is this story about? Summarize the story's theme. Have the characters changed? Explain.

Your Turn!

Need a Review? See the *Envision It! Handbook* for help with literary elements and story structure.

Ready to Try It? To enhance your comprehension, establish your own purpose for reading *Cliff Hanger*.

231

Student Edition pp. 230–231

Skill Madeline and her mother seem to have a close relationship; they go camping together as a family.

Strategy It leads Madeline to look at the stream and see the family of moose.

Skill Madeline and her mom go on a walk. They see a family of moose in a stream. The father moose herds the family away. Madeline and her mom encounter a family just like them. This will change them to hike quietly, so they can see more wildlife.

Academic Vocabulary

theme the main idea or central meaning of a piece of writing

Model Fluency
Expression

Model fluent reading

Have students listen as you read the first paragraph of "A Family Just Like Ours" with appropriate expression. Explain that you will adjust your voice level to stress important words and phrases.

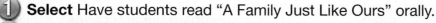

ROUTINE | Paired Reading | Team Talk

1. **Select** Have students read "A Family Just Like Ours" orally.

2. **Reader 1** Students read the entire story, switching readers at the end of each paragraph.

3. **Reader 2** Partners reread the story. This time the other student begins.

4. **Reread** For optimal fluency, have partners continue to read three or four times.

5. **Corrective Feedback** Listen as students read. Provide feedback regarding their expression and encourage them to adjust their voice level as they read.

Routines Flip Chart

English Language Learners
Literary elements Have students reread the story. Provide oral practice by having a group of students tell the three main events in the story in order. Write them on the board. Draw pictures next to each event to help students remember each event. Have them use and reuse the pictures to tell the sequence of events in the story in their own words.

Vocabulary
Tested Vocabulary

Lesson vocabulary

Have students create word rating charts using the categories *Know, Have Seen,* and *Don't Know.*

Word Rating Chart			
Word	Know	Have Seen	Don't Know
coil	✔		
descent		✔	
foresaw			✔
rappel			✔
ridge	✔		
shaft			
trekked			
void			

Activate prior knowledge

Read each word to students and have them rate their knowledge of the word by placing a checkmark in one of the three columns: *Know* (know and can use); *Have Seen* (have seen or heard the word; don't know meaning); *Don't Know* (don't know the word).

Have students provide sentences for the words in the *Know* column. By the end of the week when students have encountered all the words in their reading selections, have them revise their charts and demonstrate their understanding by using each word in a sentence in the correct context.

Preteach Academic Vocabulary

ELL **Academic Vocabulary** Write the following words on the board:

theme	**comparative adjectives**
imagery	**superlative adjectives**
thank-you note	

Have students share what they know about this week's Academic Vocabulary. Use the students' responses to assess their prior knowledge. Preteach the Academic Vocabulary by providing a student-friendly description, explanation, or example that clarifies the meaning of each term. Then ask students to restate the meaning of the Academic Vocabulary term in their own words.

Research and Inquiry
Identify Questions

Teach

Discuss the Question of the Week: *What does it take to be a hero?* Tell students they will research the life of a famous hero. They will present their report and diagram or scale drawing to the class on Day 5.

Model the Strategy

Think Aloud I'll start by brainstorming a list of heroic people. Then I'll try to narrow the list down to one person I admire. I think I'll focus on Amelia Earhart. An inquiry question could be *What made Amelia Earhart want to become a pilot?* Another question could be *What obstacles did Amelia Earhart face as a female pilot?*

Guide practice

After students have formulated open-ended inquiry questions, explain that tomorrow they will conduct research of their questions. To generate a research plan, help students identify key words that will guide their search for relevant information.

On their own

Have students work individually, in pairs, or in small groups to narrow research topics to one question and write an inquiry question.

INTERNET GUY
Don Leu

21st Century Skills

Weekly Inquiry Project

Day 1 Identify Questions

Day 2 Navigate/Search

Day 3 Analyze

Day 4 Synthesize

Day 5 Communicate

Small Group Time

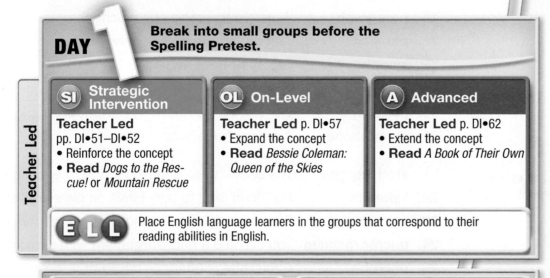

DAY 1

Break into small groups before the Spelling Pretest.

Teacher Led

SI Strategic Intervention	**OL On-Level**	**A Advanced**
Teacher Led pp. DI•51–DI•52 • Reinforce the concept • **Read** *Dogs to the Rescue!* or *Mountain Rescue*	**Teacher Led** p. DI•57 • Expand the concept • **Read** *Bessie Coleman: Queen of the Skies*	**Teacher Led** p. DI•62 • Extend the concept • **Read** *A Book of Their Own*

ELL Place English language learners in the groups that correspond to their reading abilities in English.

Practice Stations
• Read for Meaning
• Get Fluent
• Word Work

Independent Activities
• Concept Talk Video
• *Reader's and Writer's Notebook*
• Vocabulary Activities

English Language Learners
Multilingual vocabulary
Students can apply knowledge of their home languages to acquire new English vocabulary by using Multilingual Vocabulary Lists (*ELL Handbook*, pp. 431–442).

Objectives
- Spell words with Greek word parts.
- Use and understand comparative and superlative adjectives and adverbs.
- Write cursive capital letter *O* and lowercase *o* in words.

Spelling Pretest
Words with Greek Word Parts

Introduce Tell students that many words we use contain Greek word parts. This week we will spell words with Greek word parts.

Pretest Use these sentences to administer the spelling pretest. Say each word, read the sentence, and repeat the word.

1.	**telephone**	I will answer the **telephone.**
2.	**biography**	They read a **biography** of her life last week.
3.	**telescope**	I saw the moon through a **telescope.**
4.	**photograph**	I have a **photograph** of my dog.
5.	**microwave**	Please clean the **microwave** oven.
6.	**diameter**	What is the **diameter** of the circle?
7.	**barometer**	The **barometer** says it will rain.
8.	**microscope**	You can see tiny things through a **microscope.**
9.	**headphones**	Use **headphones** to listen to music.
10.	**microphone**	The singer used a **microphone** at the concert.
11.	**autograph**	I got the author's **autograph** at the book signing.
12.	**microchip**	A **microchip** can hold a lot of data.
13.	**telegraph**	The **telegraph** sent coded messages.
14.	**perimeter**	The fence surrounds the **perimeter** of the yard.
15.	**paragraph**	Write a **paragraph** about school.
16.	**phonics**	I left my **phonics** book at home.
17.	**symphony**	Our **symphony** is great.
18.	**saxophone**	I can play the **saxophone.**
19.	**periscope**	The submarine raised its **periscope.**
20.	**megaphone**	A **megaphone** is cone-shaped.

Challenge words

21.	**stethoscope**	The doctor used a **stethoscope** to examine me.
22.	**xylophone**	My friend likes to play tunes on his **xylophone.**
23.	**cacophony**	The **cacophony** of sounds made the room noisy.
24.	**microorganism**	You can see a **microorganism** with a microscope.
25.	**microbe**	A **microbe** is often the cause of disease.

Self-correct After the pretest, you can either display the correctly spelled words or spell them orally. Have students self-correct their pretests by rewriting misspelled words correctly.

On their own Use *Let's Practice It!* p. 263 on the *Teacher Resources DVD-ROM* for additional practice.

Let's Practice It!
TR DVD•263

Conventions
Comparative and Superlative Adjectives and Adverbs

Grammar Transparency 23, TR DVD

Teach | Display Grammar Transparency 23 and read aloud the explanations and examples in the box. Point out the comparative and superlative adjectives and adverbs and how they are formed.

Model | Model writing the correct form of comparative and superlative adjectives and adverbs to complete numbers 1 and 2. Apply the rules to show how you determined the correct form.

Guide practice | Guide students to complete items 3 and 4. Remind them that some adjectives and adverbs have irregular comparative and superlative forms. Record the correct responses on the transparency.

Daily Fix-It | Use Daily Fix-It numbers 1 and 2 in the right margin.

Connect to oral language | Have students read sentences 5 and 6 on the transparency and write comparative and superlative adjectives and adverbs to correctly complete each sentence.

Handwriting
Cursive Letters O and o

Model letter formation | Display the capital cursive letter *O* and the lowercase letter *o*. Follow the stroke instructions pictured to model letter formation.

Model slant | Explain that writing legibly means letters are the correct size, form, and slant. The writing has smoothness: the lines are not shaky or jagged. Point out that both lowercase and capital *O* slant to the right. Model writing this sentence: *Oliver had only one tool.* Make sure the letters have the proper spacing and slant.

Guide practice | Have students write these sentences: *Olivia is looking for a brown coat in her closet. Otto won a trophy that he keeps in his room.* Circulate around the room, guiding students.

Academic Vocabulary

Comparative adjectives compare two people, places, things, or groups. To form most comparative adjectives, add -er.

Superlative adjectives compare three or more people, places, things, or groups. To form most superlative adjectives, add -est.

Daily Fix-It

1. Have you seen this photagraph of an man climbing down a mountain? *(photograph, a)*
2. He is wearing a harness, and is smiling happy. *(harness and; happily)*

ELL

English Language Learners
Language transfer: Adjectives that compare In Spanish, Korean, and Hmong, comparisons are expressed with phrases. If students have difficulty with comparative adjectives, write phrases such as *the fast runner, the large box.* Ask students to read each phrase and identify the adjective. Then ask them to say the phrase, substituting a comparative form of the adjective.

Handwriting: Comparative adjectives To provide practice in handwriting lowercase *o* and to extend language opportunities, have students write these comparative adjectives: *older, shorter, younger.*

Writing—Thank-You Note
Introduce

MINI-LESSON

5-Day Planner
Guide to Mini-Lessons

DAY 1	Read Like a Writer
DAY 2	Developing an Outline
DAY 3	Choosing Exact Words
DAY 4	Revising Strategy: Adding
DAY 5	Proofread for Comparative and Superlative Adjectives and Adverbs

MINI-LESSON

Read Like a Writer

Reader's and Writer's Notebook p. 339

■ **Introduce** This week you will write a thank-you note to a friend for saving you when you were in a dangerous situation. Your thank-you note will be a friendly letter.

Prompt Imagine that you, not Grits, were the one Axel saved in *Cliff Hanger*. Write a thank-you note to your friend for his help.

Trait Word Choice

Mode Narrative

■ **Examine Model Text** Let's read an example of a thank-you note that thanks a friend for helping when a sailboat turned over. Have students read "Dear Anna" on p. 339 of their *Reader's and Writer's Notebook*.

■ **Key Features** A thank-you note uses letter format. Find the date, salutation, closing, and signature in the model and circle them. Have students interact by circling the parts of the thank-you note. Discuss the function of each of these parts of a friendly letter. Now let's look at the body of the letter and how the writer retells what happened. Discuss how the writer was saved.

A thank-you note has a friendly tone. Have students draw a box around a part of the letter that has a friendly tone.

A thank-you note tells why the writer is grateful. Have students underline the sentences that tell why the writer is grateful.

Explain that today people sometimes send thank-you notes by e-mail and that these notes don't always contain all the parts of a friendly letter.

Review
Key features

Review the key features of a thank-you note. You may want to post the key features in the classroom for students to refer to as they work on their thank-you notes.

Key Features of a Thank-You Note

- uses letter format
- has a friendly tone
- explains why the writer feels grateful

Write Guy
Jeff Anderson

Register Swap

Even if they don't know what to call them, students often know the difference between formal and informal registers. We talk different ways in different situations. Discuss with students the types of audiences and situations where they might use informal language and those where they might use formal language.

ROUTINE **Quick Write for Fluency** **Team Talk**

1. **Talk** Have partners participate in a short discussion on the features of a thank-you note.

2. **Write** Each student writes a short paragraph that gives details on why he or she thinks a person might write a thank-you note.

3. **Share** Partners read each other's paragraphs.

Routines Flip Chart

English Language Learners
Read the writing model aloud and help students understand it. Make sure students understand the parts of a friendly letter. Have them work with a partner and take turns suggesting other examples of a date, a salutation, and a closing.

Wrap Up Your Day

✔ **Build Concepts** Discuss what you learned about what it takes to be a hero.

✔ **Oral Vocabulary** Have students use the Amazing Words they learned in context sentences.

✔ **Homework** Send home this week's Family Times newsletter in *Let's Practice It!* pp. 264–265 on the *Teacher Resources DVD-ROM.*

Let's Practice It
TR DVD•264–265

Preview DAY 2

Tell students that tomorrow they will read a selection about a heroic rescue on a mountain.

Objectives
- Expand the weekly concept.
- Develop oral vocabulary.

Today at a Glance

Oral Vocabulary
admirable, individual

Word Analysis
Related words

Literary Terms
Imagery

Story Structure
Climax

Lesson Vocabulary
◉ Unfamiliar words

Reading
"Climbing New Heights"

Cliff Hanger

Fluency
Expression

Research and Inquiry
Navigate/Search

Spelling
Greek word parts

Conventions
Comparative and superlative
adjectives and adverbs

Writing
Thank-you note

Concept Talk

Question of the Week

What does it take to be a hero?

Expand the concept

Remind students of the weekly concept question. Tell students that today they will begin reading *Cliff Hanger*. As they read, encourage students to think about what it takes to be a hero.

Anchored Talk

Develop oral vocabulary

Use the photos on pp. 228–229 and the Read Aloud, "Heroes and She-roes," to talk about the Amazing Words *extraordinary, decency, courage,* and *valiant.* Use the context of the sentence to help you determine the meaning of these words. Add these and other concept-related words to the concept map to develop students' knowledge of the topic. Discuss the following questions. Remind students to listen attentively to other students and to answer with appropriate detail. Encourage students to build on others' ideas when they answer.

- What makes heroes *extraordinary*?
- How do people show they are acting with *decency*?
- Discuss a time when you were *valiant* or showed great *courage*.

Oral Vocabulary
Amazing Words

Amazing Words
extraordinary	individual
decency	protect
courage	secure
valiant	generous
admirable	flood

Teach Amazing Words

Amazing Words — Oral Vocabulary Routine

1 Introduce Write the Amazing Word *admirable* on the board. Have students say it aloud with you. Relate *admirable* to the photographs on pp. 228–229 and "Heroes and She-roes." How do heroes show they are *admirable*? (They help others; go above the call of duty; save lives.) Have students determine the definition of the word. A person who is admirable acts in a way that deserves respect or approval.

2 Demonstrate Have students answer questions to demonstrate understanding. What types of situations call for people to be *admirable*? (those where a person's life is at risk, those where others can see you making good or bad choices) How can you be *admirable*? (follow the rules, help others even when you don't have to)

3 Apply Have students apply their understanding. What is a synonym for the word *admirable*? (*great, honorable, respectable, deserving*)

See p. OV•3 to teach *individual*.

Routines Flip Chart

Apply Amazing Words

As students read "Climbing New Heights" on p. 233, have them think about how this *individual*, George Dunn, acts in a way that is *admirable*.

Connect to reading

Explain that today students will read about a boy who takes risks to save his dog. As they read, they should think about how the Question of the Week and the Amazing Words *admirable* and *individual* apply to the story.

ELL **Reinforce Vocabulary** Use the Day 2 instruction on ELL Poster 23 to teach Lesson Vocabulary and the lesson concept.

Objectives

• Recognize and understand the meanings of related words.

• Understand how imagery is used to help the reader experience the text.

• Summarize the main events to understand the climax of the story.

Word Analysis
Related Words

Teach related words

Tell students that related words are words that share a common morpheme and can sometimes be related in meaning. Knowing the meaning of one word is a clue that can help them determine the meaning of the other.

Model

Think Aloud Display the words *descent* and *descend*. These words are related words, words that share a common morpheme, and are sometimes related in meaning. A morpheme is the smallest unit of language to carry meaning. Underline the letters both words have in common. We know that *descent* means the "action of moving downward." The word *descend* has a similar spelling, so we can guess that it may have a similar meaning. When I look up *descend* in the dictionary, I see that it can mean "to move downward" or "to come from."

Guide practice

Word	Related Words
foresaw	foresee, foreseen, foresight
coil	coils, coiled, coiling, recoil, recoils, recoiled, recoiling
void	voided, avoid, avoiding, avoidance

Have students build more related words from the Words to Know list.

On their own

Have students check the meanings of the new words in the dictionary or glossary to verify that the related words are in fact words. Follow the Strategy for Meaningful Word Parts to teach the words *foresee* and *foresaw*.

ROUTINE Strategy for Meaningful Word Parts

1. **Introduce word parts** Circle the word *fore* in *foresaw* and *foresee*.

2. **Connect to meaning** Define *fore* as "placed in front" and *saw* as "the past tense of see."

3. **Relate the words** The words *foresaw* and *foresee* are related. *Foresee* is the present tense of *foresaw*.

Continue the routine with the words *coil* and *recoil*.

Routines Flip Chart

Literary Terms
Imagery

Teach imagery

Tell students that imagery is the use of words that help the reader experience the way things look, sound, smell, taste, or feel. These words spark the senses or imagination. Imagery is used in fiction to make characters and settings seem real.

Model imagery

Think Aloud Let's look back at "A Family Just Like Ours" on page 231. Reread the selection. What imagery does the author use? (Answers will vary. Possible responses: wide awake, curled up, snoring, whispered, trekked, nudging, splashed.)

Guide practice

Find an example of imagery in *Cliff Hanger*. Remind students that these words are details that trigger the senses or imagination.

On their own

Have students look for examples of imagery in other selections of their Student Edition. Have them list the words in a chart with the headings: look, sound, smell, taste, and feel.

Story Structure
Climax

Teach climax

In fiction, the climax is the turning point when the character does something that will bring about the conclusion of the story. It is often the most exciting part of the story.

Model the strategy

Think Aloud Understanding and summarizing the main events in the story can help us determine the climax. After reading "A Family Just Like Ours," we know the main events are: Maddy and her mother peek into the boys' tent to see they are sleeping; Maddy and her mother go for a walk past their campsite; they see a mother and baby moose in a stream; the baby moose splashes in the water; Maddy laughs and the father moose herds his family away. If we decide which event happens just before the conclusion of the story, this will likely be the story's climax.

Guide practice

Have students determine the climax of "A Family Just Like Ours."

On their own

Have students review the climaxes of other stories they have read together as a class. Encourage students to summarize the events in each story before determining the climax.

Academic Vocabulary

imagery the use of words that help the reader experience the way things look, sound, smell, taste, or feel

Objectives

◎ Use context clues to determine the meaning of unfamiliar words.

• Read aloud grade-level text with expression.

Vocabulary Strategy for
Unfamiliar Words

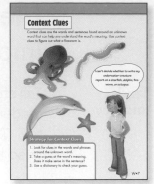

Student Edition p. W•7

Teach unfamiliar words

Envision It!

Tell students that when they encounter an unfamiliar word, they should use the strategy of context clues, or the words in the sentences around the unfamiliar word, to determine the meaning of the word. Refer students to *Words!* on p. W•7 in the Student Edition for additional practice.

Model the strategy

Write on the board: *In gym class, we learned how to use ropes and pulleys to rappel down a climbing wall.*

 Think Aloud The word *rappel* is an unfamiliar word, so I will use the strategy of looking for clues to help me figure out its meaning. The words *ropes*, *pulleys*, *down*, and *climbing wall* are words that help me determine meaning. Using them, I understand that *rappel* means "to lower yourself down."

Guide practice

Write this sentence on the board: *The hose is stored in a neat coil, wrapped tightly when not in use.* Have students determine the meaning of *coil* using context clues. Have them list the context clues they used to help them understand the meaning of *coil*. For additional support, use *Envision It! Pictured Vocabulary Cards* or *Tested Vocabulary Cards*.

On their own

Read "Climbing New Heights" on p. 233. Have students use context clues to determine the meanings of the lesson vocabulary words. For additional practice use *Reader's and Writer's Notebook* p. 340.

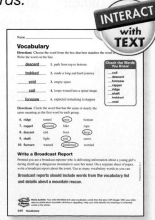

Reader's and Writer's Notebook p. 340

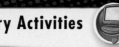
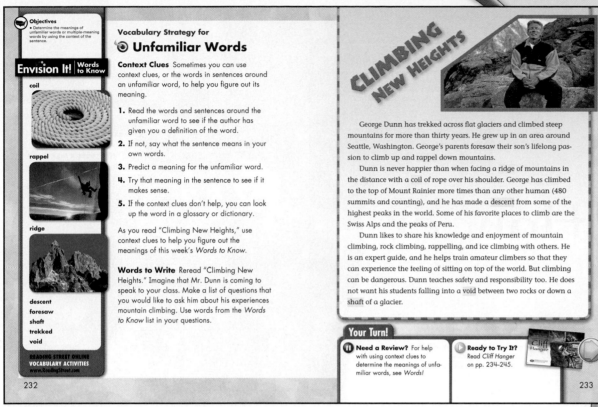

Student Edition pp. 232–233

Reread for Fluency
Expression

Model fluent reading

Have students listen as you read paragraph 1 of "Climbing New Heights" with appropriate expression. Explain that you will adjust your voice level to stress important words and phrases.

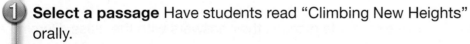

ROUTINE **Paired Reading**

1. **Select a passage** Have students read "Climbing New Heights" orally.

2. **Reader 1** Students read the entire story, switching readers at the end of each paragraph.

3. **Reader 2** Partners reread the story, slowing down to be sure they comprehend the text. This time the other student begins.

4. **Corrective Feedback** Listen as students read. Provide feedback regarding their expression and encourage them to adjust their voice level to stress important words and phrases.

Routines Flip Chart

Differentiated Instruction

SI Strategic Intervention

Context clues Have students work with a partner to read "Climbing New Heights" and find the context clues that help them understand the meaning of the lesson vocabulary words.

Lesson Vocabulary

coil to wind around and around, forming a pile

descent the act of moving down from a higher to a lower place

foresaw saw or knew beforehand

rappel to lower yourself down the face of a cliff by means of a rope fastened to the top of the cliff and placed around your body, so that the rope can be gradually lengthened

ridge the long narrow upper part of something

shaft a long, narrow, usually vertical hole

trekked traveled slowly by any means

void an empty space

Objectives

- Understand the elements of realistic fiction.
- Use text features to preview and predict.
- Set a purpose for reading.

JEAN CRAIGHEAD GEORGE

ILLUSTRATED BY WENDELL MINOR

Cliff Hanger

Genre **Realistic fiction** tells about events that could really happen. To enhance your comprehension, think about your own desired outcome for reading this story and establish your purpose for reading it.

Question of the Week
What does it take to be a hero?

234

235

Student Edition pp. 234–235

Build Background

Discuss heroes

Team Talk Have students turn to a partner and discuss the Question of the Week and these questions about heroes. Remind students to ask and answer questions with appropriate detail and to give suggestions that build on the ideas of others.

- What makes a person a hero?
- What qualities do heroes have?
- Who is your hero?

Connect to selection

Have students discuss their answers with the class. Remind students to listen attentively to speakers and to make relevant, pertinent comments. Possible responses: Heroes are people who put others before themselves. They display courage, take risks, do what is right, and do more than what is expected of them. For additional opportunities to build background, use the Background Building Audio.

Prereading Strategies

Genre Explain that **realistic fiction** is fictional writing with believable characters, setting, and events. Explain that *Cliff Hanger* is a realistic adventure story.

Preview and predict Have students preview the title and photographs in *Cliff Hanger*. Encourage students to use lesson vocabulary words as they make their predictions.

Set purpose To enhance comprehension prior to reading, tell students to establish their own purposes for reading *Cliff Hanger* based upon their own desired outcome. Purposes could include learning about rock climbing or about what it takes to be heroic.

Strategy Response Log

Have students use p. 29 in the *Reader's and Writer's Notebook* to review the elements of story structure. As they read, have them begin filling out the plot map.

Small Group Time

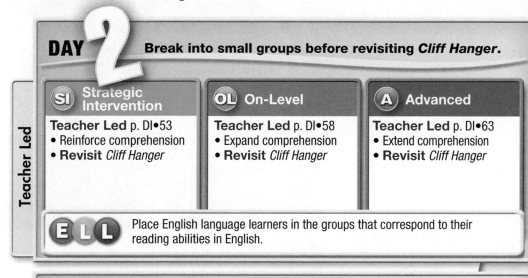

DAY 2 Break into small groups before revisiting *Cliff Hanger*.

Teacher Led

SI Strategic Intervention
Teacher Led p. DI•53
• Reinforce comprehension
• Revisit *Cliff Hanger*

OL On-Level
Teacher Led p. DI•58
• Expand comprehension
• Revisit *Cliff Hanger*

A Advanced
Teacher Led p. DI•63
• Extend comprehension
• Revisit *Cliff Hanger*

ELL Place English language learners in the groups that correspond to their reading abilities in English.

Practice Stations
• Words to Know
• Get Fluent
• Word Wise

Independent Activities
• Background Building Audio
• *Reader's and Writer's Notebook*
• Research and Inquiry

Differentiated Instruction

 Strategic Intervention

Set purpose Work with students to set a purpose for reading, or if time permits, have students work with partners to set a purpose.

A Advanced

Compare heroes Using a Venn diagram, have students compare and contrast the accomplishments of two heroes.

 Multidraft Reading

For **Whole Group** instruction, choose one of the reading options below. For each reading, have students set the purpose indicated.

Option 1
Day 2 Read the selection. Use Guide Comprehension to monitor and clarify understanding.
Day 3 Reread the selection. Use Extend Thinking to develop higher-order thinking skills.
Option 2
Day 2 Read the first half of the selection, using both Guide Comprehension and Extend Thinking instruction.
Day 3 Read the second half of the selection, using both Guide Comprehension and Extend Thinking instruction.

English Language Learners
Build background To build background, review the selection summary in English *(ELL Handbook, p. 163)*. Use the Retelling Cards to provide visual support for the summary.

Objectives

◎ Summarize the plot's main events to better understand the story's structure.

Guide Comprehension Skills and Strategies

Teach Story Structure

 Story Structure Tell students that good readers use story structure to help them understand and predict what they read. Story structure is how the story is organized. Tell students that as they read, they should note how the story begins, how it builds, and how it ends. Have students read pp. 236–237 of *Cliff Hanger* and use story structure to summarize the plot's main events so far.

Corrective Feedback

If... students are unable to summarize the main events,

then... use the model to guide students in summarizing.

Model the Strategy

Think Aloud After reading, I'll pause to think about what I've learned so far about the story structure. Axel is the main character, and the setting is the mountains.

Axel washed his tin cup at the hand pump outside the Teton Mountains Climbing School hut and looked up. A storm cloud darkened Death Canyon. Lightning flashed. Axel was glad he wasn't rock climbing now.

236

Student Edition pp. 236–237

Extend Thinking Think Critically

Higher-Order Thinking Skills

 Story Structure • Analysis What do you think the problem in this story will be? What details did you use to make this prediction? Possible response: Axel has to figure out a way to get his dog off the mountain before the storm comes. The author says that Axel is upset that the climbers left Grits on the mountain.

 Character, Plot, and Theme • Synthesis How would the story be different if Axel wasn't the main character in the story? Possible response: It would change the entire story. If the main character were a professional mountain climber, the story may not be as exciting.

The events that have happened so far are that Axel notices a storm coming and two climbers tell him his dog is still on the mountain. Since I know that most stories have a problem the main character must resolve, I can predict the problem in this story.

"Axel!"

Two mountain climbers ran down the trail. "Your dog followed us up the mountain," one of the women said. "We had to leave him at the top of Cathedral Wall."

"You left Grits?" Axel was upset.

"That storm's bad," she said looking over her shoulder. "We had to get out of there."

237

Imagery • Analysis What imagery is used to help you better experience the story? What senses do the words trigger? Possible response: The words *darkened*, *lightning*, and *flashed* help me "see" what is happening.

On Their Own

Remind students that summarizing what they know so far about story structure will help them fully comprehend what they're reading.

Differentiated Instruction

 Strategic Intervention

Author's craft Explain that the author tells the story in the third person so readers have an understanding of all characters in the story.

A **Advanced**

Critical Thinking Have students make a prediction about how the setting will affect the plot and read on to check predictions.

Connect to Science

Grand Teton National Park is located in northwestern Wyoming. The climate consists of short, warm summers, and long, bitterly cold winters with temperatures as low as –63° F. The sixty-one species of mammals that have adapted to this harsh climate include moose, elk, bison, and deer.

English Language Learners

Activate prior knowledge Create a KWL chart to record students' knowledge of mountain climbing, what they want to learn about it, and what they have learned about it. Provide this question: What do you know about mountain climbing? In the K column of the chart, record students' answers. In the W column, record what students would like to learn as they read. In the L column, list what students learned about mountain climbing as a result of what they read.

Objectives

◎ Use context clues to determine the meanings of unfamiliar words.

Reader's and Writer's
Notebook p. 344

OPTION 1 Skills and Strategies, continued

Teach Unfamiliar Words

🔊 **Unfamiliar Words** Have students read p. 238. Write the word *carabiner* on the board. Ask students to search for clue words within and around the sentence to help them determine the meaning of the word.

Corrective Feedback

If... students are unable to determine the meaning of the word,

then... use the model to help them understand unfamiliar words.

Model the Skill

Think Aloud I can use context clues to help me determine the meaning of an unfamiliar word. I read that Dag "put on his belt, which jangled with climbing nuts and carabiners, and shouldered his rope and backpack."

Axel's father, Dag, the leader of the school, heard the news. He closed the registration book and stepped outside.

Lightning exploded.

Dag counted slowly.

". . . thirty-eight, thirty-nine, forty. . . ."

"A mile for every five counts," Dag said. "The storm's eight miles away. We've got enough time to get Grits."

Dag put on his belt, which jangled with climbing nuts and carabiners, and shouldered his rope and backpack.

Axel looked at his dad. "Thanks," he said, and put on his own mountain-climbing gear.

Axel and Dag trekked steadily up the wooded trails, climbed over rock avalanches, and finally arrived at the bottom of the shaft of rock that is Cathedral Wall. A lightning bolt split open the black cloud.

"One, two, three ..."

Kaboom.

"The storm's only a half mile away," Dag said. "Too close. We'd better wait it out here."

From high on the wall came a howl. Axel looked up.

"Look! Grits got down to Monkey Ledge. If he tries to come on down, he'll fall. Let's go."

"No," said Dag. "We can't make that climb. It's too difficult. We'll go back to the trail split and up the ridge."

"That'll take too long," Axel said. "I can do it." He tied the rope to his belt and placed his foot in a crack. He reached up.

238

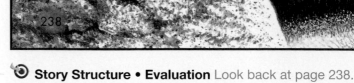

Student Edition pp. 238–239

OPTION 2 Think Critically, continued

Higher-Order Thinking Skills

🔊 **Unfamiliar Words • Synthesis** What does the word *bracing* mean on page 239? What prior knowledge of the base word *brace* do you have to help you understand its meaning? Possible response: *Bracing* means to support something. In this sentence, Dag braces his foot against a rock to support himself. I know that a brace can be worn around a broken leg to allow it to heal and support it in the process.

🔊 **Story Structure • Evaluation** Look back at page 238. What is the problem in the story? What textual evidence does the author give to help me understand the problem? Possible response: The problem the characters must solve is how to get Grits down from the mountain before the storm endangers people. At the beginning of the story, it looks like Axel will have enough time to get Grits before the storm moves in. As they climb, the storm is only a half a mile away. Dag thinks they had better wait to make the climb. Axel decides Grits can't wait until the storm is over to be rescued.

I can predict that a carabiner is something needed for rock climbing, but I don't know exactly what it is. When I look up *carabiner* in the dictionary, I find that it is "a metal link with a safety closure used by climbers to join or secure safety ropes."

Dag had no choice. His son was climbing. He picked up the top coil of Axel's rope and took a deep breath.

"Think out your moves," he said, wrapping the rope around his waist and bracing his foot against a rock.

"On belay," he called out.

"Climbing!" Axel answered.

Axel climbed slowly, from crack to crack to ledge to crack, moving like a ballet dancer. His father let out rope as he climbed.

When Axel was fifteen feet up, he jammed a climber's nut securely into a crack. He clipped a carabiner into the nut, and his rope in the carabiner. He relaxed. If he fell now, the nut, the carabiner, and his dad would stop him from plunging to his death. He climbed on.

239

Draw Conclusions • Analysis Why does Dag allow Axel to make the dangerous climb to rescue Grits? Possible response: Dag realizes that nothing can stop Axel. He knows that Axel is a skilled climber and wants to save his dog.

On Their Own

Have students find other unfamiliar words on pp. 238–239. Ask them to use context clues to determine the meaning of each word. Encourage them to use a dictionary or glossary, if necessary. For additional practice, use *Reader's and Writer's Notebook* p. 344.

Connect to Science

An electrical storm starts when moving water molecules cause a storm cloud to become magnetically charged. The negatively charged electric field at the bottom of the cloud is attracted to Earth's positive charge. It also causes the air to become separated into positive ions and electrons. These electrons help create a path for lightning to follow. Meanwhile, Earth creates a positive charge. When this positive charge meets the negative electrical field, lightning strikes.

Six Pillars of Character

Responsibility We show responsibility when we think before we act and are accountable for our actions. Have students discuss whether they think Axel acted responsibly when he climbed the cliff, and why.

English Language Learners
Professional development: What ELL experts say about Think-alouds "Think-alouds can be particularly informative when used with second-language students. Through this type of dialogue, the teacher can discover not only the types of challenges that students encounter with the text, but also how they deal with such challenges." —*Dr. Georgia Earnest García*

Objectives

◎ Use story structure to summarize the literary elements: character, plot, and theme.

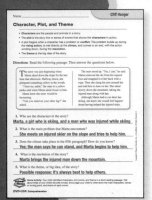

Let's Practice It!
TR DVD•266

OPTION 1 Skills and Strategies, continued

Teach Literary Elements

◉ **Literary Elements: Character, Plot, and Theme** Have students read pp. 240–241. Then ask them to think about the important elements of the story, such as character and plot. Tell them that understanding the character and plot can help them summarize the theme of the story.

Corrective Feedback

If... students are unable to summarize or explain the theme of the story, **then...** use the model to help them summarize and explain.

Model the Skill

Think Aloud To summarize the first half of this selection, I'll tell about the characters and the main plot events including the problem and solution. The characters are Axel, Dag, and Grits.

Axel looked up. Grits was crouched on the ledge, about to jump to him. "Stay!" Axel yelled.

Splats of rain hit the wall. Axel climbed very carefully. Using the tips of his fingers and the edges of his climbing shoes, he pulled himself upward until his hand found the rim of Monkey Ledge. The next move was dangerous. Climbers had fallen here.

Thinking clearly, Axel placed both hands firmly on the ledge and concentrated. Slowly he pressed on them. His body rose. When his arms were straight, he placed his right foot beside his right hand, then his left foot beside his left hand.

Student Edition pp. 240–241

240

◉ **Unfamiliar Words • Analysis** What is the meaning of the word *relief* on page 241? What context clues did you use to help you? Possible response: Meaning: a feeling of relaxation and safety after a dangerous or worrisome event has passed. Clues: "breathed a sigh," "Grits was safe"

OPTION 2 Think Critically, continued

Higher-Order Thinking Skills

◉ **Literary Elements: Character, Plot, and Theme • Synthesis** What have you learned about Axel and Grits from the text? Possible response: Axel is a brave boy who stops at nothing to save his dog. He is a skilled climber. Dag is Axel's father. He has a lot of trust in Axel's climbing ability and lets him rescue Grits.

The problem is that Axel needs to reach Grits on a ledge before the storm puts them both in danger. Axel solves the problem by using his climbing skills to climb up the rock wall. He reaches Grits just as the storm arrives. He holds Grits until the storm goes away. So far, the theme, or message, of the story is having courage in a difficult situation.

On Their Own

Have partners summarize the main events. For additional practice, use the *Let's Practice It!* page 266 on the *Teacher Resources DVD-ROM.*

Differentiated Instruction

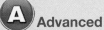

Strategic Intervention

Context clues If students have trouble figuring out the meanings of unfamiliar words, remind them that context clues are facts or details surrounding an unfamiliar word in the text that can help them figure out its meaning.

A Advanced

Debate Have pairs of students debate whether it was a good idea for Dag to allow Axel to make the climb. One student should support Dag's decision and the other should oppose it. Have each student consider the story details and personal knowledge that support his or her position before debating his or her partner.

Bent like a hairpin, he found his balance and stood up. Grits wagged his tail but did not move. He was scared.

Lightning buzzed across the sky.

"One . . ."

KABOOM. Grits shivered.

"A quarter mile away."

Axel put a nut and carabiner in the wall and roped himself to them. He sat down beside Grits and breathed a sigh of relief. Grits was safe.

Axel picked up his little dog and hugged him.

The cloud opened, and rain poured down. Grits whimpered.

"It's all right," Axel whispered into his fur. "It's all right."

The sky flashed. *KABOOM!*

"No count," said Axel. "It's here, Grits. We're right in the center of the storm." Crackling electricity lifted the hair straight up on Axel's head and arms. The air hummed. Sparks snapped from his ears to the rocks.

He hugged Grits closer.

Flash.

". . . seven, eight, nine, ten . . ."

Kaboom.

"Two miles," said Axel. "The storm's going away."

241

Background Knowledge • Evaluation • Text to Self Think about the events in the story. When have you been in a storm? What was it like? Answers will vary, but students should describe a time when they got caught in a storm and what it was like.

Check Predictions Have students look back at the predictions they made earlier and discuss whether they were accurate. Then have students preview the rest of the selection and either adjust their predictions accordingly or make new predictions.

English Language Learners

Build vocabulary Bring students' attention to the words that describe the sounds of the storm on p. 241. Provide examples of the sounds for students: *buzzed* (a buzzing clock alarm or mobile phone), *crackling* (a piece of plastic or paper being crushed), *hummed* (demonstrate humming with your mouth), *snapped* (demonstrate by snapping your fingers).

If you want to teach this selection in two sessions, stop here.

Objectives
- Find pertinent information from online sources.
- Recognize and correctly use comparative and superlative adjectives and adverbs.
- Practice correctly spelling words with Greek word parts.

Research and Inquiry
Navigate/Search

Teach

Have students search the Internet and books, using their inquiry questions and keywords from Day 1. Tell them to skim and scan each site and resource for information that helps answer their inquiry question or helps them locate specific information that will be useful. Bolded or italicized words may be clues to what kind of information a Web site will provide. Have students look for other features, such as headings, captions, or highlighting. Remind students to take notes as they gather information.

Model

Think Aloud Listing keywords that apply to my subject will help me do effective research. The more specific the keywords, the more specific my results will be. To learn about Earhart's life, I will use the keywords *Amelia Earhart*, *childhood*, *education*, and *women pilots*.

Guide practice

Have students continue their review of Web sites and resources they identified. Explain that Web addresses ending in *.gov*, *.org*, or *.edu* are more likely to have reliable information than Web addresses ending in *.com*. Make sure students understand the importance of using valid and reliable sources so that their information is accurate. Circulate around the classroom to verify that the Web sites students have found are appropriate to their topics.

On their own

Have students write down Web addresses, book titles, publication dates, authors, and the dates the Web sites were last updated to create a Works Cited page.

Conventions
Comparative and Superlative Adjectives and Adverbs

Teach

Write these sentences on the board: *The louder clap of thunder caused him to climb more quickly. When he saw the brightest flash of lightning, he felt most frightened.* Point out the comparative and superlative adjectives and adverbs and explain that a comparative compares two things, while a superlative compares three or more.

Guide practice

Write these phrases on the board. Have students supply a comparative and superlative adjective or adverb to complete each.

the _____ ledge	climbed _____ carefully
the _____ rain	rained _____ heavily

Daily Fix-It

Use Daily Fix-It numbers 3 and 4 in the right margin.

Connect to oral language

Have students look for and read aloud comparative adjectives in *Cliff Hanger*. (*closer*, p. 241; *wider*, p. 243)

On their own

For additional practice, use *Reader's and Writer's Notebook* p. 341.

Reader's and Writer's Notebook p. 341

Spelling
Greek Word Parts

Teach

Remind students that words with the same Greek word parts share related meanings. On the board, write *telephone* and *megaphone*. Point out that both have to do with "sound" because they share the same Greek word part, *phone*.

Guide practice

Write the word parts -*graph*, -*meter*, -*scope*, *micro-*, *mega-*, and *tele-* on the board. Discuss the meaning of each. Have students create a chart with a row for each word part and complete the chart by writing spelling words that share the word part in the correct row.

Reader's and Writer's Notebook p. 342

On their own

For additional practice, use *Reader's and Writer's Notebook*, p. 342.

Daily Fix-It
3. A friend of mine has this actors audograph *(actor's; autograph)*

4. Wow. How much money is it worth! *(Wow!; worth?)*

ELL

English Language Learners
Conventions To provide students with practice using comparative and superlative adjectives and adverbs, use the modified grammar lessons in the *ELL Handbook* and Grammar Jammer online at: www.ReadingStreet.com.

Language transfer: Comparisons Monitor sentences written or spoken by speakers of Spanish, Korean, and Hmong. Check for errors with comparisons, such as *That mountain is more hard to climb.*

Objectives
- Organize ideas to prepare for writing.

Writing—Thank-You Note
Writing Trait: Word Choice

Introduce the prompt

Review the key features of a thank-you note. Remind students that they should think about these features as they begin their writing. Explain that they will begin generating ideas for a thank-you note today. Read aloud the writing prompt.

Writing Prompt

Imagine that you, not Grits, were the one Axel saved in *Cliff Hanger*. Write a thank-you note to your friend for his help.

Choose words

Think Aloud To help you choose descriptive words as you write your thank-you note, let's use a chart. Display a T-chart. I'll head the columns *What happened* and *How Axel acted*. In *Cliff Hanger,* we read about how Axel saves his dog Grits. What happened first? How did Axel act? What happened next? How did Axel act? Have students think of words that give a clear picture of what happened and how Axel acted. Fill in the chart as they give information. To help students generate ideas for an outline and first draft, discuss the character traits of heroes and what happens during a rescue.

Remember to keep this chart as the students will refer back to it tomorrow as they draft.

What happened	How Axel acted
Friends told Axel his dog was in trouble.	Although Axel was upset, he acted calmly.
A storm was coming and Grits was stuck on a ledge on a mountain.	Axel climbed carefully and skillfully up to his dog.

Corrective feedback

Circulate among the students as they use the chart to note vivid words they might use in their thank-you note. Talk briefly with students who are having difficulty thinking of strong descriptive words. Ask struggling students to use a thesaurus to help them find a stronger word than one they are thinking of.

MINI-LESSON

Developing an Outline

■ **Display an outline.** I'm going to write a note to thank a friend for rescuing me when I fell through the ice. I'll use an outline to organize my note. I'll write *Salutation* on the title line of my outline and a salutation I might use.

■ In sections A–C, I'll write the most important information I want to include in the note. On line A, I'll write *I fell through the ice*. On line B, I'll write *What you did to help me*. On line C, I'll write *Why I'm thanking you*. Then on lines 1, 2, and 3 under each section, I'll write details for each section.

■ Below section C, I'll write *Closing*. Under that I'll write some closings I might want to use in my thank-you note.

Have students begin their own outlines using p. 343 of their *Reader's and Writer's Notebook.*

Differentiated Instruction

 Advanced

Brainstorm Challenge small groups of students to brainstorm characteristics of heroes.

Teacher Tip

Do a check of students' outlines to make sure they are on task and following the proper format.

Reader's and Writer's Notebook p. 343

ROUTINE **Quick Write for Fluency** **Team Talk**

1 **Talk** Have pairs discuss how they might feel if Axel rescued them.
2 **Write** Each student writes two sentences about his or her feelings.
3 **Share** Partners read their sentences to each other.

Routines Flip Chart

Wrap Up Your Day

✔ **Build Concepts** What did you learn about Axel's attempts to rescue Grits?

✔ **Character, Plot, Theme** How do Axel's character traits help you predict what will happen next?

✔ **Story Structure** How might the setting affect the story's structure?

Preview DAY 3

Tell students that tomorrow they will continue reading about a heroic rescue on a mountain.

Today at a Glance

Oral Vocabulary
protect, secure

Comprehension Check/Retelling
Discuss questions

Reading
Cliff Hanger

Think Critically
Retelling

Fluency
Expression

Research and Study Skills
Diagram/scale drawing

Research and Inquiry
Analyze

Spelling
Greek word parts

Conventions
Comparative and superlative adjectives and adverbs

Writing
Thank-you note

Concept Talk

Question of the Week
What does it take to be a hero?

Expand the concept

Remind students of the weekly concept question. Discuss how the question relates to heroes. Remind students to make pertinent comments in a discussion. Help students establish a purpose for reading to enhance their comprehension. Tell them that today they will read about how Axel rescues Grits and gets down from the mountain. Encourage students to think about how admirable Axel's actions were during the rescue.

Anchored Talk

Develop oral vocabulary

Use illustrations to review pp. 234–241 of *Cliff Hanger*. Discuss *admirable* and *individual*. Add these and other concept-related words to the concept map. Use the following questions to develop students' understanding of the concept. Remind students to ask and answer questions with appropriate detail and to give suggestions based on the ideas of others.

- Axel is an *individual* whose actions show he is *admirable*. How are other rescue workers *admirable*?

- Think about the heroes you know. How are they *admirable*?

Oral Vocabulary
Amazing Words

Teach Amazing Words

Routines Flip Chart

Apply Amazing Words

As students read pp. 242–245 of *Cliff Hanger,* have them consider how the Amazing Words *protect* and *secure* apply to Grits's rescue.

Connect to reading

Explain that today students will read about Axel's courage as he climbs down the cliff to safety before the storm hits. As they read, students should think about this week's concept question and how the Amazing Words *protect* and *secure* apply to his climb.

⭐ Amazing Words

extraordinary	individual
decency	protect
courage	secure
valiant	generous
admirable	flood

E L L Expand Vocabulary Use the Day 3 instruction on ELL Poster 23 to help students expand vocabulary.

E L L Poster 23

Cliff Hanger **242b**

Comprehension Check

Have students discuss each question with a partner. Ask several pairs to share their responses.

☑ **Genre • Synthesis**

What makes this story realistic fiction? Possible response: The events could really happen in real life.

☑ **Literary Elements: Character, Plot, and Theme • Analysis**

What is the theme of the story based on what you have read so far? Explain how the plot helps you understand the theme. Possible response: The theme of the story is that kids can be heroes and be brave in the face of danger. Thinking about the events in the story helps me understand what the story is all about.

☑ **Story Structure • Analysis**

What problem does Axel solve at the end of the story? Possible response: After Axel gets Grits down the mountain safely, he must climb down himself before the storm gets worse. During the last part of his climb, he climbs down without a rope before landing safely.

☑ **Unfamiliar words • Analysis**

Use what you learned about mountain climbing and any context clues to define the word *belay*. Check your definition in a dictionary or glossary. *Belay* means "to fix a climbing rope around a cleat, pin, rock, or other object to secure it."

☑ **Connect text to self**

Axel had to use his climbing skills to rescue his dog and then himself. What important skills do you have that may help you save someone else? Possible response: I am a strong swimmer, so I can help bring someone to safety if they fall into a pool.

Strategy Response Log

INTERACT with TEXT

Have students add story elements for *Cliff Hanger* to the plot map on p. 29 in the *Reader's and Writer's Notebook*.

Check Retelling

Have students retell Day 2 of *Cliff Hanger*, summarizing information in the text in a logical order. Encourage students to use text features in their retellings.

Corrective feedback

If... students leave out important details,
then... have students look back through the illustrations in the selection.

Small Group Time

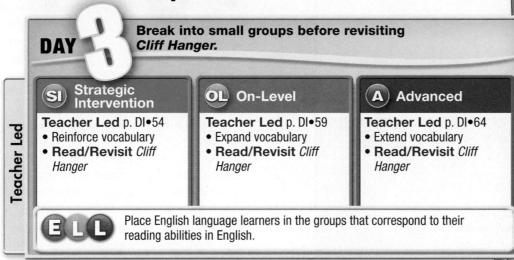

DAY 3 — Break into small groups before revisiting *Cliff Hanger.*

Teacher Led

SI Strategic Intervention
Teacher Led p. DI•54
• Reinforce vocabulary
• **Read/Revisit** *Cliff Hanger*

OL On-Level
Teacher Led p. DI•59
• Expand vocabulary
• **Read/Revisit** *Cliff Hanger*

A Advanced
Teacher Led p. DI•64
• Extend vocabulary
• **Read/Revisit** *Cliff Hanger*

ELL Place English language learners in the groups that correspond to their reading abilities in English.

Practice Stations
• Let's Write
• Get Fluent
• Word Work

Independent Activities
• AudioText: *Cliff Hanger*
• *Reader's and Writer's Notebook*
• Research and Inquiry

English Language Learners
Check retelling To support retelling, review the multilingual summary for *Cliff Hanger* with appropriate Retelling Cards to scaffold understanding.

Objectives

◎ Use story structure to summarize the main events and problem in the story.

OPTION 1 Skills and Strategies, continued

Teach Story Structure

Story Structure Have students summarize the plot's main events in the second half of the story and determine the problem and predict a possible solution.

Corrective Feedback

If... students are unable to summarize and determine the problem and solution,

then... model how to find the problem and make a prediction about how it will be solved.

Multidraft Reading

If you chose...

Option 1 Return to Extend Thinking instruction starting on p. 236–237.
Option 2 Read pp. 242–245. Use the Guide Comprehension and Extend Thinking instruction.

Student Edition pp. 242–243

OPTION 2 Think Critically, continued

Higher-Order Thinking Skills

Story Structure • Analysis Can you summarize the main events on pages 242–243? Possible response: Axel attached a dog harness to Grits and lowered him down the mountain. Axel worked to swing back and forth to find a secure spot to balance. He had to free climb to get to the bottom of the mountain.

Model the Strategy

Think Aloud The problem Axel needs to solve in this half of the selection is how to get Grits down from the cliff and how to get himself down safely, too. This seems as if it could be very tricky.

Axel took a dog harness from his pocket and slipped it over Grits's head and shoulders.

The rain stopped. The sun came out. Axel picked up Grits and eased him over the edge of the ledge. Grits clawed the air.

"Dog on belay!" he called to his dad. Slowly Axel let out the rope, lowering Grits down through space

"Got him!" Dag finally shouted, and looked up. "Axel," he shouted, "when you double your rope to rappel, you'll only have enough rope to get halfway down."

"I know it, but it's OK. I see a good ledge where the rope will end."

Axel wrapped the rope around an outcrop and clipped it to his harness. Then he put his back to the void and leaned out. Holding one end of the rope, letting out the other, he jumped out, dropped, caught himself, jumped out, dropped, caught himself.

And then he came to the end of the rope.

The planned route was still ten feet below.

Dag saw the problem. He studied the wall.

"If you can swing out to your left," he said quietly, "you'll find a good route."

Axel swung across the face of the wall. He reached but could not find a handhold near the route. He swung back. Dag foresaw a disaster.

"Stay where you are," he said. "I'm going for help."

"It'll be too dark," Axel answered. "I'll try again."

242

Literary Elements: Character, Plot, and Theme • Evaluation
What characteristics does Axel have that help him rescue Grits? Possible response: Axel is brave, daring, able to remain calm in a dangerous situation, and good at solving problems. He's also skilled and knowledgeable about mountain climbing. For example, he knows how much rope he has and how far down the mountain the rope will get him.

I predict that Axel will have to use his skills and knowledge about mountain climbing. His father may also help. I'll keep reading to find out what his solution to the problem is.

On Their Own

Have students read to find out how Axel solves the problem of getting Grits down from the mountain.

Axel ran like a track star back and forth across the vertical wall, back and forth. He swung wider and wider. When he was over Dag's route, he jammed his fist in a crack. He did not swing back.

Axel forced his toes into another crack. When he was secure and firmly balanced, he untied the rope from his waist, pulled it from the boulder on Monkey Ledge, and let it fall to his dad.

No nut, carabiner, or rope was there to save him if he made a mistake. From this moment on, he must free climb.

He began his descent.

243

 Literary Elements: Character, Plot, and Theme • Analysis How has the main problem in the plot changed from what it was at the beginning of the story to what it is on page 243? Possible response: At the beginning of the story, the main problem in the plot was how to rescue Grits from the cliff in the storm. Now that the storm has passed and Grits has been rescued, Axel's problem is how to get himself down without having enough climbing rope.

Differentiated Instruction

 Strategic Intervention

Story structure If students have difficulty identifying a problem and a solution, remind them that a problem is a difficult situation that a character must resolve, and a solution is the answer to a problem. The plots of most stories include one or more problem and solution. Often, a character must work through a problem and try several times to solve it before coming to a solution that finally works.

A **Advanced**

Story structure Have students work with a partner to discuss how the main events in the second half of the story support their prediction for how the story will end and the problem that will be solved.

Connect to Science

Friction climbers use belays to keep each other safe when they fall. To work, belays depend on friction, the stopping effect that an object or surface has when moving over another object or surface. When a climber falls, friction between the rope, the belay anchor, and between the rope and the belayer's hands helps slow the climber's fall.

 ELL

English Language Learners

Plot If students have difficulty understanding the pattern of main events of the story, have them draw pictures to go along with each event in logical order.

Objectives

• Understand and explain the author's purpose for writing.

Let's Practice It!
TR DVD•267

OPTION 1 — Skills and Strategies, continued

Teach Author's Purpose

Review Author's Purpose Have students think about the author's purpose in writing this selection. Why did the author write this story?

Corrective Feedback

If... students have difficulty determining the author's purpose,
then... model how to identify the author's purpose.

Model the Skill

Think Aloud I know this story is realistic fiction and that it tells about events that could happen in real life. I think the author wanted to entertain his audience and describe how an ordinary boy with the gift of climbing could be a hero.

Student Edition pp. 244–245

he was scared of losing Grits forever. This shows that he cares for his dog. It also shows that he was more scared of losing Grits than he was of the storm or the climb. He trusted Dag to help him rescue Grits. He and his father have a good relationship.

OPTION 2 — Think Critically, continued

Higher-Order Thinking Skills

Review Author's Purpose • Synthesis Why do you think the author wrote this story by creating a feeling of suspense throughout the story. Possible response: The author thought the story would best be told as a suspense story since it's about an adventure on a mountain during a storm. By creating a feeling of suspense, he keeps readers engaged throughout the story, wondering what will happen next.

Literary Elements: Character, Plot, and Theme • Analysis What does the last paragraph of the story tell you about Axel's character and feelings? What kind of relationship does he have with Dag? Possible response: Axel says

The author wants us to realize that you don't have to be a sports star or adult to be a hero.

Dag watched. The old pro said not one word, for fear of breaking his son's concentration.

When Axel was three feet from the ground, he whooped and jumped down to his father.

"Did it!"

"That was so close, I can't talk about it," Dag said. There was a flash in the canyon. Axel hugged Grits.

". . . twenty-one, twenty-two, twenty-thr—" *Kaboom!*

"The storm's at the hut," Dag said. "Let's wait it out here. I'm beat." He lit his small gas stove and made soup with clear stream water and instant mix. He poured some into a cup for Axel.

"I'll bet Grits sleeps well tonight," Dag said when he finally relaxed. "He was one scared dog."

"I don't know about Grits," Axel answered. "But I was sure scared. I thought I had lost my friend forever."

245

On Their Own

Have students work with a partner to discuss the authors' purpose for writing other stories in the Student Edition. For additional practice, use *Let's Practice It!* p. 267 on the *Teacher Resources DVD-ROM*.

Differentiated Instruction

 Strategic Intervention

Author's purpose Tell students that identifying important ideas in the story will help them figure out the author's purpose for writing. Have students work in pairs to discuss the important idea on pp. 244–245. Have them look for details to support the important idea.

 Advanced

Explore Have a small group discuss why they think Axel is or isn't a hero. Ask them to think about people and actions they themselves consider heroic. Then ask them to discuss which of Axel's characteristics are heroic and which, if any, are not heroic.

ELL

English Language Learners
Contractions Point out the contractions *can't* (can not), *storm's* (storm is), *let's* (let us) and *I'll* (I will) on p. 245. Explain that a contraction is two words shortened into one word with an apostrophe replacing the letters that are removed when the two words are combined.

Comprehension Check

Spiral Review

Generalize • Synthesis Based on what you read in this story and your prior knowledge, what generalization could you make about mountain climbing? Possible response: Mountain climbing is a dangerous sport that requires a lot of skill, knowledge, and concentration.

Inferring • Evaluation Do you think Axel is a hero? Why or why not? Answers will vary but should be supported by evidence from the text and personal knowledge.

Check Predictions Have students return to the predictions they made earlier and confirm whether they were accurate.

Objectives

⦿ Identify and use literary elements to aid in comprehension.

⦿ Use story structure to understand the sequence of events.

Check Retelling

SUCCESS PREDICTOR

Objectives
● Read independently for long periods of time and paraphrase the reading, including the order in which events occur. ● Write responses to texts using details to show understanding.

Envision It! Retell

READING STREET ONLINE
STORY SORT
www.ReadingStreet.com

246

Think Critically

1. The willingness to take risks is an important quality of heroic people. Think of a real-life hero you've seen interviewed on TV or read about in a newspaper. What qualities does that person have that make him or her a hero? Explain. **Text to World**

2. On pages 240–241, the author tries to give readers a sense of how dangerous mountain climbing can be, particularly during a storm. How does the author make you feel like you are with Axel on his adventure? Find sample sentences that made you feel this way. **Think Like an Author**

3. What do the actions and words of Axel and his dad tell you about their relationship? **Literary Elements**

4. In this story, one event leads to the next event. Why do you think that this type of structure is important in the telling of Axel's adventure? **Story Structure**

5. **Look Back and Write** Look back at pages 238–239. How can you tell that Axel is an experienced mountain climber? Provide evidence to support your answer. **TEST PRACTICE Extended Response**

Meet the Author

Jean Craighead George

Jean Craighead George was born in 1919, in Washington, D.C. She has written more than one hundred books in her long, busy career.

When Ms. George was a young girl, her father would take her to the Potomac River to learn about plants and animals. Her father, an entomologist and ecologist, taught her how to identify the edible plants along the river and how to make homemade fishhooks and lean-tos to sleep in. Ms. George cherished these trips with her father. She says she had "a glorious childhood."

Her trips with her father into the wilderness inspired many of her books, including the award-winning *My Side of the Mountain* and *Julie of the Wolves*. She says, "Children are still in love with nature, and I am too." Ms. George's advice to young writers is to "read, write, and talk to people, hear their knowledge, hear their problems. Be a good listener. The rest will come."

Here are other books by Jean Craighead George.

Choose a book from the library and read independently for a sustained period of time. Record your reading by paraphrasing in a logical order what you have read. Be sure what you write maintains meaning.

247

Student Edition pp. 246–247

Plan to Assess Retelling

☑ **Week 1** Assess Strategic Intervention students.

☑ **Week 2** Assess Advanced students.

☑ **This week assess Strategic Intervention students.**

☐ **Week 4** Assess On-Level students.

☐ **Week 5** Assess any students you have not yet checked during this unit.

Retelling

Envision It!

Scoring rubric

Have students work in pairs to retell the selection, using the Envision It! Retelling Cards as prompts. Remind students that they should accurately describe the character, plot, and theme, and use key vocabulary in their retellings. Monitor students' retellings.

> **Top-Score Response** A top-score response makes connections beyond the text, describes the character, plot, and theme, and draws conclusions from the text.

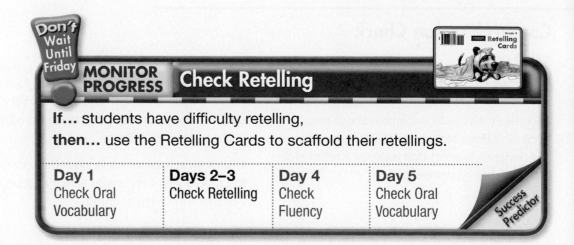

Don't Wait Until Friday

MONITOR PROGRESS Check Retelling

Retelling Cards

If... students have difficulty retelling,

then... use the Retelling Cards to scaffold their retellings.

Day 1	Days 2–3	Day 4	Day 5
Check Oral Vocabulary	Check Retelling	Check Fluency	Check Oral Vocabulary

Success Predictor

Think Critically

Text to world

1. Possible response: Martin Luther King Jr. is a hero who fought for equal rights for all people. He stood up to injustices, made speeches about inequality, and worked to bring people together.

Think like an author

2. Responses will vary, but should include details from the text to support the students' opinions and demonstrate understanding.

Literary elements

3. Possible response: The way Axel and his dad work together to rescue Grits and then get Axel down the mountain safely show they have a good relationship. Axel's dad is proud of Axel and his climbing abilities.

Story structure

4. Possible response: The events in this story need to be told in logical order from beginning to end so I can understand how Axel rescues Grits and himself.

5. **Look Back and Write** To build writing fluency, assign a 10–15 minute time limit.

Suggest that students use a prewriting strategy, such as brainstorming or using a graphic organizer, to organize their ideas. Remind them to establish a topic sentence and support it with facts, details, or explanations. As students finish, encourage them to reread their responses, revise for organization and support, and proofread for errors in grammar and conventions.

Scoring rubric

Top-Score Response A top-score response uses details to tell about Axel's mountain climbing abilities.

A top-score response should include:

- Axel was moving like a ballet dancer as he climbs.
- As he was climbing, he relaxed, knowing that his equipment and dad would stop him from plunging to his death if he fell.
- Axel thinks clearly and carefully about his moves as he climbs to stay safe.

Differentiated Instruction

 **Strategic Intervention**

Have students work in pairs to make a list of details that illustrate how they know Axel was an experienced mountain climber.

Meet the Author

Have students read about the author Jean Craighead George on p. 247. Ask students what it is about her wilderness trips with her father that may have inspired her to write *Cliff Hanger*.

Independent Reading

After students enter their independent reading information into their Reading Logs, have them paraphrase a portion of the text they have just read. Remind students that when we paraphrase, we express the meaning of a passage in other words and maintain logical order.

ELL

English Language Learners
Retelling Use the Retelling Cards to discuss the selection with students. Place the cards in an incorrect order and have volunteers correct the mistake. Then have students explain where each card should go as they describe the sequence of the selection.

Objectives

- Read grade-level text with expression.
- Reread for fluency.
- Explain information displayed in a diagram or scale drawing.

Model Fluency
Expression

Model fluent reading

Have students turn to p. 237 of *Cliff Hanger.* Have students follow along as you read the page. Tell them to listen to the expression of your voice as you read about Axel's reaction when he learns that Grits is stuck at the top of the cliff. Adjust your voice to show where the story includes excitement and emotion.

Guide practice

Have the students follow along as you read the page again. Then have them reread the page as a group without you until they read with the right expression and with no mistakes. Ask questions to be sure students comprehend the text. Continue in the same way on p. 238.

Reread for Fluency

Corrective feedback

If... students are having difficulty reading with the right expression, **then...** prompt:

- Which word is a problem? Let's read it together.
- Read the sentence again to be sure you understand it.
- Tell me the sentence. Now read it as if you are speaking to me.

ROUTINE Paired Reading | Team Talk

1. **Select a passage** For *Cliff Hanger,* use p. 239.
2. **Reader 1** Partners read the page, switching readers at the end of each paragraph.
3. **Reader 2** Partners reread the page. This time the other student begins.
4. **Corrective Feedback** Listen as students read. Provide feedback regarding their expression and encourage them to adjust their tone of voice as they read.

Routines Flip Chart

Research and Study Skills
Diagram/Scale Drawing

Teach

Ask students when it is a good time to use a diagram or scale drawing. Students may mention that diagrams can be used to show how something works, to show the parts of something, or to show size relationships between two or more things. Then review these terms and characteristics of diagrams and scale drawings.

- A **diagram** is a drawing that shows how something is made, how objects or parts relate to one another, or how something works.

- Diagrams use labels, which are descriptive or identifying words or phrases, to identify their parts. They may also include other text to help readers understand what is shown.

- Steps or parts in a diagram may be identified with numbers to show the order of steps or to identify the parts.

- A **scale drawing** is a diagram that uses a mathematical scale. For example, on a scale drawing of an object, one inch in the drawing might represent one foot on the actual object.

Guide practice

Discuss these questions:

How can you locate information presented in a diagram? (Numbers, labels, and other text features identify parts shown in a diagram.)

How are steps in a diagram labeled? (with numbers)

Display a few diagrams or scale drawings and ask questions about the information they contain. Have students use text features to locate specific steps or parts and explain the information that is being presented graphically.

On their own

Have students review p. 345 and complete p. 346 of the *Reader's and Writer's Notebook*.

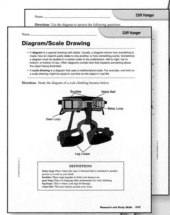

Reader's and Writer's Notebook pp. 345–346

ELL

English Language Learners
Diagrams Have students draw a diagram of something they use often. Some options: a bicycle, a phone, a video game system. Encourage students to label all important parts with words or phrases.

Objectives

- Analyze data for usefulness.
- Identify and correctly use comparative and superlative adjectives and adverbs.
- Spell frequently misspelled words.

Research and Inquiry
Analyze

Teach

Tell students that today they will analyze their findings and may need to change the focus of their original inquiry question in order to narrow down the topic even further.

Model

Think Aloud Originally I thought I would research the background and education of Amelia Earhart. I will refocus my inquiry question in order to narrow it down to one topic and will include information from my research. Now my inquiry question is *What makes Amelia Earhart a hero?*

Guide practice

Have students analyze their findings. They may need to refocus their inquiry question to better fit the information they found. Remind students that if they have difficulty improving and narrowing their focus, they can ask a reference librarian for other reference texts that will provide additional information as they get ready to write their report.

Remind students that they can make a scale drawing or diagram to provide a visual representation of their findings with their report.

On their own

Have students survey one another about what makes a person a hero. Students should then compare their research results to the survey they conducted in class.

Conventions
Comparative and Superlative Adjectives and Adverbs

Review

Remind students that this week they learned about comparative and superlative adjectives and adverbs.

- A comparative adjective tells how two things are alike or different. A comparative adverb compares two actions.

- A superlative adjective compares three or more things. A superlative adverb compares three or more actions.

- Some adjectives and adverbs have irregular comparative and superlative forms.

Daily Fix-It

Use Daily Fix-It numbers 5 and 6 in the right margin.

Connect to oral language

Have students select three items of a similar type. Ask them to compare two of them and then to compare three.

On their own

For additional support, use *Let's Practice It!* p. 268 on the *Teacher Resources DVD-ROM.*

Let's Practice It!
TR DVD•268

Differentiated Instruction

SI Strategic Intervention

Conventions Working with a small group, create a 3-column chart. Head the columns *Adjective or Adverb, Comparative,* and *Superlative.* Model filling in the chart by suggesting an adjective or adverb and having a student give the comparative and superlative forms. Students can then suggest adjectives and adverbs to add to the chart and complete the process of filling it in.

Daily Fix-It

5. The boy climbed down the rock wall, the others sitted down below. *(wall. The [or wall, and]; sat)*

6. They climbing very slow. *(climb or climbed; slowly)*

Spelling
Greek Word Parts

Frequently misspelled words

The words *friend* and *then* seem simple, but are often misspelled. The words *headphones* and *symphony* from your spelling list are also difficult to spell. I'm going to read a sentence. Choose the correct word to complete the sentence and then write it correctly.

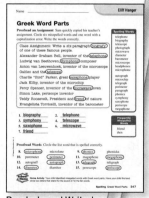

Reader's and Writer's Notebook, p. 347

1. My _____ and I like to ice-skate. (friend)

2. I'll use _____ so I don't disturb you. (headphones)

3. The _____ orchestra gave a great performance (symphony)

4. They ate and _____ went out to play (then)

On their own

For additional support, use *Reader's and Writer's Notebook* p. 347.

Objectives

- Understand the criteria for writing an effective thank-you note.
- Begin draft of thank-you note.

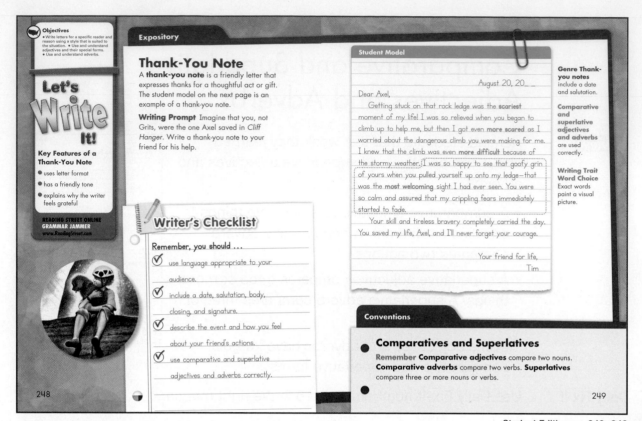

Student Edition pp. 248–249

Let's Write It!
Thank-You Note

Teach

Use pp. 248–249 in the Student Edition. Direct students to read the key features of a thank-you note, which appear on p. 248. Then have students read the remainder of the page. Remind students that they can refer to the information in the Writer's Checklist as they write their thank-you note.

Read the student model on p. 249. Point out the date, the salutation, the body of the note, and the closing.

Connect to conventions

Remind students that most comparative adjectives and adverbs are formed by adding -*er*. Review that most superlative adjectives and adverbs are formed by adding -*est*. Point out that *more* or *most* is used with longer adjectives to form comparatives or superlatives. When an adverb ends in -*ly*, *more* or *most* is used to form a comparative or superlative. Point out the correct use of comparative and superlative adjectives and adverbs in the model. Explain that these words create imagery, a picture in the reader's mind.

Writing—Thank-You Note
Writer's Craft: Word Choice

Display rubric

Display Scoring Rubric 23 from the Teacher's Resource DVD and go over the criteria for each trait under each score. Then, using the student writing model in the Student Edition, choose students to explain why the model should score a 4 for one of the traits. If a student thinks that the model should score below 4 for a particular trait, the student should offer support for that response. Remind students that this is the rubric that will be used to evaluate the thank-you note they begin writing today.

Scoring Rubric: Thank-You Note

	4	3	2	1
Focus/Ideas	Clear focus on one event; good supporting details	Mostly clear focus on one event; some details	Sometimes unfocused account; few details	Rambling account of event; no details
Organization	Organized in a logical pattern	Organized in a mostly logical pattern	Organizational pattern attempted but not clear	No organizational pattern evident; hard to follow
Voice	Sincere and personal voice	Mostly sincere and personal voice	Mostly impersonal voice	Writer does not express personal feelings
Word Choice	Vivid, precise word choices	Word choices generally good	Generally vague and limited language	Vague, dull, or misused words
Sentences	Varied, well-crafted sentences	Generally smooth sentences with some variety	Choppy or wordy sentences; lacks variety	No sentence variety; many incomplete sentences
Conventions	Excellent use of comparative and superlative adjectives and adverbs	Good use of comparative and superlative adjectives and adverbs	Sparse and incorrect use of comparative and superlative adjectives and adverbs	Serious errors in use of comparative and superlative adjectives and adverbs

Outline

Have students get out the outlines they worked on yesterday. If their outlines are not complete, have them complete them now.

Write

You will be using your outline as you write the paragraphs for the first draft of your thank-you note. When you are drafting, don't worry if your note does not sound exactly as you want it. You will have a chance to revise tomorrow.

Differentiated Instruction

 Advanced

Compare Have students compare a business letter with a thank-you note.

English Language Learners
Comparing actions Use gestures to demonstrate the meaning of comparative and superlative adverbs such as *high, higher, highest; fast, faster, fastest.* Say a sentence to describe each action. Then have pairs take turns demonstrating an adverb, saying the comparative and superlative forms, and using them in sentences.

Objectives

- Write a first draft of a thank-you note.
- Use exact words to create imagery.
- Include the date, salutation, and closing.
- Use friendly language.

Writing, continued
Writer's Craft: Word Choice

MINI-LESSON

Choosing Exact Words

■ **Introduce** Explain to students that good writers choose strong and exact words to create pictures in their reader's mind. They select strong adjectives to describe a character or setting and strong verbs and adverbs to describe actions. By including comparative and superlative adjectives and adverbs, they create clear imagery, a visual picture in their reader's mind. Display the Drafting Tips for students. Tell them that the focus of drafting is to get their ideas down in an organized way. Then display Writing Transparency 23A.

Dear Janis,
    I'll never forget this past New Year's Day. Walking out onto the pond was probably the most foolish thing I could have done. I saw the flag that meant it wasn't safe, but I ignored it. As I began to fall through, I felt more terrified than I can ever remember.
    When you saw me disappearing into the hole, you did the most smart thing anyone could do. First, you shouted, Help!" to get an adult's attention. But then you picked up the tree limb lying on the ground near the pond. By laying flat on your stomit, you got into a best position to push the branch to me. I caught onto it, but pulling me out was more hard than you thought
    A booming voice behind you suddenly yelled, I'll get that!" Our neighbor, Bill Johnson, had heard you cry for help. He grabbed the tree branch and since he was stronger than you, he was able to pull me out.
    Your quick thinking kept me from drowning. I'm so lucky you were with me. Janis, I'll always remember what you did.

        Roy

Unit 5: Cliff Hanger   Writing: Model **23A**

Writing Transparency 23A,
TR DVD

Drafting Tips

✔ Review your outline.

✔ Keep in mind your purpose for writing and your audience.

✔ Choose words that will create a picture in your reader's mind.

Think Aloud I'm going to begin my thank-you note. When I draft, I refer to my outline and develop my ideas. I don't worry about revising or proofreading, because those tasks will come later. I will refer to my outline to make sure I include a salutation, the text for the body of the note, and a closing.

Direct students to use the drafting tips to guide them in writing their drafts. Remind them to choose vivid, lively words that will create imagery, a picture in their reader's mind.

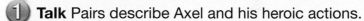

ROUTINE   **Quick Write for Fluency**   **Team Talk**

1. **Talk** Pairs describe Axel and his heroic actions.

2. **Write** Each student writes a brief paragraph about Axel, using comparative and superlative adjectives and adverbs to describe him.

3. **Share** Partners read each other's writing and discuss words that help them picture Axel.

Routines Flip Chart

Write Guy
Jeff Anderson

Show Off— in a Good Way

Post students' successful sentences or short paragraphs. Celebrate them as writers. Select a sentence of the week, and write it large! Display it as a poster inside or outside the classroom door. Students learn from each other's successes.

Academic Vocabulary

Imagery is the use of exact language that helps the reader experience the way things look, sound, smell, taste, or feel. Imagery makes characters and settings seem real and familiar.

Wrap Up Your Day

✔ **Build Concepts** Discuss what you learned about what makes Axel a hero.

✔ **Character, Plot, Theme** How did the story's plot help you understand the theme?

✔ **Story Structure** How did the story's structure help you understand its setting and plot?

Preview DAY 4

Tell students that tomorrow they will read a selection about rock climbing.

Objectives
- Expand the weekly concept.
- Develop oral vocabulary.

Today at a Glance

Oral Vocabulary
generous, flood

21st Century Skills
Online sources

Reading
"Rock Climbing"

Let's Learn It!
Fluency: Expression

Vocabulary: Unfamiliar words

Listening and speaking: How-to Demonstration

Research and Inquiry
Synthesize

Spelling
Greek word parts

Conventions
Comparative and superlative adjectives and adverbs

Writing
Thank-you note

Concept Talk

Question of the Week

What does it take to be a hero?

Expand the concept

Remind students that this week they have read about ways people have been heroic. Tell students that today they will read about rock climbing and evaluating online sources.

Anchored Talk

Develop oral vocabulary

Use text illustrations to review pp. 242–245 of *Cliff Hanger*. Discuss the Amazing Words *protect* and *secure*. Add these and other concept-related words to the concept map. Use the following questions to develop students' understanding of the concept. Remind students to ask and answer questions with appropriate detail and to build on other students' answers.

- How can heroes *protect* themselves when they help others? (practice rescuing people, train to help others, wear necessary protective gear, have a plan)

- Why is it important for a rescue team to make others feel *secure* and safe? (They need the people to stay calm during a difficult situation so they can focus on helping them.)

Strategy Response Log

INTERACT with TEXT

Have students complete p. 29 in the *Reader's and Writer's Notebook*. Then have students work in pairs to summarize *Cliff Hanger*.

Oral Vocabulary
Amazing Words

Amazing Words

Amazing Words

extraordinary	individual
decency	protect
courage	secure
valiant	generous
admirable	flood

Teach Amazing Words

Amazing Words   Oral Vocabulary Routine

1 **Introduce** Write the concept word *generous* on the board. Have students say it aloud with you. We read about how heroes are *generous.* In what way are heroes *generous*? (They give their time to help others.) Provide a student friendly definition. To be *generous* is to be willing to give or share.

2 **Demonstrate** Have students answer questions to demonstrate understanding. My grandfather is very *generous;* he volunteers to help charities and helps family members whenever he can. It is hard for my little sister to be *generous* when it comes to sharing her toys with others.

3 **Apply** Have students apply their understanding. What is something a *generous* person would do? (serve food to the homeless; provide a home to a stray dog)

See p. OV•3 to teach *flood*.

Routines Flip Chart

Apply Amazing Words

As students read "Rock Climbing" on pp. 250–253, have them think about the words *generous* and *flood*.

Connect to reading

As students read today's selection about rock climbing, have them think about how this week's concept question and the Amazing Words *generous* and *flood* apply to the text.

ELL **Produce Oral Language** Use the Day 4 instruction on ELL Poster 23 to extend and enrich language.

ELL Poster 23

21st Century Skills
Online Sources

Introduce online sources

Explain to students that technology is all around us. Tell them that online sources are one type of technology we use today. Ask students to share what they already know about online sources, such as what they are and what types of information they provide.

Discuss the skill

Discuss with students how online sources have changed the way we learn about topics. For example, ask: How could you get information on a topic for a report? (Possible responses: check out books from the library, interview an expert, research the topic on the Internet) Explain: In the past, people weren't able to use the Internet to research a topic, the Internet didn't exist. People relied on locating appropriate books or articles, or to speak to experts to get the information. Let's take a closer look at the similarities and differences between online sources and books.

On the board, draw a Venn diagram like the one below. Label the sides *Online Sources* and *Books.* Ask the following questions.

• How do you find and use online sources when researching a topic? Possible responses: go to the Internet, type in my topic in a search engine, and visit reliable Web sites to read more about the topic.

• How do you use books when researching a topic? Possible responses: look up the location of books on the topic in an online card catalog in the library, go to that section in the library, look through the books to see which ones I think will give me more information on the topic, and check out the books I will need.

• How are the two types of sources alike? Possible responses: both provide information on topics; both include pictures, photographs, and graphics; both are organized by topic.

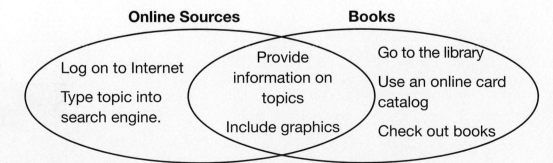

Online Sources		Books
Log on to Internet	Provide information on topics	Go to the library
Type topic into search engine.	Include graphics	Use an online card catalog
		Check out books

Guide practice

Then have pairs list the benefits of using both online sources and books to get information. Ask them to share their lists with the class.

Connect to reading

Tell students that they will now read about how to evaluate reliable online sources to get information. Have the class think about times when using online sources might be helpful.

Small Group Time

DAY 4 Break into small groups before reading or revisiting "Rock Climbing."

Teacher Led

SI Strategic Intervention	**OL On-Level**	**A Advanced**
Teacher Led p. DI•55	**Teacher Led** p. DI•60	**Teacher Led** p. DI•65
• Practice retelling	• Practice retelling	• Genre focus
• Genre focus	• Genre focus	• **Read/Revisit** "Rock Climbing"
• **Read/Revisit** "Rock Climbing"	• **Read/Revisit** "Rock Climbing"	

ELL Place English language learners in the groups that correspond to their reading abilities in English.

Practice Stations
• Read for Meaning
• Get Fluent
• Words to Know

Independent Activities
• AudioText: "Rock Climbing"
• *Reader's and Writer's Notebook*
• Research and Inquiry

ELL

English Language Learners
Cognates The Spanish word for *tecnología* may be familiar to Spanish speakers as the cognate for *technology.*

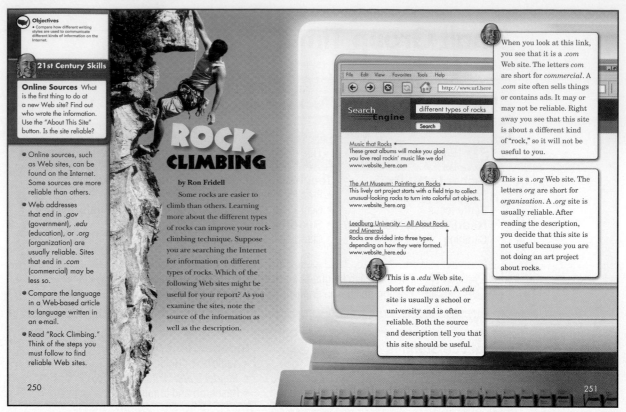

Student Edition pp. 250–251

Guide Comprehension
Skills and Strategies

Teach online sources

21st Century Skills: Online Sources Have students preview "Rock Climbing" on pp. 250–251. Have them look at the different types of Web sites listed. Then ask: Why would the Web site that ends in *.edu* be most helpful when looking for information about different kinds of rocks?

Corrective feedback

If... students are unable to explain why the site would be most helpful, **then...** use the model to guide students in evaluating online sources.

Model the skill

Think Aloud

I know that the first two Web sites are not useful for the report because they are about different topics—rock music and an art project with rocks. So even though the second site ends in *.org,* it would not be useful. The third site is about the three types of rocks and where they are formed. It's also an *.edu* site from a school or university, so it should be reliable.

On their own

Have pairs work to evaluate online sources on a particular topic and to identify the importance of citing reliable information. For example, students might want to learn more about the equipment needed for rock climbing.

Extend Thinking
Think Critically

Higher-order thinking skills

Monitor and Clarify • Analysis What should you look for to decide if a Web site is reliable? Why is it important that the sources be reliable? Possible response: A site that ends in *.org, .gov,* or *.edu* is usually reliable. A site that ends in *.com* is usually less reliable. It is important in a report that the information you present be factual.

Fact and Opinion • Evaluation How can you distinguish whether these Web sites provide statements of fact or opinion? How can you verify the statements of fact? Possible response: If the information seems like it could be proven, it may be a statement of fact. To verify the statements of fact, I could look up the same information on a different site to see if both sources provide the same information.

Differentiated Instruction

 Strategic Intervention

Ask questions Ask students to think about questions they would ask themselves when evaluating online sources, such as: Who owns or publishes the Web site? Are the statements of fact and opinion well supported? Does the site use persuasive language?

 Advanced

Online sources Have students search and evaluate online sources for a project they are doing for another class. Ask them to make a list of the sites they evaluated, which ones they plan to use, and why they will use them.

English Language Learners

Access content In some languages, such as Spanish, abbreviations are seldom or never used. Explain that an abbreviation is a shortening of a longer word. Review the abbreviations *.edu, .org,* and *.com* in the lesson. Make sure students understand what the abbreviations stand for and what they mean.

Online research Work with students to research rock climbing to help build concept attainment. If time allows, help them find audio that helps reinforce the concept.

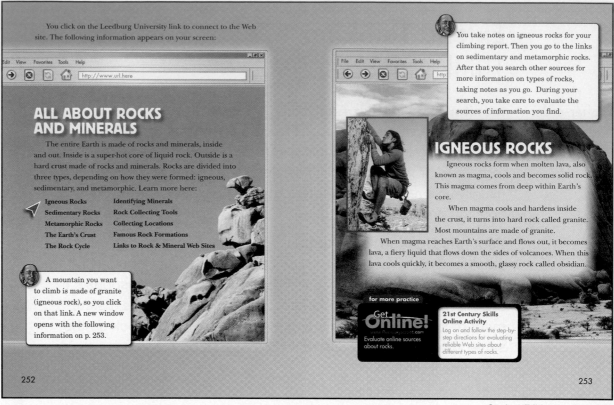

Student Edition pp. 252–253

Guide Comprehension
Skills and Strategies

Teach online sources

21st Century Skills: Online Sources Explain that large or bold headings act as guide words and can help online readers locate the information they are searching for. Then ask: How would you use headings to look for information on the page?

Corrective feedback

If... students are unable to explain how to use headings as guide words, **then...** use the model to guide students in using headings.

Model the skill

When I look for information on a Web page, I scan the headings. I keep my research topic in mind and ask myself *Will this section tell me what I want to know?* Then I decide which sections probably contain the most useful information and read those sections first. I skip sections that are not related to my research topic. If none of the headings on the Web page seem relevant, I try a different page or Web site.

On their own

Have students discuss what the headings on p. 252 tell about the information on the Web page.

Extend Thinking
Think Critically

Higher-order thinking skills

Inferring • Synthesis What can you infer about igneous rocks after reading the paragraphs on page 253? Possible response: I can infer that the mountains I saw in Colorado are made out of granite.

Fact and Opinion • Analysis Does the information on the Web page about igneous rocks include factual information or opinion? How do you know? How could you verify the facts? Possible response: It contains facts. The author backs up statements with details. No persuasive language is used. I could check other reputable Web sites or books to make sure these facts are valid.

21st Century Skills
Online Sources

For more practice

Show students how to locate the Web site by clicking on the appropriate links. Be sure that they follow the step-by-step directions for evaluating reliable Web sites about different types of rocks. Discuss with students how to determine if a Web site is reliable.

ELL

English Language Learners
Guide practice Help students make connections between the steps they are following in order to use headings to locate information and related vocabulary terms. Ask them to describe their interactions using vocabulary terms. Also ask questions such as *Where is the window on the page? What should you type into it?*

DAY 4 Read and Comprehend

Objectives

- Read with fluency and comprehension.
- Use context clues to determine the meaning of unfamiliar words.
- Perform a demonstration.

Check Fluency WCPM

SUCCESS PREDICTOR

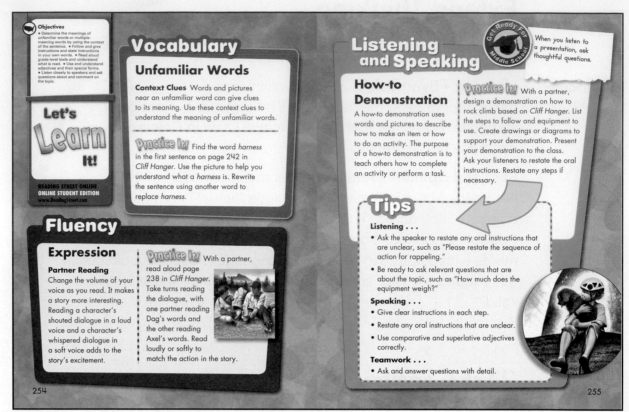

Objectives
- Determine the meanings of unfamiliar words or multiple-meaning words by using the context of the sentence. • Follow and give instructions and state instructions in your own words. • Read aloud grade-level texts and understand what is read. • Use and understand adjectives and their special forms. • Listen closely to speakers and ask questions about and comment on the topic.

Let's Learn It!

READING STREET ONLINE
ONLINE STUDENT EDITION
www.ReadingStreet.com

Vocabulary

Unfamiliar Words

Context Clues Words and pictures near an unfamiliar word can give clues to its meaning. Use these context clues to understand the meaning of unfamiliar words.

Practice It! Find the word *harness* in the first sentence on page 242 in *Cliff Hanger*. Use the picture to help you understand what a *harness* is. Rewrite the sentence using another word to replace *harness*.

Fluency

Expression

Partner Reading
Change the volume of your voice as you read. It makes a story more interesting. Reading a character's shouted dialogue in a loud voice and a character's whispered dialogue in a soft voice adds to the story's excitement.

Practice It! With a partner, read aloud page 238 in *Cliff Hanger*. Take turns reading the dialogue, with one partner reading Dag's words and the other reading Axel's words. Read loudly or softly to match the action in the story.

Listening and Speaking

Get Ready For Middle School
When you listen to a presentation, ask thoughtful questions.

How-to Demonstration

A how-to demonstration uses words and pictures to describe how to make an item or how to do an activity. The purpose of a how-to demonstration is to teach others how to complete an activity or perform a task.

Practice It! With a partner, design a demonstration on how to rock climb based on *Cliff Hanger*. List the steps to follow and equipment to use. Create drawings or diagrams to support your demonstration. Present your demonstration to the class. Ask your listeners to restate the oral instructions. Restate any steps if necessary.

Tips

Listening . . .
- Ask the speaker to restate any oral instructions that are unclear, such as "Please restate the sequence of action for rappeling."
- Be ready to ask relevant questions that are about the topic, such as "How much does the equipment weigh?"

Speaking . . .
- Give clear instructions in each step.
- Restate any oral instructions that are unclear.
- Use comparative and superlative adjectives correctly.

Teamwork . . .
- Ask and answer questions with detail.

254

255

Student Edition pp. 254–255

Fluency
Expression

Guide practice

Use the Student Edition activity as an assessment tool. Make sure the reading passage is at least 200 words in length. As students read aloud with partners, walk around to make sure their expression is appropriate and that it changes to enhance the meaning of what they are reading.

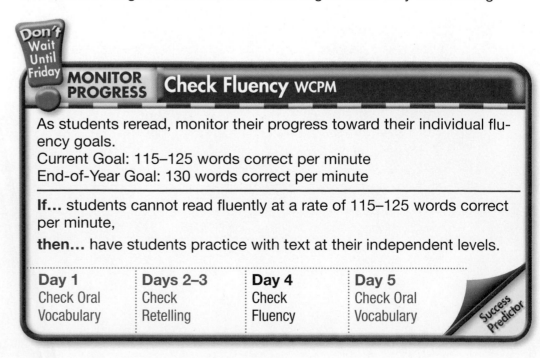

Don't Wait Until Friday

MONITOR PROGRESS — Check Fluency WCPM

As students reread, monitor their progress toward their individual fluency goals.
Current Goal: 115–125 words correct per minute
End-of-Year Goal: 130 words correct per minute

If... students cannot read fluently at a rate of 115–125 words correct per minute,

then... have students practice with text at their independent levels.

Day 1	Days 2–3	Day 4	Day 5
Check Oral Vocabulary	Check Retelling	Check Fluency	Check Oral Vocabulary

Success Predictor

Vocabulary
◎ Unfamiliar Words

Teach context clues

Context Clues Help students find this sentence on p. 240 of *Cliff Hanger: Grits was crouched on the ledge, about to jump to him*. Direct students to use context clues and illustrations to determine the meaning of *crouched*.

Guide practice

Have students use the context clues and illustration to understand the meaning of *crouched*.

On their own

Ask students to use context clues and illustrations in *Cliff Hanger* to determine the meaning of another unfamiliar word. Have students tell the meaning of the word and the context clues they used.

Listening and Speaking
How-to Demonstration

Teach

Explain that the purpose of a how-to demonstration is to teach others how to complete a task. Tell students that speakers often express opinions about the activity based on their own experiences. Speakers may also display drawings or diagrams to illustrate each step in order.

Guide practice

To guide students as they prepare for their presentations, model restating and following oral instructions given by a speaker. Name each rock-climbing step the speaker gives, show a picture of it, and pantomime the actions in sequence.

On their own

Have students make a list of the series of related sequences of action they will demonstrate for the class. Be sure they include the equipment needed. Then have them share their how-to demonstrations by giving oral instructions that involve a series of related sequences of actions and present accompanying drawings/diagrams. Direct audience members to listen attentively, restate the oral instructions, and then follow the oral instructions, or series of actions, by pantomiming each step in sequence. Have audience members ask relevant questions related to important details in the instructions.

How-to Demonstration

Remind students that the purpose of a how-to activity is to teach others how to do something. Tell students that they should give oral instructions that involve a series of related sequences of action. Tell them that adding pictures, diagrams, or demonstrations can help their listeners understand how to perform the task.

Have listeners pay close attention to details in the presentation. Have them ask relevant questions about the rock-climbing demonstration, such as "Do you have to follow the actions in sequence?"

E L L

English Language Learners

Act out vocabulary Have students act out the word *crouched* and other unfamiliar words to help them understand their meaning. Encourage students to use each word in a sentence of their own.

Success Predictor

Objectives

- Use a diagram or scale drawing to present information.
- Review comparative and superlative adjectives and adverbs.
- Spell words with Greek word parts.

Research and Inquiry
Synthesize

Teach

Have students synthesize their research findings and results. Suggest that students create a scale drawing or diagram as a visual aid to accompany their report. Review how to decide what information in the report would be useful to have in the form of a diagram or scale drawing.

Guide practice

Have students use a word processing program and poster board to prepare for their reports for Day 5. If students are using diagrams, check to see that students are labeling them correctly. Review with students how to do scale drawings.

On their own

Have students write a brief explanation of their research findings. Then have them organize and combine information and write their reports. Remind them to draw conclusions in their report about what makes their person a hero and to include a works cited page.

Conventions
Comparative and Superlative Adjectives and Adverbs

Test practice

Remind students that grammar skills, such as knowing comparative and superlative adjectives and adverbs, are often assessed on important tests. Remind students that comparative adjectives compare two people, places, or things. Superlative adjectives compare three or more people, places, or things. Review that comparative and superlative adverbs are used to compare actions. Review adding *-er* and *-est* or using the words *more* and *most*. Point out that some adjectives and adverbs, such as *good* and *well,* have irregular comparative and superlative forms.

Daily Fix-It

Use Daily Fix-It numbers 7 and 8 in the right margin.

On their own

For additional practice, use *Reader's and Writer's Notebook* p. 348.

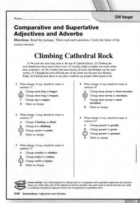

Reader's and Writer's Notebook p. 348

Daily Fix-It

7. Can you polished this man's shoes. *(polish; shoes?)*

8. She was only 16 years old, her brother moved far away *(old when her; away.)*

Spelling
Greek Word Parts

Practice spelling strategy

Have pairs of students write the following Greek word parts on cards*: -graph, -meter, -phon, tele-.* Have students turn the cards face down, mix them up, and turn over one card. Using the Greek word part on the card, have each student list words that contain that Greek word part. If needed, allow students to use a dictionary. Have students repeat with each of the remaining cards.

On their own

For additional practice, use *Let's Practice It!* p. 269 on the *Teacher Resources DVD-ROM.*

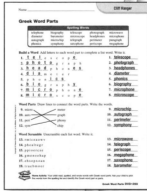

Let's Practice It! TR DVD•269

Objectives

- Revise draft of a thank-you note.
- Apply revising strategy of adding.
- Include descriptive and exact words that create imagery.

Writing—Thank-You Note
Revising Strategy

MINI-LESSON

Revising Strategy: Adding

■ Yesterday we wrote a thank-you note. Today we will revise our drafts. The goal is to make your writing clearer, more interesting, and to express your appreciation.

Writing Transparency 23B, TR DVD

■ Display Writing Transparency 23B. Remind students that revising does not include corrections of grammar and mechanics. Tell them that this will be done tomorrow as they proofread their work. Then introduce the revising strategy of adding.

When you revise, ask yourself *Where do I need to add missing letter parts or words to help my reader picture what I'm trying to communicate?* Adding is a revising strategy in which more information is included. Let's look at the first part of my note. It includes the salutation but not the date. Some of the sentences need words added to create an image in the reader's mind.

■ Use revising marks to add information. Then read the sentences aloud. Reread your thank-you note looking for places to add information so that the form of the letter is correct and the reader will easily understand why you wrote the note.

Tell students that as they revise, not only should they look for places where they might add missing letter parts, but they should also add strong, descriptive words to create imagery. Remind them to make sure their notes include friendly language.

Revising Tips

✔ Make sure to include all the parts of a friendly letter.

✔ Review writing to make sure the language is friendly.

✔ Add strong words to clearly describe your feelings.

Peer conferencing

Peer Revision Have pairs of students exchange papers for peer revisions. Students should write three questions about their partner's writing, focusing on where their partner could revise by adding information. Refer to the *Reader's and Writer's Notebook* for more information about peer conferencing.

Have students revise their notes using the questions their partner wrote during Peer Revision as well as the key features of a thank-you note to guide them. Be sure that students are using the revising strategy of adding.

Corrective feedback

Circulate around the room to monitor students and meet with them as they revise. Remind any students correcting errors that they will have time to edit tomorrow. They should be working on content and word choice today.

ROUTINE — Quick Write for Fluency — Team Talk

1. **Talk** Pairs discuss what it takes to be a hero.
2. **Write** Each student writes several sentences summarizing his or her discussion.
3. **Share** Students read aloud their sentences to their partner. Partners check to see if the writing is a summary of their discussion.

Routines Flip Chart

Wrap Up Your Day

✔ **Build Concepts** What are common characteristics of heroic people?

✔ **Oral Vocabulary** Monitor students' use of oral vocabulary as they respond to this question: How can we prepare for adventures?

✔ **Story Structure** Discuss how setting and plot add realism to the story.

ELL

English Language Learners
Modify the prompt Allow students with limited language skills to work with a partner who has greater skills. Have them revise their letters by using the strategy of adding. Students may dictate their suggestions and have their partner add them to the writing.

Differentiated Instruction
Review the parts of a thank-you note. Working with a small group, have students identify each part in their own writing. If they have left out a part, have them add it. Then ask them to point to each part and name it.

Preview DAY 5

Remind students to continue thinking about heroes. Tomorrow they will read about a boy who becomes a hero.

Objectives
- Review the weekly concept.
- Review oral vocabulary.

Today at a Glance

Oral Vocabulary

Comprehension
◉ Literary Elements: character, plot, theme

Lesson Vocabulary
◉ Unfamiliar words

Assessment
Fluency:
"Stuck at the Top"

Comprehension:
"The Train Trip"

Spelling
Greek word parts

Conventions
Comparative and superlative adjectives and adverbs

Writing
Thank-you note

Check Oral Vocabulary
SUCCESS PREDICTOR

Concept Wrap Up

Question of the Week
What does it take to be a hero?

Review the concept

Have students look back at the reading selections to find examples that demonstrate what it takes to be a hero.

Review Amazing Words

Display, discuss, and review this week's concept map. Remind students that this week they have learned ten Amazing Words related to heroism. Have students use the Amazing Words and the concept map to answer with appropriate detail the question *What does it take to be a hero?*

What it takes to be a hero

Heroic People	Heroic Acts	Heroic Qualities
rescue workers	make others feel secure	extraordinary
teachers	protect citizens	valiant
firefighters	fight fires	courage
parents	emergency volunteer	decency
police	rescue	generous
soldiers	help others	admirable

 **Visual Learning: Check Concept and Language** Use the Day 5 instructions on ELL Poster 23 to monitor students' understanding of the lesson concept.

ELL Poster 23

Amazing Ideas

Connect to the Big Question

Have pairs of students discuss how the Question of the Week connects to the Big Question: *What makes an adventure?* Tell students to use the concept map and what they have learned from this week's Anchored Talks and reading selections to form an Amazing Idea—a realization or "big idea" about Heroism. Remind partners to pose and answer questions with appropriate details and to give suggestions that build on each other's ideas. Then ask pairs to share their Amazing Idea with the class.

Amazing Ideas might include these key concepts:

- Heroism means accomplishing heroic acts and having heroic qualities.

- Heroic acts might be helping others, making others feel secure, or rescuing someone from a dangerous situation, such as a flood, storm, mountain, or fire.

- Different types of individuals can be heroic, such as parents, police, firefighters, and teachers.

- Heroes are generous and valiant; they also have extraordinary courage and decency.

Write about it

Have students write a few sentences about their Amazing Ideas beginning with "This week I learned…" Remind students to establish the central idea of their composition in their topic sentence.

Amazing Words

extraordinary	individual
decency	protect
courage	secure
valiant	generous
admirable	flood

It's Friday

MONITOR PROGRESS — Check Oral Vocabulary

Have individuals use this week's Amazing Words to describe heroism. Monitor students' abilities to use the Amazing Words and note which words you need to reteach.

If… students have difficulty using the Amazing Words,

then… reteach using the Oral Vocabulary Routine, pages 229a, 232b, 242b, 250b, OV•3.

Day 1	Days 2–3	Day 4	Day 5
Check Oral Vocabulary	Check Retelling	Check Fluency	Check Oral Vocabulary

Success Predictor

ELL

English Language Learners
Concept map Work with students to add new words to the concept map.

Oral Vocabulary

Success Predictor

Objectives
◉ Review literary elements: character, plot, and theme.
◉ Review unfamiliar words.
• Review related words.
• Review imagery.

Comprehension Review
↻ Literary Elements: Plot, Character, and Theme

Teach literary elements

Review the definitions of character, plot, and theme on p. 230. Remind students that the characters are the people in a story and the plot is the sequence of events. A story's theme is the most important idea. For additional support have students review p. EI•11 on literary elements.

Envision It!

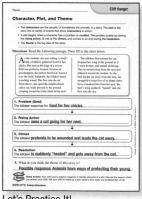

Student Edition p. EI•11

Guide practice

Have partners work together to describe the inter-action of the characters in *Cliff Hanger* and the changes they go through. Have them summarize and sequence the plot's main events. Then, looking at the characters and plot, have students summarize and explain the main message, or theme, of the story.

On their own

For additional practice with literary elements, use *Let's Practice It!* p. 270 on the *Teacher Resources DVD-ROM*.

Vocabulary Review
↻ Unfamiliar Words

Teach unfamiliar words

Remind students that an unfamiliar word is a word for which they do not know the meaning. Tell students that when they come across an unfamiliar word in their reading, sometimes they can use context clues or illustrations to help them determine the meaning. Other times, they may need to look the word up in a dictionary or glossary.

Let's Practice It!
TR DVD•270

Guide practice

Review with students how to use context clues and illustrations or a dictionary or glossary to figure out the meaning of an unfamiliar word.

On their own

Have students look at this week's Amazing Words that appear in "Heroes and She-roes": *extraordinary, decency, courage,* and *valiant.* Have them identify context clues that could help a reader understand their meanings in the poem.

Word Analysis Review
Related Words

Teach related words

Review the definition of related words with students. Discuss how the words *void* and *avoid* are related.

Guide practice

Display the following words: *extra, hero, extraordinary, heroic, extracurricular, heroism, extract,* and *heroine.* Review with students the steps of the Strategy for Meaningful Word Parts using the word *heroic.*

ROUTINE **Strategy for Meaningful Word Parts**

1. **Introduce word parts** Circle the base word *hero* and underline the ending *-ic.*

2. **Connect to meaning** I see the base word *hero.* I know that it is a noun meaning "someone who is admired for great courage or special achievements." Adding the ending *-ic* turns the noun into an adjective meaning "very brave" or "like a hero."

3. **Read the word** Blend the meaningful word parts together to read *heroic.*

Routines Flip Chart

On their own

Have students work in pairs to divide the words into two groups of related words and determine which word part each of the related words has in common. Then have students work together to determine the meaning of each of the words.

Literary Terms Review
Imagery

Teach imagery

Have students reread *Cliff Hanger* on pp. 239–240. Remind students that imagery is the use of words that help the reader experience the way things look, sound, smell, taste, or feel.

Guide practice

Find an example of imagery. Discuss why the author included those words. Have students find other examples of imagery.

On their own

Have students make a list of other words that illustrate imagery.

Lesson Vocabulary

coil to wind around and around, forming a pile

descent the act of moving down from a higher to a lower place

foresaw saw or knew beforehand

rappel to lower yourself down the face of a cliff by means of a rope fastened to the top of the cliff and placed around your body, so that the rope can be gradually lengthened

ridge the long. narrow upper part of something

shaft a long, narrow, usually vertical hole

trekked traveled slowly by any means

void an empty space

English Language Learners
Related words If students have trouble identifying the related words in the list, ask: Which words have similar word parts? Which words have the base word *hero*? Which words have the base word *extra*?

Objectives
• Read grade-level text with fluency.

Assessment

Check words correct per minute

Fluency Make two copies of the fluency passage on page 255k. As the student reads the text aloud, mark mistakes on your copy. Also mark where the student is at the end of one minute. To check the student's comprehension of the passage, have him or her retell you what was read. To figure words correct per minute (WCPM), subtract the number of mistakes from the total number of words read in one minute.

WCPM

Corrective feedback

If... students cannot read fluently at a rate of 115–125 WCPM,
then... make sure they practice with text at their independent reading level. Provide additional fluency practice by pairing nonfluent readers with fluent readers.

If... students already read at 130 WCPM,
then... have them read a book of their choice independently.

Plan to Assess Fluency

☑ **Week 1** Assess Advanced students.

☑ **Week 2** Assess Strategic Intervention students.

☑ **This week assess On-Level students.**

☐ **Week 4** Assess Strategic Intervention students.

☐ **Week 5** Assess any students you have not yet checked during this unit.

Set individual goals for students to enable them to reach the year-end goal.

• Current Goal: 115-125 WCPM

• Year-End Goal: 130 WCPM

Small Group Time

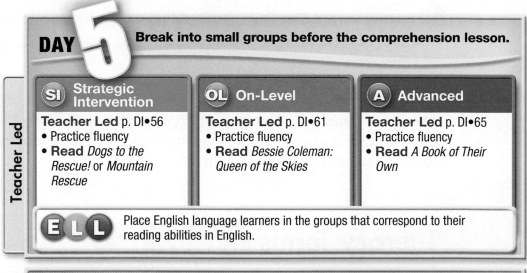

DAY 5 **Break into small groups before the comprehension lesson.**

Teacher Led

SI Strategic Intervention
Teacher Led p. DI•56
• Practice fluency
• **Read** *Dogs to the Rescue!* or *Mountain Rescue*

OL On-Level
Teacher Led p. DI•61
• Practice fluency
• **Read** *Bessie Coleman: Queen of the Skies*

A Advanced
Teacher Led p. DI•65
• Practice fluency
• **Read** *A Book of Their Own*

ELL Place English language learners in the groups that correspond to their reading abilities in English.

Practice Stations
• Words to Know
• Get Fluent
• Read for Meaning

Independent Activities
• Grammar Jammer
• Concept Talk Video
• Vocabulary Activities

Stuck at the Top

"Kelsey will take me!" said Ashley. She turned toward her big sister. 12

Ashley had seen the Ferris wheel from far away. Ever since the 24

Cooley family had gotten to the fair, it was all she had talked about. 38

"Yes, I'll take you," said Kelsey. Ashley squealed with delight. 48

Soon the girls got into one of the swinging cages. They sat down 61

and put on the straps. They waved goodbye to their parents. 72

"Here we go!" said Kelsey as the cage began moving. 82

"Look at the fair!" cried Ashley. "You can see everything!" 92

As the cage reached the very top, the Ferris wheel stopped. The 104

cage rocked back and forth. A voice came over the speaker: "Sit tight. 117

We'll have you moving again soon." 123

"What is going on?" said Ashley. Her voice was very small. Her 135

eyes were very big. "I'm scared!" 141

Kelsey grabbed her hand. "Scared? Why, we have the best seats in 153

the world!" Kelsey started pointing things out to her little sister. Ashley's 165

fear soon turned back into excitement. 171

"These are great seats!" said Ashley as they began moving again. 182

The happy little girl never knew that her big sister was very scared 195

herself. She only knew that the Ferris wheel was the best ride in the 209

world. 210

Objectives
• Read grade-level text with comprehension.

Assessment

Check literary elements

⊙ Literary Elements: Character, Plot, and Theme Use "The Train Trip" on p. 255m to check students' understanding of the literary elements of character, plot, and theme.

1. What caused the lady to choke? Response: The lady choked when a large nut got stuck in her throat.

2. Who are the main characters in the story? Response: The main characters are Alma, Carlos, and the woman choking.

3. What is the theme of the story? Possible response: Kids can be heroes; you never know how you'll be able to help someone.

4. What is the most exciting part of the story? Possible response: The most exciting part is when Carlos saves the woman's life.

Corrective feedback

If… students are unable to answer the comprehension questions, **then…** use the Reteach lesson in the *First Stop* book.

The Train Trip

As the train began moving, Alma felt a lump in her throat. She pressed her cheek against the window. Her parents grew smaller as the train picked up speed.

"It's okay," Alma's big brother Carlos said. "We'll have a great adventure."

Alma smiled shakily. It was not like her brother to be so kind. She guessed he was nervous too. It was their first trip to their grandparents' house without their parents.

Alma looked at the other passengers in their train car. There was no one her age. Alma decided that looking outside would be more interesting. Like Carlos, she put in her earphones, turned on her music, and looked at the sights rushing by.

Suddenly, Carlos nudged Alma and motioned for her to listen to him.

"I think something's wrong," he whispered as he pointed to a woman Alma had noticed earlier. The woman's eyes were wide, and she was grabbing at her throat with both hands.

"She's choking!" Alma gasped.

Carlos quickly stood up and ran to the woman. Using a move he had learned in health class, he soon got the woman to cough up a large nut that had lodged in her throat.

Alma brought the woman a bottle of water, and Carlos asked a man to find help. Very soon, someone arrived, and the woman was taken to another car where she could lie down. Before she left, she grabbed Carlos's hands. She said, "You saved my life!"

As Carlos and Alma went back to their seats, Alma looked at her brother. "I never thought we'd have this kind of adventure!" she grinned. "You are a hero!"

MONITOR PROGRESS   • Character, Plot, and Theme

Objectives
- Communicate inquiry results.
- Administer spelling test.
- Review comparative and superlative adjectives and adverbs.

Research and Inquiry
Communicate

Present ideas Have students share their inquiry results by presenting their reports to the class. Have them display any scale drawings or diagrams they created on Day 3 to go along with their report. Remind them to explain the factual information presented graphically in their drawings or diagrams.

Listening and speaking Remind students how to be good speakers and how to communicate effectively with their audience.

- Use pitch to add emphasis to important points.
- Speak clearly and loudly.
- Keep eye contact with audience members.

Remind students of these tips for being a good listener.

- Wait until the speaker has finished before raising your hand to ask a relevant question or make a comment.
- Listen attentively and be polite, even if you disagree.

 **Go Digital! Grammar Jammer**

Spelling Test
Greek Word Parts

Spelling test — To administer the spelling test, refer to the directions, words, and sentences on p. 231c.

Conventions
Extra Practice

Teach — Remind students that comparative adjectives compare two things and superlative adjectives compare three or more things. Review that a comparative adverb compares two actions and a superlative adverb compares three or more actions. To form comparatives, add -er or use the word more with the adjective or adverb. To form superlatives, add -est or use the word most with the word. Point out that some adjectives and adverbs have irregular comparative and superlative forms, such as good, bad, far, and many.

Guide practice — Working in pairs, have students take turns saying a sentence that includes an adjective or adverb that has an irregular comparative or superlative form. Have the partner change the adjective or adverb to a comparative or superlative form and identify the changed word.

Daily Fix-It — Use Daily Fix-It numbers 9 and 10 in the right margin.

On their own — Write these sentences. Have students use comparative and superlative adjectives or adverbs to fill in the blanks. Remind students to pay attention to whether two or three or more items are being compared. Students should complete Let's Practice It! p. 271 on the Teacher Resources DVD-ROM.

Let's Practice It!
TR DVD•271

1. I felt _____ than I did the last time I rescued a hiker. (more scared)

2. Axel picked up his little dog and hugged him _____ than he had before. (closer)

3. This would be the _____ descent of the many he had made. (longest)

4. The storm was the _____ they had ever seen. (fiercest)

Daily Fix-It

9. Sal and me think this book is more good than the last one we read. (I; better)

10. I'll be gladly to learn more About rock climbing. (glad; more about)

Objectives

- Proofread revised drafts of thank-you notes, including correct use of comparative and superlative adjectives and adverbs.
- Create and present final draft.

Writing—Thank-You Note
Writer's Craft: Comparative and Superlative Adjectives and Adverbs

Review Revising

Remind students that yesterday they revised their thank-you notes using the strategy of adding. Today they will proofread their thank-you notes.

MINI-LESSON

Proofread for Comparative and Superlative Adjectives and Adverbs

■ **Teach** When we proofread, we look closely at our work, searching for errors in mechanics such as spelling, capitalization, punctuation, and grammar. Today we will focus on making sure that comparative and superlative adjectives and adverbs are used correctly.

■ **Model** Let's look at a paragraph from the note we revised yesterday. Display Writing Transparency 23C. Explain that you will look for errors in the use of comparatives and superlatives. In the first sentence, the phrase *most smart* is not correct. I should add *-est* to *smart* to form the superlative. Also I can see that an opening quotation mark is needed before *Help*. Explain to students that they should read their thank-you notes a number of times, each time checking on different types of errors: spelling, punctuation, capitalization, and grammar.

Writing Transparency 23C, TR DVD

Proofread

Display the Proofreading Tips. Ask students to proofread their thank-you notes, using the Proofreading Tips and paying particular attention to comparative and superlative adjectives and adverbs. Circulate and answer students' questions. When students have finished, have pairs proofread one another's thank-you note.

Proofreading Tips

✓ Use comparative and superlative adjectives and adverbs correctly.

✓ Use language appropriate to your audience.

✓ Include a date, salutation, body, closing, and signature.

✓ Check spelling.

Present

Have students incorporate revisions and proofreading edits into their thank-you note to create a final draft. Remind students to make sure that they have used the correct conventions and language for a thank-you note.

Give students two options for publishing and presenting:

Options	
send to a friend or family member by e-mail	photocopy and mail to family or friends

If they are sending their note by e-mail, students need to input the note, making sure they keep the correct form. They should check to see that they have the proper e-mail address of the person to whom they are sending it. They also need to remember to attach their note to their e-mail message. If they are sharing the note by mailing it, they should check to be sure they have the correct mailing address of the person to whom they're sending it. When students have finished, have each complete the Writing Self-Evaluation Guide.

ROUTINE **Quick Write for Fluency** **Team Talk**

1) **Talk** Pairs discuss what they learned about the actions of heroes this week.

2) **Write** Each student writes a list of the most interesting things he or she learned.

3) **Share** Partners read their lists to one another.

Routines Flip Chart

Teacher Note

Writing Self-Evaluation Make copies of the Writing Self-Evaluation Guide on p. 39 of the *Reader's and Writer's Notebook* and hand out to students.

English Language Learners
Support proofreading
Brainstorm and record adjectives and adverbs on a chart. Discuss the comparative and superlative forms of each. Have students use in a sentence those words that need *more* and *most*.

Poster preview Prepare students for next week by using Week 4 ELL Poster 24. Read the Talk-Through to introduce the concept and vocabulary. Ask students to identify and describe actions in the art.

Selection summary Send home the summary of *Antarctic Journal,* in English and the students' home languages, if available. They can read the summary with family members.

Preview
NEXT WEEK

Tell students that next week they will read a journal about a trip to Antarctica.

Weekly Assessment

Use pp. 170–177 of *Weekly Tests* to check:

✔ **Word Analysis** Related Words

✔ 🎯 **Comprehension Skill** Literary Elements: Character, Plot, and Theme

✔ Review **Comprehension Skill** Author's Purpose

✔ **Lesson Vocabulary**

coil	ridge
descent	shaft
foresaw	trekked
rappel	void

Weekly Tests

A Advanced

OL On-Level

SI Strategic Intervention

Differentiated Assessment

Use pp. 133–138 of *Fresh Reads for Fluency and Comprehension* to check:

✔ 🎯 **Comprehension Skill** Literary Elements: Character, Plot, and Theme

✔ Review **Comprehension Skill** Author's Purpose

✔ **Fluency** Words Correct Per Minute

Fresh Reads for Fluency and Comprehension

Managing Assessment

Use *Assessment Handbook* for:

✔ **Weekly Assessment Blackline Masters for Monitoring Progress**

✔ **Observation Checklists**

✔ **Record-Keeping Forms**

✔ **Portfolio Assessment**

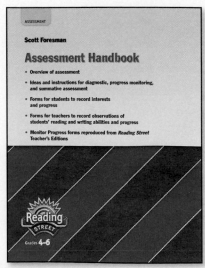

Assessment Handbook

Teacher Notes

Small Group Time

Pacing Small Group Instruction

15–20 min

3-Day Plan: Eliminate the shaded box.

SI *Strategic Intervention*

DAY 1

Build Background

■ **Reinforce the Concept** Explore possible answers to the weekly question *What does it take to be a hero?* One way to be a hero is to save an animal or a person from danger. For example, if your cat was trapped in a tree, you could be a hero by climbing the tree to save it. Many times, police officers and firefighters are called heroes because they rescue people from dangerous situations, such as being in an accident or a burning building. **Discuss the words in the concept map.**

■ **Connect to Reading** This week you will read about people who could have been discouraged by dangerous situations. These people didn't walk away, though. Instead, they used their knowledge and a little creativity to deal with the danger. From the poem "Heroes and She-roes," what did you learn that could explain people who face danger instead of avoiding it? (*Such people put their fear aside, do what they do because of a "sense of decency," and are giving instead of selfish.*)

Objectives
• Participate in teacher-led discussions by answering questions with appropriate detail.

For a complete literacy instructional plan and additional practice with this week's target skills and strategies, see the **Leveled Reader Teaching Guide.**

Concept Literacy Reader

■ **Read** *Dogs to the Rescue!*

■ **Before Reading** Preview the book with students, focusing on key concepts and vocabulary. Then have them set a purpose for reading.

■ **During Reading** Read the first two pages of the book aloud while students track the print. If students are able, have them read and discuss the remainder of the book with a partner.

■ **After Reading** After students finish reading the book, connect it to the weekly question *What does it take to be a hero?* What do these dogs do that makes them heroes?

Below-Level Reader

■ **Read** *Mountain Rescue*

■ **Before Reading** Have students preview the story using the illustrations. Encourage them to predict what the story will be about. Then have students set a purpose for reading.

■ **During Reading** Do a choral reading of pp. 3–5. Then have students finish reading the story with a partner. Ask partners to discuss these questions.

• What emergency do Al and Marisa face as they hike in the Grand Tetons? (*They have to save a lamb that is trapped below a cliff.*)

• Why does Marisa have to carry the lamb all the way back to Abuela's farm? (*Al had fallen and injured his arm.*)

■ **After Reading** Have students look at and discuss the concept map. Connect the Below-Level Reader to the weekly question *What does it take to be a hero?* In *Mountain Rescue,* how do Marisa and Al act as heroes? (*They save the lamb at some risk to themselves.*)

MONITOR PROGRESS

If... students have difficulty reading the selection with a partner,

then... have them follow along as they listen to the Leveled Readers DVD-ROM.

If... students have trouble understanding why Marisa lowers Al down the cliff,

then... reread pp. 8–11 and discuss the situation together.

Objectives
• Participate in teacher-led discussions by answering questions with appropriate detail.

Small Group Time

More Reading

Use additional Leveled Readers or other texts at students' instructional levels to reinforce this week's skills and strategies. For text suggestions, see the Leveled Reader Database or the Leveled Readers Skills Chart on pp. CL 24–CL 29.

Reinforce Comprehension

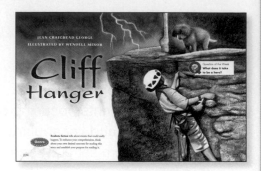

◉ **Skill Literary Elements: Character, Plot, and Theme** Review with students *Envision It!* pp. EI•10–EI•11 on Literary Elements. Then use p. 230 to review the definitions of character, plot, and theme. In a story, the characters, plot, and theme are all related to one another. Characters make events happen. The way characters solve a problem gives clues about the theme.

◉ **Strategy Story Structure** Review the definition of story structure. Remind students to think about what they already know about the topic as they read the story. For additional support, refer students to *Envision It!* p. EI•22.

■ **Revisit** *Cliff Hanger* on pp. 234–241. Have students begin reading aloud *Cliff Hanger* with a partner. As they read, have them apply the comprehension skill and strategy to the story.

- Where are Axel and Dag at the beginning of this story? (*at the Teton Mountains Climbing School*)

- What is the first problem Axel and his father face? (*Axel's dog, Grits, is trapped on a high ledge during a storm and has to be rescued.*)

- How do they plan to solve this problem? (*They plan to use their rock-climbing skills to get to Grits.*)

Use the During Reading Differentiated Instruction for additional support for struggling readers.

> **MONITOR PROGRESS**
>
> **If…** students have difficulty reading along with the group,
> **then…** have them follow along as they listen to the AudioText.

Objectives
- Summarize the lesson or message of a work of fiction as its theme.
- Sequence the plot's main events.

 **Strategic Intervention** **DAY 3**

Reinforce Vocabulary

 Unfamiliar Words/Context Clues Say the word *belay* as you write it on the board. Direct students' attention to p. 239 and the context surrounding this word. I see that right before Dag says "On belay," he has been wrapping rope around his waist and holding himself steady. Then Axel responds "Climbing!" and starts climbing as his father lets out rope. The context tells me that the word *belay* is a command that has something to do with rock-climbing teamwork.

Student Edition, p. W•7

■ **Revisit** *Cliff Hanger* on pp. 242–245. Review *Words!* on p. W•7. Then have students finish reading *Cliff Hanger.* Prompt them to use context clues to figure out the meaning of any unfamiliar words. Look at the words *rim* and *ledge* on p. 240. How do you know that they mean about the same thing? (*Both words are used to describe where Axel has put his hands.*)

• What dangerous thing happens after Axel saves his dog? (*Axel has to free climb for the last ten feet of his climb down.*)

• How do you know Axel is brave? (*He saves his dog even though he must put himself in danger to do so.*)

• What do you think is the main theme, or meaning, of the story? (*The bond between a boy and his dog can be very strong.*)

Use the During Reading Differentiated Instruction for additional support for struggling readers.

MONITOR PROGRESS

If... students need more practice with the lesson vocabulary,

then... use *Envision It! Pictured Vocabulary Cards*.

More Reading

Use additional Leveled Readers or other texts at students' instructional levels to reinforce this week's skills and strategies. For text suggestions, see the Leveled Reader Database or the Leveled Readers Skills Chart on pp. CL 24–CL 29.

Objectives
• Use the context of the sentence to determine meaning of an unfamiliar word.

Small Group Time

Practice Retelling

■ **Retell** Have students work in pairs and use the Retelling Cards to retell *Cliff Hanger.* Monitor retelling and prompt students as needed.

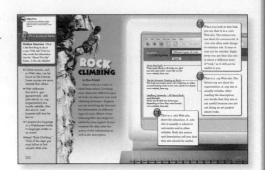

- Who are the main characters in the story?

- What problem do they try to solve?

If students struggle, model a fluent retelling.

Genre Focus

■ **Before Reading or Revisiting** "Rock Climbing" on pp. 250–253, read aloud the genre information about online sources on p. 250. Not all online sources are reliable, or trustworthy. The last three letters in a Web address give clues about the reliability of the source.

Help students preview "Rock Climbing." Look at the boxes on the first computer screen. What do they tell you? (*additional information about the Web sites listed on the screen*) Have students set a purpose for reading based on their preview.

■ **During Reading or Revisiting** Have students read along with you while tracking the print. Stop to discuss any unfamiliar words, such as *evaluate* and *obsidian.*

■ **After Reading or Revisiting** Have students share their reactions to the information about online sources. Then guide them through the online activity.

- What is the text trying to teach you? (*to evaluate online sources for usefulness and reliability*)

- What does this article have in common with *Cliff Hanger*? (Cliff Hanger *is a realistic fictional story about a boy who goes rock climbing. "Rock Climbing" is an article on evaluating online sources related to rocks.*)

MONITOR PROGRESS

If... students have difficulty retelling the selection,
then... have them review the story using the illustrations.

Objectives
• Compare various written conventions used for digital media.

For a complete literacy instructional plan and additional practice with this week's target skills and strategies, see the **Leveled Reader Teaching Guide.**

Concept Literacy Reader

Dogs to the Rescue!

■ **Model** Demonstrate expression for students. Ask students to listen carefully as you read aloud the first three pages of *Dogs to the Rescue!* Have students note how you vary your tone of voice, adjusting the pitch and inflection to emphasize the examples in the photograph.

■ **Fluency Routine**

1. Have students reread passages from *Dogs to the Rescue!* with a partner.

2. For optimal fluency, students should reread three to four times.

3. As students read, monitor fluency and provide corrective feedback.

See *Routines Flip Chart* for more help with fluency.

■ **Retell** Have students retell *Dogs to the Rescue!* Prompt as necessary.

Below-Level Reader

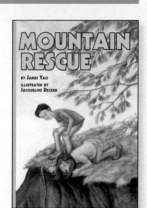

Mountain Rescue

■ **Model** Ask students to listen carefully as you read aloud pp. 3–4 of *Mountain Rescue,* emphasizing appropriate expression.

■ **Fluency Routine**

1. Have students reread passages from *Mountain Rescue* with a partner or individually.

2. For optimal fluency, students should reread three to four times.

3. As students read, monitor fluency and provide corrective feedback. Discuss how varying your tone of voice, pitch, and inflection can make the selection livelier and more interesting.

See *Routines Flip Chart* for more help with fluency.

■ **Retell** For additional practice, have students retell *Mountain Rescue* page by page using the illustrations. Prompt students as necessary. What problem do the characters face, and how do they solve it?

MONITOR PROGRESS

If... students have difficulty reading fluently,

then... provide additional fluency practice by pairing nonfluent readers with fluent ones.

Objectives
• Read aloud grade-level stories with fluency.

Small Group Time

5-Day Plan

DAY 1	• Expand the concept • Read On-Level Reader
DAY 2	• Character, Plot, and Theme • Story Structure • Revisit Student Edition pp. 234–241
DAY 3	• Unfamiliar Words • Revisit Student Edition pp. 242–245
DAY 4	• Practice Retelling • Read/Revisit Student Edition pp. 250–253
DAY 5	• Reread for fluency • Reread On-Level Reader

3- or 4-Day Plan

DAY 1	• Expand the concept • Read On-Level Reader
DAY 2	• Character, Plot, and Theme • Story Structure • Revisit Student Edition pp. 234–241
DAY 3	• Unfamiliar Words • Revisit Student Edition pp. 242–245
DAY 4	• Practice Retelling • Read/Revisit Student Edition pp. 250–253 • Reread for fluency • Reread On-Level Reader

3-Day Plan: Eliminate the shaded box.

OL On-Level — DAY 1

Build Background

■ **Expand the Concept** Connect to the weekly question *What does it take to be a hero?* and expand the concept. One quality that all heroes share is courage. That doesn't mean that heroes are never afraid. It takes courage to go ahead with an action even if you are afraid. Have students add new words to the concept map.

On-Level Reader

For a complete literacy instructional plan and additional practice with this week's target skills and strategies, see the **Leveled Reader Teaching Guide.**

■ **Before Reading** *Bessie Coleman: Queen of the Skies,* have students preview the book by looking at the title, subtitle, and pictures inside.

Bessie Coleman: Queen of the Skies

- What is the topic of this book?

- Do you think it was easy or difficult for an African American woman to become a pilot? Why?

Have students create time lines titled *Bessie Coleman,* starting with 1892 and ending with 2000. This book tells about the life of Bessie Coleman. As you read, look for dates and events and record them on your time line. Also ask yourself how ideas about women and careers have changed over time.

■ **During Reading** Read aloud pp. 3–4 of the book as students follow along. Then have students finish reading the book on their own. Remind students to add dates and events to their time lines as they read.

■ **After Reading** Have partners compare their time lines.

- How did Bessie Coleman achieve her dreams? (*She worked hard and never gave up, even when flying schools in the U.S. rejected her. She went to France to study aviation. She returned to the United States and put on air shows.*)

- How does the topic relate to the weekly question *What does it take to be a hero?*

Objectives
• Participate in teacher-led discussions by answering questions with appropriate detail.

 On-Level

DAY **2**

Expand Comprehension

◉ **Skill Literary Elements: Character, Plot, and Theme** Use p. 230 to review the definitions for character, plot, and theme. Authors do not always tell readers direct information about characters. Instead, readers pick up clues about characters from what the characters do and say. For additional review, see *Envision It!* Skill pp. EI•10–EI•11.

Student Edition, p. EI•11

◉ **Strategy Story Structure** Review the definition of story structure. Encourage students to be aware of story structure as they read. During reading, use the Extend Thinking questions for additional support. For additional support, refer students to the *Envision It! Strategy* p. EI•22.

■ **Revisit** *Cliff Hanger* on pp. 234–241. As students begin reading aloud *Cliff Hanger,* have them apply the comprehension skill and strategy to the story.

• The two women leave Axel's dog at the top of the mountain. What does this tell you about them? (*They have no attachment to the dog and care more about keeping themselves safe.*)

• Even though his father says it's "too difficult," Axel starts to climb up the mountain. What does this tell you about Axel? (*He is willing to take a risk to save his dog.*)

• What is the relationship between Axel and his father? How can you tell? (*They cooperate with each other. Even when they disagree, they trust each other and give each other support.*)

More Reading

Use additional Leveled Readers or other texts at students' instructional levels to reinforce this week's skills and strategies. For text suggestions, see the Leveled Reader Database or the Leveled Readers Skills Chart on pp. CL 24–CL 29.

Objectives
• Summarize the lesson or message of a work as its theme.
• Sequence the plot's main events.

Small Group Time

Student Edition, p. W•7

More Reading

Use additional Leveled Readers or other texts at students' instructional levels to reinforce this week's skills and strategies. For text suggestions, see the Leveled Reader Database or the Leveled Readers Skills Chart on pp. CL 24–CL 29.

Expand Vocabulary

🌀 **Unfamiliar Words/Context Clues** Write the word *carabiner* as you say it aloud (pronounced *kar uh BEE ner*). Every mountain climber knows that a carabiner is a necessary tool. Without it, rock climbing would be completely unsafe. Based on what I have just said, what is a carabiner? (*a safety device used in rock and mountain climbing*) What context clues helped you answer the previous question? (*"necessary tool," "without it . . . completely unsafe"*)

■ **Revisit** *Cliff Hanger* on pp. 242–245. As students finish reading *Cliff Hanger,* encourage them to apply their knowledge of context clues. Look at the word *harness* on p. 242. What context clues in the sentence help you understand what a harness is? (*"over Grits's head and shoulders"*)

• What is the tensest moment in the plot? (*when Axel is making his final descent without ropes*)

• Why doesn't Dag talk to Axel as Axel finishes his descent? (*He doesn't want to break his concentration.*)

• How are the characters Dag and Axel similar? (*Both are courageous when it comes to making sure the people or pets they love are safe.*)

Objectives
• Use the context of the sentence to determine meaning of an unfamiliar word.

 On-Level

DAY **4**

Practice Retelling

■ **Retell** To assess students' comprehension, use the Retelling Cards. Monitor retelling and prompt students as needed.

Genre Focus

■ **Before Reading or Revisiting** "Rock Climbing" on pp. 250–253, read aloud the genre information about online sources on p. 250. Have students preview "Rock Climbing" and set a purpose for reading.

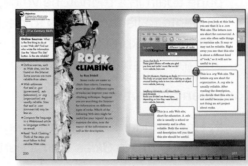

- What features do you see that are different from features in other articles you read? (*computer screens, information in boxes, photographs of rocks and rock climbers*)

- Why do you think the writer put some text in boxes? (*to point out specific parts in the Web site and separate the boxed text from the Web site it is explaining*)

■ **During Reading or Revisiting** Have students read along with you while tracking the print.

- What are four different types of Web addresses, and what does each one mean? (*addresses that end in .gov [government], .edu [education], .org [organization], and .com [commercial]*)

- What information about reliability does the article give? (*Web addresses ending in .gov, .edu, and .org are generally more reliable than those that end in .com.*)

■ **After Reading or Revisiting** Have students share their reactions to the article. Then have them write a short evaluation of a Web site they have used.

Objectives
• Compare various written conventions used for digital media.

Small Group Time

On-Level Reader

■ **Model** Read aloud p. 3 of *Bessie Coleman: Queen of the Skies,* emphasizing appropriate expression. Then read the page again in a monotone voice, without expression. Ask students to list adjectives to describe each reading. Discuss how using expression makes a reading easier to understand and more enjoyable to listen to.

Bessie Coleman: Queen of the Skies

■ **Fluency Routine**

1. Have students reread passages from *Bessie Coleman: Queen of the Skies* with a partner.

2. For optimal fluency, students should reread passages three to four times.

3. As students read, monitor fluency and provide corrective feedback. Have students note the tone, pitch, and inflection of your voice. Discuss how using appropriate expression makes the reading livelier.

See *Routines Flip Chart* for more help with fluency.

■ **Retell** For additional practice, have students use the book's photographs as a guide to retell *Bessie Coleman: Queen of the Skies.* Prompt as necessary.

• What sequence of events do the photographs show?

• What was Bessie Coleman's life like?

• Why would some people at the time have thought Bessie's life was unusual?

Objectives
• Read aloud grade-level stories with fluency.

A Advanced **DAY 1**

Build Background

■ **Extend the Concept** Invite students to draw some conclusions based on the weekly question *What does it take to be a hero?* Heroes possess many qualities, such as courage, selflessness, and devotion to an important cause or belief. What is one way a fourth-grader could be a hero? (*stand up to a bully, participate in a fund-raiser for a good cause, rescue an animal from the animal shelter*)

Advanced Reader

For a complete literacy instructional plan and additional practice with this week's target skills and strategies, see the **Leveled Reader Teaching Guide.**

■ **Before Reading** *A Book of Their Own,* preview the book with students. Today you will read about a girl who finds a way to be a local hero. Have students study the illustrations and use them to predict what will happen in the text. Then have students set a purpose for reading.

A Book of Their Own

■ **During Reading** Have students read the book independently.

• What do you think of Mrs. Jackson's punishment for what Toni did in the library?

• How did Mrs. Jackson's experience as a child prepare her for her career as a school librarian? (*She knew the value of books.*)

• How does Toni change from the beginning of the story to the end? (*She learns to appreciate books and works hard to get books for children who can't afford them.*)

■ **After Reading** Have students review the concept map and explain how *A Book of Their Own* helps answer the weekly question *What does it take to be a hero?*

• Why does the newspaper reporter call Toni a "local hero"?

• What positive effects resulted from Toni's actions?

■ **Now Try This** Ask students to collaborate on a plan to provide books to people who cannot afford them. Challenge them to write a short description of their plan.

Objectives
• Participate in teacher-led discussions by answering questions with appropriate detail.

Pacing Small Group Instruction
15–20 min

5-Day Plan

DAY 1	• Extend the concept • Read Advanced Reader
DAY 2	• ⦿ Character, Plot, and Theme • ⦿ Story Structure • Revisit Student Edition pp. 234–241
DAY 3	• ⦿ Unfamiliar Words • Revisit Student Edition pp. 242–245
DAY 4	• Genre Focus • Read/Revisit Student Edition pp. 250–253
DAY 5	• Reread for fluency • Reread Advanced Reader

3- or 4-Day Plan

DAY 1	• Extend the concept • Read Advanced Reader
DAY 2	• ⦿ Character, Plot, and Theme • ⦿ Story Structure • Revisit Student Edition pp. 234–241
DAY 3	• ⦿ Unfamiliar Words • Revisit Student Edition pp. 242–245
DAY 4	• Genre Focus • Read/Revisit Student Edition pp. 250–253 • Reread for fluency • Reread Advanced Reader

3-Day Plan: Eliminate the shaded box.

More Reading

Use additional Leveled Readers or other texts at students' instructional levels to reinforce this week's skills and strategies. For text suggestions, see the Leveled Reader Database or the Leveled Readers Skills Chart on pp. CL 24–CL 29.

A *Advanced* **DAY 2**

Extend Comprehension

🔁 **Skill Literary Elements: Character, Plot, and Theme** Review the definitions of character, plot, and theme on p. 230. To broaden students' understanding, discuss how all three work together. As the plot progresses in a story, characters' personalities are revealed. The outcome of the story often gives clues about the theme. The plot may include one or more flashbacks, or events that happened in the past. Think of the book *A Book of Their Own* that you just read. How does the flashback regarding Mrs. Jackson move the plot along?

🔁 **Strategy Story Structure** Review the definition of the strategy. Remind students to be aware of story structure as they read the rest of *Cliff Hanger.*

■ **Revisit** *Cliff Hanger* on pp. 234–241. Tell students to be aware of character, plot, and theme as they read.

■ **Critical Thinking** Encourage students to think critically, noting how the characters' personalities affect the plot and how the plot reveals their strengths.

• Why did Axel climb the mountain despite the danger of the storm? (*because he wanted to save his dog*)

• Which word would you say better describes Axel's character—*determined* or *cautious*? Why? (*Most students will choose determined because even though Axel is careful, he cares so much about his dog that he will take risks.*)

During reading, use the Extend Thinking questions and the During Reading Differentiated Instruction for additional support.

Objectives
• Summarize the lesson or message of a work as its theme.
• Sequence the plot's main events.

A Advanced

DAY **3**

Extend Vocabulary

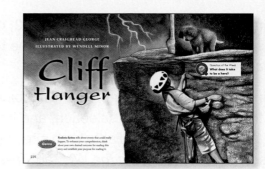

Unfamiliar Words/Context Clues Direct students' attention to a passage with a possibly unfamiliar word and some context clues, such as the first paragraph of *A Book of Their Own.* Model how to use context clues to unlock meaning. I'm not sure what *procrastinated* means, but I notice that Toni is nervous about finishing her report by tomorrow. Obviously, she has put off doing her work until the last minute. *Procrastinated* must mean "postponed (something unpleasant) until a later time."

■ **Revisit** *Cliff Hanger* on pp. 242–245. As students finish reading, have them apply the vocabulary skill. Encourage them to also think about character, plot, and theme.

- What context clues in the story help you understand what it means to "free climb" on p. 243? (*"No nut, carabiner, or rope was there to save him if he made a mistake."*)

- What is the most dramatic point in the story? Explain.

■ **Creative Thinking** Invite students to imagine different outcomes based on shifts in the characters or the plot.

- If the weather had been good, how would the story have changed? (*The dog would have faced less danger. Axel and his father would have taken the long way up to the ridge.*)

- If the hikers had not told Axel about his dog, what might have been different? (*Axel would have worried about the missing animal before thinking of where it might be.*)

- If Axel's father had been a businessman rather than a climbing instructor, how would the plot have changed? How might Axel's character be different?

More Reading

Use additional Leveled Readers or other texts at students' instructional levels to reinforce this week's skills and strategies. For text suggestions, see the Leveled Reader Database or the Leveled Readers Skills Chart on pp. CL 24–CL 29.

Objectives
• Use the context of the sentence to determine meaning of an unfamiliar word.

Small Group Time

A Advanced — DAY 4

Genre Focus

■ **Before Reading or Revisiting** "Rock Climbing" on pp. 250–253, read the panel information on online sources. Then have students use the text features to set a purpose for reading.

■ **During Reading or Revisiting** Have students read "Rock Climbing" on their own. Ask students to share their reactions to the selection, and jot notes on the board. What steps must you follow to find reliable Web sites? (*Evaluate the sources for reliability based on the endings in the Web addresses and the information at "About This Site." Evaluate the sources for usefulness based on what you're looking for.*)

■ **After Reading or Revisiting** Have students do the Get Online! activity independently.

"Rock Climbing"

Objectives
• Compare various written conventions used for digital media.

A Advanced — DAY 5

■ **Reread for Fluency** Have students silently reread passages from *A Book of Their Own.* Then have them reread aloud with a partner or individually. As students read, monitor fluency and provide corrective feedback. If students read fluently on the first reading, they do not need to reread three to four times. Assess the fluency of students in this group using p. 255j.

■ **Retell** Have students summarize the main idea and key details from the Advanced Reader *A Book of Their Own.*

■ **Now Try This** Have the group finish its written description. You may wish to review the plan to see if students need additional ideas. Ask the group to share the plan with classmates.

A Book of Their Own

Objectives
• Read aloud grade-level stories with fluency.

 English Language Learners

The ELL lessons are organized by strands. Use them to scaffold the weekly curriculum of lessons or during small group time instruction.

Academic Language

Students will hear or read the following academic language in this week's core instruction. As students encounter the vocabulary, provide a simple definition or concrete example. Then ask students to suggest an example or synonym of the word and identify available cognates.

Skill Words	character	theme
	plot	comparative (*comparativo*)
	climax	superlative
Concept Words	hero (*héroe*)	rescue
	concentrate (*concentrar*)	

* *Spanish cognates in parentheses*

Concept Development

What does it take to be a hero?

■ **Preteach Concept** Follow this routine to give students support in developing background knowledge needed to comprehend language.

• **Prior Knowledge** Have students turn to pp. 228–229 in the Student Edition. Call attention to the picture of the man holding the dog and tap into students' knowledge of people who help others. Who are some people that help other people? How can a parent or friend help you? Has anyone ever helped you? Who was it?

• **Discuss Concept** Elicit students' knowledge and experience of heroes. What kind of people are heroes? Can you name any heroes that you know? What do you need to do in order to be a hero? Supply background information as needed.

• **Poster Talk-Through** Read the Poster Talk-Through on ELL Poster 23 aloud and work through the Day 1 activities.

■ **Daily Concept and Vocabulary Development** Use the daily activities on ELL Poster 23 to build concept and vocabulary knowledge.

Objectives
• Internalize new basic and academic language by using and reusing it in meaningful ways in speaking and writing activities that build concept and language attainment.

Content Objectives
• Use content vocabulary related to what it takes to be a hero.

Language Objectives
• Express ideas in response to art and discussion.

Daily Planner

DAY 1	• **Frontload Concept** • **Preteach** Comprehension Skill, Vocabulary, Phonics/Spelling, Conventions • **Writing**
DAY 2	• **Review Concept,** Vocabulary, Comprehension Skill • **Frontload Main Selection** • **Practice** Phonics/Spelling, Conventions/Writing
DAY 3	• **Review Concept,** Comprehension Skill, Vocabulary, Conventions/Writing • **Reread Main Selection** • **Practice** Phonics/Spelling
DAY 4	• **Review Concept** • **Read ELL/ELD Readers** • **Practice** Phonics/Spelling Conventions/Writing
DAY 5	• **Review Concept,** Vocabulary, Comprehension Skill, Phonics/Spelling, Conventions • **Reread ELL/ELD Readers** • **Writing**

*See the ELL Handbook for ELL Workshops with targeted instruction.

Concept Talk Video

Have students listen to and view the Concept Talk Video to build and reinforce the concept attainment relating to what it takes to be a hero.

Language Objectives

- Understand and use basic vocabulary.
- Learn meanings of grade-level vocabulary.

Cognates

For Spanish speakers, point out that the word for *descent* is spelled *descenso* in Spanish. Reinforce the concept that these languages share many words that are the same or similar.

ELL Workshop

Provide practice for students to better comprehend English vocabulary used in written classroom materials with *Learn New Words (ELL Handbook,* pp. 402–403).

ELL English Language Learners

Basic Vocabulary

■ **High-Frequency Words** Use the vocabulary routines and the high-frequency word list on p. 454 of the *ELL Handbook* to systematically teach newcomers the first 300 sight words in English. Students who began learning ten words per week at the beginning of the year are now learning words 221–230. The *ELL Handbook* (p. 446) contains a bank of strategies that you can use to ensure students' mastery of high-frequency words.

Lesson Vocabulary

■ **Preteach** Help students internalize new language by having them use it in the following meaningful speaking activity:

1. Distribute copies of this week's Word Cards *(ELL Handbook,* p. 161).

2. Display ELL Poster 23 and reread the Poster Talk-Through.

3. Using the poster illustrations, model how a word's meaning can be expressed with other similar words: To be safe, the rock climbers *rappel*, or move down using a rope.

4. Use these sentences to reveal the meaning of the other words.

- The group *trekked* across the desert. (traveled slowly, with difficulty)
- When Marcus saw black clouds, he *foresaw* a storm. (predicted)
- We had a great view from the *ridge*. (long, narrow top of a mountain)
- She wound the rope into a *coil*. (series of circles)
- Climbing was hard, but the *descent* was harder. (going down)
- They stood on the cliff and looked into the *void*. (empty space)
- A column is a *shaft* that holds up a roof. (tall, thin part of a building)

Objectives

- Internalize new basic and academic language by using and reusing it in meaningful ways in speaking and writing activities that build concept and language attainment.

ELL English Language Learners

■ **Reteach** Ask questions to check and reinforce students' understanding of the vocabulary.

- If you *trekked*, would it be easy? (no)

- Do mountain climbers make their *descent* first or last? (last)

- Could you wrap a hose into a *coil*? (yes)

- What would the *shaft* of a pine tree be called? (the trunk)

- Is a ridge high or low? (high)

- Is there a *void* in outer space? (yes)

- What do rock climbers need to *rappel*? (rope)

- How would you act if one of your friends told you they *foresaw* some trouble? (I'd be worried.)

To help students further understand the general meaning of spoken language in familiar and unfamiliar situations, have students turn to p. 232 of the Student Edition. Have students look at the pictures on the page. Have students use their newly acquired language to describe what is happening in the pictures. If students are unfamiliar with what is happening in the pictures, have them describe the picture the best they can using words that are familiar to them.

■ **Writing** Place the Word Cards that relate to mountains and rock climbing face up. Divide students into two groups of mixed proficiency. Using the word grid, have one group pick out the Word Cards that relate to mountains and the other group pick the cards that relate to rock climbing. Have each group work together to draw a picture showing and labeling both words and to write one sentence about the picture using both words. Select a spokesperson from each group to explain their drawing to the other group. Have another spokesperson from each group read their sentence.

Beginning Have students cooperate to draw their group's picture. Then have each student write the Lesson Vocabulary words.

Intermediate Ask this group to advise students about what to draw and label the drawings.

Advanced/Advanced High Assign these students to write their group's sentence. Have them underline the vocabulary words.

Language Objectives

- Produce drawings, phrases, or short sentences to show understanding of Lesson Vocabulary.

- Understand the general meaning of spoken language in familiar and unfamiliar situations.

ELL Teacher Tip

Grouping words that relate to an activity, quality, or theme helps students learn new words. Use the word grid to help students classify words into meaningful groups and create visual references.

Graphic Organizer

Words related to mountains	ridge, void
Words related to rock climbing	rappel, descent

Objectives
- Understand the general meaning, main points, and important details of spoken language ranging from situations in which topics, language, and contexts are familiar to unfamiliar.
- Share information in cooperative learning interactions.

Cliff Hanger **DI•68**

Content Objectives

• Monitor and adjust oral comprehension.

Language Objectives

• Use accessible language to discuss oral passages.

• Use a graphic organizer to take notes.

• Learn new and essential language.

Graphic Organizer

What heroes do	What heroes do or don't do	How to honor a hero

ELL Teacher Tip

Students may be used to nouns that are masculine or feminine in their home language. For example, in Spanish, *hero* is *héroe* and *heroine* is *heroína*.

ELL Workshop

Encourage students to demonstrate listening comprehension of the Read Aloud and other spoken messages. Provide *Retell or Summarize* (*ELL Handbook,* pp. 408–409) for practice.

ELL English Language Learners

Listening Comprehension

Heroes and Heroines

Heroes and Heroines may be scared, / but they do not act scared. / They listen to people. / They help people with tough problems.

Heroes and heroines / do not leap tall buildings like Superman. / They share their abilities with everyone. / Any place, any time, for anyone— / they do what has to be done.

They do not boast about it later. / Say thank you to these heroes / they are not zeroes.

Honor them by cheering, / and clapping, and rolling out a red / carpet for them to walk on. / Heroes have acted very brave. / In simple words—they gave.

Prepare for the Read Aloud The modified Read Aloud above prepares students for listening to the oral reading "Heroes and She-roes" on p. 229b.

■ **First Listening: Listen to Understand** Write the title of the Read Aloud on the board. Help students use accessible language and learn new and essential language in the process. This is about heroes and heroines. Listen to find out what heroes and heroines do and do not do. How can we honor a hero or a heroine? Afterward, ask the question again and have students use accessible language to share their answers.

■ **Second Listening: Listen to Check Understanding** Make a three-column chart and read the headings. Now listen again for things we can put under each heading. Stop reading after each statement, and fill in the boxes under the appropriate heading together. When students suggesting answers, encourage them to use new language learned listening to the read aloud.

Objectives
• Use accessible language and learn new and essential language in the process.
• Ask and give information ranging from using a very limited bank of high-frequency, high-need, concrete vocabulary, including key words and expressions needed for basic communication in academic and social contexts, to using abstract and content-based vocabulary during extended speaking assignments.

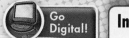

 English Language Learners

Phonics and Spelling

■ **Greek Word Parts** Use Sound-Spelling Card 155 to teach the pronunciation, spelling, and meaning of the Greek prefix *micro-*.

• **Teach** Display Card 155 to teach *micro-*. This is *micro-*. Say it with me: *micro-*. Point to the letters *micro-*. The prefix *micro-* is spelled *m-i-c-r-o,* pronounced /m/ + /ī/ + /k/ + /r/ + /ō/. Have students say *micro-* several times as you point to *micro-*. What is the sound for these letters?

• **Model** Write *micro* on the board. *Micro-* is from the Greek word for tiny. Add *scope* to make the word *microscope.* This word is *microscope.* When you look through a microscope, you can see something very tiny. Under *microscope,* write *microphone.* This word is *microphone.* A microphone makes a small sound much louder.

■ **Reteach** To give students more practice speaking grade-level content area vocabulary to build academic language proficiency, have students turn to p. W•9 in the Student Edition for additional practice with Greek word parts. Have them complete the activity on the page.

Word Analysis: Related Words

■ **Preteach and Model** Point to the underlined portion of the words <u>micro</u>scope and <u>micro</u>phone on the board. *Microscope* and *microphone* are related words because they begin with the same Greek word part *micro.* Next to them, write <u>tele</u>scope and <u>tele</u>phone. *Tele-* is a prefix from a Greek word that means "at a distance" or "far away." A *telephone* carries the sound of a voice a long way. A *telescope* lets people see distant stars. So *telescope* and *telephone* are related words.

■ **Practice** Point to the final syllable of *microscope* and *telescope* as you say the words. Are these related words? (yes) Why? (because they both end with *scope)* What do you think *scope* means? (something you look through) So you look through a microscope to see small things up close, and you look through a telescope to see big things far away. Direct students to brainstorm and say other words that contain *micro-, tele-,* or *-scope.*

Content Objectives

• Identify and define Greek parts of words.

• Review related words with Greek parts.

Language Objectives

• Speak using grade-level content and vocabulary.

• Discuss meaning of words with Greek parts.

 Transfer Skills

Spanish also uses the prefix *micro-* in the cognates *microscopio* and *micrófono.*

Explain to students that the prefix came to both languages from Greek. Because *microscope* and *microphone* start with the same prefix, they are related words.

ELL Teaching Routine

For more practice with word parts, use the Word Parts Strategy Routine *(ELL Handbook,* p. 473).

Objectives
• Speak using grade-level content area vocabulary in context to internalize new English words and build academic language proficiency.

Support for English Language Learners

Content Objectives
- Identify literary elements of character, plot, and theme.

Language Objectives
- Demonstrate understanding of main points and important details of spoken language.
- Retell plot of a picture story.
- Write sentences about plot and theme of story.

ELL Workshop
Encourage students to ask questions to monitor their understanding of instruction of comprehension skills. Use *Ask Clarifying Questions* (*ELL Handbook,* pp. 404–406) for practice.

Comprehension
Literary Elements: Character, Plot, Theme

■ **Preteach** Help students understand the main points and important details of spoken language by explaining literary elements to them. Plot is what happens. The characters start with a problem and work to solve it in the end. Theme is the big idea of the story. We can look at the characters and plot of a story to figure out the theme. Have students turn to Envision It! on pp. EI•10 and EI•11 of the Student Edition. Do a picture walk through p. EI•10. Then help students gain more experience understanding the main points and important details of spoken language by reading p. EI•11 to them. Have students demonstrate their understanding of spoken language by identifying the characters, setting, plot, and theme.

■ **Reteach** Distribute copies of the Picture It! (*ELL Handbook,* p. 144.) Ask students to describe the illustration. Then read the text aloud twice. Prepare students for the first reading by asking them to listen for the characters and setting. For the second reading, done chorally, have students tell what the plot is. Guide students in completing the practice exercises at their language proficiency level. (1. Amelia Earhart 2. the Pacific Ocean 3. She was never heard from again.)

Beginning/Intermediate Have Beginning students say a sentence about the characters in the story. Direct Intermediate students to help them form the sentence about the main character and write it down.

Advanced/Advanced High Tell students to each write a sentence about the story's plot. Then have them share their sentences and agree on one to show the other groups.

 **English Language Learners**

Reading Comprehension
Cliff Hanger

Student Edition pp. 234–235

■ **Frontloading** Read the title aloud. Ask students what they think it means. I wonder if this boy has what it takes to be a hero. Let's look through the story for clues. Guide pairs of students on a picture walk through *Cliff Hanger* to develop background knowledge. Ask students to predict whether Axel will rescue the dog and get down safely. During reading, pause and invite students to adjust their predictions. Give students a two-column chart to fill out as they read.

Sheltered Reading To give students support comprehending increasingly challenging language, ask the following questions:

• p. 237 How did Grits get stuck on the cliff? (He followed some girls. They came down because of the storm.)

• p. 238 Why did Axel climb the rock instead of taking the trail? (He was afraid Grits would fall off before he got to him.)

• p. 241 How does Axel know when the storm is right overhead? (There is no time between the lightning and thunder.)

• p. 245 What was Axel most afraid of? (losing his dog)

■ **Fluency: Read with Expression** Tell students that in order to read with expression they need to understand implicit ideas in the text. Read p. 245. Model the exultation and relief in your voice when you read "Did it!" and the exhaustion when you read "I'm beat." Explain how you used the implicit ideas in the text to understand how the characters in the story felt. Explain how this helped guide your expression. Have pairs choose a paragraph on p. 245. Have students read expressively while their partners listen and offer feedback. Encourage them to talk about the implicit ideas that helped guide their expression.

After Reading Help students summarize the text with the Retelling Cards. Ask questions that prompt students to summarize the text.

Content Objectives
• Monitor and adjust comprehension.
• Make and adjust predictions.

Language Objectives
• Read grade-level text with expression.
• Distinguish intonation patterns in English.

Graphic Organizer

How does Axel act like a hero?	When does he take risks?

Audio Support
Students can prepare for reading *Cliff Hanger* by using the eSelection or the AudioText CD (*ELL Handbook*, p. 477).

English Opportunity
Intonation Patterns Write *Did it!* and *Did it?* on the board. Show how the intonation of your voice differs based on the punctuation. Have students practice distinguishing the intonation patterns by reading the two sentences aloud with correct intonation.

Objectives
• Distinguish sounds and intonation patterns of English with increasing ease.
• Demonstrate listening comprehension of increasingly complex spoken English by following directions, retelling or summarizing spoken messages, responding to questions and requests, collaborating with peers, and taking notes commensurate with content and grade-level needs.

Support for English Language Learners

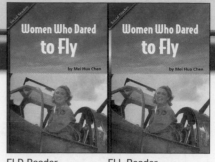

For additional leveled instruction, see the **ELL/ELD Reader Teaching Guide.**

Comprehension
Women Who Dared to Fly

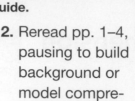

ELD Reader   ELL Reader

■ **Before Reading** Distribute copies of the ELL and ELD Readers, *Women Who Dared to Fly,* to students at their reading level.

- **Preview** Read the title aloud with students: This is a nonfiction text about brave women who flew planes.

- **Set a Purpose for Reading** Let's read to figure out why these women pilots made history.

■ **During Reading** Follow the Reading Routine for both reading groups.

1. Read the entire Reader aloud slowly.

2. Reread pp. 1–4, pausing to build background or model comprehension. Have Beginning students finger-point as you read. Use the questions in the chart to check students' comprehension.

3. Have students do a choral rereading of pp. 1–5.

4. Repeat steps 2–3 above for pp. 5–8 of the Reader.

■ **After Reading** Use the exercises on the inside back cover of each Reader and invite students to share their writing. In a whole-group discussion, ask students Why do you think one of these women is a heroine? Record their answers on the board and invite them to point to pictures in the book to support their answers.

ELD Reader Beginning/Intermediate

■ **p. 5** During which war did women first fly war planes? (during World War II)

■ **p. 6** Who was the first woman Space Shuttle pilot? (Eileen Collins) Read the sentence that gives the answer aloud. (p. 6)

Writing What fact about the women in the story is the most interesting to you? Find the sentence in the book that tells about the fact. Copy the sentence. Then read it aloud with your partner.

ELL Reader Advanced/Advanced High

■ **p. 5** When did women start flying war planes? (during World War II) Read the sentences that tell you the answer aloud. (p. 5)

■ **p. 6** What is Eileen Collins famous for? (being the first woman Space Shuttle pilot) Read the sentence that gives the answer aloud. (p. 6)

Study Guide Distribute copies of the ELL Reader Study Guide (*ELL Handbook,* p. 166). Scaffold comprehension of setting and plot by helping students complete the chart. Review their responses together. (See *ELL Handbook*, pp. 209–212.)

Objectives
• Expand and internalize initial English vocabulary by learning and using high-frequency English words necessary for identifying and describing people, places, and objects, by retelling simple stories and basic information represented or supported by pictures, and by learning and using routine language needed for classroom communication.

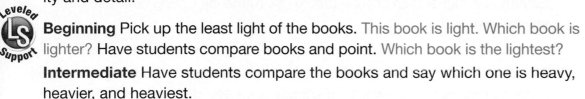 English Language Learners

Conventions
Comparative and Superlative Adjectives

■ **Preteach** Show students three books of different thicknesses. *This book is thick. This book is thicker. This book is the thickest.* Tell students that you have used comparative and superlative adjectives to explain with increasing specificity and detail.

■ **Practice** Show students three small books of varying weights. Have students use comparative and superlative adjectives to explain with increasing specificity and detail.

Beginning Pick up the least light of the books. *This book is light. Which book is lighter?* Have students compare books and point. *Which book is the lightest?*

Intermediate Have students compare the books and say which one is heavy, heavier, and heaviest.

Advanced/Advanced High Have students compare the books and write sentences about which title is light, lighter, and lightest.

■ **Reteach** Write *thick, thicker,* and *thickest* on the board. Point to the *er* and tell students this is the comparative form of the adjective. Tell them *est* is the superlative form. Tell students some longer adjectives use "more" in front for comparative and "most" for superlative. List adjectives such as *important* and *courageous.* Have students take turns making the adjectives comparative and superlative.

■ **Practice** Display a chart to illustrate comparative and superlative adjectives.

Article	Comparative Form	Superlative Form
brave	braver	bravest
happy	happier	happiest
interesting	more interesting	most interesting

Beginning/Intermediate Have pairs write one comparative adjective from p. 241 of *Cliff Hangers* and another on p. 243. Have them write the superlative form of each.

Advanced/Advanced High Have students write three sentences comparing the storm clouds in the pictures on pp. 236, 237, and 238.

Content Objectives
• Decode, use, and form comparative and superlative adjectives.

Language Objectives
• Speak and write sentences with comparative and superlative adjectives.

 ## Transfer Skills
In English, some longer adjectives use *more* instead of -*er* and *most* instead of -*est*. As African and Asian languages may use both constructions, some students may say "more stronger" or "most fastest."

Grammar Jammer
For more practice with adjectives, use the Grammar Jammer for this target skill. See the Grammar Jammer Routine (*ELL Handbook,* p. 478) for suggestions on using this learning tool.

ELL Workshop
Students may need extra practice using language structures heard during classroom interactions. *Use Prepositions and Adjectives in Your Speaking* (*ELL Handbook,* pp. 426–427) provides extra support.

Content Objectives

- Choose the most exact word.

Language Objectives

- Write an e-mail using exact words and details to explain.
- Write using content-based vocabulary.

ELL Teaching Routine

For practice spelling words related to heroes, use the Spelling Routine (*ELL Handbook*, p. 476).

ELL *English Language Learners*

Using Exact Words

■ **Introduce** Exact words explain and give a clear picture of people, places, things, and actions. For example, *He climbed up the mountain* gives a better idea of what he did than *He walked up the mountain.* Display the model paragraph and read it aloud. Do you see some words that could be more exact? What words would you choose to replace them? Erase the inexact words and replace with the exact words. (Possible answers: *did tricks, soared, raced*)

Writing Model

Some women became flying heroes. Harriet Quimby flew at air shows. Amelia Earhart flew higher than anyone before her. Katherine Chung flew faster than anyone else had.

■ **Practice** Write this incomplete paragraph on the board. Work together to fill in the blanks with exact words. (Possible answers: *disappeared, crashed, landed, found*)

Amelia Earhart and her plane _____ over the Pacific Ocean. What happened? Most people think she _____ into the water. Some people think she _____ on an island but was never _____.

■ **Write** Have students write a detailed e-mail to a friend about a hero they learned about this week. For ideas, have students use a content-based vocabulary word from *Cliff Hangers* or *Women Who Dared to Fly*. Give students support in using content-base vocabulary by using the following leveled support strategies.

Beginning Have students write the name of a hero from *Cliff Hangers* or *Women Who Dared to Fly* at the top of their paper. Then have them draw that hero in action. Ask them to dictate one or more sentences about the drawing. Write the sentences and have students type them into their e-mail.

Intermediate Supply students with this sentence frame: [Name of hero] is a hero because _____. Have partners work together to explain details about what their hero did. Encourage them to use exact words to explain this to a friend who doesn't know about their hero.

Advanced/Advanced High Direct students to write their e-mails independently. Have partners switch places to point out where more exact words could be used before sending.

Objectives

- Write using newly acquired basic vocabulary and content-based grade-level vocabulary.
- Narrate, describe, and explain with increasing specificity and detail to fulfill content area writing needs as more English is acquired.

E-Pen Pals

Introduce genre and key features

Writing Project Correspond by e-mail with an e-pen pal to share a travel experience by land, air, or water.

Purpose enhance skills in writing formal e-mail and using word processing applications

Audience teacher and a student in another fourth-grade class

In this workshop, we will write an e-mail to an e-pen pal telling about a travel adventure and asking the e-pen pal to share a similar experience. We will use the Internet to match our class with another fourth-grade class, to set up e-mail accounts, and to send e-mails. We will draft, revise, and edit our e-mails using tools at the e-mail account site.

Key Features of E-mail

- sent over the Internet from one computer to another
- contains a greeting, body, closing, and signature just like a friendly letter
- requires use of exact e-mail address
- calls for use of correct English both as a courtesy and to be understood

Academic Vocabulary

E-pen pal An e-pen pal is a person with whom one communicates by e-mail on a regular basis.

Differentiated Instruction

 Strategic Intervention

Compare E-mail to Letter Invite students to share their experiences in sending and receiving e-mail. Discuss similarities between a letter and an e-mail. Display an example of each form and have students circle parallel parts in the forms (date, greeting, body, etc.).

Technology Tip

Setting Up E-Pen Pal Site Use search words *e-pen pals, connected classrooms* to locate an online educational organization that safely connects students as e-pen pals. Teacher registration on such a site allows you to match by classroom and topic or interest, to control access, and to monitor content for student safety.

English Language Learners
English Conventions of Punctuation Use 21st Century Writing Transparency TC8 to model the use of a comma after the greeting and closing of an e-mail and to show English conventions in the use of the question marks and quotation marks. Ask students to tell how these conventions differ in their first language.

UNIT 5 21st Century Writing

Objectives

• Understand and identify the features of an e-mail.

• Organize ideas to prepare for writing.

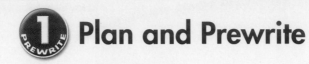

① Plan and Prewrite

MINI-LESSON

Reading Like a Writer

■ **Examine Model Text** Use a projector to display 21st Century Transparency TC8. Point out and discuss the parts of an e-mail and appropriate conventions for entering text in each part. Online e-mail service programs can vary slightly. In this program, the e-mail address of the sender appears in the first box on the e-mail form. In the second box we type the e-mail address of the person who is to receive the e-mail. In the third box, we enter a phrase that describes what the e-mail is about. The message or letter goes in the large box below these boxes. To get from one box to another, we press the "Tab" key or use the mouse to position the cursor.

■ Read aloud the e-mail, asking students to identify the greeting, closing, and signature. Make sure students understand that an e-mail to an e-pen pal is like a friendly letter and should use standard English grammar, spelling, and mechanics.

21st Century Transparency
TC8, TR DVD

List topics

You will write e-mails to a new pen pal. These e-mails will tell about an adventure you have had on land, in the air, or on water. Your e-mail will include an anecdote, or brief personal story, to help you introduce yourself. First, we need to choose an experience to write about. Remind students that their adventures might have taken place on a vacation, on a quick shopping trip, or on a bus ride across town. Ask students to list some travel experiences, including travels by land, air, or water.

Choose a topic

Now list some exciting or funny events that happened while you were traveling. Give students time to brainstorm; suggest that they list details about each experience they name. Then pair students and have them share their ideas to get feedback that will help them select one adventure to write about.

Academic Vocabulary

Anecdote An anecdote is a brief story about a personal experience told to entertain or to make a point.

Differentiated Instruction

 Advanced

Focusing on a Trait Remind students that their anecdote introduces them to a new friend. Have students include in their word web the personality trait that their adventure reveals about them.

English Language Learners
Vocabulary Check students' familiarity with vocabulary words they may need to write about travel: *bus, plane, car, truck, ship, highway, route, ticket, gas station, ride, drive, fly,* and so on. Have students illustrate word cards for the words they want to use and post them near their computer.

21st Century Writing

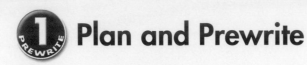

Objectives

- Brainstorm details about and sequence events in a personal experience.
- Fill out required information in an e-mail form.
- Type a correct greeting.

1 PREWRITE Plan and Prewrite

MINI-LESSON

Brainstorming Anecdote Details

Think Aloud To write about an adventure I have had while traveling, I need to remember the important details. I can use a word web to write them quickly as I think of them. Then I can list events in the order they happened.

▪ Using a projector, create a word web and model using it to brainstorm anecdote details and list events in order, or display 21st Century Transparency TC9.

▪ Have students create their own word webs. Then have them refer to their webs as they use a word processing application to sequence events in their anecdote.

21st Century Transparency
TC9, TR DVD

① Plan and Prewrite

Using an Educational Internet Site for E-Pen Pals

- ▣ **Using an Educational Internet Site for E-Pen Pals** Study the partner class you have selected to match each student in your classroom with an e-pen pal. Give each student his or her individual e-mail address as well as the e-mail address and name of his or her e-pen pal. Explain that everyone will begin by filling out the fields in the e-mail form.

- ▣ **Using an E-mail Format** Log on to the Internet e-pen pal site you have chosen and model for students how to use the e-mail function. Display the e-mail form on a projector. The boxes on the e-mail form must be filled out correctly in order for an e-mail to be sent. The first box is for my e-mail address. I enter my e-mail address carefully and then move the cursor to the box labeled "To." I type the e-mail address of my e-pen pal in this box. Then I move the cursor to the box labeled "Subject" and type a phrase describing what the e-mail is about. **Fill in each field with appropriate examples.** Next, I press the Tab key again and type in the greeting to my e-mail. Here I will use the name of my e-pen pal. **Enter a standard greeting and point out proper punctuation.**

- ▣ Have students open an e-mail form and type their e-mail address, their e-pen pal's e-mail address, and the subject of their e-mail.

Academic Vocabulary

Greeting In a friendly letter or e-mail, the greeting identifies the recipient and opens the letter.

Teacher Tip

Student Safety Online
Familiarize yourself with your school's policy about e-mail communications among students. Discuss with students the need to avoid sending personal information such as telephone numbers and street addresses over the Internet.

Objectives

- Write a first draft of an anecdote.
- Check drafts for appropriate chronological order of events.
- Revise drafts to include adequate detail.
- Correct sentence fragments.

2 Draft

Getting started

Give students the name of their e-pen pal and have them access their e-mail site to write a greeting and an introductory paragraph for their e-mail. Remind them that they are introducing themselves to someone for the first time. Suggest that they think about what they would say if they met the person face to face.

Have students look at their word web and list and think of a beginning for their anecdote that will tell about themselves. Then they can enter into their e-mail sentences that tell what happened in their travel adventure. Encourage them to refer back to details in their web as they write.

Examine model text

Display 21st Century Transparency TC8 and review the body of the e-mail.

 Think Aloud This student begins by introducing himself to his e-pen pal. Then he describes things he likes and tells about his dog. This leads him to tell the story about how he got his dog. The details of the story are given in order. Last, the student asks about his e-pen pal's likes and adventures. He ends with a closing and signature.

21st Century Transparency TC8, TR DVD

Develop draft

Remind students that in a draft they get ideas down in rough form. There will be time to improve their writing by adding or subtracting when they revise.

③ Revise

Use Chronological Order

■ One way to revise writing is to check that ideas are in a logical order. In a story or anecdote, events are described in the order in which they happened. Telling events in random order confuses readers. Read these examples to students:

Confused order	I saw a tiny brown dog. A big dog barked. The little dog wagged his tail slowly. The little dog growled at him like a tiger.
Logical order	I saw a tiny brown dog. The little dog wagged his tail slowly. A big dog barked. The little dog growled at him like a tiger.

■ Discuss with students how the reordered details make the incident clear.

Peer conferencing

Have students share their drafts with their partners for peer revision. Explain that an outside reader can help a writer revise by pointing out what is not clear. Ask each partner to note places where events may be in the wrong order or lack enough detail to be clear. Encourage students to write at least two suggestions for revision.

Revise drafts

Now we will revise our e-mail drafts. When we revise, we try to make our writing clearer and more interesting. As you revise, think about your partner's comments and whether more details are needed to make your anecdote clear.

Corrective feedback

If... students have difficulty including sufficient detail in their anecdotes,

then... have them visualize the scene and answer the following questions: *What exactly is happening? What sights, sounds, smells, and feelings are important?*

Differentiated Instruction

SI Strategic Intervention

Elaborating with Descriptive Details If students have difficulty generating specific details about each event in their anecdote, have them quickly sketch the main events in comic-strip style and write two words or phrases under each picture that give details about what is happening.

Technology Tip

Copying and Pasting Review with students the operations for highlighting text and moving the cursor. Explain that the computer "remembers" the last text copied and pastes it when the paste command is given.

Objectives
- Correct sentence fragments.
- Fill out required information in an e-mail form.
- Edit drafts.
- Type a correct closing.

4 Edit

MINI-LESSON

Using the Computer to Edit

■ The spelling checker can help you find some errors in spelling in your draft. When the checker highlights a problem, reread the word to check whether you have made an error. Some e-mail programs have dictionaries that can make suggestions. **Have students use the spelling checker in the e-mail program to check their draft.**

Type the following passage and display it on a projector:

My family driveing Abuela to her home.
In El Paso, Texas.

First, I will use the spelling checker to check for errors. **Use the spelling checker and identify the results.** The spelling checker caught the words "driveing" and "Abuela." "Driveing" is spelled incorrectly. I will change it. "Abuela" is spelled correctly, but since it is a Spanish word, the spelling checker does not recognize it. **Make the changes.**

■ Most e-mail programs have a spelling checker, but not a grammar checker. I will have to check the passage for grammar on my own. **Read the fragments aloud.** These groups of words do not sound complete. In the first group of words I see that I left out the word *was* before *driving*. This word group is a sentence fragment. A sentence fragment lacks a subject or a predicate or both. **Make the correction. Then read the second fragment aloud.** This group of words does not express a complete idea. I can see that it is really a phrase that belongs in the first sentence. This means I should delete the period and change the uppercase letter *I* to a lowercase *i*. **Make the correction. Read the corrected sentence aloud.**

■ Ask students to edit their own draft using the spelling checker in the e-mail program. Then have them read their drafts to check for errors in grammar, punctuation, and capitalization.

Corrective feedback | **If...** students have difficulty correcting sentence fragments,
then... have them complete simple sentence frames in which a subject or predicate is missing and explain why they needed to add words.

⑤ Publish and Present

MINI-LESSON

Completing the Body of the E-mail

■ **Add a Closing** To end your e-mail, you will add a closing. The closing is a word or phrase such as "Sincerely" or "Your e-pen pal." Place a comma after the closing. Then type your name on the line below the closing. Model adding an appropriate closing and signature line. Then instruct students to write their closing and add their names to their e-mails.

■ **Check Format** Have students check their e-mail to be sure it is complete and correct. Have them check the following items:

- Are the *To* and *Subject* lines completed correctly? Am I sure the e-mail address is correct?

- Does the greeting spell the e-pen pal's name correctly and end with a comma?

- Does each paragraph of the e-mail have a space before and after it?

- Is there a closing line that ends with a comma?

- Did I type my name at the end?

Explain that you will check the e-mails to be sure they are correct and appropriate and then send them on to each e-pen pal.

Academic Vocabulary

Closing The closing of an e-mail is a phrase placed below the last line of the letter or e-mail and followed by a comma. Example: *Your friend,*

Sentence Fragment A sentence fragment lacks a subject, a predicate, or both.

Differentiated Instruction

 Strategic Intervention

Using Verbs Correctly Explain that the *-ing* form of a verb is used with a helping verb (*is, was, were, am*). Used by itself, the *-ing* form acts as an adjective (*racing* bike, *helping* verb). Have students identify and correct errors in these sentences:
They following us into town.
Shantay feeling sleepy.

ELL

English Language Learners
Identifying Subjects and Predicates Help students understand what makes a sentence complete using these sentence frames:
My mom ___. (*What did she do?*)
___ makes me laugh. (*Who or what makes you laugh?*)

Explain that the subject tells who or what does something. The predicate tells what the subject did. Have partners find subjects and predicates for sentences in their drafts.

Objectives
- Plan and journal for future e-mails.
- Analyze and evaluate the process of writing an e-mail.

⑤ Publish and Present

Options for publishing

Students may choose from the following options for presenting their e-mail.

Print out a copy of their e-pen pal e-mail to share with their families and to display in the classroom.	Send the e-mail to their e-pen pal and save and store the e-mail in their folder at the school e-mail site.

E-Pen Pal possibilities

Explain to students that e-pen pal correspondence can continue, with each student sending and receiving an e-mail. When students' e-pen pals respond, it will be your student's turn to write a second e-mail.

Discuss with students possible subjects they might like to discuss with their e-pen pals and information they might like to find out about the e-pen pal's school or interests. Explain that e-pen pals can even work together on projects, keeping in touch and sharing ideas by e-mail.

Encourage students to record information they want to share, information they want to learn, and possible projects they would like to suggest in a writing journal or e-journal. They can refer to their journals when replying to their e-pen pals.

Contents

Pacing Guide

This chart shows the instructional sequence from *Scott Foresman Reading Street* for Grade 4. You can use this pacing guide as is to ensure you are following a comprehensive scope and sequence. Or, you can adjust the sequence to match your calendar, curriculum map, or testing schedule.

Grade 4

REVIEW WEEK

READING	UNIT 1					UNIT 2	
	Week 1	Week 2	Week 3	Week 4	Week 5	Week 1	Week 2
Comprehension Skill	Sequence	Author's Purpose	Literary Elements (Character, Setting, Plot)	Author's Purpose	Main Idea/ Details	Cause/Effect	Draw Conclusions
Comprehension Strategy	Summarize	Questioning	Background Knowledge	Story Structure	Text Structure	Background Knowledge	Story Structure
Vocabulary Skill/ Strategy	Suffixes/ Word Structure	Word Endings/ Word Structure	Multiple-Meaning Words/ Dictionary	Synonyms, Antonyms/ Context Clues	Suffixes -ist, -ive, -ness/ Word Structure	Prefixes & Suffixes/ Word Structure	Unknown Words/ Dictionary-Glossary
Fluency Skill	Expression	Appropriate Phrasing/ Punctuation Cues	Rate/Accuracy	Expression	Appropriate Phrasing	Appropriate Phrasing	Expression
Spelling/ Word Work	Short Vowels VCCV	Long *a* and *i*	Long *e* and *o*	Long *e*	Long *u*	Adding -s, -es	Irregular Plurals

REVIEW WEEK

	UNIT 4					UNIT 5	
	Week 1	Week 2	Week 3	Week 4	Week 5	Week 1	Week 2
Comprehension Skill	Compare/ Contrast	Compare/ Contrast	Sequence	Graphic Sources	Literary Elements (Character, Plot)	Author's Purpose	Compare/ Contrast
Comprehension Strategy	Visualize	Summarize	Important Ideas	Predict and Set Purpose	Monitor and Clarify	Important Ideas	Visualize
Vocabulary Skill/ Strategy	Synonyms & Antonyms/ Context Clues	Multiple-Meaning Words/ Context Clues	Unknown Words/ Dictionary-Glossary	Greek & Latin Roots/ Word Structure	Synonyms & Antonyms/ Context Clues	Homographs/ Dictionary-Glossary	Greek & Latin Roots/ Word Structure
Fluency Skill	Expression	Appropriate Phrasing/ Punctuation Cues	Expression	Appropriate Phrasing	Expression	Rate and Accuracy	Appropriate Phrasing
Spelling/ Word Work	Contractions	Final Syllable Patterns	Consonant Digraph /sh/	Consonants /j/, /ks/, /kw/	Prefixes un-, dis-, in-	Multisyllabic Words	Words with Double Consonants

Are you the adventurous type? Want to use some of your own ideas and materials in your teaching? But you worry you might be leaving out some critical instruction kids need? **Customize Literacy** *can help.* **"**

Planning

REVIEW WEEK **REVIEW WEEK**

UNIT 3

Week 3	Week 4	Week 5	Week 1	Week 2	Week 3	Week 4	Week 5
Draw Conclusions	Fact and Opinion	Main Idea/ Details	Graphic Sources	Fact/ Opinion	Generalize	Cause and Effect	Generalize
Questioning	Monitor & Clarify	Inferring	Important Ideas	Text Structure	Visualize	Predict and Set Purpose	Inferring
Prefixes/ Word Structure	Unknown Words/ Dictionary-Glossary	Unknown Words/ Dictionary-Glossary	Multiple-Meaning Words/ Context Clues	Multiple-Meaning Words/ Context Clues	Unfamiliar Words/ Context Clues	Root Words/ Word Structure	Suffixes/ Word Structure
Expression	Expression	Expression	Expression	Expression	Appropriate Phrasing	Appropriate Phrasing/ Punctuation Cues	Appropriate Phrasing/ Punctuation Cues
Words with *ar, or*	Consonant Patterns *ng, nk, ph, wh*	Words with *ear, ir, our, ur*	Adding *-ed, -ing*	Homophones	Vowel Sound in *shout*	Compound Words	Possessives

REVIEW WEEK **REVIEW WEEK**

UNIT 6

Week 3	Week 4	Week 5	Week 1	Week 2	Week 3	Week 4	Week 5
Literary Elements (Character, Plot, Theme)	Main Idea/ Details	Draw Conclusions	Cause/Effect	Fact/Opinion	Sequence	Generalize	Graphic Sources
Story Structure	Text Structure	Monitor and Clarify	Questioning	Summarize	Inferring	Predict and Set Purpose	Background Knowledge
Unfamiliar Words/ Context Clues	Greek & Latin Prefixes/Word Structure	Synonyms/ Context Clues	Root Words/ Word Structure	Multiple-Meaning Words/ Dictionary-Glossary	Unfamiliar Words/ Context Clues	Unfamiliar Words/ Context Clues	Multiple-Meaning Words/ Context Clues
Expression	Expression	Rate and Accuracy	Appropriate Phrasing	Expression	Expression	Appropriate Phrasing/ Punctuation Cues	Rate and Accuracy
Greek Word Parts	Latin Roots	Related Words	Schwa	Prefixes *mis-, non-, pre-, re-*	Suffixes *-less, -ment, -ness*	Suffixes *-ful, -ly, -ion*	Silent Consonants

Pacing Guide

LANGUAGE ARTS

UNIT 1 / REVIEW WEEK

	Week 1	Week 2	Week 3	Week 4	Week 5
Speaking and Listening	Dramatic Retelling	Introduction	Advertisement	Oral Report	Travel Show
Grammar	Declarative and Interrogative Sentences	Imperative and Exclamatory Sentences	Complete Subjects and Predicates	Compound Sentences	Clauses and Complex Sentences
Weekly Writing	Realistic Fiction	Expository Composition	Parody	Friendly Letter	Personal Narrative
Trait of the Week	Organization	Organization	Voice	Conventions	Voice
Writing	E-Newsletter/Personal Narrative				

UNIT 2

	Week 1	Week 2
Speaking and Listening	Sportscast	Newscast
Grammar	Common and Proper Nouns	Regular Plural Nouns
Weekly Writing	Poetry	News Article
Trait of the Week	Figurative Language	Focus/Ideas

UNIT 4 / REVIEW WEEK

	Week 1	Week 2	Week 3	Week 4	Week 5
Speaking and Listening	Advertisement	TV Commercial	Interview	Retelling	Newscast
Grammar	Singular and Plural Pronouns	Pronouns	Pronouns and Antecedents	Possessive Pronouns	Contractions and Negatives
Weekly Writing	Mystery	Song	Instructions	Problem-Solution Essay	Adventure
Trait of the Week	Word Choice	Word Choice	Organization	Focus/Ideas	Word Choice
Writing	Story Exchange/Story				

UNIT 5

	Week 1	Week 2
Speaking and Listening	Dramatization	Radio Announcement
Grammar	Adjectives and Articles	Adverbs
Weekly Writing	Fantasy	Legend
Trait of the Week	Conventions	Sentences

REVIEW WEEK

Week 3	Week 4	Week 5
Readers' Theater	Interview	Panel Discussion
Irregular Plural Nouns	Singular Possessive Nouns	Plural Possessive Nouns
Poetry: Free verse, cinquain	Expository Composition	Persuasive Essay
Figurative Language	Organization	Organization

Podcast/How-to Report

UNIT 3

REVIEW WEEK

Week 1	Week 2	Week 3	Week 4	Week 5
Persuasive Speech	Interview	Readers' Theater	Weather Broadcast	How-to Demonstration
Action and Linking Verbs	Main and Helping Verbs	Subject-Verb Agreement	Past, Present, and Future Tenses	Irregular Verbs
Narrative Poem	Invitation	Myth	Formal Letter	Summary
Organization	Voice	Sentences	Organization	Sentences

Photo Essay/Compare and Contrast Essay

REVIEW WEEK

Week 3	Week 4	Week 5
How-to Demonstration	Panel Discussion	Talk Show
Comparative & Superlative Adjectives, Adverbs	Time Order Words	Prepositions and Prepositional Phrases
Thank-You Note	Persuasive Ad	Personal Narrative
Word Choice	Focus/Ideas	Sentences

Electronic Pen Pals/Persuasive Essay

UNIT 6

REVIEW WEEK

Week 1	Week 2	Week 3	Week 4	Week 5
Panel Discussion	How-to Demonstration	Debate	Readers' Theater	Informational Speech
Conjunctions	Capitalization and Abbreviations	Commas	Quotations and Quotation Marks	Titles
Cause-and-Effect Essay	Review	Skit	Play	Literary Nonfiction
Focus/Ideas	Sentences	Word Choice	Word Choice	Conventions

Blog/Research Report

Teaching Record Chart

This chart shows the critical comprehension skills and strategies you need to cover. Check off each one as you provide instruction.

Reading/Comprehension	DATES OF INSTRUCTION		
Summarize and explain the lesson or message of a work of fiction is its theme.			
Compare and contrast the adventures or exploits of characters (e.g., the tricksters) in traditional and classical literature.			
Explain how the structural elements of poetry (e.g., rhyme, meter, stanzas, line breaks) relate to form (e.g., lyrical poetry, free verse).			
Describe the structural elements particular to dramatic literature.			
Sequence and summarize the plot's main events and describe their influence on future events.			
Describe the interaction of characters including their relationships and the changes they undergo.			
Identify whether the narrator or speaker of a story is first or third person.			
Identify similarities and differences between the events and characters' experiences in a fictional work and the actual events and experiences described in an author's biography or autobiography.			
Identify the author's use of similes and metaphors to produce imagery.			
Read independently for a sustained period of time and paraphrase what the reading was about, maintaining meaning and logical order (e.g., generate a reading log or journal; participate in book talks).			
Explain the difference between a stated and implied purpose for an expository text.			

> " Tired of using slips of paper or stickies to make sure you teach everything you need to? Need an easier way to keep track of what you have taught, and what you still need to cover? **Customize Literacy** can help. "

Reading/Comprehension	DATES OF INSTRUCTION		
Summarize the main idea and supporting details in texts in ways that maintain meaning.			
Distinguish fact from opinion in a text and explain how to verify what is a fact.			
Describe explicit and implicit relationships among ideas in texts organized by cause-and-effect, sequence, or comparison.			
Use multiple text features (e.g., guide words, topic and concluding sentences) to gain an overview of the contents of text and to locate information.			
Explain how an author uses language to present information to influence what the reader thinks or does.			
Determine the sequence of activities needed to carry out procedure (e.g., following a recipe).			
Explain factual information presented graphically (e.g., charts, diagrams, graphs, illustrations).			
Establish purposes for reading selected texts based on own or others' desired outcome to enhance comprehension.			
Ask literal, interpretive, and evaluative questions of text.			
Monitor and adjust comprehension (e.g., using background knowledge, creating sensory images, rereading a portion aloud, generating questions).			
Make inferences about text and use textual evidence to support understanding.			
Summarize information in text, maintaining meaning and logical order.			
Make connections (e.g., thematic links, author analysis) between literary and informational texts with similar ideas and provide textual evidence.			

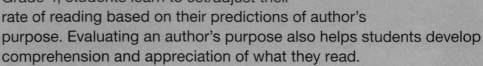

Author's Purpose

What is it? An author may write to persuade, to inform, to entertain, or to express a mood or feeling. Readers can infer an **author's purpose** from text features and from specific language the author uses. At Grade 4, students learn to set/adjust their rate of reading based on their predictions of author's purpose. Evaluating an author's purpose also helps students develop comprehension and appreciation of what they read.

Student Edition p. EI•2

How Good Readers Use the Skill Students know that they read different kinds of selections for different reasons. Teachers can build on these experiences by introducing specific purposes for writing and helping readers classify things they read. At first, students learn that authors write to inform or entertain. More sophisticated readers learn other purposes; they learn that an author may have several purposes. Eventually we want readers to preview a selection for hints to author's purpose, for example, graphics, dialogue, and sample text. They also think critically about whether an author met his or her purpose.

Texts for Teaching

Student Edition
- *Lewis and Clark and Me,* 4.1, pages 52–61
- *The Horned Toad Prince,* 4.1, pages 116–129
- *Smokejumpers,* 4.2, pages 178–191

Leveled Readers
- See pages 24–29 for a list of Leveled Readers.

Objectives:

- Students understand that an author writes for one or more purposes.
- Students identify purposes for writing.
- Students infer an author's purpose from text features and specific language used.
- Students use author's purpose to set a reading rate.

Mini-Lesson 1

Teach the Skill

Use the **Envision It!** lesson on page EI•2 to visually review author's purpose.

Remind students that:
- an author may write to **persuade,** to **inform,** to **entertain,** or to **express** a mood or feeling.
- readers can infer an **author's purpose** from text features and language.

Practice

Ask students to name some movies, books, and TV shows they have read or seen lately. Join in, adding your experiences. Together, work to classify the list according to purpose. Have students ask: *Was this created to teach me something? to entertain me? to persuade me to think or act in a certain way? to express a certain mood or feeling?* Talk briefly about what parts of the movie, book, or TV show students used to decide on its purpose. Make a chart for your responses.

If... students have difficulty identifying the purpose,

then... provide two choices for a particular book or show and have students select from the choices.

Apply

As students read the assigned text, have them look at the classification chart you made and think about what purpose the author might have had.

Writing

Students can write their own definitions for *persuade, inform, express,* and *entertain* to use when classifying selections.

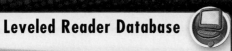

Mini-Lesson 2

Teach the Skill
Use the **Envision It!** lesson on page EI•2 to visually review author's purpose.

Remind students that:
- an author may write to **persuade,** to **inform,** to **entertain,** or to **express** a mood or feeling.
- readers can infer an **author's purpose** from text features and from specific language the author uses.
- an author may have more than one purpose for writing.

Practice
Provide some examples of different reading materials. Include one or more nonfiction informational articles, fictional stories, a poem or two, and at least one advertisement. Have students work in small groups to first decide on the purpose behind the piece and then to point out language or text features to support their opinions. Bring the groups together and have them explain their ideas. Write down some of the language they cite for each kind of writing. Ask: Could an author have more than one purpose for writing? What makes you think as you do?

If... students have difficulty determining purpose from text features and language,

then... have them look at one kind of writing at a time and list some text features and language that help them make an inference about author's purpose.

Apply
As students read the text, have them complete a graphic organizer to record details to use to figure out author's purpose.

Writing
Students can write a few sentences with a purpose in mind and have a classmate say what the purpose is.

Mini-Lesson 3

Teach the Skill
Use the **Envision It!** lesson on page EI•2 to visually review author's purpose.

Remind students that:
- an author may write to **persuade,** to **inform,** to **entertain,** or to **express** a mood or feeling.
- readers can infer an **author's purpose** from text features and from specific language the author uses.
- an author may have more than one purpose for writing.
- understanding the author's purpose can help them determine their reading rate.

Practice
Model reading aloud a portion of a nonfiction article to show students how to determine challenging reading rate. Think aloud as you preview the article to determine your reading rate. Ask questions: What is this all about? What text features does the author include? Why might the author have written this? Will I read slowly or quickly? As you read, explain to students how you will set your reading rate based on the difficulty of the text and the author's purpose.

If... students have difficulty understanding that previewing can help determine author's purpose and reading rate,

then... go through a nonfiction selection and list text features, discussing their use in the article.

Apply
As students read, have them set their reading rate based on the author's purpose.

Writing
Students review a piece of their writing to determine purpose.

Instruction

Compare and Contrast

Student Edition p. EI•5

What is it?

Comparing and **contrasting** means finding likenesses and/or differences between two or more people, places, things, or ideas. At Grade 4, students are using clue words such as *like, but, unlike,* and *as* to help identify likenesses and differences in text, but they are also seeing likenesses and differences in text without clue words. They understand that looking for comparisons can help them remember what they read. They begin to compare text with their own prior knowledge and ideas.

How Good Readers Use the Skill

Comparing and contrasting are basic reasoning devices. We try to understand an unknown using the known—i.e., a likeness or difference. At first, students notice likenesses and differences. Older students begin to use clue words as signals for comparisons. They learn about similes and metaphors, which are literary comparisons. Students also learn that authors sometimes use comparison and contrast as a way to organize their writing.

Texts for Teaching

Student Edition
- *The Case of the Gasping Garbage,* 4.2, pages 26–41
- *Encantado: Pink Dolphin of the Amazon,* 4.2, pages 58–71
- *Lost City: The Discovery of Machu Picchu,* 4.2, pages 206–217

Leveled Readers
- See pages 24–29 for a list of Leveled Readers.

Objectives:
- Students define *compare* and *contrast.*
- Students identify some clue words that can help them see comparisons.
- Students can identify comparisons even when clue words are not used.
- Students make comparisons between text and prior knowledge and ideas.

Mini-Lesson 1

Teach the Skill

Use the **Envision It!** lesson on page EI•5 to visually review compare and contrast.

Remind students that:
- to **compare** means to tell how things are the same or almost the same.
- to **contrast** means to tell how things are different.
- they can group things by comparing and contrasting.

Practice

Have students visualize two vehicles, such as a bicycle and a bus. Draw a Venn diagram (two overlapping circles) on the board with these labels: *Bicycle, Both Vehicles, Bus.* Work together to list qualities that are unique to each and then list the qualities the two vehicles share. Help get students started by asking: How are the two vehicles alike? How are they different? Students can name shape, size, number of wheels, purpose, and so on.
If... students have difficulty identifying likenesses and differences of two vehicles in their mind,
then... show pictures and have them begin with color, shape, and size.

Apply

As students read on their own, have them think about how places and people they read about are alike and different.

Writing

Students can write a paragraph using the information in the diagram.

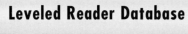

Mini-Lesson 2

Teach the Skill

Use the **Envision It!** lesson on page EI•5 to visually review compare and contrast.

Remind students that:

• to **compare** means to tell how things are the same or almost the same.

• to **contrast** means to tell how things are different.

• clue words in text can help them see when an author is comparing or contrasting people, places, things, or ideas.

• some comparison/contrast texts have no clue words and you need to figure out the comparison on your own.

Practice

Write the following paragraph on the board and read it with students.

Juan and Jamie are in the same grade. Juan goes to North School, but Jamie goes to West School. They like sports, although neither plays on a team yet. Juan likes baseball and hopes to make the team in the spring, while Jamie prefers soccer. Unlike Juan, however, Jamie practices every day.

Circle the words *but, neither, while,* and *unlike.* Explain that these are clues to comparisons. Reread the sentences and use the information to complete a Venn diagram about the boys.

If... students have difficulty identifying likenesses,

then... have them ask themselves: *Are they alike in this way? Are they different?*

Apply

As students read on their own, have them make charts or diagrams to note comparisons and contrasts.

Writing

Students can turn their sentences into a paragraph or short story.

Mini-Lesson 3

Teach the Skill

Use the **Envision It!** lesson on page EI•5 to visually review compare and contrast.

Remind students that:

• to **compare** means to tell how things are the same or almost the same.

• to **contrast** means to tell how things are different.

• clue words in text can help them see when an author is comparing or contrasting people, places, things, or ideas.

• some comparison/contrast texts have no clue words and you need to figure out the comparison on your own.

Practice

With students, think of two things to compare. As a class, create a Venn diagram, deciding on specific qualities for each thing you are comparing and deciding on qualities they share. Have partners write sentences using the qualities. Review clue words that help their readers see comparisons.

Words for Comparing	Words for Contrasting
like alike similarly in addition same also	unlike on the other hand however but different

Have partners share their sentences. Talk about how finding comparisons and contrasts as they read will help them better understand what they read.

If... students have difficulty writing sentences with clue words,

then... provide sentence starters, for example, *The king loved gold, but the queen loved _____.*

Apply

As students read, have them make charts to note comparisons and contrasts.

Writing

Students can turn their sentences into a short story.

Instruction

Section 2 Instruction

Literary Elements

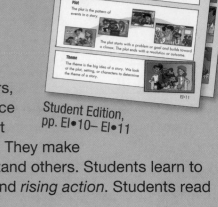

*Student Edition,
pp. EI•10– EI•11*

Objectives:
- Students understand that fictional selections include characters, a setting, and a plot.
- Students identify or infer setting and traits and motives of characters.
- Students follow the plot in a story.
- Students identify the theme of a story.

What is it?   **Literary elements** include the characters, setting, plot, and theme of a fictional piece of writing. At Grade 4, students learn that the elements of a story are often related. They make inferences about one element to understand others. Students learn to identify plot elements, such as *conflict* and *rising action*. Students read pieces with no directly stated theme.

How Good Readers Use the Skill   Students need experience in understanding the relationships between characters and setting and how they impact plot and theme. Identifying these elements is the first step. Readers ask questions, such as *What is the character's goal? Does he or she achieve it? What message might the author have for me, the reader?* Students learn to use the literary elements and language in a story to preview and make connections as they read. Understanding theme is a way readers connect a story to their own experiences or those of others. Older readers connect themes within stories and make connections between stories that share similar themes.

Texts for Teaching

Student Edition
- *On the Banks of Plum Creek,* 4.1, pages 84–99
- *Encyclopedia Brown and the Case of the Slippery Salamander,* 4.2, pages 146–155
- *Cliff Hanger,* 4.2, pages 234–245

Leveled Readers
- See pages 24–29 for a list of Leveled Readers.

Teach the Skill
Use the **Envision It!** lesson on pp. EI•10–EI•11 to visually review literary elements.

Remind students that:
- **characters** are the people or animals in stories. You learn about characters through their words and actions and through how other characters act toward them.
- the **setting** is the time and place in which a story takes place.
- the **plot** is the pattern of events in a story that lead to a character fulfilling a goal or solving a problem.

Practice
Explain that what happens in a story can often cause a character to change. Provide an example from a story you have read. Begin a web about the character, listing details from the story at the beginning of the story and at the end. Ask: What was the character like at the beginning? Did the character change? How? Why? Compare the characters with each other and with real people.
If... students have difficulty identifying character traits,
then... suggest two traits, such as curious and uninterested, and have students select the one that fits best. Make sure students explain their choices.

Apply
As students read the assigned text, have them record traits of the main character on a graphic organizer. They can use this to talk about how characters change in the story.

Writing
Students can write a paragraph describing a character and how that character changes in a story.

Go Digital!   Leveled Reader Database   Envision It! Animations

Customize Literacy

Mini-Lesson 2

Teach the Skill

Use the **Envision It!** lesson on pages EI•10–EI•11 to visually review literary elements.

Remind students that:

- **characters, setting,** and **plot** are the *who*, *where*, and *what* of a story.
- the **plot** is the pattern of events in a story that leads to a character fulfilling a goal or solving a problem.
- the character begins to solve the problem or reach the goal in what is called **rising action.**
- the turning point—usually the most important event in a story—is called the **climax.**
- the **resolution** is the outcome.

Practice

Supply students with a familiar story. Have volunteers retell the story. Jot down the events student recall on a graphic organizer, such as a plot line or story sequence chart. Identify the problem, rising action, climax, and resolution. Ask questions to help students understand kinds of problems characters face: Is there a conflict between two characters? Is there a conflict between a character and something in nature? Is the conflict inside the character, as when a character needs to make a decision about something?

If... students have difficulty identifying parts of the plot,

then... have students work with figuring out these two parts first: the problem or goal and the resolution.

Apply

As students read the assigned text, have them record plot events on a graphic organizer. They can use this to summarize the story.

Writing

Students can write a summary of a favorite book or story, including the story's problem, rising action, climax, and resolution.

Instruction

Mini-Lesson 3

Teach the Skill

Use the **Envision It!** lesson on pages EI•10–EI•11 to visually review literary elements.

Remind students that:

- **characters, setting,** and **plot** are the *who*, *where*, and *what* of a story.
- the **theme** is the underlying meaning of a story. Readers use information about characters, setting, and plot from the story to understand this big idea.
- the **theme** is the *why* of a story, or the point the author is trying to make. It may be a generalization, such as, "Honesty is the best policy."
- sometimes themes are not stated.

Practice

Using a familiar story, have students think about what the theme might be. First, have them retell the plot of the story. Then brainstorm with students a general topic for the story. Ask: Is the story about friendship? about growing up? about disappointment? *About being steadfast?* When students choose one or two topics, have them locate details in the story that would support that topic. Together, think about a theme for the story. Write it as a sentence.

If... students have difficulty choosing a theme,

then... provide one or two choices and have students select one and tell why it is a good choice.

Apply

As students read the assigned text, have them first look to see if the author states a theme; if not, have them think about why the author wrote the story.

Writing

Students can write a paragraph about the theme of a favorite story, including why they think as they do.

Text Structure

Mini-Lesson

Student Edition p. EI•24

Objectives:

- Students recognize that texts can be organized in sequential order, by description, comparison/contrast, or cause-effect.
- Students use clue words and other text features that signal a text's organization.
- Students ask questions to help them determine text structure.

Texts for Teaching

Student Edition

- *Letters Home from Yosemite,* 4.1, pages 144–155
- *Adelina's Whales,* 4.1, pages 350–361
- *Antarctic Journal,* 4.2, pages 262–277

Leveled Readers

- See pages 24–29 for a list of Leveled Readers.

Understand the Strategy

Text structure refers to how a nonfiction article is organized. Externally, nonfiction articles include titles, subheads, graphics, and so on. Internally, a nonfiction article is organized in a way that best presents the content. This organization may be sequential, comparative, explanatory (cause-effect), or descriptive. Recognizing text structure helps readers understand and recall ideas.

Teach

Use the **Envision It!** lesson on page EI•24 to visually review text structure with students.

Remind students that authors organize information in various ways. Provide examples of the following organizational patterns for students.

Organization Patterns of Text

Pattern	Word Clues	Text Features
Sequential	dates; times; *first, then, before*	timelines, flow charts, maps
Comparison/Contrast	*however, as well as, similarly*	comparison charts
Cause-Effect	*because, since, as a result*	diagrams
Description	*for example, most important*	photos, captions

Practice

Supply students with a short piece of nonfiction, such as a biographical sketch. Read the selection together and call attention to the text features, clue words, and any other evidence to support its organization pattern (sequential). Then have students reread the piece and work in pairs to locate these features on their own. Bring the group together and summarize the piece, using sequential order. On subsequent occasions, use a different nonfiction piece, such as a science article that explains a process. Over time, have them work with all the patterns listed in the chart.

If... students have difficulty recognizing sequential text structure,

then... chunk the text for them and have them look for clue words. They can put chunks together to see more examples of clue words for sequence.

Apply

Ask students to think about possible text structure as they preview and get ready to read. Then have them revise their ideas if necessary after reading.

Anchor Chart

Anchor charts help students make their thinking visible and permanent. With an anchor chart, the group can clarify their thinking about how to use a strategy. Display anchor charts so readers can use them and add to them as they read. Here is a sample chart for figuring out text structure.

Text Structure

1. Look over the article before you start to read. Ask: *What is the topic? What text features are there? Can they help me figure out text structure?*

2. Read the subheads. They can be clues to text structure.

3. Look for clue words as you read.
Sequence clue words: *before, after, first, next, last*
Compare/contrast clue words: *both, neither, on the other hand, likewise*
Cause-effect clue words: *because, consequently, as a result, this led to*
Description clue words: *most important, also, for example*

4. Look for patterns as you read.
Sequence: Information is told in time order.
Compare/contrast: The author tells how things or places or people are the same and/or different.
Cause-effect: The author explains how things work or what happens and why.
Description: The author tells all about one thing, person, or place.

5. If you think you know the structure, use a graphic organizer that fits and take notes on it.

6. Write a summary and try to use the same text structure.

Anchor Chart

Using Multiple Strategies

Good readers use multiple strategies as they read. You can encourage students to read strategically through good classroom questioning. Use questions such as these to help students apply strategies during reading.

Answer Questions

- Who or what is this question about?

- Where can you look to find the answer to this question?

Ask Questions

- What do you want to know about _____?

- What questions do you have about the _____ in this selection? Use the words *who, what, when, where, why,* and *how* to ask your questions.

- Do you have any questions after reading?

Graphic Organizers

- What kind of graphic organizer could you use to help you keep track of the information in this selection?

Monitor and Clarify

- Does the story or article make sense?

- What don't you understand about what you read?

- Do you need to reread, review, read on, or check a reference source?

- Do you need to read more slowly or more quickly?

- What is a _____? Where could you look to find out?

Predict/Confirm Predictions

- What do you think this story or article will be about? Why do you think as you do?

- What do you think you will learn from this selection?

- Do the text features help you predict what will happen?

- Based on what has happened so far, what do you think will happen next?

- Is this what you thought would happen?

- How does _____ change what you thought would happen?

Preview

- What do the photographs, illustrations, or graphic sources tell about the selection?

- What do you want to find out? What do you want to learn?

Background Knowledge

- What do you already know about _____?
- Have you read stories or articles by this author before?
- How is this selection like others that you have read?
- What does this remind you of?
- How does your background knowledge help you understand _____?
- Did the text match what you already knew? What new information did you learn?

Story Structure

- Who are the characters in this story? the setting?
- What is the problem in this story? How does the problem get solved?
- What is the point of this story?

Summarize

- What two or three important ideas have you read so far?
- How do the text features relate to the important ideas?
- Is there a graphic organizer that can help you organize the information before you summarize?

Text Structure

- How has the author organized the writing?
- What clues tell you that the text is structured _____?

Visualize

- When you read this, what do you picture in your mind?
- What do you hear, see, or smell?
- What do you think _____ looks like? Why do you think as you do?

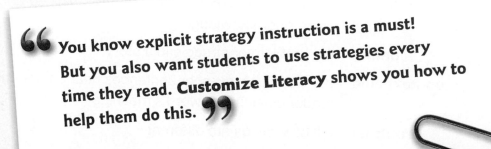

" You know explicit strategy instruction is a must! But you also want students to use strategies every time they read. **Customize Literacy** shows you how to help them do this. "

Glossary of Literacy Terms

This glossary lists academic language terms that are related to literacy.
They are provided for your information and professional use.

A

alliteration	the repetition of a consonant sound in a group of words, especially in poetry
allusion	a word or phrase that refers to something else the reader already knows from history, experience, or reading
animal fantasy	a story about animals that talk and act like people
answer questions	a reading strategy in which readers use the text and prior knowledge to answer questions about what they are reading
antonym	a word that means the opposite of another word
ask questions	a reading strategy in which readers ask themselves questions about the text to help make sense of what they read
author's point of view	the author's opinion on the subject he or she is writing about
author's purpose	the reason the author wrote the text
autobiography	the story of a real person's life written by that person

B

background knowledge	the information and experience that a reader brings to a text
biography	the story of a real person's life written by another person

C

cause	why something happens
character	a person, an animal, or a personified object in a story
chronological order	events in a selection, presented in the order in which they occurred
classify and categorize	put things, such as pictures or words, into groups
climax	the point in a story at which conflict is confronted
compare	tell how things are the same
comprehension	understanding of text being read—the ultimate goal of reading
comprehension strategy	a conscious plan used by a reader to gain understanding of text. Comprehension strategies may be used before, during, or after reading.
conclusion	a decision or opinion arrived at after thinking about facts and details and using prior knowledge
conflict	the problem or struggle in a story
context clue	the words, phrases, or sentences near an unfamiliar word that give the reader clues to the word's meaning
contrast	tell how things are different

details   small pieces of information

dialect   form of a language spoken in a certain region or by a certain group of people that differs from the standard form of that language

dialogue   written conversation

diary   a day-to-day record of one's activities and thoughts

draw conclusions   arrive at decisions or opinions after thinking about facts and details and using prior knowledge

D

effect   what happens as the result of a cause

etymology   an explanation of the origin and history of a word and its meaning

exaggeration   a statement that makes something seem larger or greater than it actually is

expository text   text that contains facts and information. Also called *informational text*.

E

fable   a story, usually with animal characters, that is written to teach a moral, or lesson

fact   piece of information that can be proved to be true

fairy tale   a folk story with magical characters and events

fantasy   a story that could not really happen

fiction   writing that tells about imaginary people, things, and events

figurative language   the use of language that gives words a meaning beyond their usual definitions in order to add beauty or force

flashback   an interruption in the sequence of events of a narrative to include an event that happened earlier

folk tale   a story that has been passed down by word of mouth

foreshadowing   the use of hints or clues about what will happen later in a story

F

generalize   make a broad statement or rule after examining particular facts

graphic organizer   a drawing, chart, or web that illustrates concepts or shows how ideas relate to each other. Readers use graphic organizers to help them keep track of and understand important information and ideas as they read. Story maps, word webs, Venn diagrams, and K-W-L charts are graphic organizers.

graphic source   a chart, diagram, or map within a text that adds to readers' understanding of the text

G

Instruction

H

historical fiction	realistic fiction that takes place in the past. It is an imaginary story based on historical events and characters.
humor	writing or speech that has a funny or amusing quality
hyperbole	an exaggerated statement not meant to be taken literally, such as *I'm so hungry I could eat a horse.*

I

idiom	a phrase whose meaning differs from the ordinary meaning of the words. *A stone's throw* is an idiom meaning "a short distance."
imagery	the use of language to create beautiful or forceful pictures in the reader's mind
inference	conclusion reached on the basis of evidence and reasoning
inform	give knowledge, facts, or news to someone
informational text	writing that contains facts and information. Also called *expository text.*
interview	a face-to-face conversation in which someone responds to questions
irony	a way of speaking or writing in which the ordinary meaning of the words is the opposite of what the speaker or writer is thinking; a contrast between what is expected and what actually happens

J

jargon	the language of a special group or profession

L

legend	a story coming down from the past about the great deeds of a hero. Although a legend may be based on historical people and events, it is not regarded as historically true.
literary elements	the characters, setting, plot, and theme of a narrative text

main idea	the big idea that tells what a paragraph or a selection is mainly about; the most important idea of a text
metacognition	an awareness of one's own thinking processes and the ability to monitor and direct them to a desired goal. Good readers use metacognition to monitor their reading and adjust their reading strategies.
metaphor	a comparison that does not use *like* or *as*, such as *a heart of stone*
meter	the pattern of beats or accents in poetry
monitor and clarify	a comprehension strategy by which readers actively think about understanding their reading and know when they understand and when they do not. Readers use appropriate strategies to make sense of difficult words, ideas, or passages.
mood	the atmosphere or feeling of a written work
moral	the lesson or teaching of a fable or story
motive	the reason a character in a narrative does or says something
mystery	a story about mysterious events that are not explained until the end, so as to keep the reader in suspense
myth	a story that attempts to explain something in nature

M

narrative	a story, made up or true, that someone tells or narrates
narrator	the character in a selection who tells the story
nonfiction	writing that tells about real things, real people, and real events

N

onomatopoeia	the use of words that sound like their meanings, such as *buzz* and *hum*
opinion	someone's judgment, belief, or way of thinking
oral vocabulary	the words needed for speaking and listening
outcome	the resolution of the conflict in a story

O

paraphrase	retell the meaning of a passage in one's own words
personification	a figure of speech in which human traits or actions are given to animals or inanimate objects, as in *The sunbeam danced on the waves.*
persuade	convince someone to do or to believe something
photo essay	a collection of photographs on one theme, accompanied by text
play	a story that is written to be acted out for an audience

P

P

plot	a series of related events at the beginning, middle, and end of a story; the action of a story
poem	an expressive, imaginative piece of writing often arranged in lines having rhythm and rhyme. In a poem, the patterns made by the sounds of the words have special importance.
pourquoi tale	a type of folk story that explains why things in nature came to be. *Pourquoi* is a French word meaning "why."
predict	tell what a selection might be about or what might happen in a text. Readers use text features and information to predict. They confirm or revise their predictions as they read.
preview	look over a text before reading it
prior knowledge	the information and experience that a reader brings to a text. Readers use prior knowledge to help them understand what they read.
prop	an item, such as an object, picture, or chart, used in a performance or presentation

R

reading vocabulary	the words we recognize or use in print
realistic fiction	a story about imaginary people and events that could happen in real life
repetition	the repeated use of some aspect of language
resolution	the point in a story where the conflict is resolved
rhyme	to end in the same sound(s)
rhythm	a pattern of strong beats in speech or writing, especially poetry
rising action	the buildup of conflicts and complications in a story

S

science fiction	a story based on science that often tells what life in the future might be like
semantic map	a graphic organizer, often a web, used to display words or concepts that are meaningfully related
sensory language	the use of words that help the reader understand how things look, sound, smell, taste, or feel
sequence	the order of events in a selection or the order of the steps in which something is completed
sequence words	clue words such as *first*, *next*, *then*, and *finally* that signal the order of events in a selection

setting	where and when a story takes place
simile	a comparison that uses *like* or *as*, as in *as busy as a bee*
speech	a public talk to a group of people made for a specific purpose
stanza	a group of lines in a poem
steps in a process	the order of the steps in which something is completed
story map	a graphic organizer used to record the literary elements and the sequence of events in a narrative text
story structure	how the characters, setting, and events of a story are organized into a plot
summarize	give the most important ideas of what was read. Readers summarize important information in the selection to keep track of what they are reading.
supporting detail	piece of information that tells about the main idea
symbolism	the use of one thing to suggest something else; often the use of something concrete to stand for an abstract idea

S

Instruction

tall tale	a humorous story that uses exaggeration to describe impossible happenings
text structure	the organization of a piece of nonfiction writing. Text structures of informational text include cause/effect, chronological, compare/contrast, description, problem/solution, proposition/support, and ask/answer questions.
theme	the big idea or author's message in a story
think aloud	an instructional strategy in which a teacher verbalizes his or her thinking to model the process of comprehension or the application of a skill
tone	author's attitude toward the subject or toward the reader
topic	the subject of a discussion, conversation, or piece of text

T

visualize	picture in one's mind what is happening in the text. Visualizing helps readers imagine the things they read about.

V

Leveled Readers Skills Chart

Scott Foresman Reading Street provides more than six hundred leveled readers. Each one is designed to:

- Practice critical skills and strategies
- Build fluency
- Build vocabulary and concepts
- Develop a lifelong love of reading

Grade 4

Title	Level*	DRA Level	Genre	Comprehension Strategy
Florida Everglades: Its Plants & Animals	K	20	Expository Nonfiction	Summarize
The Long Journey West	K	20	Expository Nonfiction	Questioning
From Sea to Shining Sea	K	20	Realistic Fiction	Background Knowledge
Flash Flood	K	20	Realistic Fiction	Story Structure
America's National Parks	K	20	Expository Nonfiction	Text Structure
Cheers for the Cheetahs	K	20	Realistic Fiction	Background Knowledge
Ranches in the Southwest	L	24	Expository Nonfiction	Background Knowledge
What It Takes to Stage a Play	L	24	Expository Nonfiction	Questioning
Animal Helpers	L	24	Nonfiction	Monitor and Clarify
A Trip to Capitol Hill	L	24	Expository Nonfiction	Inferring
Looking For Changes	L	24	Expository Nonfiction	Important Ideas
The Gray Whale	L	24	Expository Nonfiction	Text Structure
Day For Night	M	28	Narrative Nonfiction	Visualize
Surviving Hurricane Andrew	M	28	Realistic Fiction	Predict
Saving Trees Using Science	M	28	Nonfiction	Inferring
Mini Microbes	M	28	Expository Nonfiction	Visualize
Dolphins: Mammals of the Sea	M	28	Expository Nonfiction	Summarize
Speaking in Code	M	28	Expository Nonfiction	Important Ideas
The Rosetta Stone: The Key to Ancient Writings	M	28	Expository Nonfiction	Predict and Set Purpose
Something to Do	N	30	Realistic Fiction	Summarize
Lewis, Clark, and the Corps of Discovery	N	30	Biography	Questioning
Protecting Wild Animals	N	30	Realistic Fiction	Background Knowledge
From Spain to America	N	30	Expository Nonfiction	Story Structure
Top Hat Tompkins, the Detective	N	30	Mystery Fiction	Monitor and Clarify
Putting a Stop to Wildfires	N	30	Expository Nonfiction	Important Ideas
Let's Get to Know the Incas	N	30	Expository Nonfiction	Visualize
Mountain Rescue	N	30	Fiction	Story Structure
Plants and Animals in Antarctica	N	30	Expository Nonfiction	Text Structure
Stuart's Moon Suit	N	30	Realistic Fiction	Monitor and Clarify
The Wonders of Western Geography	O	34	Expository Nonfiction	Text Structure

* Suggested Guided Reading Level. Use your knowledge of students' abilities to adjust levels as needed.

The chart here and on the next few pages lists titles of leveled readers appropriate for students in Grade 4. Use the chart to find titles that meet your students' interest and instructional needs. The books in this list were leveled using the criteria suggested in *Matching Books to Readers* and *Leveled Books for Readers, Grades 3–6* by Irene C. Fountas and Gay Su Pinnell. For more on leveling, see the *Reading Street Leveled Readers Leveling Guide*.

Target Comprehension Skill	Additional Comprehension Instruction	Vocabulary
Sequence	Draw Conclusions	Word Structure/Suffixes
Author's Purpose	Main Idea and Details	Word Structure/Endings
Setting and Plot	Sequence	Dictionary/Glossary/Multiple Meanings
Author's Purpose	Main Idea and Details	Context Clues/Synonyms/Antonyms
Main Idea and Details	Generalize	Word Structure/Suffixes
Cause and Effect	Plot	Word Structure/Prefixes/Suffixes
Draw Conclusions	Graphic Sources	Unknown Words/Dictionary/Glossary
Draw Conclusions	Generalize	Word Structure/Prefixes/Suffixes
Fact and Opinion	Draw Conclusions	Unknown Words/Dictionary/Glossary
Main Idea and Details	Generalize	Unknown Words/Dictionary/Glossary
Graphic Sources	Compare and Contrast	Context Clues/Multiple Meanings
Fact and Opinion	Main Idea and Details	Context Clues/Multiple Meanings
Generalize	Cause and Effect	Context Clues/Unfamiliar Words
Graphic Sources	Plot and Character	Root Words/Word Structure
Generalize	Main Idea and Details	Word Structure/Suffixes
Compare and Contrast	Fact and Opinion	Context Clues/Synonyms and Antonyms
Compare and Contrast	Generalize	Context Clues/Multiple Meanings
Sequence	Author's Purpose	Unknown Words/Dictionary/Glossary
Graphic Sources	Draw Conclusions	Word Structure/Greek and Latin Roots
Sequence	Draw Conclusions	Word Structure/Suffixes
Author's Purpose	Compare and Contrast	Word Structure/Endings
Setting and Plot	Sequence	Dictionary/Glossary/Multiple Meanings
Author's Purpose	Compare and Contrast	Context Clues/Synonyms/Antonyms
Character and Plot	Fact and Opinion	Context Clues/Synonyms/Antonyms
Author's Purpose	Fact and Opinion	Homographs/Dictionary/Glossary
Compare and Contrast	Main Idea and Details	Word Structure/Greek and Latin Roots
Character, Plot, Theme	Cause and Effect	Context Clues/Unfamiliar Words
Main Idea and Details	Graphic Sources	Word Structure/Greek and Latin Roots
Draw Conclusions	Main Idea and Details	Synonyms/Context Clues
Main Idea and Details	Graphic Sources	Word Structure/Suffixes

Grade 4

Title	Level*	DRA Level	Genre	Comprehension Strategy
Amazing Female Athletes	O	34	Biography	Background Knowledge
Ranching in the Great American Desert	O	34	Expository Nonfiction	Story Structure
The Black Ensemble Theater	O	34	Nonfiction	Questioning
Dogs on the Job	O	34	Nonfiction	Monitor and Clarify
We Shall Overcome	O	34	Expository Nonfiction	Questioning
The Sauk and Fox Native Americans	O	34	Expository Nonfiction	Summarize
Living with Grandpa Joseph	O	34	Realistic Fiction	Inferring
To Be a Star	O	34	Realistic Fiction	Predict and Set Purpose
Earth's Closest Neighbor	O	34	Expository Nonfiction	Background Knowledge
The United States Government	P	38	Expository Nonfiction	Inferring
Storm Chasers	P	38	Nonfiction	Important Ideas
Migration Relocation	P	38	Expository Nonfiction	Text Structure
Darkness into Light	P	38	Expository Nonfiction	Visualize
Severe Weather: Storms	P	38	Expository Nonfiction	Predict and Set Purpose
Maine Now and Then	P	38	Expository Nonfiction	Inferring
Mysterious Monsters	Q	40	Expository Nonfiction	Visualize
Come Learn About Dolphins	Q	40	Expository Nonfiction	Summarize
The Super Secret Surprise Society	Q	40	Realistic Fiction	Important Ideas
Code Breakers: Uncovering German Messages	Q	40	Expository Nonfiction	Predict and Set Purpose
The Missing Iguana Mystery	Q	40	Mystery	Monitor and Clarify
The Grizzly Bear Hotshots	Q	40	Fiction	Important Ideas
Pompeii, the Lost City	R	40	Expository Nonfiction	Visualize
Bessie Coleman: Queen of the Skies	R	40	Historical Fiction	Story Structure
Let's Explore Antarctica!	R	40	Expository Nonfiction	Text Structure
To the Moon!	R	40	Science Fiction	Monitor and Clarify
The Civil Rights Movement	R	40	Expository Nonfiction	Questioning
The Story of Libraries	S	40	Expository Nonfiction	Summarize
Two Powerful Rivers	S	40	Expository Nonfiction	Questioning
Exploring the Moon	S	40	Realistic Fiction	Background Knowledge
The Diné	S	40	Expository Nonfiction	Story Structure

* Suggested Guided Reading Level. Use your knowledge of students' abilities to adjust levels as needed.

You know the theory behind leveled books: they let you match books with the interest and instructional levels of your students. You can find the right reader for every student with this chart. ""

Target Comprehension Skill	Additional Comprehension Instruction	Vocabulary
Cause and Effect	Author's Purpose	Dictionary/Prefixes/Suffixes
Draw Conclusions	Main Idea and Details	Unknown Words/Dictionary/Glossary
Draw Conclusions	Fact and Opinion	Word Structure/Prefixes
Fact and Opinion	Compare and Contrast	Unknown Words/Dictionary/Glossary
Cause and Effect	Sequence	Root Words/Word Structure
Fact and Opinion	Plot and Theme	Multiple Meanings/Dictionary/Glossary
Sequence	Character	Context Clues/Unfamiliar Words
Generalize	Cause and Effect	Context Clues/Unfamiliar Words
Graphic Sources	Main Idea and Details	Multiple Meanings/Context Clues
Main Idea and Details	Generalize	Unknown Words/Dictionary/Glossary
Graphic Sources	Sequence	Context Clues/Multiple Meanings
Fact and Opinion	Draw Conclusions	Context Clues/Multiple Meanings
Generalize	Compare and Contrast	Context Clues/Unfamiliar Words
Cause and Effect	Graphic Sources	Root Words/Word Structure
Generalize	Fact and Opinion	Word Structure/Suffixes
Compare and Contrast	Main Idea and Details	Context Clues/Synonyms and Antonyms
Compare and Contrast	Fact and Opinion	Context Clues/Multiple Meanings
Sequence	Cause and Effect	Unknown Words/Dictionary/Glossary
Graphic Sources	Main Idea and Details	Word Structure/Greek and Latin Roots
Character and Plot	Cause and Effect	Context Clues/Synonyms and Antonyms
Author's Purpose	Sequence	Homographs/Dictionary/Glossary
Compare and Contrast	Generalize	Word Structure/Greek and Latin Roots
Character, Plot, Theme	Generalize	Context Clues/Unfamiliar Words
Main Idea and Details	Generalize	Word Structure/Greek and Latin Affixes
Draw Conclusions	Compare and Contrast	Context Clues/Synonyms
Cause and Effect	Sequence	Root Words/Word Structure
Sequence	Main Idea and Details	Word Structure/Suffixes
Author's Purpose	Compare and Contrast	Word Structure/Endings
Setting and Plot	Sequence	Dictionary/Glossary/Multiple Meanings
Author's Purpose	Compare and Contrast	Context Clues/Synonyms

Matching Books & Readers

Grade 4

Title	Level*	DRA Level	Genre	Comprehension Strategy
Becoming a Melting Pot	S	40	Expository Nonfiction	Summarize
The Seahaven Squids Host a Pet Wash	S	40	Realistic Fiction	Inferring
Birthday Surprise	S	40	Realistic Fiction	Predict and Set Purpose
One Giant Leap	S	40	Narrative Nonfiction	Background Knowledge
John Muir: Protector of the Wilderness	T	50	Biography	Text Structure
Equality in American Schools	T	50	Expository Nonfiction	Background Knowledge
The Legacy of César Chávez	T	50	Biography	Story Structure
Journey to Hong Kong	T	50	Nonfiction	Questioning
Danger! Children at Work	T	50	Expository Nonfiction	Monitor and Clarify
The Power of the People	T	50	Expository Nonfiction	Inferring
Sharing Our Planet	U	50	Expository Nonfiction	Important Ideas
Birds Take Flight	U	50	Expository Nonfiction	Text Structure
Orbiting the Sun	U	50	Expository Nonfiction	Visualize
Wondrously Wild Weather	U	50	Narrative Nonfiction	Predict and Set Purpose
The Alaskan Pipeline	U	50	Expository Nonfiction	Inferring
What in the World Is That?	U	50	Expository Nonfiction	Visualize
How Does Echolocation Work?	U	50	Expository Nonfiction	Summarize
The Incredible Alexander Graham Bell	U	50	Historical Fiction	Important Ideas
The Navajo Code Talkers	V	50	Expository Nonfiction	Predict and Set Purpose
The Salamander Stumper	V	50	Realistic Fiction	Monitor and Clarify
Thor Heyerdahl's Incredible Raft	V	50	Narrative Nonfiction	Important Ideas
Meet the Maya	V	50	Expository Nonfiction	Visualize
A Book of Their Own	V	50	Realistic Fiction	Story Structure
Danger: The World Is Getting Hot!	V	50	Expository Nonfiction	Text Structure
Life on Mars: The Real Story	V	50	Realistic Fiction	Monitor and Clarify
The Women's Movement	V	50	Expository Nonfiction	Questioning
Jim Thorpe: The World's Greatest Athlete	W	60	Biography	Summarize
A New Home	W	60	Realistic Fiction	Inferring
The Show Must Go On!	W	60	Realistic Fiction	Predict and Set Purpose
The Mysteries of Space	W	60	Expository Nonfiction	Background Knowledge

* Suggested Guided Reading Level. Use your knowledge of students' abilities to adjust levels as needed.

Target Comprehension Skill	Additional Comprehension Instruction	Vocabulary
Fact and Opinion	Sequence	Multiple Meanings/Dictionary/Glossary
Sequence	Author's Purpose	Context Clues/Unfamiliar Words
Generalize	Fact and Opinion	Context Clues/Unfamiliar Words
Graphic Sources	Cause and Effect	Context Clues/Homonyms
Main Idea and Details	Generalize	Word Structure/Suffixes
Cause and Effect	Sequence	Word Structure/Prefixes/Suffixes
Draw Conclusions	Sequence	Unknown Words/Dictionary/Glossary
Draw Conclusions	Graphic Sources	Word Structure/Prefixes
Fact and Opinion	Draw Conclusions	Unknown Words/Dictionary/Glossary
Main Idea and Details	Draw Conclusions	Unknown Words/Dictionary/Glossary
Graphic Sources	Theme	Context Clues/Multiple Meanings
Fact and Opinion	Author's Purpose	Context Clues/Multiple Meanings
Generalize	Main Idea and Details	Context Clues/Unfamiliar Words
Cause and Effect	Compare and Contrast	Root Words/Word Structure
Generalize	Sequence	Word Structure/Suffixes
Compare and Contrast	Author's Purpose	Context Clues/Synonyms and Antonyms
Compare and Contrast	Cause and Effect	Context Clues/Multiple Meanings
Sequence	Character and Setting	Unknown Words/Dictionary/Glossary
Graphic Sources	Author's Purpose	Word Structure/Greek and Latin Roots
Character and Plot	Fact and Opinion	Context Clues/Synonyms and Antonyms
Author's Purpose	Fact and Opinion	Homographs/Dictionary/Glossary
Compare and Contrast	Draw Conclusions	Word Structure/Greek and Latin Roots
Character, Plot, Theme	Generalize	Context Clues/Unfamiliar Words
Main Idea and Details	Fact and Opinion	Word Structure/Greek and Latin Roots
Draw Conclusions	Graphic Sources	Synonyms/Context Clues
Cause and Effect	Draw Conclusions	Word Structure/Root Words
Fact and Opinion	Author's Purpose	Multiple Meanings/Dictionary/Glossary
Sequence	Plot	Context Clues/Unfamiliar Words
Generalize	Main Idea and Details	Context Clues/Unfamiliar Words
Graphic Sources	Fact and Opinion	Multiple Meanings/Context Clues

Matching Books & Readers

What Good Readers Do

You can use the characteristics and behaviors of good readers to help all your students read better. But what are these characteristics and behaviors? And how can you use them to foster good reading behaviors for all your students? Here are some helpful tips.

Good Readers enjoy reading! They have favorite books, authors, and genres. Good readers often have a preference about where and when they read. They talk about books and recommend their favorites.

Develop this behavior by giving students opportunities to respond in different ways to what they read. Get them talking about what they read, and why they like or dislike it.

This behavior is important because book sharing alerts you to students who are somewhat passive about reading or have limited literacy experiences. Book sharing also helps you when you select books for the class.

Good Readers select books they can read.

Develop this behavior by providing a range of three or four texts appropriate for the student and then letting the student choose.

This behavior is important because students gain control over reading when they can choose from books they can read. This helps them become more independent in the classroom.

Good Readers read independently for longer periods of time.

Develop this behavior by taking note of the level of support students need during guided reading. Use this information to gauge independent reading time accordingly.

This behavior is important because students become better readers when they spend time reading many texts at their independent level.

Good Readers use text features to help them preview and set purposes.

Develop this behavior by having students use the title and illustrations in fiction texts or the title, contents, headings, and other graphic features in nonfiction texts to make predictions about what they will be reading.

This behavior is important because previewing actually makes reading easier! Looking at features and sampling the text enables readers to predict and set expectations for reading.

" Want to improve student performance by fostering good reading behaviors? **Customize Literacy can help. "**

Good Readers predict and ask questions before and while they read.

Develop this behavior by asking questions. After reading a passage, ask students what they think will happen next in a fiction text. Have them ask a question they think will be answered in a nonfiction text and read on to see if it is.

This behavior is important because when students predict and ask questions as they read, they are engaged. They have a purpose for reading and a basis for monitoring their comprehension.

Good Readers read meaningful phrases aloud with appropriate expression.

Develop this behavior by giving students lots of opportunities to read orally. As they read, note students' phrasing, intonation, and attention to punctuation and give help as needed.

This behavior is important because reading fluently in longer, meaningful phrases supports comprehension and ease in reading longer, more complex texts.

Good Readers read aloud at an appropriate reading rate with a high percent of accuracy.

Develop this behavior by timing students' oral reading to calculate their reading rates. You can also record students' miscues to determine a percent of accuracy. This will help identify problems.

This behavior is important because when students read fluently texts that are "just right," they find reading more enjoyable. A fluent reader is able to focus more on constructing meaning and is more likely to develop a positive attitude toward reading.

Matching Books & Readers

Good Readers use effective strategies and sources of information to figure out unknown words.

Develop this behavior by teaching specific strategies for figuring out unknown words, such as sounding out clusters of letters, using context, reading on, and using references.

This behavior is important because when readers have a variety of strategies to use, they are more able to decode and self-correct quickly. Readers who do these things view themselves as good readers.

CH-
QU-
ST-

Good Readers construct meaning as they read and then share or demonstrate their understanding.

Develop this behavior by having students retell what they read or write a summary of what they read in their own words.

This behavior is important because the ability to retell or write a summary is essential for success in reading. It shows how well a student has constructed meaning.

Good Readers locate and use what is explicitly stated in a text.

Develop this behavior by asking questions that require students to go back into the text to find explicitly stated information.

This behavior is important because the ability to recall, locate, and use specific information stated in a text enables readers to respond to literal questions as well as to support opinions and justify their responses.

Good Readers make connections.

Develop this behavior by asking questions to help students make connections: *What does this remind you of? Have you ever read or experienced anything like this?*

This behavior is important because making connections helps readers understand and appreciate a text. Making connections to self, the world, and other texts supports higher-level thinking.

Good Readers interpret what they read by making inferences.

Develop this behavior by asking questions to help students tell or write about what they think was implied in the text: *Why do you think that happened? What helped you come to that conclusion?*

This behavior is important because the ability to go beyond the literal meaning of a text enables readers to gain a deeper understanding. When students make inferences, they use background knowledge, their personal knowledge, and the text to grasp the meaning of what is implied by the author.

Good Readers determine importance and evaluate what they read.

Develop this behavior by always having students identify what they think is the most important message, event, or information in a text.

This behavior is important because readers must be able to sort out important from interesting information. The ability to establish and/ or use criteria and provide support when making judgments is an important critical-thinking skill.

Good Readers support their responses using information from a text and/or their own background knowledge.

Develop this behavior by always asking students to give the reason(s) they identified an event, message, or idea as most important.

This behavior is important because the ability to justify one's response is important for all learners. It enables others to know the basis for a decision and provides an opening for further discussion.

Conversation Starters

Asking Good Questions When students read interesting and thought-provoking books, they want to share! You can encourage students to think critically about what they read. Use questions such as the following to assess comprehension as well as evoke good class/group discussions.

Author's Purpose

- Why did the author write this piece?

- How does figuring out the author's purpose help you decide how to read the text?

Cause and Effect

- Why did these events happen? How might they have been different if the causes had been different?

- Are there several causes that result in a single effect?

- Is there a single cause that has several effects?

Compare and Contrast

- What clue words show the author is comparing and/or contrasting in this article?

- How are the fictional characters and events in this story like and/or different from real people and events you know of?

Draw Conclusions

- Based on what you have read, seen, or experienced, what can you conclude about this event in the selection?

- This story seems to be a fantasy. Why might you conclude this?

- What words help you draw conclusions about the relationship between the characters?

Fact and Opinion

- What clue word or words signal that this is a statement of opinion?

- How could this statement of fact be proved true or false?

Generalize

- What generalization can you make about the story or the characters in it? What examples lead to that generalization?

- What details, facts, and logic does the author use to support this generalization?

- Is this a valid or a faulty generalization? Explain your ideas.

Graphic Sources

- How does the author use graphic sources (chart, maps, illustrations, time lines, and so on) to support ideas and opinions?

- This selection has many graphic sources. Which one or ones best help you understand the events or ideas in the selection? Why?

Literary Elements: Character, Setting, Plot, Theme

- Describe the main character at the beginning of the story and at the end of the story. How and why does he or she change?

- How is the setting important to the story? How might the story be different if its time or its place were different?

- What does the main character want at the beginning of the story? How does the main character go about trying to achieve this?

- A plot has a conflict, but the conflict isn't always between two characters. What is the conflict in this story? How is it resolved?

- In a few sentences, what is the plot of the story?

- What is the theme of the story? Use details from the story to support your statement.

Main Idea and Details

- What is the main idea of this paragraph or article? What are some details?

- The author makes this particular statement in the article. What details does the author provide to support that statement?

Sequence

- How is the sequence of events important in the text?

- Is the order of events important in this story? Why or why not?

- Based on what has already happened, what will most likely happen next?

Connecting Science and Social Studies

Scott Foresman Reading Street Leveled Readers are perfect for covering, supporting, or enriching science and social studies content. Using these books ensures that all students can access important concepts.

Grade 4 Leveled Readers

Science

Earth and Space Science

Nonfiction Books
- *Danger: The World Is Getting Hot!*
- *Darkness Into Light*
- *Day for Night*
- *Earth's Closest Neighbor*
- *Let's Explore Antarctica!*
- *Looking For Changes*
- *The Mysteries of Space*
- *One Giant Leap*
- *Orbiting the Sun*
- *Putting a Stop to Wildfires*
- *Severe Weather: Storms*
- *Storm Chasers*
- *Wondrously Wild Weather*

Fiction Books
- *Exploring the Moon*
- *Flash Flood*
- *Life on Mars: The Real Story*
- *Stuart's Moon Suit*
- *Surviving Hurricane Andrew*
- *To the Moon!*

Life Science

Nonfiction Books
- *Birds Take Flight*
- *Come Learn About Dolphins*
- *Dolphins: Mammals of the Sea*
- *Florida Everglades: Its Plants and Animals*
- *The Gray Whale*
- *How Does Echolocation Work?*
- *Migration Relocation*
- *Mini Microbes*
- *Mysterious Monsters*
- *Plants and Animals in Antarctica*
- *Saving Trees Using Science*
- *Sharing Our Planet*
- *What in the World Is That?*

Life Science

Fiction Books
- *The Missing Iguana Mystery*
- *Protecting Wild Animals*
- *The Salamander Stumper*
- *Top Hat Tompkins, the Detective*

Grade 4 Leveled Readers

Social Studies

Citizenship

Nonfiction Books
- Equality in American Schools
- Danger! Children at Work
- Dogs on the Job

Fiction Books
- Mountain Rescue
- The Super Secret Surprise Society

Culture

Nonfiction Books
- The Black Ensemble Theater
- The Diné
- From Spain to America
- What It Takes to Stage a Play

Fiction Books
- A Book of Their Own
- A New Home
- Birthday Surprise
- Cheers for the Cheetahs
- The Grizzly Bear Hotshots
- Living with Grandpa Joseph
- The Show Must Go On!
- Something to Do
- To Be a Star

Economics

Nonfiction Books
- The Alaskan Pipeline
- Ranches in the Southwest
- Ranching in the Great American Desert
- Two Powerful Rivers

Fiction Books
- The Seahaven Squids Host a Pet Wash

History

Nonfiction Books
- Becoming a Melting Pot
- The Civil Rights Movement
- Code Breakers: Uncovering German Messages
- Let's Get to Know the Incas
- The Long Journey West
- Meet the Maya
- The Navajo Code Talkers
- Pompeii, the Lost City
- The Rosetta Stone: The Key to Ancient Writing
- The Sauk and Fox Native Americans
- Speaking in Code
- The Story of Libraries
- Thor Heyerdahl's Incredible Raft
- We Shall Overcome
- The Women's Movement

History

Fiction Books
- Bessie Coleman
- The Incredible Alexander Graham Bell

Geography

Nonfiction Books
- America's National Parks
- Maine, Now and Then
- A Trip to Capital Hill
- The Wonders of Western Geography

Fiction Books
- From Sea to Shining Sea

Government

Nonfiction Books
- The Power of the People
- The United States Government

More Great Titles

Biography
- Amazing Female Athletes
- Jim Thorpe
- John Muir
- The Legacy of César Chávez
- Lewis and Clark and the Corps of Discovery

Connecting Science and Social Studies

Need more choices? Look back to Grade 3.

Grade 3 Leveled Readers

Science

Earth and Space Science

Nonfiction Books
- *The Frozen Continent: Antarctica*
- *Fun with Hobbies and Science!*
- *Gemstones Around the World*
- *Grandpa's Rock Kit*
- *How to Measure the Weather*
- *Measuring the Earth*
- *Meet the Stars*
- *Pictures in the Sky*

Fiction Books
- *What a Day!*
- *Journey Across the Arctic*

Life Science

Nonfiction Books
- *A Pet Bird*
- *All About Birds*
- *All About Penguins*
- *Animal Tracking: Learn More About It*
- *Animals of the Concrete Jungle*
- *Coral Reefs*
- *Desert Life*
- *The Field Trip*
- *Free in the Sea*
- *Growing Vegetables*
- *Ice Fishing in the Arctic*
- *Largest, Fastest, Lightest, Longest*
- *Life in the Arctic*
- *Raisins*
- *Rescuing Whales*
- *These Birds Can't Fly!*
- *Whales and Other Amazing Animals*

Life Science

Fiction Books
- *The Best Field Trip Ever!*
- *Bills and Beaks*
- *Buddy Ran Away*
- *Grape Season*
- *The Hunters and the Elk*
- *In the Fields*
- *Swimming in a School*
- *Swimming Like Buck*
- *Toby the Smart Dog*

Grade 3 Leveled Readers

Social Studies

Citizenship

Nonfiction Books
- Sweet Freedom!
- Symbols, Signs, and Songs of America

Fiction Books
- Buddy Goes to School
- Camping with Aunt Julie
- The Opposite Cousins
- Our Garden
- Puppy Problems

Culture

Nonfiction Books
- A Child's Life in Korea
- A Walk Around the City
- Celebrate Around the World
- China's Special Gifts to the World
- His Favorite Sweatshirt
- Let's Go Have Fun!
- Life Overseas
- Mixing, Kneading, and Baking
- New York's Chinatown
- The French Connection
- The World of Bread!

Fiction Books
- A Tea Party with Obâchan
- Bobby's New Apartment
- Cowboy Slim's Dude Ranch
- E-mail Friends

Culture

Books
- Grandmother Spider Steals the Sun
- Iguana Takes a Ride
- Kapuapua's Magic Shell
- The Last Minute
- Lily's Adventure Around the World
- The Magic of Coyote
- One Forest, Different Trees
- The Road to New York
- The Three Bears and Goldilocks
- The Thunder and Lightning Men

Economics

Nonfiction Books
- It's a Fair Swap!
- It's a World of Time Zones
- Let's Make a Trade
- What's Money All About?

Fiction Books
- A Family of Collectors
- Joanie's House Becomes a Home
- Let's Surprise Mom
- The Market Adventure
- The Metal Detective
- Mr. Post's Project
- The Shopping Trip

History

Nonfiction Books
- Across the English Channel
- Celebrate Independence Day/Celebra El Día de la Independencia
- Changing Times: Women in the Early Twentieth Century
- Greek Myths
- The Statue of Liberty: A Gift From France

Fiction Books
- A Trip
- The Winning Point
- With a Twist

More Great Titles

Biography
- Extraordinary Athletes
- Great Women in U. S. History
- Thomas Hart Benton: Painter of Murals

Connecting Science and Social Studies

Need more choices? Look ahead to Grade 5.

Grade 5 Leveled Readers

Science

Earth and Space Science

Nonfiction Books
- Aim High: Astronaut Training
- Astronauts and Cosmonauts
- Can Humans Make a Home in Outer Space?
- Cheaper, Faster, and Better
- Dangerous Storms
- Explore with Science
- The Inside Story of Earth
- Sailing the Stars
- The Shaping of the Continents
- Space Travel Inventions
- Storm Chasing Challenges
- Traveling by Plane
- Weather Forecasting

Fiction Books
- The Journey Through the Earth
- The Signs

Life Science

Nonfiction Books
- Changing for Survival: Bird Adaptations
- Driven to Change
- How the Wolves Saved Yellowstone
- The Kudzu Invasion
- Mixed-Up Vegetables
- Our Essential Oceans
- Paleontology: Digging for Dinosaurs and More
- Sea Life
- Searching for Dinosaurs
- Surviving the Elements: Animals and Their Environments
- What's New with Dinosaur Fossils?

Fiction Books
- The Long Trip Home
- Toby's California Vacation

Physical Science

Nonfiction Books
- George Ferris's Wheel
- The Magic of Makeup: Going Behind the Mask
- Philo and His Invention
- The Search to Build a Perpetual Motion Machine

Fiction Books
- A Happy Accident
- Jenna and the High Dive

Grade 5 Leveled Readers

Social Studies

Citizenship

Nonfiction Books

- Helping Others
- The National Guard: Today's Minutemen
- The New Kid at School

Fiction Books

- Bill Lucks Out
- Giant Pumpkin on the Loose
- The Sandwich Brigade

Culture

Nonfiction Books

- Art's Inspiration
- China: Today and Yesterday
- Computers in Filmmaking: Very Special Effects
- The Root of the Blues
- Special Effects in Hollywood
- Strange Sports with Weird Gear
- The Talker
- Unexpected Music
- A Visit to the Navajo Nation

Fiction Books

- Abuela's Gift
- Grandma Betty's Banjo
- The Medicine Harvest
- Moving
- Moving to Mali

Culture

- Nathaniel Comes to Town
- Operation Inspiration
- Our Village
- Playing the Game

Economics

Nonfiction Books

- Ancient Gold from the Ancient World
- The Oceans' Treasures
- Precious Goods: From Salt to Silk

History

Nonfiction Books

- The Blues Evolution
- The California Gold Rush
- The Flight Over the Ocean: Yesterday and Today
- From Territory to Statehood
- The Golden Spike
- The Italian Renaissance and Its Artists
- Jazz, Jazz, Jazz
- The Land of Opportunity
- Let the Games Begin: History of the Olympics
- The Most Dangerous Woman in America

History

- Paul Revere and the American Revolutionary War
- Paul Revere's Ride
- A Railroad Over the Sierra
- Rube Foster and the Chicago American Giants
- Saving an American Symbol
- A Spy in Disguise
- Stop That Train!
- Titanic: The "Unsinkable" Ship
- The United States Moves West
- What Makes Great Athletes?

Fiction Books

- From Slave to Soldier
- The Golden Journey
- Journey to the New World
- The Land of Plenty

More Great Titles

Biography

- Blues Legends
- The Designs of Da Vinci
- Famous Women in Sports
- The Journey of African American Athletes
- Wilma Rudolph: Running to Win

Planning Teacher Study Groups

Adventurous teachers often have good ideas for lessons. A teacher study group is a great way to share ideas and get feedback on the best way to connect content and students. Working with other teachers can provide you with the support and motivation you need to implement new teaching strategies. A teacher study group offers many opportunities to collaborate, support each other's work, share insights, and get feedback.

Think About It

A weekly or monthly teacher study group can help support you in developing your expertise in the classroom. You and a group of like-minded teachers can form your own study group. What can this group accomplish?

- Read and discuss professional articles by researchers in the field of education.
- Meet to share teaching tips, collaborate on multi-grade lessons, and share resources.
- Develop lessons to try out new teaching strategies. Meet to share experiences and discuss how to further improve your teaching approach.

Let's Meet!

Forming a study group is easy. Just follow these four steps:

1. **Decide on the size of the group.** A small group has the advantage of making each member feel accountable, but make sure that all people have the ability to make the same commitment!

2. **Choose teachers to invite to join your group.** Think about whom you want to invite. Should they all teach the same grade? Can you invite teachers from other schools? Remember that the more diverse the group, the more it benefits from new perspectives.

3. **Set goals for the group.** In order to succeed, know what you want the group to do. Meet to set goals. Rank goals in order of importance and refer often to the goals to keep the group on track.

4. **Make logistical decisions.** This is often the most difficult. Decide where and when you will meet. Consider an online meeting place where group members can post discussion questions and replies if people are not able to meet.

What Will We Study? Use the goals you set to help determine what your group will study. Consider what materials are needed to reach your goals, and how long you think you will need to prepare for each meeting.

How Will It Work? Think about how you structure groups in your classroom. Then use some of the same strategies.

- **Assign a group facilitator.** This person is responsible for guiding the meeting. This person comes prepared with discussion questions and leads the meeting. This could be a rotating responsibility dependent on experience with various topics. This person might be responsible for providing the materials.

- **Assign a recorder.** Have someone take notes during the meeting and record group decisions.

- **Use the jigsaw method.** Not everyone has time to be a facilitator. In this case, divide the text and assign each portion to a different person. Each person is responsible for leading the discussion on that particular part.

Meet Again Make a commitment to meet for a minimum number of times. After that, the group can reevaluate and decide whether or not to continue.

> " Have some great teaching tips to share? Want to exchange ideas with your colleagues? Build your own professional community of teachers. **Customize Literacy** gets you started. "

Trial Lessons

Use your colleagues' experiences to help as you think about new ways to connect content and students. Use the following plan to create a mini-lesson. It should last twenty minutes. Get the support of your colleagues as you try something new and then reflect on what happened.

Be Creative! As you develop a plan for a mini-lesson, use these four words to guide planning: *purpose, text, resources,* and *routine*.

- **Purpose:** Decide on a skill or strategy to teach. Define your purpose for teaching the lesson.

- **Text:** Develop a list of the materials you could use. Ask your colleagues for suggestions.

- **Resources:** Make a list of the available resources, and consider how to use those resources most effectively. Consider using the leveled readers listed on pages CL24–CL29 and CL36–CL41 of Customize Literacy.

- **Routine:** Choose an instructional routine to structure your mini-lesson. See the mini-lessons in Customize Literacy for suggestions.

Try It! Try out your lesson! Consider audio- or videotaping the lesson for later review. You may wish to invite a colleague to sit in as you teach. Make notes on how the lesson went.

How Did It Go? Use the self-evaluation checklist on page CL45 as you reflect on your trial lesson. This provides a framework for later discussion.

Discuss, Reflect, Repeat Solicit feedback from your teacher study group. Explain the lesson and share your reflections. Ask for suggestions on ways to improve the lesson. Take some time to reflect on the feedback. Modify your lesson to reflect what you have learned. Then try it again.

Checklist for Teacher Self-Evaluation

How Well Did I ...	Very Well	Satisfactory	Not Very Well
Plan the lesson?			
Select the appropriate level of text?			
Introduce the lesson and explain its objectives?			
Review previously taught skills?			
Directly explain the new skills being taught?			
Model the new skills?			
Break the material down into small steps?			
Integrate guided practice into the lesson?			
Monitor guided practice for student understanding?			
Provide feedback on independent practice?			
Maintain an appropriate pace?			
Assess student understanding of the material?			
Stress the importance of applying the skill as they read?			
Maintain students' interest?			
Ask questions?			
Handle student questions and responses?			
Respond to the range of abilities?			

Building Community

Books for Teachers

Students aren't the only ones who need to read to grow. Here is a brief list of books that you may find useful to fill your reading teacher basket and learn new things.

A Professional Bibliography

Afflerbach, P. "Teaching Reading Self-Assessment Strategies." *Comprehension Instruction: Research-Based Best Practices.* The Guilford Press, 2002.

Bear, D. R., M. Invernizzi, S. Templeton, and F. Johnston. *Words Their Way.* Merrill Prentice Hall, 2004.

Beck, I. L., and M. G. McKeown. *Improving Comprehension with Questioning the Author: A Fresh and Expanded View of a Powerful Approach.* Scholastic, 2006.

Beck, I., M. G. McKeown, and L. Kucan. *Bringing Words to Life: Robust Vocabulary Instruction.* The Guilford Press, 2002.

Blachowicz, C. and P. Fisher. "Vocabulary Instruction." *Handbook of Reading Research,* vol. III. Lawrence Erlbaum Associates, 2000.

Blachowicz, C. and D. Ogle. *Reading Comprehension: Strategies for Independent Learners.* The Guilford Press, 2008.

Block, C. C. and M. Pressley. "Best Practices in Comprehension Instruction." *Best Practices in Literacy Instruction.* The Guilford Press, 2003.

Daniels, H. *Literature Circles.* 2nd ed. Stenhouse Publishers, 2002.

Dickson, S. V., D. C. Simmons, and E. J. Kame'enui. "Text Organization: Instructional and Curricular Basics and Implications." *What Reading Research Tells Us About Children with Diverse Learning Needs: Bases and Basics.* Lawrence Erlbaum Associates, 1998.

Diller, D. *Making the Most of Small Groups: Differentiation for All.* Stenhouse Publishers, 2007.

Duke, N. and P. D. Pearson. "Effective Practices for Developing Reading Comprehension." *What Research Has to Say About Reading Instruction,* 3rd ed. Newark, DE: International Reading Association, 2002.

Fillmore, L. W. and C. E. Snow. *What Teachers Need to Know About Language.* Office of Educational Research and Improvement, U.S. Department of Education, 2000.

Fountas, I. C. and G. S. Pinnell. *Guiding Readers and Writers Grades 3–6: Teaching Comprehension, Genre, and Content Literacy.* Heinemann, 2001.

Guthrie, J. and E. Anderson. "Engagement in Reading: Processes of Motivated Strategic, Knowledgeable, Social Readers." *Engaged Reading: Processes, Practices, and Policy Implications.* Teachers College Press, 1999.

Harvey, S. and A. Goudvis. *Strategies That Work: Teaching Comprehension to Enhance Understanding.* 2nd ed. Stenhouse Publishers, 2007.

Keene, E. O. and S. Zimmerman. *Mosaic of Thought.* 2nd ed. Heinemann, 2007.

Leu Jr., D. J. "The New Literacies: Research on Reading Instruction with the Internet and Other Digital Technologies." *What Research Has to Say About Reading Instruction,* 3rd ed. International Reading Association, 2002.

McKeown, M. G. and I. L. Beck. "Direct and Rich Vocabulary Instruction." *Vocabulary Instruction: Research to Practice.* The Guilford Press, 2004.

McTighe, J. and K. O'Connor. "Seven Practices for Effective Learning." *Educational Leadership,* vol. 63, no. 3 (November 2005).

Nagy, W. E. *Teaching Vocabulary to Improve Reading Comprehension.* International Reading Association, 1998.

National Reading Panel. *Teaching Children to Read.* National Institute of Child Health and Human Development, 1999.

Ogle, D. and C. Blachowicz. "Beyond Literature Circles: Helping Students Comprehend Information Texts." *Comprehension Instruction: Research-Based Practices.* The Guilford Press, 2001.

Pressley, M. *Reading Instruction That Works: The Case for Balanced Teaching,* 3rd ed. The Guilford Press, 2005.

Stahl, S. A. "What Do We Know About Fluency?" *The Voice of Evidence in Reading Research.* Paul H. Brookes, 2004.

Taylor, B. M., P. D. Pearson, D. S. Peterson, and M. C. Rodriguez. "The CIERA School Change Framework: An Evidence-Based Approach to Professional Development and School Reading Improvement." *Reading Research Quarterly,* vol. 40, no. 1 (January/February/March 2005).

Valencia, S. W. and M. Y. Lipson. "Thematic Instruction: A Quest for Challenging Ideas and Meaningful Learning." *Literature-Based Instruction: Reshaping the Curriculum.* Christopher-Gordon Publishers, 1998.

Building Community

Smokejumpers

Amazing Words Oral Vocabulary Routine

DAY 1

deserted

1 **Introduce** If something is *deserted* it is abandoned or left vacant.

2 **Demonstrate** The ranch looked like it had been *deserted* for years.

3 **Apply** Have students tell about areas of the school that are *deserted* at certain times.

hurricane watch

1 **Introduce** A *hurricane watch* is to look carefully for a coming storm.

2 **Demonstrate** Thanks to the *hurricane watch,* the people evacuated the town in time.

3 **Apply** Have students use a map to show places where there might be a *hurricane watch.*

dangerous

1 **Introduce** If something is *dangerous*, it is not safe.

2 **Demonstrate** The ocean currents made the waters very *dangerous* for swimming.

3 **Apply** List areas in your town that can be *dangerous*.

DAY 2

medical

1 **Introduce** If something is *medical*, it is about healing and medicine.

2 **Demonstrate** When she broke her leg, she had a *medical* excuse for not attending.

3 **Apply** Ask students to name jobs that are in the *medical* profession.

DAY 3

ignite

1 **Introduce** To *ignite* means "to set on fire."

2 **Demonstrate** If you want a campfire you need to *ignite* the wood.

3 **Apply** Identify common things used to *ignite* a fire.

DAY 4

gear

1 **Introduce** *Gear* is equipment.

2 **Demonstrate** We brought along all of our volleyball *gear*.

3 **Apply** Have students name *gear* used for camping.

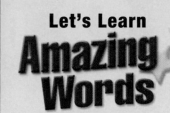
Lost City

Amazing Words Oral Vocabulary Routine

cultivate

1 **Introduce** To *cultivate* means "to help plants grow by caring for them."

2 **Demonstrate** They learned to *cultivate* all sorts of vegetable in the garden.

3 **Apply** Discuss the steps needed to *cultivate* a garden.

adobe

1 **Introduce** *Adobe* is brick made of clay and baked in the sun.

2 **Demonstrate** The farmer built an *adobe* home.

3 **Apply** Have students name things that are made with *adobe*.

highland

1 **Introduce** A *highland* is a country or region that is higher than the neighboring country.

2 **Demonstrate** The *highlands* get colder than other areas.

3 **Apply** Have students identify places that have *highlands*.

century

1 **Introduce** A *century* is one hundred years.

2 **Demonstrate** During that *century* there were no cars.

3 **Apply** Identify several event that happened in the previous *century*.

legend

1 **Introduce** A *legend* is a story from the past, which is based on real people and events.

2 **Demonstrate** The *legend* of Davy Crockett is exciting and funny.

3 **Apply** Have students tell about a *legend* they know of.

records

1 **Introduce** *Records* are information that have been written or kept.

2 **Demonstrate** Our *records* show that he moved a lot during those years.

3 **Apply** Have students identify places that keep *records*.

Cliff Hanger

Amazing Words Oral Vocabulary Routine

DAY

decency

1 **Introduce** Showing *decency* means treating people well or behaving properly.

2 **Demonstrate** He had the *decency* to apologize for his mistakes.

3 **Apply** Have students tell what it means to treat people with *decency*.

courage

1 **Introduce** *Courage* is the ability to meet danger instead of running from it.

2 **Demonstrate** His *courage* during the disaster was an inspiration to everyone.

3 **Apply** Have students talk about someone who they think shows *courage*.

valiant

1 **Introduce** If you are *valiant*, you are brave and courageous.

2 **Demonstrate** The *valiant* firefighters worked nonstop to put out the fire.

3 **Apply** Have student name a situation in which they were *valiant*.

DAY

individual

1 **Introduce** An *individual* is a single person, animal, or thing.

2 **Demonstrate** He is an *individual* who is filled with happiness.

3 **Apply** Ask students how many *individuals* are in the classroom.

DAY

secure

1 **Introduce** To be *secure* means "to be safe and protected."

2 **Demonstrate** He felt *secure* when the doors were locked.

3 **Apply** What steps do schools take to make sure everyone is *secure*?

DAY

flood

1 **Introduce** A *flood* is a huge flow of water over what is usually dry land.

2 **Demonstrate** The *flood* washed away the farmhouse.

3 **Apply** Have students identify where a *flood* might occur.

UNIT 5

Acknowledgments

Acknowledgments

Text

Grateful acknowledgment is made to the following for copyrighted material:

A&C Black Publishers

"Who Knows" by Fatou Ndiaye Sow, translated by Véronique Tadjo from *Talking Drums: A Selection Of Poems From Africe South Of The Sahara* edited and illustrated by Véronique Tadjo. Used by permission of A & C Black Publishers.

Alfred A. Knopf a div of Random House & Harold Ober Associates

"Dream Dust" from *The Collected Poems Of Langston Hughes* by Langston Hughes edited by Arnold Rampersand with David Roessel, Associate Editor, copyright © 1994 by The Estate of Langston Hughes. Used by permission.

Ben Bova

"Moonwalk" by Ben Bova from *Boy's Life, November 2002. Pp 29–31.* Copyright © 2002 by Ben Bova. Reprinted by permission of Ben Bova.

Chronicle Books

From *The Man Who Went to the Far Side of the Moon,* copyright © 1999 by Bea Uusuma Schyffert. Used with permission of Chronicle Books LLC. San Francisco. Visit ChronicleBooks.com.

Clairon Books an imprint of Houghton Mifflin Harcourt Publishing Company

"The Best Paths" from *Toasting Marshmallows: Camping Poems* by Kristine O'Connell George. Text copyright © 2001 by Kristine O'Connell George. Reprinted by permission of Clarion Books, an imprint of Houghton Mifflin Harcourt Publishing Company. All rights reserved.

Curtis Brown, Ltd

"Roller Coasters", Copyright © 1991 by X.J. Kennedy. First appeared in *The Kite That Braved Old Orchard Beach,* published by Margaret K. McElderry Books. "Martin Luther King Day", Copyright © 1991 by X.J. Kennedy. First appeared in *The Kite That Braved Old Orchard Beach,* published by Margaret K. McElderry Books. "First Men on the Moon", Copyright © 1999 by J. Patrick Lewis. First appeared in *Lives: Poems About Famous Americans,* published by HarperCollins. Now appears in *A Burst of Firsts,* published by Dial Books for Young Readers. Reprinted by permission of Curtis Brown, Ltd.

Dutton Children's Books a div of Penguin Group (USA)

The Case of the Gasping Garbage by Michele Torrey, illustrated by Barbara Johansen Newman, copyright © 2001 by Michele Torrey, text. "Mr. Talberg's Famous Bread Recipe" from *The Case of the Gasping Garbage* by Michelle Torrey, illustrated by Barbara Johansen Newman, copyright © 2001 by Michele Torrey, text. Used by permission of Dutton Children's Books, A Division of Penguin Young Readers Group, A Member of Penguin Group (USA) Inc., 345 Hudson Street, New York, NY 10014. All rights reserved.

G.P. Putnam's Sons a div of Penguin Group (USA)

"Fall Football", from *Fearless Fernie: Hanging Out With Fernie & Me* by Gary Soto, copyright © 2002 by Gary Soto. Used by permission of G.P. Putnam's Sons, A Division of Penguin Young Readers Group, A Member of Penguin Group (USA) Inc., 345 Hudson Street, New York, NY 10014. All rights reserved.

Harold Ober Associates

"Poetry" from *Eleanor Farjeon's Poems For Children* by Eleanor Farjeon. Reprinted by permission of Harold Ober Associates Incorporated. Copyright 1938 by Eleanor Farjeon. Copyright renewed 1966 by Gervase Farjeon

HarperCollins Publishers

"Antarctic Journal: Four Months at the Bottom of the World" by Jennifer Owings Dewey. Text copyright © 2001 by Jennifer Dewey. Used by permission of HarperCollins Publishers.

HarperCollins Publishers & Curtis Brown, Ltd

"Cliff Hanger" by Jean Craighead George. Text copyright © 2004 by Jean Craighead George. First appeared in *Cliff Hanger,* published by HarperCollins. Used by permission.

Houghton Mifflin Harcourt Publishing Company

Abridged from *Encantado: Pink Dolphin Of The Amazon* by Sy Montgomery with photographs by Dianne Taylor-Snow. Text copyright © 2002 by Sy Montgomery. Photographs copyright © 2002 by Dianne Taylor-Snow. From *Seeker Of Knowledge: The Man Who Deciphered Egyptian Hieroglyphics* by James Rumford. Copyright © 2000 by James Rumford. Reprinted by permission of Houghton Mifflin Harcourt Company. All rights reserved.

Lee & Low Books

"Jim Thorpe's Bright Path". Text copyright © 2004 by Joseph Bruchac. Illustrations copyright © 2004 by S.D. Nelson. Permission arranged with Lee & Low Books, Inc. New York, NY 10016. Used by permission.

Marian Reiner Literary Agent

"The Seed" from *Always Wondering* by Aileen Fisher. Copyright © 1991 by Aileen Fisher. Inc. "Carolyn's Cat" from *When Whales Exhale and Other Poems* by Constance Levy. Copyright © 1996 by Constance Kling Levy. "Martin Luther King" from *No Way of Knowing Dallas Poems* by Myra Cohn Livingston. Copyright © 1980 by Myra Cohn Livingston. Used by permission of Marian Reiner.

Penguin Group, Ltd (UK)

"The Door" (26 lines) (p. 62) from *Miroslav Holub: Selected Poems,* translated by Ian Milner and George Theiner (Penguin Books, 1967) Copyright © Miroslav Holub 1967, Translation copyright © Penguin Books, 1967. Introduction Copyright © A Alvarez. Reproduced by permission by Penguin Books Ltd.

Philomel Books a div of Penguin Group (USA)

From *Lost City: The Discovery Of Machu Picchu* by Ted Lewin, copyright © 2003 by Ted Lewin. Used by permission of Philomel Books, A Division of Penguin Young Readers Group, A Member of Penguin Group (USA) Inc., 345 Hudson Street, New York, NY 10014. All rights reserved.

Picture Window/Compass Point Books

"Navajo Code Talkers" by Andrew Santella. Copyright © 2004 by Compass Point Books. Used by permission. All rights reserved.

Random House Children's Books a div of Random House

From *Encyclopedia Brown And The Case Of The Slippery Salamander* by Donald J. Sobol and illustrated by Warren Chong, copyright © 1999 by Donald J. Sobol. Illustration © 1999 by Warren Chang. Used by permission of Random House Children's Books, a division of Random House, Inc.

The Rosen Publishing Group

"Smokejumpers: Life Fighting Fires" by Mark Beyer, copyright 2001 by the Rosen Publishing Group, Inc. Used by permission.

Simon & Schuster Books for Young Readers an imprint of Simon & Schuster Publishing Div & The Jennifer Lyons Literary Agency, LLC

From *My Brother Martin: A Sister Remembers* by Christine King Farris. Copyright © 2003 by Christine King Farris. Used by permission.

Simon & Schuster Books for Young Readers & Sandford Lyne

"My Life Is a Buried Treasure" by Dawn Withrow, from *Ten Seconds Rainshowers: Poems for Young People,* compiled by Sandford Lyne, Simon & Schuster Books for Young Readers, 1996.

Skipping Stone Magazine

"Haiku" by Cristina Beecham. "When You Hope and Trust" by Ek Ongkar K. Khalsa. Reprinted with permission from Skipping Stones Magazine, Sept-Oct. 2003, Vol 15, No 4.

Susan Berholz Literary Services

Two Happy Months in Vermont" from *How Tia Lola Came To Visit/Stay.* Copyright © 2001 by Julia Alvarez. Published by Dell Yearling and in hardcover by Alfred A Knopf Children's Books, a division of Random House, New York. Reprinted with the permission of Susan Berholz Literary Services, New York and Lamy, NM. All rights reserved.

Times Books a div of Random House & Sanford J. Greenburger Associates

"Sadaharu Oh: a Zen Way of Baseball" from *Sadaharu Oh: A Zen Way Of Baseball* by Sadaharu Oh and David Falkner, copyright © 1984 by Sadaharu Oh and David Falkner. Used by permission.

Writer's House

"I Have a Dream" by Dr. Martin Luther King Jr. Copyright © 1963 Martin Luther King Jr., Copyright renewed © 1991 Coretta Scott King. Used by permission of The Estate of Martin Luther King, Jr.c/o Writer's House as agent for the proprietor New York, NY.

Note: Every effort has been made to locate the copyright owner of material reproduced on this component. Omissions brought to our attention will be corrected in subsequent editions.

Illustrations

Cover: Tim Jessel; **EI1–EI13** Bill McGuire; **EI16–EI25** Kenny Kiernan; **26–44** Barbara Johansen Newman; **146–154** Brett Helquist; **166–168** Joel Nakamura; **262–264** Jennifer Owings Dewey; **294–304** Peter Bollinger; **316–318** Franklin Hammond; **346** Stephen Daigle; **388–406** Macky Pamintuan; **408–410** SuLing Wang; **420–434** Erwin Madrid; **468, 476** Rafael Lopez; **W2–W15** Leslie Harrington.

Photographs

Every effort has been made to secure permission and provide appropriate credit for photographic material. The publisher deeply regrets any omission and pledges to correct errors called to its attention in subsequent editions.

Unless otherwise acknowledged, all photographs are the property of Pearson Education, Inc.

Photo locators denoted as follows: Top (T), Center (C), Bottom (B), Left (L), Right (R), Background (Bkgd)

Acknowledgments

18 (C) ©ChiselVision/Corbis; **20** (TL) ©Alistair Scott/Alamy, (B) ©Kathie Atkinson/PhotoLibrary Group, Ltd.; **23** (TR) ©DK Images, (BR) ©Lyn Balzer and Tony Perkins/Getty Images; **24** (CL) ©fStop/Alamy, (TL) ©Heinrich van den Berg/Getty Images, (BL) Jupiter Images; **25** (B) Jupiter Images; **52** (BL) ©Erich Kuchling/Westend61/Jupiter Images, (B) Jupiter Images; **53** (BR) ©Steve Kaufman/Corbis; **56** (CL) ©David Tipling/Getty Images, (BL) ©Ingo Wagner/dpa/Corbis, (TL) ©mm-images/PhotoLibrary Group, Ltd.; **58** (C) ©Todd Pusser/Nature Picture Library; **60** (CR) ©Wolfgang Kaehler/Corbis; **61** (CR) Getty Images; **62** (TL) Getty Images; **63** (TL) ©Dianne Taylor-Snow; **66** (CL) Jupiter Images; **67** (C) Andre Bartschi; **68** (TL) ©Royalty-Free/Corbis; **71** (B) ©Jay Dickinson/Corbis; **76** (BR) ©Darek Karp/Animals Animals/Earth Scenes, (TR) ©Dr. Morley Read/Photo Researchers, Inc.; **77** (CR) Andy Crawford/©DK Images, (TR, BR) Getty Images; **78** (B) ©William Grenfell/Visuals Unlimited; **79** (T) ©Manfred Klindwort GDT/Visuals Unlimited; **82** (TL) ©Bettmann/Corbis, (BC) ©Cindy Miller Hopkins/Danita Delimont/Alamy Images; **86** (CL) ©Enigma/Alamy, (BL) ©Gray Mortimore/Getty Images, (TL) ©Pat Doyle/Corbis; **88** Marine Corps/Department of Defense; **90** (TR) ©Hulton Archive/Getty Images, (B) National Archives; **91** Courtesy of FDR Library, Hyde Park, NY; **92** (CL) ©Underwood & Underwood/Corbis, (TL) Marine Corps/Department of Defense; **93** (BL) Cline Library, Northern Arizona University; **94** (B) National Archives; **95** National Archives; **98** Museum of Northern Arizona; **99** Cline Library, Northern Arizona University; **100** ©Bettmann/Corbis; **101** J. L. Burns/Marine Corps/U.S. Department of Defense; **102** (TR) ©AFP/Getty Images, (TL) Joe Rosenthal, Associated Press/Navy/U.S. Department of Defense; **105** (BR) ©DK Images, (TR, CR) Library of Congress; **108** (Bkgd) ©Dennis Hallinan/Alamy Images, (BR) ©Jose Luis Palaez, Inc./Corbis; **112** (B) ©Bettmann/Corbis, (CL) ©Stefan Sollfors/Alamy Images; **113** (BR) ©Myrleen Ferguson Cate/PhotoEdit; **116** (CL) ©Jim Sugar/Corbis, (TL) ©Jon Arnold Images Ltd/Alamy, (BL) ©Phil Boorman/Getty Images; **120** (CL) Getty Images; **123** Getty Images; **132** (TL) ©Kenneth Garrett/National Geographic Image Collection; **134** (BR) ©The Print Collector/Alamy Images; **135** (TR) ©Mike Nelson/epa/Corbis, (CR) ©Ron Watts/Corbis; **140** (B) ©Dirk Anschutz/Getty Images, (CL) ©Corbis/Jupiter Images, (TL) Getty Images; **144** (CL) ©Juniors Bildarchiv/Alamy, (TL) ©Phil Degginger/Alamy Images, (CL) ©Westend61/Alamy; **161** (TCR) ©Royalty-Free/Corbis; **162** (TL) ©Becky Shink/Lansing State Journal, (BC) Getty Images; **163** (CC) Getty Images; **165** (BR) ©Michael Krasowitz/Getty Images; **170** (C) Corbis; **172** (BL) ©Reuters/Corbis, (B) Getty Images; **173** (TR) USDA Forest Service, Missoula, MT; **176** (TL) ©Alex Mares-Manton/Getty Images, (CL) ©Matthias Clamer/Getty Images, (BL) ©Panoramic Images/Getty Images; **178** ©Kevin R. Morris/Corbis; **180** ©Mike McMillan/Spotfire Images; **181** (TR) ©Mike McMillan/Spotfire Images; **182** (T) ©Mike McMillan/Spotfire Images; **185** ©Mike McMillan/Spotfire Images; **186** (T) ©Mike McMillan/Spotfire Images; **187** (B) ©Mike McMillan/Spotfire Images; **188** (T) ©Mike McMillan/Spotfire Images; **189** (B) ©Mike McMillan/Spotfire Images; **191** (B) ©Kevin R. Morris/Corbis; **193** (CC) ©Rainer Holz/zefa/Corbis; **200** (BL) ©ImageGap/Alamy; **201** (BR) ©Ron Levine/Getty Images; **204** (CL) ©Angelo Cavalli/zefa/Corbis, (BL) ©Helene Rogers/Alamy Images, (CL) ©Travelshots/Alamy Images; **222** (C) ©Jim Erickson/Corbis; **224** (B) ©Dave Wilhelm, (CR) ©Roman Soumar/Corbis; **225** (TR) ©Francesco Venturi/Corbis, (CL) ©Kevin Schafer/Corbis; **228** (B) ©Bo Zaunders/Corbis, (BL) ©Marcel Antonisse/epa/Corbis; **229** (TR) ©Image Source Limited; **232** (TL) ©david sanger photography/Alamy Images; **247** (CR) Ian O'Leary/©DK Images; **250** ©Ant Strack/Corbis; **252** ©Christophe Boisvieux/Corbis; **253** ©Hoberman Collection/Corbis, **(Inset)** ©Jim Arbogast/Corbis; **256** (CL) ©Bill Hatcher/National Geographic Image Collection, (B) ©Patrick Robert/Corbis, (BC) National Science Foundation; **260** (BL) ©ImageState/Alamy Images; **264** (Bkgd) Getty Images; **266** (CR) Jennifer Owings Dewey; **268** (BR) Jennifer Owings Dewey, (TR, CL, BC) National Science Foundation; **270** (BL, BC) Jennifer Owings Dewey; **271** (TR) National Science Foundation; **273** (TR) National Science Foundation; **274** (TR) National Science Foundation; **275** (BR) National Science Foundation; **276** (CL) National Science Foundation; **277** (B) National Science Foundation; **282** (Bkgd) Corbis; **283** (CR) ©Gabriella Miotto; **284** (TL) ©Gabriella Miotto, (BR) AP/Wide World Photos; **285** (Bkgd) Corbis; **288** (B) ©Bloomimage/Corbis, (TL) Corbis; **289** (BR) ©NASA/Roger Ressmeyer/Corbis; **292** (TL) ©Kari Marttila/Alamy Images, (CL) ©Michael Coyne/Getty Images, (BL) ©Nigel Cattlin/Alamy Images; **310** (Bkgd) Getty Images; **311** (CR) Getty

Images; **312** (CL) Getty Images, (B) Original image courtesy of NASA/Corbis; **313** (TL) Getty Images, (CR) NASA/Corbis; **320** (C) ©Michael Wong/Corbis; **322** (B) ©Bob E. Daemmrich/Sygma/Corbis, (CC) ©Enigma/Alamy; **326** (BL) ©ImageState/Alamy Images, (CL) ©Roger Day/Alamy Images, (TL) Jupiter Images; **350** (BC) ©LWA-Dann Tardif/Corbis, (B) Corbis/Jupiter Images; **351** (BC) Jupiter Images; **354** (TL) ©David Joel/Getty Images, (B) ©Paul Doyle/Alamy Images, (CL) ©Tim Tadder/Corbis; **370** (CR, CL, BR) Cumberland County Historical Society, Carlisle, PA, (TL) Getty Images; **371** (TL, CC, BR) Cumberland County Historical Society, Carlisle, PA, (BC) Getty Images; **376** (T) ©Joseph Sohm/ChromoSohm Inc/Corbis, (BC) ©Reuters/Corbis; **377** (B) ©Stephane Cardinale/Corbis; **378** (BL, B) ©Jonathan Nourok/PhotoEdit, (TR) ©Kathleen Kliskey-Geraghty/Index Stock Imagery, (TL) ©Robert W. Ginn/PhotoEdit; **379** (TR) ©The Daily Oakland Press/AP/Wide World Photos, (TR) ©The Times/AP/Wide World Photos; **381** (BR) ©PCN Photography/Alamy; **382** (BL) ©Bettmann/Corbis, (B) ©Mickael Parpet/Sygma/Corbis; **383** (BR) ©Chuck Place/Alamy Images; **386** (TL) ©Robert W. Ginn/Alamy Images, (BL) ©Corbis/Jupiter Images, (CL) ©Image100/Jupiter Images; **414** (BC) ©Colin Underhill/Alamy Images, (B) ©Sean Justice/Corbis, (BL) Corbis; **417** (TR) George E. Marsh Album/NOAA; **418** (TL) ©Oote Boe Photography/Alamy Images, (BL) ©ScotStock/Alamy Images, (CL) ©Thom Lang/Corbis; **419** (TR) ©Bananastock/Jupiter Images; **437** (BR) Neil Fletcher/©DK Images; **444** (B) ©Roger Ressmeyer/Corbis, (BL) Jupiter Images; **445** (TR) NASA; **448** (TL) ©Jon Arnold Images Ltd/Alamy Images, (CL) ©Nik Keevil/Alamy, (BL) STS-122 Shuttle Crew/NASA; **451** (R) NASA; **453** (CR, BL) NASA; **454** (TC) NASA; **455** (CC) NASA; **457** (C) NASA; **459** (BR) NASA; **460** (TR) N.ASA; **461** NASA; 462 (BC) ©Time Life Pictures/Getty Images; **463** (C) ©Time Life Pictures/Getty Images; **473** Original image courtesy of Buzz Aldrin/NASA/Corbis; **478** ©Corbis/Jupiter Images; **479** Digital Vision; **480** (L) ©FogStock/Index Open, (R) Getty Images; **481** ©Matthew Mawson/Alamy; **482** (R) ©FogStock/Index Open, (L) ©Kitt Cooper-Smith/Alamy; **483** (L) ©Keith Levit Photography/Index Open, (R) Getty Images; **484** (L) Index Open; **485** (R) Corbis/Jupiter Images, Getty Images; **486** (R) NASA; **488** (BR) DFRC/NASA; **489** (TR) ©Mark J. Terrill/AP Images, (CR) ©Tim Johnson/AP Images.

Teacher's Edition

Text

Grateful acknowledgment is made to the following for copyrighted material:

Cricket Magazine Group a div of Carus Publishing Company

"Coconuts" by Dagmar Kost from *Spider Magazine, August 2006, Vol. 13, No. 8.* Copyright © 2006. Used by permission of Carus Publishing Company.

Dial Books for Young Readers a div of Penguin Group (USA) & Curtis Brown, Ltd

"Give Thanks to the Heroes and She-Roes," from *Heroes and She-roes: Poems of Amazing and Everyday Heroes* by J. Patrick Lewis, illustrated by Jim Cooke. Copyright 2005 by J. Patrick Lewis. First appeared in *Heroes and She-roes: Poems of Amazing Everyday Heroes*, published by Dial. Used by permission.

Franklin Watts an imprint of Scholastic Library Publishing, Inc

From *The Incas* by Shirlee P. Newman. Copyright © 1992, Franklin Watts. All rights reserved. Reprinted by permission of Franklin Watts, an imprint of Scholastic Library Publishing, Inc.

Note: Every effort has been made to locate the copyright owner of material reproduced on this component. Omissions brought to our attention will be corrected in subsequent editions.

KWL Strategy: The KWL Interactive Reading Strategy was developed and is used by permission of Donna Ogle, National-Louis University, Skokie, Illinois, co-author of *Reading Today and Tomorrow*, Holt, Rinehart & Winston Publishers, 1988. (See also the *Reading Teacher*, February 1986, pp. 564–570.)

Understanding by Design quotes: Wiggins, G. & McTighe, J. (2005). *Understanding by Design*. Alexandria, VA: Association for Supervision and Curriculum Development.

Illustrations

Cover Tim Jessell

Running Head Linda Bronson

Photographs

Every effort has been made to secure permission and provide appropriate credit for photographic material. The publisher deeply regrets any omission and pledges to correct errors called to its attention in subsequent editions.

Unless otherwise acknowledged, all photographs are the property of Pearson Education, Inc.